Money
1989

Money
1989

By the Editors of MONEY Magazine

Oxmoor House®

Library of Congress Catalog Number: 87-659006
ISBN: 0-8487-0752-4
ISSN: 0891-172X

Manufactured in the United States of America
First Printing 1989

Published by arrangement with Oxmoor House, Inc.
Book Division of Southern Progress Corporation
P.O. Box 2463, Birmingham, Alabama 35201

Executive Editor: Ann H. Harvey
Production Manager: Jerry Higdon
Associate Production Manager: Rick Litton
Art Director: Bob Nance

Money 1989
Compiled and Edited by Junius Ellis

Editor: Clark Scott
Assistant Editor: Margaret Allen Northen
Editorial Assistants: L. Amanda Owens, Pamela Whyte
Senior Designer: Cynthia R. Cooper
Designer: Nancy Johnson

To order *Money* magazine, write to: *Money*, P.O. Box
54429, Boulder, CO 80322-4429

Money Staff
Managing Editor: Landon Y. Jones
Executive Editor: Frank Lalli
Assistant Managing Editors: Richard A. Burgheim,
Frank B. Merrick
Senior Editors: Joseph S. Coyle, Caroline Donnelly,
Richard Eisenberg, Diane Harris, Augustin Hedberg,
Tyler Mathisen, Kevin S. McKean, Michael Sivy, Robert
Wool
Art Director: Eric Seidman
Picture Editor: Deborah Pierce
Editor, Investor's Scorecard: Pauline Tai
Senior Writers: Jerry Edgerton, Marlys Harris, Walter L.
Updegrave
Staff Writers: Greg Anrig Jr., Beth Kobliner, Robert
McNatt, Marsha Meyer, Robin Micheli, Jeanne L. Reid,
Eric Schurenberg, Suzanne Seixas, Marguerite T. Smith,
John Stickney, Leslie N. Vreeland, Clint Willis
Chief of Reporters: Katharine B. Drake
Senior Reporters: Jordan E. Goodman, Lani Luciano,
Holly Wheelwright
Reporters: Martha J. Mader (deputy chief), Jan
Alexander, Sian Ballen, Debra Wishik Englander, Carla
A. Fried, Beth M. Gilbert, Jersey Gilbert, Mary
Granfield, J. Howard Green, Bruce Hager, Elizabeth M.
MacDonald, Prashanta Misra, Daphne D. Mosher
(letters), D. Jacqueline Smith
Design and Picture Departments: Traci Churchill
(associate art director), Mark Shafer (designer), Warren
Isensee, Michael Olson, Miriam Hsia (deputy picture
editor), Leslie Yoo
Director of Editorial Operations: Anne R. Davis
Copy Desk: Patricia A. Feimster, Andrew Schwartz
(deputy chiefs), Sukey Rosenbaum (senior coordinator),
Eve Sennett, Suzanne Justin Riggio, Mark Hudson Giles,
Margaret J. Stefanowicz, Kathleen Beakley, Bill
O'Connor, Judith Ryan, Edward M. Gay Jr., Sarah Plant,
Jane Rigney
Editorial Production Manager: Karen Harper Diaz
Editorial Production: Sally Boggan, Gary S. Costello

Editor's Note

Welcome to the 1990s. To be sure, your calendar does not yet acknowledge the first tremors of the new decade—and your personal planning may not yet mirror the new landscape ahead—but I can assure you that your finances have already been reordered by a seismic upheaval that has forever altered the economic landscape of the 1980s.

Are you prepared to prosper in a decade that has arrived faster than anyone ever thought it could? In 1988 we elected a new President, confronted the lowest marginal tax rates in a half-century—and faced up to the end of the bull market of the 1980s. After all, the 1990s effectively began on October 19, 1987, the day the stock market crashed and brought down with it any illusions that financial security could be bought easily. Now we know better. Anyone who plans to get ahead in the coming decade will need a full command of every personal-financial tool available: astute tax planning, sophisticated investment strategy, and the careful crafting of long-term financial goals. At the same time, you may need to raise a war chest to pay college tuition for your children, to provide for your elderly parents, or to guarantee your own financial security in retirement.

It is the purpose of *Money 1989* to give you the winning edge over the next decade. This volume, the third in the series the Editors of *Money* have prepared with Oxmoor House, brings to you in permanent form the best insights we have gathered over the past twelve months. We have organized and selected dozens of articles that represent the most practical and lasting advice found in *Money*. Here you will find information— we list our 100 best ideas for the 1990s—as well as advice on insurance, real estate, investing, taxes, college admissions, retirement, and even how to organize your home office into a formidable resource.

We have worked hard this past year to save you time and effort as you face the vital decisions that will determine your financial security. We are convinced that *Money 1989* is an invaluable distillation of these efforts. We wish you good fortune as you pursue your goals—and we look forward to congratulating you on your success as you enter the next decade.

Landon Y. Jones

LANDON Y. JONES
Managing Editor, *Money*

Contents

Colleen Duffley

Success Strategies for the 1990s

"An era can be said to end," observed playwright Arthur Miller, "when its basic illusions are exhausted." By that standard, the 1980s are over. Already weakened by Wall Street's insider-trading scandals, the decade's self-indulgent all-gain, no-pain philosophy collapsed under the weight of the October 1987 Armageddon in the Dow Jones industrial average. Thus, even though the calendar says 1989, we have begun the 1990s.

What most likely will be the economic shape of the next decade? Although the 1990s will probably get off to a wobbly start, it will be better remembered for what emerges afterward—a period of moderate inflation, low interest rates, steady growth, and full employment. No economic Elysian fields, to be sure, but a very favorable setting for a new bull market in stocks and bonds. This chapter will tell you what you should do now to make money in the coming decade.

The overriding issue that will determine the nation's prosperity is how we deal with the aftermath of our consumption binge of the 1980s. During the past five years, we Americans spent roughly 3.5% a year more than we produced and saddled ourselves with the infamous twin towers—a budget deficit that has nearly doubled to $150 billion a year since 1980 and an annual trade deficit that has almost quadrupled to $170 billion since 1982. This staggering debt load is not only costly (the interest meter on all federal debt ticks away at $155 billion a year) but it forces us to keep interest rates higher than we would otherwise to attract desperately needed foreign capital. High interest payments siphon off money that could be used to expand our economy and raise our standard of living.

Near term, there is yet another threat. Classical business-cycle theory holds that expansions last roughly three or four years. Therefore, the current one, which completed its sixth year in 1988, appears vulnerable to recession. Some economists believe the debt we piled up in the profligate 1980s could tip us into a 1930s-style depression.

Fortunately, a massive, economywide shift from consumption to saving may already be under way. This is crucial, since increased savings by individuals and corporations will provide American business with the money it needs to build and modernize factories and otherwise lay the groundwork for growth. For the year that ended in June 1988, business investment jumped 13.5%, while consumer spending rose only 2.4%. What's more, a fledgling export boom in the first seven months of last year has begun narrowing our Mount Fuji-size trade gap.

And while a recession is unquestionably a painful period, it can also be highly therapeutic, because it allows the economy to cool down and frees productive capacity for the inevitable economic recovery.

What to Expect in the Next Decade

Get ready for an era of steady growth, moderate inflation, and low unemployment.

Ye of little faith take note: Just as every bust is followed by a boom, every bear market ushers in a bull. What's more, if you miss the initial stages of a stock market boom, you can drastically reduce your returns. A study by the investment firm Sanford C. Bernstein & Co. notes that people who remained fully invested between 1975 and 1984 earned an impressive 14.8% compound annual return. But had an investor missed the five months when the market had its largest returns—three of which were at the beginning of the two major market upturns of this 10-year period—the annual rate of return would have dropped to less than 9%. That is the same return earned during the period on risk-free Treasury bills.

Moral: Since no one knows when the market will make its next great leap forward, investors who want to ride the bull market of the 1990s should begin positioning themselves now before stocks bolt from the gate. To explore the shape of the 1990s—and how individuals can prepare themselves to profit from the coming expansion—*Money* interviewed approximately 300 economists, demographers, investment analysts, futurists, and others who monitor trends and forecast change. The most convincing scenario for the years ahead unfolds like this:

There will be a recession in 1989 or 1990 but only a mild one. With the economy lately humming along at a 3.3% annualized growth rate, analysts have pushed their recession forecasts into late 1989 at the earliest. Some of them even predict no economic stall until 1991. Whenever the next recession begins, though, economists generally agree it will be mild.

There are two reasons: The steady demand for services—the service industry now accounts for 67% of our gross national product and 90% of newly created jobs—tends to make recessions shorter and shallower, as opposed to the boom-and-bust cycles associated with manufacturing. And today's increasingly deregulated global economy tends to be more self-correcting. When an overheating economy sends out a whiff of escalating inflation, bondholders worldwide immediately dump their bonds and drive up interest rates. The higher rates squelch the boom and strangle the inflation threat.

After the recession, we will enjoy a period of moderate inflation and steady, modest growth. Coming out of the next downturn, the U.S. economy may boom along at a 4% or so rate for a few quarters but then slow to a cruising speed of roughly 2.5%. That's respectable, though lower than our historical growth rate of about 3%. What's more, less ebullient consumer spending and worldwide surpluses in many raw materials, including oil and petrochemicals, will keep inflation tamed at a 3% to 5% annual rate.

The U.S. dollar will bottom out after another slight drop. After sliding as much as 44% against major currencies since 1985, the U.S. dollar finally rallied in summer 1988 some 13.5% against the Japanese yen and climbed to its highest point against the German mark since December 1986. That strength won't last, however. As the dollar rises, our exports become more expensive, making U.S. products—and the dollars needed to buy them—less attractive worldwide. Still, most economists don't expect a repeat of the free-falls of recent years. Instead, they see the dollar stabilizing by early 1990 at 115 yen and 1.6 Deutsche marks—down roughly 16% from late 1988 levels. With a stable, cheaper dollar, the U.S. trade deficit will continue to shrink, dipping as low as $100 billion in 1990. But improvement from there will get sticky if, in the euphoria of the next expansion, consumers gorge themselves on imports as they did in the 1980s.

The President will raise taxes. Within two years, despite all the vows politicians have made, economists assert that a tax hike is preordained because there is no other way to rein in the budget deficit. Faced with already-scheduled budget increases and under pressure to spend for education, anti-pollution, and drug-abuse programs, the President will start raising taxes by the end of his first year in office—the fourth quarter of 1989. Look for him to disguise the boost in taxes as much as possible. Rather than increase income tax rates, he might scale back the mortgage deduction on first homes and eliminate it for second homes, while ratcheting up excise taxes on alcohol, cigarettes, and gasoline. If these moves don't generate enough revenue by 1991, he will then be forced to abandon sleight-of-hand tactics and raise taxes on corporations and boost the personal income tax rate for the top-earning taxpayer from 28% to 33%. But the increases will be phased in gradually to avoid triggering a slump in consumer spending and hastening or worsening the recession.

Interest rates will peak at 10.5% and then sink as low as 5%. An export-driven manufacturing boom has strained U.S. factories—recently operating at 84% of capacity—and rekindled inflation fears. As a result, long-term interest rates climbed from 8.3% in February 1988 to 9% in September 1988. Economists expect another uptick before rates peak at 10.5% or 11%. Once the recession begins, however, interest rates will head into a long downward spiral.

Beyond decreased demand for credit that normally occurs during a recession, the biggest pressure to lower rates will come from a demographic shift—specifically, the transformation of baby boomers from people who only spend to people who save as well for their families' future. The key is the boomers' own babies, some 40 million since 1978. As baby boomers move into their peak earning years, their income should outpace consumer spending and the personal savings rate, which dipped 2.2% in 1987, should jump to 10% in the next five years.

As that cash flows into the financial markets, rates will fade to as low as 5% by 1993, their lowest level since the 1960s. In addition to reducing interest rates on everything from car

What Could Go Wrong

Whereas optimists see a revitalized U.S. economy charging into a decade that promises unprecedented affluence, many well-meaning skeptics warn of a system on the verge of collapse. Some see not only a recession, but a depression not unlike the one this country went through in the 1930s. If this bleak view of the future becomes reality, the U.S. economy will shrink rapidly and then remain stagnant for a decade. Unemployment will surge to double-digit levels and the Dow Jones industrial average could crash to 800 or lower—more than 50% below its bottom on Black Monday.

The Cassandras attribute the potential calamity to two now familiar factors: our record levels of debt and the stunning rise in bank failures. If the worst were to occur, the most likely scenarios are:

Faulty U.S. government policy chokes off economic growth. Most economists believe that in order to reduce the towering budget deficit, the President inevitably will have to raise taxes. With consumers already strapped by high levels of debt, a tax increase could easily cause a limited cutback in consumer spending, which can lead to a slowdown in business activity, unemployment, and negative growth—that is, recession. But a severe cutback in spending caused by a too-burdensome tax hike could set off a deep recession or depression. Similarly, the Federal Reserve could overreact to inflation fears and jack up interest rates too far too fast. That would cause consumer demand and business activity, which are both fueled by credit, to drop precipitously.

Bank-bust fears paralyze consumers. A dramatic rise in the number of bank failures could cause a lack of confidence in our financial system that might lead consumers to cut back spending drastically. But a crisis of consumer confidence could also occur as a result of the collapse of only a few banks— if they are large enough. In fact, the solvency of several of the nation's largest banks is tenuous if one takes into account their huge loans to economically crippled countries such as Argentina, Brazil, Chile, Mexico, and Venezuela. Most money center banks have increased their loan-loss reserves to help absorb the impact of possible future defaults. But despite the increase in reserves, a default on the $7.6 billion of loans to less developed countries held by Manufacturers Hanover or the $8.3 billion held by Chase Manhattan, for example, would virtually wipe out the banks' equity.

The economy becomes a trade-war casualty. The export boom ignited by the dollar's decline abroad has helped mute the cries for protectionist legislation. But the calls for higher tariffs and import quotas could easily resurface if an invigorated U.S. dollar quashes the boom and the trade deficit widens. The planned unification of European countries into a single $5 trillion economic market by 1992 could also unleash fresh protectionist sentiments there. Were the U.S. to retaliate, world trade could conceivably dry up. Since exports have accounted for nearly two-thirds of the 3.3% annualized increase in our Gross National Product in the first half of 1988, shutting them off would devastate our economic growth. As world trade closed down, our trading partners—who are even more reliant on exporting to the U.S.—would suffer an even worse economic shock that ultimately could result in a severe worldwide recession or depression.

Japanese stock market crash launches a tidal wave that capsizes the U.S. economy. Although the Tokyo market escaped with only a 15% dive in October 1987 and has since rebounded to new highs, many analysts believe the Japanese market's inflated price/earnings ratios of 50 or higher (about four times those of the U.S. market) leave it highly vulnerable to a Black Monday-style crash. Should Tokyo's market topple, the ensuing margin calls could cause a liquidity crisis. To raise cash, Japanese investment firms would likely begin dumping billions of dollars' worth of U.S. Government bonds and blue-chip stocks. This would drive U.S. interest rates sky-high and send our economy into a tailspin.

to home loans, such a precipitous drop would also offer investors huge capital gains as bond prices boom. For example, owners of long-term bonds yielding 9% would enjoy capital gains of 42% if rates dropped to 6% and gains of 62% if they went as low as 5%.

The Dow Jones industrial average will hit 3000 early in the 1990s. As interest rates and bond yields fall, more money moves to stocks, which pushes up prices. Stocks also benefit because lower rates cut companies' borrowing costs and improve corporate earnings. Increased takeovers by foreigners will add fuel to rekindled share prices. The Japanese could account for as much as 25% of the takeover activity in the early 1990s. Reason: The strong yen makes U.S. companies seductively cheap to cash-rich Japanese investors. To prepare for a future role as major acquirers of U.S. companies, the Japanese have recently spent more than $1.4 billion to buy stakes in U.S. investment banking firms specializing in mergers and acquisitions. But don't be surprised if the stock market turns tail and retreats in anticipation of the next recession before heading for the rarefied air of 3000.

Gold will plunge in value while the returns on other traditional inflation hedges will lag as well. A rapidly growing supply and weak demand—not to mention the forecast for moderate inflation—point to a tarnished outlook for gold. Real estate returns will merely mirror the inflation rate or barely beat it. The demographic trends that virtually guaranteed real estate investors double-digit returns in the 1970s and early 1980s are history. For example, the annual number of new household formations—a key determinant of single-family housing demand—will decline by as much as 37% between now and 1995. As for rental housing, 25- to 34-year-olds—the group most likely to rent—will decline by 6.6% between now and 1995 to further dim prospects in an apartment market already plagued by an 11% vacancy rate.

We increasingly will become long-term investors. In the mid-1990s, the first baby-boomlet children will begin enrolling in college. Considering the expected 6% annual rise in college costs by then, the average bill for four years' tuition, room and board, and other expenses may reach $39,500 at a state university and $85,500 at a private university. Assuming a relatively conservative 8% annual return, a parent wishing to send one child to a private university in September 1995 would have to begin stashing away $758 a month now—more than most families can muster. Thus, families will have to start saving sooner for this important goal.

A well-justified lack of confidence in the Social Security system will also spur a need for long-term investing. One Social Security Administration projection calls for an $872 billion surplus in the fund by the year 2000 that will run out in 2026, before half the baby boomers have reached age 69. And future benefits may be so heavily taxed that their value will be seriously eroded. As it becomes clear that individuals will have to rely on their own investments for retirement, the return of the fully deductible Individual Retirement Account will become economically and politically inevitable.

Anyone with a decent education and marketable skills who wants a job will have one, as the unemployment rate plunges to perhaps as low as 4%. The U.S. faces a looming labor shortage. The number of 18- to 24-year-olds—the main source of new workers—will *decline* by 10% between now and 1995 as the baby-bust generation of 45 million follows the 80 million baby boomers into the labor market. As a result, the work force will grow at an annual rate of only about 1%, roughly a third of what it did in the 1970s. Unemployment, therefore, will average around 5% for much of the next decade, compared with more than 7% for most of the 1980s.

Well-educated baby busters will benefit. Unlike boomers, who had to claw their way into their first jobs, college graduates will have greater job selection in a wide choice of careers and command far higher salaries. But those higher wages, in turn, will threaten to reignite inflation. Two potential solutions: robots and immigrants.

The fast-food industry faces a possible shortage of 1 million workers by 1992. As a result, chains such as McDonald's and Pizza Hut are turning to high-tech solutions such as so-called robomation—automated hamburger makers and programmable soft-drink dispensers and french fryers. In addition, most economists agree that the U.S. must permit greater immigration to achieve higher levels of economic growth. The number of immigrants allowed in the country will have to double to 1 million a year for most of the next decade. In addition to helping to stave off inflation by accepting low wages, the immigrants will also provide the Social Security payroll deductions needed to support retired baby boomers in the 21st century.

We will finally make some headway on solving the child-care problem. The lack of moderately priced child care has become so conspicuous that both presidential candidates made child-care programs cornerstones of their campaigns. Two out of three scarce first-time workers will be women, 80% of whom are likely to get pregnant during their working years. As a result, companies will be forced to cater to family needs in order to promote, recruit, and retain talented employees. Rather than an increase in on-site child-care facilities, expect more firms to enable employees to pay for private child care with pretax dollars through payroll deductions.

Later in the decade, however, parent care may supersede child care as the leading bene-fits issue. In the 1990s, adults over the age of 85 will continue to be the fastest-growing segment of the population, increasing 49% by 1996, and roughly one in four will require some form of long-term care. Since caring for an elderly relative can undermine a worker's productivity—one survey estimates that lost employee hours because of elder-care responsibilities cost U.S. corporations $4 billion a year—companies will come under increasing pressure to broaden their benefits packages to include such care. A few companies have already begun. American Express, for example, permits employees to purchase nursing-home insurance for parents and in-laws at group rates. The cost varies according to the dependent's age (insurance for a 60-year-old parent would cost $936 a year).

The polarization between rich and poor will increase. Unfortunately, not all of us will share equally in the rising tide of prosperity in the 1990s. While by 1995 the number of households earning $60,000 or more a year will surge by more than a third over 1985 levels, economists project that those living in impoverished households (income of less than $10,989 for a family of four) could jump nearly 20%. This would put 42 million people, 16% of the total U.S. population, below the poverty threshold.

Where to Put Your Money

The next decade will provide an extraordinary environment for stocks, bonds, and mutual funds.

Although stocks of American industrial companies were the wallflowers of the last bull market, investment strategists predict that these issues will become the life of the party in the 1990s. Increased savings and investment will give U.S. industry the capital injection it needs to modernize plant and equipment and expand production. While the next market surge will not be limited to smokestack issues, many analysts expect industrial stocks to lead the way.

The long-awaited industrial renaissance has

already started. The business investment that's needed to keep exports booming jumped 6.5% in the first half of 1988 compared with 1.7% for all of 1987. But most analysts agree we are only at the beginning of a long period of rust-belt rehabilitation. Over the past five years, U.S. factories have expanded just 0.7% a year—the lowest rate since World War II—so investors should be cautiously selective over the short term.

Capital-spending stocks typically take off late in the economic cycle as factories reach their production limits—and then stumble hard when the economy slows down. The price of many manufacturing-related shares, which rose as much as 25% in the first nine months of 1988, could slip 15% in a moderate recession. Keeping such caveats in mind, here's a rundown of the sectors that could lead the pack in the years ahead:

Machinery and machine tools. Companies that produce the machinery needed to build new manufacturing equipment and factories will get the biggest push from the expected capital-spending boom. And as long as the dollar remains relatively depressed, companies that rely on exports for growing revenues will get an extra boost. One prime example is Caterpillar, a maker of earth-moving equipment used in construction, mining, and agriculture, which gets nearly half of its revenue from foreign customers. For 15 years or so, Caterpillar has been at a disadvantage to Komatsu, its major Japanese competitor, because of a strong currency and high production costs. Now the situation is reversed.

Raw-materials suppliers. If we are going to have all this capital spending, the companies will need something to build their parts and plants from. Thus steel, copper, and aluminum companies stand to flourish. Analysts favor companies such as copper producer Phelps Dodge and Alcoa; the cost cutting of the 1980s will allow them to wring far more profits out of higher future revenues. But such companies are sensitive to recession, so investors probably should postpone buying until the next one is under way.

Automation plays. Now that U.S. industry must meet growing demand, analysts expect a

wave of American manufacturers to install robotics and computer-aided production systems. Two leaders in this field are Teradyne and Mentor Graphics, both producers of test and design equipment for electronic circuitry.

Interest-rate-sensitive issues. In addition to high dividends, banks, regional telephone companies, and electric utilities offer investors a shot at capital appreciation if interest rates decline as many experts predict. As rates fall, investors are willing to pay more for the income provided by such stocks. These shares will fall in a recession but only about half as far as the market overall.

Among electric utilities, investors should emphasize well-managed companies with steadily increasing dividends that operate in areas where power demands will grow. Examples include Dominion Resources and Ipalco, the parent company of Indianapolis Power & Light. Investors should be wary, however, of utilities such as Columbus, Ohio's American Electric Power that rely almost exclusively on coal. The dividends could go up in smoke if the acid-rain legislation that is likely to be enacted in the early 1990s requires plants to be overhauled or replaced.

Like the electric utilities, regional telephone companies provide a measure of protection during economic slowdowns—people don't pull the plug on their phone during recessions. Standouts among the so-called Baby Bells include Southwestern Bell and BellSouth. Also home in on banking stocks that will excel in a deregulated environment. Most analysts expect banks to keep moving into the securities industry even if Congress does not, as expected, repeal the Glass-Steagall Act, which prohibits banks from underwriting stocks and bonds. One leader in investment banking is J.P. Morgan.

Industrial training, environmental, and health-care stocks. American industry already spends an estimated $200 billion a year retraining workers, and this figure is expected to increase significantly in the coming decade. The industry is so young that there is only one recognized front-runner: National Education Corporation. Through a subsidiary, National trains employees for more than 90% of the

Fortune 500 companies.

With medical waste washing up on our beaches, acid rain threatening our forests and lakes, and the deteriorating ozone layer exacerbating the highly publicized greenhouse effect, environmental quality may emerge as the political issue of the 1990s. As a result, demand for waste disposal and other environmental services should double over the next five years with profits expanding by more than 20% a year. The biggest investor opportunities are in the disposal of hazardous medical and industrial wastes. Two heavyweights in this sector are Waste Management and Browning-Ferris.

An aging population and increased longevity will help push U.S. health-care spending from $500 billion in 1987 to almost $1 trillion in 1995. But despite such rampant growth, the industry is fraught with risks. Glamorous biotechnology stocks such as Genentech and Cambridge BioScience sell at price/earnings ratios more than double those of the average stock. Health-care analysts also warn that overbuilding and poor management will lead to the failures of many hospital management companies in the next few years. Still, with hospitals under increasing pressure to hold down costs, analysts say the home health-care field offers special promise. Notable companies are New England Critical Care, which provides home antibiotic treatments, and Baxter International, which manufactures home health-care products in addition to medical equipment for use in hospitals.

The catastrophic-health-care bill recently passed by Congress may boost drug company earnings, particularly when Medicare begins picking up 60% of the tab for prescription drugs in 1991. To contain costs, Medicare may insist that doctors use lower-cost generic drugs whenever possible. So look for a future surge in sales at companies such as Bolar Pharmaceutical and Mylan, which specialize in generic products.

International stocks. Analysts see ways that U.S. investors might profit big from the planned dismantling of trade barriers among European nations by 1992. For example, they expect more mergers and takeovers as European companies scramble to gain footholds in countries where they have been excluded. Most likely takeover targets are companies currently selling below their assets' value or earning power. One potential target might be Nederlandsche Middenstandsbank, a Dutch bank trading at less than 70% of book value, or net worth per share.

Since the largest gains often come in the fastest-growing countries, U.S. investors may

Turning Points for Investors

IF YOU WANT TO . . .	THEN YOU SHOULD BUY WHEN . . .
Bet on the resurgence of industrial stocks	The Federal Reserve's industrial production index rises to a level one percentage point or more above prior-year levels for two consecutive months.
Invest in high-yield stocks and total-return mutual funds	The average yield of stocks in the Dow, recently 4.1%, hits or exceeds 4.5%.
Ride the anticipated boom in small-company stocks and emerging growth funds	The federal funds rate declines at least half a percentage point, signaling an easier monetary policy that could usher in a broad economic expansion.
Snap up stocks at bargain prices before values skyrocket in the next recovery	The price/earnings ratio on Standard & Poor's 500-stock index, recently 12.1, dips below the 8.5 level.

want to dip into the markets of emerging industrialized nations such as Korea, Malaysia, Taiwan, and Thailand, where economies are expanding 5% or more each year. The easiest way for U.S. investors to get into such countries is through closed-end mutual funds. But avoid those that sell at huge premiums to net asset value. The Korea Fund, for example, recently sold at a 77% premium to net asset value; that means you are paying 77% more than the market value of the fund's stocks. Investors are generally better off finding funds that sell below net asset value, such as Templeton Emerging Growth and Asia Pacific Fund, both of which invest in emerging growth markets and recently sold at more than 15% less than their net asset value.

Bonds

Many strategists predict that bonds—long considered stodgy investments—will become 1990s superstars, rewarding investors savvy enough to buy them now with exciting returns. Thirty-year Treasury bonds, recently yielding around 9%, already rival the 10% or so annual returns that stocks have paid over the past six decades. And if interest rates drop below 6% within the next few years—as some economists believe—today's holders of long-term Treasuries could reap capital gains of 42% or more on top of those fat yields. For stocks to match these lavish gains, the Dow Jones industrial average will have to hit at least 2900.

If, however, interest rates climb as high as 10.5% by mid-1989, as many economists predict, then investors who bought long-term bonds at 9% or so could see the value of their bonds drop by about 14%. Given the outlook, investors may want to postpone some of their bond buys until rates hit double digits. Whenever you buy, here are your options, ranked from least to most risky:

Treasury bonds. Issued in denominations of $1,000 and backed by the U.S. government, Treasury bonds are safe from default and also have virtually no call risk—that is, the possibility that falling interest rates will lead to early repayment of a bond, robbing investors of

their high yields and potential capital gains. With few exceptions, Treasury bonds cannot be repaid prematurely.

Steely-nerved investors who want to take full advantage of the forecasted decline over time in interest rates should opt for Treasuries maturing in 20 to 30 years. The longer the maturity, the more the bond's price will climb as interest rates fall. For example, if you own a 30-year Treasury bond yielding 9.5% and interest rates decline to 5%, you would reap a 70% capital gain.

But interest rates also rise, reducing the bond's value. So if you reach for antacid tablets at every bond price downtick, stick with Treasuries with maturities of 10 years or less. A seven-year Treasury note, yielding 8.8%, would drop just 5% in price if interest rates rose one percentage point—half the loss on a 30-year Treasury that yields less than a quarter of a percentage point more. And by going to a two-year note, you can pick up almost 95% of the yield of 30-year Treasuries, yet limit your risk to roughly one-fifth of that of the long-term bond.

Investors should keep in mind that you pay no state or local taxes on Treasuries. If your state and local income taxes total 5%, this exemption can boost the effective yield by almost one-half of a percentage point.

Municipals. With tax-exempt municipal bonds yielding roughly 85% of comparable taxable issues lately, investors in the 28% and 33% tax brackets have an opportunity to lock in extraordinary returns. For example, 20-year munis recently yielding 7.9% represent the equivalent of an 11% taxable return to investors in the 28% bracket and 11.8% to those with a 33% marginal tax rate.

Several potential developments could also point to an even brighter future for those who buy munis. If Congress raises income taxes to help reduce the deficit, the demand for—and, therefore, the price of—munis will surge. Another argument for munis is that Congress might extend limitations on municipal bond issuers that were enacted in the Tax Reform Act of 1986, thereby cutting the supply of new munis and making existing bonds even more valuable.

But recent uncertainty and turmoil in the tax-exempt market have also increased the risks. You should avoid those bonds most likely to be called—premium bonds, which sell at a price greater than face value because of their high coupon rates. To protect yourself against the risk of default by an issuer, you should have at least five different munis in your portfolio. Since these bonds are most frequently sold in minimum denominations of $5,000, this means an initial investment of at least $25,000. If that amount is too steep, you can invest instead in a bond mutual fund.

Finally, in the event that you might have to sell some of your munis, opt for bonds from large issues—$10 million or more. Smaller issues have thinner markets. Thus, instead of charging you the usual one-percentage-point markup at sale (which is usually built into the price) on an infrequently traded bond, your broker may assess as much as 5%.

Corporates. Investors should pass up high-grade corporate bonds in favor of Treasuries for two reasons. First, the spreads between Treasury yields and those of high-grade corporates is relatively narrow, with top-drawer AA-rated corporates yielding at most one percentage point more than Treasuries of comparable maturity. Second, the wave of takeovers, restructurings, and management buy-outs has made even high-grade corporate bonds far more risky. Corporate acquisitions and restructurings usually increase a company's level of debt, which, in turn, often leads to a lower credit rating on a company's existing bonds—and a lower price. A typical downgrading can knock off 20% of a long-term bond's value. Standard & Poor's, which rates corporate bonds, downgraded 216 through the first half of 1988.

Still, you can find good values in corporate bonds by sifting through junk bonds, those rated BB or lower or not rated at all. While junk bonds present a greater risk of default than higher-rated bonds, they compensate investors with a superior yield. Recently, junk bonds yielded between 12% for the issues of relatively healthy companies, to 16% for lesser-quality companies laden with debt. Because of the default risk, junk holdings must be more widely diversified than high-grade portfolios, and investors should exercise greater caution in assessing individual bonds. As such diversification and analysis are beyond the ken of most nonprofessionals, small investors are better off playing this risky game through high-yield bond funds.

International bonds. In 1987, American

Turning Points for Bond Buyers

IF YOU WANT TO . . .	LOOK FOR . . .	AND BUY . . .
Lock in high yields and don't mind wide price swings	Treasury bond yields to hit or exceed 10%	Treasury bonds maturing in 20 to 30 years or long-term U.S. Government bond funds.
Limit risk to principal and still earn up to 97% of long-term Treasury bond yields	Nothing; you can ignore interest-rate fluctuations	Treasuries maturing in four to seven years or intermediate-term U.S. Government bond funds.
Capture tax-free yields that beat Treasury bonds on an after-tax basis	Municipal bonds to yield 80% or more of Treasury bond rates	High-quality municipals that have maturities of at least 10 years or long-term muni bond funds.
Shoot for huge capital gains	Treasury bond yields to hit or exceed 10%	Zero-coupon bonds or zero-coupon bond funds.

investors in foreign bonds saw their holdings appreciate 21% in U.S. dollars. But much of that gain resulted from the sliding greenback, and investors in foreign bonds are unlikely to see such gains again soon. Still, U.S. investors should consider diversifying by keeping at least 15% of their fixed-income portfolio in international bonds. Foreign bond markets do not move in lockstep with the U.S. bond market, so a lackluster performance in U.S. Treasuries could be offset by gains in, say, British or Japanese bonds.

For the best returns, look for countries where yields adjusted for local inflation are equal to or higher than the 5% or so real return available in the U.S. Such countries' currencies are most likely to improve relative to the U.S. dollar. Examples include France, where 10-year government bonds recently yielded 9% and inflation was just 3%, and Canada, where inflation-adjusted returns have topped 5.5%.

Small investors may lean to international bond funds. Not only do such funds diversify among assets denominated in a number of currencies, they also hedge by buying and selling currency futures contracts—a technique too costly and complex for most individuals.

Zero-coupon bonds. For those investors who have no doubts that interest rates will drop precipitously and who want to shoot for the moon, long-term zero-coupon bonds are the ideal investment vehicle. Unlike other bonds, zeros pay no interest; instead, they are sold at a deep discount and redeemed at full face value at their maturity. A $1,000-denomination 20-year zero-coupon Treasury bond, for example, sold in August 1988 for $157, resulting in a yield to maturity of 9.5%. Since zeros withhold all interest until their due dates, their prices are far more volatile than are conventional bonds. A two-percentage-point rate drop in six months would increase the price of that $157 zero to $239, giving its holder a 46% capital gain. But you can get seriously hurt if interest rates go the wrong way. The value of that same bond would drop 31% if interest rates were to increase by two points—just about double the loss on a conventional 20-year Treasury bond.

The unique characteristics of zeros also allow them to play a role in conservative investors' portfolios. Such investors can match the maturity of zeros to coincide with specific financial goals—say, retirement or a child's education. They can then ignore any seesawing in the security's price, content knowing exactly how much their investment will be worth when it matures.

Zero-coupon bonds do have a drawback. Although you don't receive any interest until the bonds' maturity, you are taxed as though you received a portion of it every year. This is not a problem, however, if you park your zeros in an Individual Retirement Account, Keogh, or other tax-deferred account. If you want to invest outside such accounts, you should look into tax-exempt zero-coupon municipal bonds.

Mutual Funds

Want to know which stock mutual funds will lead the charge in the next decade? Simple. Just rank the types of funds by their performance in the last bull market and turn the list upside down. That's right: Small-company growth funds, the also-rans of the mutual fund world since 1983, have moved into the favorite's slot among analysts.

Why relatively risky, small-company funds? For one thing, small, adaptable companies respond quickly to change and typically zoom ahead in the early stages of a bull market. In addition, after being largely ignored in the last market advance, shares in small and medium-size companies are relatively cheap. Small-company stocks often sport price/earnings ratios that are twice that of the average stock, as investors willingly pay a premium for the prospect of big future earnings. In July 1988, however, the average P/E of the stocks in T. Rowe Price's small-company fund, New Horizons, was only 20% above that of Standard & Poor's 500-stock index.

To help you put together the right mix of funds for the 1990s, here is a look at some of the best choices in the best five categories:

Growth funds. Buy-and-hold investors should

make growth funds the core of their portfolios. The best beat the stock market averages over periods of five years or more. Invested in companies whose earnings are chugging along at an annual 15% or more, these funds stick to larger, more established firms than small-company growth funds. Be mindful, though, of the short-term risk: if recession wrecks the market, growth funds' net asset values will plunge, though not as much as the small-company ones will.

If you want a fund that will respond quickly to a surging market, concentrate on the high-risk end of the spectrum—funds that invest in cyclicals and high fliers. For example, Ken Heebner, manager of New England Growth, racked up superior gains in the last bull market by stuffing his portfolio with cyclical stocks such as Ford and Bethlehem Steel. You can take a smoother trip to long-term gains by investing in growth funds that look for shares of undervalued companies—generally companies selling at low P/Es or at market prices that are below book value, or net worth per share.

Small-company growth funds. You can lower your risk in this category by selecting funds that hunt for undervalued small-company shares. For example, Chuck Royce, manager of Pennsylvania Mutual and Royce Value funds, looks for small companies selling at a discount to book value or with P/Es that are as much as 15% below the market's. Some of the best bargains are in closed-end funds—mutual funds whose shares trade on exchanges like stocks and sometimes sell at a discount to their net asset values. For example, Nicholas Applegate recently sold at a 14% discount and Quest for Value Capital Appreciation at a 27% discount. If small-company stocks do lead the next bull market, closed-end owners could get a bonus as the discounts disappear.

Total-return funds. In the last bull market, this catchall category that invests in blue-chip stocks and high-quality bonds actually beat their riskier growth fund counterparts. While this anomaly is not likely to repeat in the next stock market surge, you can count on these funds to provide consistently superior returns for their level of risk. If interest rates plunge over the next few years, these funds will enjoy a double-barreled boost as bond and stock prices rise. Standouts include Evergreen Total Return, a growth and income fund that favors bank stocks and convertible bonds, and Fidelity Equity Income, which invests in utilities and emerging growth stocks.

Bond funds. The expected decline in interest rates in the 1990s could propel button-down bond funds to the top. If you are an unflappable big-gain hunter, set your sights on long-term U.S. Government bond funds, specifically those that buy Treasury bonds with maturities of 10 years or longer. If interest rates drop just two percentage points, the share price of funds with average maturities of 15 years or longer could increase by at least 18%. If interest rates rise first, you can minimize the damage by sticking to government bond funds with intermediate-term maturities of four to seven years. Ultraconservative investors can reduce risk even further by stepping down to funds with average maturities of two to five years.

For investors in the 28% and 33% tax brackets, long-term municipal bond funds offer tax-equivalent yields as high as 12.7%. You can reduce interest-rate risk by going to intermediate-term muni funds. With high-yield corporate bond funds—otherwise known as junk bond funds—you can grab yields as high as 13.2%. Avoid the funds with the highest yields (they usually hold the riskiest bonds). Instead, go for ones whose superior performances testify to their managers' research and credit analysis skills.

International funds. The key to international investing over the next few years is to find funds whose management can seek out the countries and stocks with strong fundamentals now that the currency play has ended. One such fund is Vanguard Trustees International Commingled, which seeks both income and capital gains. The fund recently was invested primarily in Japan, the United Kingdom, Canada, and West Germany. Stick to foreign bond funds that spread their holdings among a minimum of six countries. Top performers include T. Rowe Price International Bond and Fidelity Global Bond.

Your 100 Best Investments

Although there's something for everybody among these picks, what's best for you depends on what you plan to be doing in the 1990s—and your personal aspirations.

Investors who are looking ahead to the 1990s must worry not only about the economic big picture but also about the fine brushwork of their own financial situations. How you invest will depend on how old you are, whether you have children, and what you expect to be doing in the 1990s. The best choices will be somewhat different for everyone. Thus, the following list of the 100 stocks, bonds, mutual funds, and other investments that ought to do especially well in coming years is divided according to the investment goals they address and the levels of risk they present.

The group whose objective is *potential big scores* combines stocks of small, fast-growing companies with those of big industrial firms. (A listing of just a company's name indicates common stock. All stocks are traded on the New York Stock Exchange unless otherwise indicated. The notation for American Stock Exchange is ASE; OTC stands for over the counter.) The small-company picks here are concentrated in some of the most promising industries for the 1990s. But these stocks are among the riskiest: Investors with high expectations will dump them fast if growth targets are not met. Most of the mutual funds in this category invest in small-company stocks.

The bigger firms have cut costs in the 1980s and are now booming; they expect to continue doing so into the 1990s. Nonetheless, their business and their stocks could suffer in an economic downturn. With such cyclical stocks, investors should buy after a recession is under

way and decide on a target price—the price at which they would sell. Included in the listings, where appropriate, are reasonable target prices.

The *steady gains* category contains a selection of large, well-known companies with consistent growth records where analysts project earnings gains of 15% or more a year. In addition, some entries are banks and other financial institutions that stand to benefit if interest rates plummet, as expected, because their cost of money would fall faster than the rates they offer their borrowers. Many of this category's choices maintained earnings growth during past recessions. A few issues, such as the waste-disposal stocks, have the advantage of being in an explosive area in addition to being resistant to downturns. While some of the mutual funds listed here buy such stocks, others follow different investment approaches. One way or the other, all have performed relatively well through both past bull and bear markets.

The least risky kinds of investments often get part or all of their returns from income. The *growth with income* category includes stocks that pay a dividend near 4%; most have projected annual earnings increases of at least 10% for the next three to five years. *Dependable income* features mainly stocks with dividends of 6% or more—electric utilities and real estate investment trusts—plus bonds and bond funds. The *tax savings* category contains tax-exempt municipal bonds, as well as other tax-advantaged investments.

In general, younger investors with strong career prospects and no family responsibilities can afford to take more risk and go for bigger returns. Whatever your age and circumstances, however, you would be wise to pick from more than one group. A professional couple in their thirties trying to build assets for a distant retirement, for instance, might put 50% into stocks or mutual funds from the steady-gains class, 25% in the potential big scores, and 25% in dependable income. A couple in their forties with teenage children, on the other hand, might put 10% to 20% into zero-coupon bonds with maturities matched to the years when their kids' college tuition payments come due. The balance, earmarked for a retirement that's only 20 years away, might be split evenly among the steady gainers, growth and income, and dependable income.

Potential Big Scores

Some of these risky issues could more than double:

Aluminum Co. of America. The capital-spending boom is expected to boost Alcoa's sales from $9.2 billion in 1988 to $11.5 billion by 1993. Recent price: $51. Target: $95

ALZA Corp. Controlled-release systems, such as skin patches, that deliver steady doses of medicine will be increasingly used. ALZA, with $100 million in sales, provides such systems. Recent price: $22. Target: $40 (ASE)

Baxter International. Growing sales of Baxter's medical supplies, especially overseas, figure to keep earnings growing 25% a year. Recent price: $21.50. Target: $55

Bolt Beranek & Newman. New Army and Navy contracts are projected to power 28% annual earnings growth for this $325 million computer and communications firm. Recent price: $15.75. Target: $45

CareerCom. The growing need for vocational training will boost CareerCom, which has $135 million in annual sales. Recent price: $12. Target: $30

Caterpillar. A weaker dollar has restored Caterpillar's profitability in heavy machinery. Lean operations after '80s cutbacks may bring

18% average annual earnings gains. Recent price: $56. Target: $100

Compaq Computer. Analysts think Compaq's new products will keep it competitive with rival IBM. Recent price: $55.50. Target: $120

Cooper Industries. Expanding manufacturing companies will buy Cooper's cables and compressors. Recent price: $53. Target: $100

Dresser Industries. A pared-down Dresser is picking up sales for its oil field equipment as U.S. drilling continues to rebound. Recent price: $29.50. Target: $60

Fidelity Magellan Fund. This $9.3 billion fund could surge with the small-company stocks manager Peter Lynch favors. Ten-year record: up an average 28.8% a year.

General Nutrition. Expansion through franchising and boutiques in larger stores will increase sales for this $360 million retailer of vitamins. Recent price: $5.63. Target: $16

Harnischfeger Industries. Heavy spending for the manufacturing equipment Harnischfeger makes could boost earnings by 35% annually. Recent price: $18.50. Target: $30

Hartwell Emerging Growth Fund. This fund's concentration on small-company stocks has paid off with gains of 15.4% a year over the past 10 years.

Johnson Controls. An auto-parts shake-out is knocking off competitors of Johnson, which manufactures seats and other parts for car makers. Recent price: $32.50. Target: $50

Mentor Graphics. Spending by semiconductor makers for computer-aided design equipment may help $295 million Mentor increase its earnings an average of 20% a year. Recent price: $29.75. Target: $60 (OTC)

National Education Corp. Companies' burgeoning need to retrain workers could fuel 25% annual earnings growth at National Education. The firm, the field's leader, has $440 million in sales. Recent price: $28. Target: $50

New England Critical Care. Doctors will increasingly approve treatments at home instead of in hospitals. Companies such as this will deliver such treatment. Recent price: $22.75. Target: $50 (OTC)

New England Growth Fund. Fund manager Ken Heebner has a strong record of jumping into cyclical stocks at the right time. The fund gained an average of 20.8% annually over the past 10 years.

Phelps Dodge. The largest U.S. copper producer will benefit from the capital-spending boom. Recent price: $38.25. Target: $100

Poster for the movie *Chinatown.* Collectors expect these unusually beautiful ads, which appeared in moviehouse lobbies during the hit film's 1974 run, to gain 15% a year. Recent price: $250. Target: $500

T. Rowe Price International Stock Fund. This fund is positioned to gain from the phaseout of European trade barriers in 1992.

Regal-Beloit. This cutting-tool manufacturer with $155 million in sales will benefit from the rust-belt renaissance. Recent price: $16.75. Target: $25 (ASE)

Teradyne. Testing equipment from Teradyne is selling well to the booming semiconductor and phone equipment industries. Recent price: $15. Target: $35

Trinity Industries. The major U.S. supplier of railcars, Trinity is poised to cash in on growing demand as shipments of capital equipment increase. Recent price: $31.50. Target: $55

Twentieth Century Select Fund. The fund managers' stock picking has produced a 10-year record of 20.3% annual gains.

U.S. postage stamps of 1847 to 1919. Specialists expect mint condition issues to rise in value by about 15% annually. Recent price: around $50 a stamp and up.

Zero-coupon U.S. Treasury bonds. Thirty-year zeros will go up more than twice as much as regular Treasuries when interest rates decline. Potential capital gain: 114% if rates fall two points over three years.

Steady Gains

These time-tested stocks and funds offer solid growth prospects:

American Express. An increased savings rate is expected to help the company's investment divisions. Recent price: $29.25. Target: $50

Banc One. Ohio-based Banc One is expanding in the booming Midwest. Recent price: $25.25. Target: $45

Barnett Banks. Growing business across affluent Florida is likely to allow Barnett to extend its 12-year streak of rising profits. Recent price: $35. Target: $50

Boeing. As airlines replace aging fleets, Boeing's order backlog, now $18 billion, will stay high. Recent price: $62. Target: $95

Bolar Pharmaceutical. Earnings are expected to leap 20% a year on the strength of Bolar's bargain-priced generic-drug offerings. Recent price: $19.75. Target: $40 (ASE)

Browning-Ferris Industries. Acquisition of smaller firms has provided this waste-disposal company with hard-to-obtain landfill sites. Analysts project 20% annual earnings gains. Recent price: $27.75. Target: $50

Community Psychiatric Centers. This operator of psychiatric hospitals is building new facilities. Recent price: $23.75. Target: $50

Walt Disney. Disney's management, which has created a series of blockbuster movies and is opening theme parks in Europe and Asia, is expected to keep profits surging 20% a year. Recent price: $62.75. Target: $125

Dow Chemical. As strong demand for chemicals continues, Dow's earnings are projected to climb 25% a year. Recent price: $86.25. Target: $165

Dun & Bradstreet. Recent acquisitions, including a drug-marketing information firm, will keep D&B in the forefront of the business information field. Profits could grow 13% a year. Recent price: $50.25. Target: $100

John H. Harland Co. Harland has added Scantron, a maker of machines that score standardized tests, to its check-printing business. The mix is expected to produce 14% annual earnings growth. Recent price: $20.25. Target: $40

International Dairy Queen. This chain is charging higher franchise fees and opening new outlets. Recent price: $32.50. Target: $60 (OTC)

Kelly Services. A manpower firm, Kelly is likely to benefit from the long-term corporate trend toward hiring temporary workers. Recent price: $40.50. Target: $72 (OTC)

Masco. Long dominant in kitchen and

bathroom fixtures, Masco's acquisitions of two furniture lines could boost profits 13% a year. Recent price: $25.25. Target: $50

McDonald's. McProfits continues to open foreign outlets. Recent price: $46.75. Target: $90

Merck. By spending more on research than any other drug company does, Merck will keep profits rising at least 20% a year. Recent price: $58. Target: $130

Mutual Shares. Manager Michael Price has a 10-year record of average annual returns of 20.4%.

Mylan Laboratories. Powered by the success of its generic drugs, Mylan ought to be able to produce 20% annual earnings gains into the 1990s. Recent price: $10.25. Target: $40

Neuberger & Berman Partners. Fund managers have produced an annual total return of 18.9% over the past 10 years.

Pennsylvania Mutual. Fund manager Charles Royce's pursuit of stocks selling below asset value has produced a 10-year average annual return of 17.6%.

PepsiCo. The world's second largest soft-drink maker has protected itself further against recession by diversifying into food businesses. Recent price: $37. Target: $50

Prime Motor Inns. The operator or franchisor of more than 500 motels nationwide, Prime Motor Inns continues to grow at least 20% a year. Recent price: $33.50. Target: $70

SoGen International. By switching assets among U.S. and foreign securities and cash, this fund has posted an average annual return of 19.6% over the past 10 years.

Student Loan Marketing Association. This federally chartered but publicly owned corporation will be able to lock in steady profits on guaranteed student loans. Earnings will grow about 25% a year. Recent price: $79.75. Target: $145

Wal-Mart. Wal-Mart is building on its base of small-town stores with new warehouse-style hypermarkets in large cities. Analysts project profit growth of 25% a year. Recent price: $31.50. Target: $70

Waste Management. Waste Management handles both garbage and chemical-waste disposal. Profits are expected to rise at least 20%

a year. Recent price: $39.75. Target: $65

Growth with Income

The choices listed here pay you while you wait for capital gains:

Bank of Boston. Sporting a 4% dividend yield, Bank of Boston could produce 20% annual earnings growth as its business prospers along with the New England region. Recent price: $27.25. Target: $50

Bristol-Myers. Bristol-Myers has a number of important cancer drugs among its products. Its yield last month was 3.9%. Recent price: $43.50. Target: $85

Consolidated Natural Gas. Sales of Consolidated's clean-burning natural gas will get a boost from environmental concerns. This financially strong company has a 4.5% yield. Recent price: $37.75. Target: $60

Dreyfus Convertible Securities. By investing at least 65% of its assets in convertible bonds—which will rise along with stock prices in the 1990s—this mutual fund has achieved an average annual return of 14.1% over the past 10 years.

Evergreen Total Return Fund. This nine-year-old stock and bond fund has produced a 15.1% average annual return over the past five years. The portfolio currently includes utilities and other stocks that gain from lower rates.

Exxon. Exxon's dividend, which produces a 4.8% yield, is expected to rise 7% a year. The stock will reward you further if oil prices increase. Recent price: $45. Target: $60

Fidelity Equity Income. Manager Bruce Johnstone kept this fund a top performer throughout much of the 1970s and 1980s. The fund's 10-year average annual total return: 19.4%.

Gilbert Associates. Cost cutting plus acquisitions have improved prospects for Gilbert's consulting and engineering businesses serving utility and industrial clients. Gilbert, with $265 million in sales, has a 4.4% yield. Recent price: $18.25. Target: $28 (OTC)

J.P. Morgan. With its roster of blue-chip corporate clients, Morgan is set to thrive in a deregulated environment that may allow banks to underwrite securities. Its yield is 4%. Recent price: $38.50. Target: $60

Pfizer. High research outlays have positioned Pfizer to capitalize on the anticipated prescription drug boom. Its dividend yield is 3.7%. Recent price: $53.50. Target: $140

Royal Dutch Petroleum. Low-cost production and exploration could enlarge Royal Dutch's dividend, producing a 6.7% current yield, by as much as 10% a year. Recent price: $109.75. Target: $155

Safeco Income Fund. Investments in high-yield stocks plus convertible bonds have produced a 16.4% average annual total return over the past 10 years.

St. Paul Cos. This property and casualty insurance company with a 4.7% dividend yield would cash in on lower interest rates. Recent price: $42.50. Target: $75 (OTC)

Servicemaster. A longtime provider of institutional cleaning service, Servicemaster is expanding into more profitable household cleaning. The master limited partnership, recently yielding 6.1%, is forecast to raise its payout 10% annually. Recent price: $27.75. Target: $50

South Jersey Industries. Population growth around Atlantic City is expected to enhance this gas utility's profits. It recently yielded 7.2%. Recent price: $18.25. Target: $28

Strong Total Return Fund. This seven-year-old fund has a five-year average annual total return of 15.1%.

Travelers. A diversified insurance company with a 7.1% yield, Travelers has a large bond portfolio that could benefit from falling rates. Recent price $34. Target: $75

United Dominion Realty Trust. A real estate investment trust with a 6.1% yield, United Dominion buys and renovates properties in high-growth areas in Virginia and the Carolinas. Recent price: $17.50. Target: $30 (OTC)

United Telecommunications. This operator of telephone utilities with a 5.8% yield also owns 80% of the Sprint long-distance network, where profits figure to start flowing in the early 1990s. Analysts predict 25% annual earnings growth. Recent price: $38. Target: $65

Washington REIT. With properties in the prosperous Washington, D.C. area, this REIT recently yielded 5.2%. Rent increases could boost its dividend 8% a year. Recent price: $27. Target: $40 (ASE)

Dependable Income

Many of these investments will raise their payouts:

American Insured Mortgage Investors. This partnership finances properties, receiving a portion of the rent as part of its return. By targeting properties due for rent increases, AIM may boost its payout from 7% to 9%.

Bell Atlantic. Earnings and dividends of this regional telephone company are projected to grow 7% annually as its Mid-Atlantic area continues to prosper. Recent yield: 5.8%

BellSouth. Friendly regulators in the South will continue to allow BellSouth to earn high rates of return. Dividends are forecast to rise 7% annually. Recent yield: 5.9%

Capital Preservation Treasury Trust. This mutual fund invests in U.S. Government obligations with maturities of no more than 10 years. Recent yield: 7.7%

Central & South West. The Southwest's resurgent economy is likely to help this Texas-based electric utility. Recent yield: 7.9%

Commonwealth Edison. Because of regulatory problems involving its nuclear plants, investors have labeled this Illinois-based electric utility as risky. Most analysts, however, think its dividend is secure. Recent yield: 9.8%

Consolidated Edison. Financially solid Con Ed will not need to lay out money for new plants, thereby allowing the New York City-based company to raise its dividend at least 7% a year into the 1990s. Recent yield: 7.4%

Financial Bond Shares High Yield Fund. This fund's manager produces its high return with careful credit analysis of so-called junk bonds. Recent yield: 11.7%

Florida Progress Corp. Florida's swelling population of affluent retirees assures continued growth for this electric utility. Analysts project dividend increases of 4% a year. Recent yield: 7%

Houston Industries. Past problems involving two nuclear plants have depressed this electric utility's stock price and boosted its yield. Recent yield: 10.2%

Intermediate-term Treasury bonds. Seven-to-10-year Treasuries pay 8.9%, or 95% of the yield of longer, more volatile bonds.

Krupp Insured Mortgage. By buying federally insured so-called participating mortgages, which allow investors to profit from rising rents, this partnership is likely to lift its annual payout from 8% to 11% over 10 years.

MGI Properties. With more than half of this mortgage REIT's industrial properties in the booming Midwest, annual dividend growth of 5% or more from increasing rents seems probable. Recent yield: 8.3%

Mortgage & Realty Trust. This REIT is expected to maintain its high 10.8% yield from long-term mortgages already on its books.

PacifiCorp. A holding company with electric and telephone utility subsidiaries in eight western states, PacifiCorp will produce enough growth for 3.5% annual dividend increases. Recent yield: 7.6%

Prudential-Bache Gov. Intermediate. This mutual fund contains U.S. Government issues with average 10-year maturities. Recent yield: 9.4%

SCE Corp. Dividends are projected to rise 4% a year as this Southern California electric utility benefits from the area's diversified economy. Recent yield: 7.6%

Strong Government Securities. This no-load mutual fund contains bonds with varying maturities. Recent yield: 6.7%

Texas Utilities. The imminent opening of a new nuclear plant will permit this utility to raise its dividend. Recent yield: 10.2%

Wisconsin Energy. As it capitalizes on the rust-belt revival, Wisconsin Energy ought to be able to raise its dividend 6.5% a year. Recent yield: 5.8%

Tax Savings

These investments defer income taxes or avoid them entirely:

Cuyahoga County, Ohio bonds of 2000. Zero-coupon municipal bonds such as these avoid the tax problems of Treasury zeros. Recently selling at $423 per $1,000 of face value, this zero had a yield to maturity of 7.25%, the equivalent of a 10.1% taxable yield for someone in the 28% bracket.

Diversified Historic Investors VI. Investors in this real estate partnership will get two tax credits—one for rehabilitating historic buildings and a second for creating low-income housing for the elderly. Credits in the first three years may add up to more than 30% of your initial investment. The expected total annualized return over 10 years, including tax credits: 9% to 10%. Minimum investment: $3,000

Fidelity Limited Term Bond Fund. This municipal bond fund has an average maturity of less than 11 years, long enough for a yield of 6.5% (equivalent to a 9% taxable yield in the 28% bracket) but short enough to reduce the risk of loss should interest rates rise.

Lincoln Benefit Life Annuity. Single-premium annuities permit deferral of taxes on investment earnings. Lincoln's version has lower fees and withdrawal charges than some competitors' offerings. With a minimum $5,000 investment, this plan was recently guaranteeing 8.25% for the first three years.

Nuveen Intermediate Trust. This soon-to-be-available unit trust, similar to those issued by other sponsors, will contain a diversified selection of municipal bonds with average 10-year maturities. Expected yield: 6.7%, the equivalent of a 9.3% taxable yield for taxpayers in the 28% bracket. Minimum investment: $5,000. Single-state trusts are also available.

Puerto Rico 7.75% bonds of 2013. A special congressional proviso makes Commonwealth of Puerto Rico bonds exempt from state and local taxes everywhere in the U.S. (You can get a similar exemption if you buy your home-state bonds.) Selling at par, the Puerto Rico bond's 7.75% yield is the equivalent of a taxable 10.8% in the 28% bracket. The bond is callable in 1998.

Vanguard Muni Bond—Long Term. This fund holds high-grade municipals with 20-year average maturities. Its broad portfolio will cushion it if some bonds are called early. Recent yield: 7.4%, the equivalent of a taxable 10.3% in the 28% bracket.

Career and Entrepreneurial Opportunities

Success will come to those who are most adept at communicating—with consumers, the elderly, trade-minded foreigners, or computers.

Attention, prospective job applicants. For plentiful opportunities and lucrative wages, consider professions that are sizzling already, such as electrical engineering and computer programming, or those that are just beginning to take off, namely health care, job training, and travel services. The best opportunities for starting a business will be in the same fields that will provide the most promising jobs. In addition, the 1990s' booming service economy, dominated by small companies, will boost the survival rate of the next crop of ambitious entrepreneurs.

The following four themes are likely to dominate employment trends you'll see in the 1990s:

● The better you communicate, the stronger your job prospects. For example, college grads who can speak to computers will be able to find jobs easily. So will anyone fluent in foreign languages, as nearly every U.S. industry expands overseas.

● Go with the demographic flow by seeking to serve the growing legions of people over 40 or working parents.

● If you are in middle management, start acquiring unique employment skills to preserve your paycheck when educated baby boomers turn 40 and come around competing for your job.

● If your field has been hot, it runs a risk of

being overcrowded tomorrow. Therefore, you should think twice before becoming an investment banker or courting a law degree, for example. The American Bar Foundation expects the number of attorneys to grow by 27% by 1995, hitting 900,000. Competition could force most of the 237,000 new lawyers of the 1990s to settle for relatively low pay, tedious work, or a career in the boondocks. There are at least seven fields that seem poised to benefit from these major trends. Here they are in alphabetical order, complete with appropriate entrepreneurial opportunities:

Child Care. You don't have to be a futurist to figure out that there will be an enormous need for child-care centers in the next decade. More than two-thirds of the 1990s' new workers will be women of child-bearing age. Industry analysts expect the number of child-care centers—now a paltry 65,000—to grow 15% a year from now through 1993. Child-care workers typically get meager wages, but employees at day-care centers catering to upper-income families will continue receiving salaries about 15% to 25% higher than those at other centers. Managers of child-care centers can expect to earn $25,000 to $40,000. Ideal job candidates are teachers with good heads for business.

For the entrepreneur: Significant opportunities abound in strong economic areas such as the mid-Atlantic states, North Carolina, and

Southern California. Start-up costs for a 100-child facility run a minimum of $250,000 or so, mostly to pay for rent, salaries, liability insurance, advertising, and supplies. It typically takes nine to 18 months before your earnings exceed expenses. The most likely to make it will be persons with successful histories of operating centers, so it pays to start now. Then if your center catches on, you might be able to sell it for 1.25 times your gross annual revenues.

Computers. As computer use expands, technology-related jobs will increase by about 15% a year. Among the most desirable careers are assemblers, service technicians, and systems analysts. Earning an undergraduate degree in computer science is not mandatory. But you should get some training in operating the machines in college or on the job. Salaries in computer fields could climb 1.5 to two times faster than the inflation rate as demand for trained pros picks up. For example, in 1995 a programmer in bioengineering who has 10 years of experience might earn more than $90,000 a year in today's dollars, compared with $70,000 or so now.

For the entrepreneur: Some of the best prospects revolve around creating independent computer-repair companies that service companies or individuals. It takes as little as $100 worth of tools to launch one, and the only experience you need is training from a technical school or an employer in fixing popular hardware or mainframes. Software programming start-ups also require relatively modest up-front capital—typically no more than the cost of a personal computer —but they face vicious competition. The riskiest businesses will be retailing computer hardware and software, an overcrowded field. You'll need more than $100,000 to buy inventory and cover at least eight months' worth of expenses.

Engineering. Anyone with a bachelor's degree in science or mathematics may be able to get a high-paying job as an engineer during the 1990s. Foreigners already seem to know this; nearly half the nation's engineering graduate students today come from outside the U.S. Electrical engineers will be in the greatest demand, rising in number by 48% from 1986 to

2000. Reason: The growth of new technology requires electrical systems designed by more engineers. Mechanical and industrial engineers can also expect a choice of job offers as manufacturers hire them to create more complex, cost-cutting technological machinery—including robots—to replace humans.

Other engineering specialties will flourish, depending on what national concerns the federal government decides to address during the next decade. If Congress chooses to overhaul the nation's infrastructure, civil engineers will benefit. If it directs more money toward finding a cure for AIDS, biomedical engineers will be in demand. Increased spending on Star Wars strategic defense initiative will help physicists and electrical engineers. And the major push to increase investments in environmental cleanup will boost chemical and mechanical engineers. Many engineers can readily learn specific skills within a couple of years to move into their field of choice.

For the entrepreneur: Setting up a private consulting practice makes sense only for those experienced engineers who have a network of corporate contacts. But if you qualify, odds are that your business will eventually provide more than you could earn working for a corporation.

Financial Services. As the average age of the population rises, more Americans will need financial planning help. Older families tend to have more savings but face such challenges as paying their children's college bills and providing for their own retirement. The hot job categories are likely to be financial planners and actuaries.

Most financial planners get their start at brokerage houses, insurance companies, banks, and accounting firms. Those who go on to get degrees from the demanding College for Financial Planning in Denver will be most highly sought after. Actuaries make calculations regarding life-span probabilities that determine insurance premiums and payouts plus annuities, among other things. The most valuable education is a bachelor's degree in math or statistics. The 12,000 actuaries will go on enjoying limited competition; a great many students consider the profession boring.

For the entrepreneur: The most successful self-employed financial planners will continue to earn well over $100,000. But independent planners will require more than just salesmanship to succeed. Evolving regulatory standards will force planners to take ongoing education classes to stay in business.

Health Care. A person's need for medical services rises substantially after age 40, a stage already reached by the oldest baby boomers, with another 41 million to follow during the decade. Nearly all types of health-care professionals will have the luxury of weighing a multitude of high-paying job possibilities. Even physicians who have found it tougher to build their practices during the past five years can look forward to more patients and higher incomes. Many medical schools, which face openings as students turn away from becoming doctors, have begun easing their admissions standards. Two other fast-growing health-care occupations will be physical therapy and medical-record technology.

The current shortage of registered nurses may foretell similar crises in other areas. Within just two years, Americans will require one additional registered nurse for every two of the 1.4 million nurses now employed. And R.N.s' traditionally poor salaries are rising rapidly to lure people into the profession. In 1988, unionized nurses in San Francisco won a 21% pay raise over 34 months, which will ultimately bring top salaries for night nurses to $52,000.

For the entrepreneur: Health care will be one of the hottest fields for entrepreneurs in the 1990s. Some people are getting in on this trend early. Many nurses have become so disillusioned with hospital staffing shortages that they have decided to launch their own home health-care services.

Job Training. If teaching appeals to you but instructing rambunctious youths for low pay does not, consider training employed adults. At least 400 large companies, such as Chrysler and Manufacturers Hanover, already have programs to train workers to perform their jobs more effectively. Private firms may soon spend more than $60 billion a year on classes for employees, approaching the total expenditures of the nation's four-year colleges. More than 10 million employees are now being trained or retrained, compared with 12 million undergraduate students.

The types of courses taught in corporate classrooms will range from the three Rs to highly technical instruction. As a result, job candidates with teaching skills will be in demand throughout the decade. Starting salaries may not be much better than those at public schools, but some companies now pay mid-level instructors as much as $50,000 a year and program supervisors more than $100,000.

For the entrepreneur: Increasingly, the Fortune 500 corporations are hiring smaller instructional firms to train their workers. Successful start-ups will specialize in teaching subjects useful to a broad range of companies. Courses likely to remain in demand include explaining how to operate computers and ways to develop effective sales techniques. Typical start-up cost for the first six months is about $50,000, but three times that amount if you intend to offer computer training.

Travel. As more of the population prosper, Americans will splurge on vacations. They will need help getting there and then enjoying themselves after they arrive. So employment at travel agencies, hotels, and motels is expected to take off during the 1990s, with the number of jobs for hotel managers and assistants expanding 50% during the decade. The best opportunities will go to people with graduate degrees in hotel administration. As international travel accelerates worldwide, people fluent in foreign languages will be prized by domestic hotels and travel agencies. When the dollar is weak, as it has been in recent years, foreign tourists fill up U.S. hotels and motels. When the dollar strengthens, travel agencies arrange more trips abroad for Americans.

For the entrepreneur: The most successful travel agencies will be those that go beyond just booking reservations and focus, instead, on giving good advice about the best places to stay. By the way, if you share the popular dream of opening your own quaint country inn or small efficiency motel, win the lottery first. Your place could cost $25,000 to $75,000 per room.

Comstock Inc./Tom Grill

Your Investments

Successful investing begins with the premise that each of us has the opportunity—and obligation—to preserve and protect our money and to make it grow. This chapter addresses many of these opportunities as well as the risks inherent in most types of investment. The changing moods of the stock and bond markets are only two of the factors you must consider in deciding how best to deploy your assets. Most important, you want to take advantage of—or reduce your exposure to—major economic trends. In doing so, you will want to make subtle adjustments in your mix of assets as your life evolves in terms of your career, family situation, and tolerance for risk.

A lifetime plan for prudently investing your wealth and conquering risk should commence when you first start to own assets in your name, usually in your twenties. At that time, you should diversify broadly in four or five types of investments: domestic stocks and bonds, real estate, international securities, and cash. If you believe in gold's efficacy as an inflation hedge or in its power as a store of value, you might also consider adding a dollop of the heavy metal to your mix.

Since you have plenty of time to ride out periodic market downturns at this stage, you can afford to take somewhat greater risks than you would later in life. Therefore, many advisers recommend that young investors put the most substantial subset of their assets in stocks, which historically provide the highest return over time of any liquid investments. If you are not comfortable picking individual securities, choose instead a widely diversified mutual fund. And since it's unlikely that you will be able to afford investment property at this age, stick with growth-oriented real estate investment trusts (REITs), which trade like stocks, or try mutual funds that buy REIT shares.

To get international stocks into your mix, elect a no- or low-load overseas mutual fund. Such funds reduce transaction costs and spare you the need of researching foreign companies. Long-term corporate, U.S., or municipal bonds (with maturities of

20 years or more), and the funds that invest in them will give you potentially the most generous combination of high current yield and possible price appreciation. Money-market funds and certificates of deposit are the most secure and convenient stores for your cash.

No matter what your age or how you apportion your wealth among the investment areas, the challenge is to find your comfort zone—and to know that it may change. Investors with less than $20,000 should be prepared to realign their plan at least once a year. People with power portfolios of $200,000 or more should monitor their monies at least quarterly. How much time you spend noodling over your nest egg will depend largely on where it is invested. Mutual funds are easier to track, for instance, than a variety of individual securities. In any case, plan on spending at least a couple of hours each year, and maybe much more, rebalancing your holdings.

How Vulnerable Are You?

True diversification begins with an unsentimental journey into your finances.

Although many investors are haunted by fears of financial catastrophe, few recognize all the varied ways in which they are vulnerable to disasters such as a stock market crash. Even less shattering events, such as a sudden rise in interest rates or an unexpected recession, can cause big losses.

You can avoid such setbacks by taking a good look at what you own. First, you should carefully scrutinize your investments and other aspects of your financial life to determine how each affects your exposure to the five types of risk described in the box on page 33. Such risks include changes in the rate of inflation, interest rates, economic growth, financial markets, or prospects for specific industries or firms that can cause an asset to lose value. (The worksheet on page 34 will help you determine where your vulnerabilities lie.)

After uncovering the major risks in your portfolio, you can redeploy assets to reduce your exposure. Don't limit your financial inventory to investments kept in a brokerage account. Your earning power probably is by far your most valuable asset; equity in a home may come next. Many investors also have substantial assets invested in company pension plans or insurance policies with significant cash values. And entrepreneurs should take a close reading of the risks that threaten the value of their share of a small business.

Risk has a way of creeping up on even vigilant investors. Your holdings in a retirement plan or insurance policy may grow more quickly than you realize, particularly if you make regular contributions or reinvest your returns. But with this success comes a problem. Growth in one asset can throw a portfolio out of balance if other investments don't keep up. If a prolonged bull market increases the value of your stockholdings, you may need to sell some shares to restore the balance between stocks and other assets. Be particularly wary of buying large amounts of stock in the company you work for through retirement and savings plans. If the company runs into trouble, both your job and your stock could be endangered at the same time. If you live in a one-company town, the value of your home may be tied to the fortunes of that firm.

Keep a close eye on changes in your investment portfolio. A careful inspection of your portfolio may unearth important differences between investments that you thought were similar. For example, a study of mutual fund risk found that Fidelity Magellan and Twentieth Century Growth—two growth-stock funds with similar investment objectives, returns, and overall volatility—have responded quite differently when the economy has slowed. Magellan's stock holdings in large, well-established companies have held up better

The Five Faces of Risk

Most people realize that investing is a risky business, but they often fail to recognize the diversity of perils that a portfolio faces. As a result, even cautious investors overlook serious threats to their financial security. When you invest, be alert to the five major risks described below. With proper diversification, you can guard against each while maintaining the likely long-term return on your overall portfolio:

Inflation risk. Rising prices will reduce the purchasing power of an investment. An annual inflation rate of only 5% over 15 years will cut the value of $1,000 to $481. Overcautious investors who hoard all of their assets in low-yielding investments such as savings accounts and money funds may not earn enough to outpace rising prices. In addition, rising inflation erodes the value of future income on investments with fixed payments, most notably long-term bonds.

Interest-rate risk. Rising interest rates will cause investments to drop in price. For example, higher rates make yields on existing bonds less attractive, so their market values decline. Rising rates also hurt stocks by making their dividend yields look less appealing. Individuals who invest borrowed money through margin accounts or who have other floating-rate debt increase their interest-rate risk because higher borrowing costs cut into their net profits.

Economic risk. Slower economic growth will cause investments to fall in price. Shares of emerging growth companies may shrink because they require a booming economy to sustain their robust earnings gains. Cyclical companies, such as automakers and chemical producers, cannot easily cut costs during a recession, so their shares may nosedive, too. Economic downturns can also undercut junk bonds issued by financially weak firms that might default.

Market risk. This includes such factors as political developments and Wall Street fads that can batter investment markets. Tax law changes, trade agreements, program trading, and the quirks of investor psychology all contribute to market risk, which has accounted for much of the stock market's day-to-day volatility. Gold also carries considerable market risk because its price moves sharply when political or military upheavals in other countries encourage the flight of capital.

Specific risk. This covers occurrences that may affect only a particular company or industry. For example, the death of a young company's founder could send the business into a tailspin. Individuals often take on a high degree of specific risk when they invest in a real estate partnership run by inexperienced general partners or when they buy stock in a firm with a heavy debt burden. Specific risk also includes the chance that government regulation will harm a particular group of companies, such as banks or savings and loans.

Adding Up the Risks in Your Portfolio

20 QUESTIONS ABOUT YOUR PORTFOLIO

1. Are your assets diversified among fewer than four of these five major categories: stocks, real estate, gold, bonds, and cash? If yes, score one point for each risk.

2. Are more than 35% of your assets invested in any one of the five categories? If yes, score one point for each risk.

3. Is at least 10% of your portfolio in assets such as gold, natural-resource stocks, or high-grade collectibles such as rare stamps? If no, score one point for inflation risk.

4. Is at least 30% of your portfolio in investments such as growth stocks and real estate, which are likely to produce long-term capital gains that can outpace inflation? If no, score two points for inflation risk.

5. Are your real estate and gold investments held primarily in assets such as gold-mining shares, REITs, or real estate mutual funds, which fluctuate with the stock market? If yes, score one point for market risk.

6. Do you generally keep at least 15% of your portfolio in cash equivalents such as Treasury bills or money-market funds? If no, score two points for interest-rate risk.

7. Is more than 30% of your portfolio composed of assets such as long-term bonds, certificates of deposit or annuities that provide fixed payments over a period of many years? If yes, score three points each for inflation and interest-rate risk.

8. Do highly volatile zero-coupon bonds account for more than 30% of your fixed-income assets? If yes, score two points each for inflation and interest-rate risk.

9. Do emerging growth stocks or junk bonds, which may fall sharply in a recession, account for more than 25% of your portfolio? If yes, score three points for economic risk.

10. Do you switch money among different assets to try and catch the highs and lows of different investment markets? If yes, score two points for market risk.

11. Do you use dollar-cost averaging or a similar plan that involves adding money to your investment portfolio at regular intervals? If no, score two points for market risk.

12. Is more than 20% of your portfolio concentrated in a single industry? If yes, score three points each for economic risk, market risk, and specific risk.

13. Do stocks or bonds issued by one company—including the one you work for—or shares in a single limited partnership account for more than 15% of your assets? If yes, score three points each for economic risk, market risk and specific risk.

14. Does your share in a privately held business account for more than 30% of your portfolio? If yes, score one point for economic risk and four points for specific risk.

15. Does a rental property account for more than 30% of your portfolio? If yes, score one point for economic risk and three points for specific risk.

16. Do foreign stocks and shares of domestic companies with significant overseas sales account for less than 10% of your portfolio? If yes, score one point each for inflation and economic risk.

17. Will you need access in the next three to five years to principal in volatile assets such as stocks or long-term bonds? If yes, score one point each for inflation, interest-rate, economic, and market risk.

18. Do you own your home? If no, score three points for inflation risk.

19. Do you have variable-rate loans such as mortgages or credit-card debt amounting to 30% or more of the value of your portfolio? If yes, score four points for interest-rate risk.

20. Is 20% or more of your portfolio financed by loans or invested in highly leveraged assets such as options? If yes, score one point each for interest-rate and market risk.

TOTAL

	Inflation risk	Interest- rate risk	Economic risk	Market risk	Specific risk

Most people shield some of their investments against different types of risk, but few balance all of their important assets so that they are well protected. This quiz can help you identify your points of vulnerability. With each question, you will accumulate points for one or more of the five major investment risks (see the box on page 33). Write the points in the boxes at left. Then total the points for each risk and interpret your scores as follows: fewer than five points if low; five to 10 points, moderate; above 10, high. While you may want to vary your exposure to different risks somewhat, depending on your personal circumstances and the outlook for the economy, any score above 10 should set off alarm bells.

Once you have identified vulnerabilities, you can take steps to shore up your defenses. For example, say that you score high for inflation risk and low for market risk. You might balance your portfolio better by switching some money from money funds to real estate, stocks or gold. While your risk of a temporary decline in the value of your portfolio will increase, you will have a better chance of outpacing inflation over the long term.

In answering the questions, don't forget about IRA's, 401(k) plans, or any other savings or deferred-compensation plans. It may be difficult to pin down the value of some assets. Just make the best estimates that you can. It isn't necessary to be exact.

than Twentieth Century's portfolio of smaller growth-oriented firms, which are especially sensitive to changes in the level of corporate profits.

To gauge your true risk level, you will need to conduct a careful survey of your investments and other aspects of your finances. Here's a rundown of the strengths and weaknesses of various assets:

Stocks. They are vulnerable to the possibility that skittish investors will panic for some reason and drive share prices down en masse—an example of market risk. But risks related to inflation, interest rates, or economic growth may vary considerably from stock to stock. For example, a sharp increase in the inflation rate depresses stock prices because it may reduce the purchasing power of future dividends to shareholders. Also, inflation generally coincides with higher interest rates, which draw investors from stocks to bonds. Because firms such as retailers, consumer product manufacturers, and service companies can pass cost increases along to customers relatively easily, they are more likely to prosper during periods of high inflation.

Slowing economic growth hurts some firms more than others. Manufacturing companies with high overhead—known as cyclicals—cannot readily cut costs when a recession slices sales, so their earnings quickly tail off. Many emerging growth companies also require an expanding economy to sustain their earnings growth and stock prices. By contrast, firms that sell necessities such as food or clothing can often maintain sales even in a lackluster economy, and their shares tend to hold up relatively well. Since foreign stocks are at least partly immune to changes in the American economy and financial markets, they may post gains while U.S. stocks sink. But unlike domestic issues, shares denominated in foreign

Five Mistakes Investors Make

Even sophisticated investors make mistakes. Common errors include:

Having too much in your company's stock. Investors who concentrate a sizable share of their assets in any single stock are courting trouble. Many people make that mistake—often without even knowing it—because they invest heavily in the shares of the corporation they work for through vehicles such as 401(k), profit-sharing, and other deferred-compensation plans.

Leaving too much money in cash. Some investors escape the perils of stock market volatility, bond defaults, and real estate slumps by keeping the bulk of their assets in cash. But they often overlook an even more relentless threat—inflation. Cash equivalents such as Treasury bills and money-market accounts offer no chance for capital gains that can outpace rising prices.

Assembling a portfolio piecemeal. You may be a genius at spotting undervalued stocks or choosing top-performing mutual funds. But a collection of great individual investments does not always provide the balance your portfolio needs. If you have already loaded up on stocks, for example, pass up a promising new stock issue and buy some bonds, CDs, gold, or real estate instead.

Buying more investments than you can monitor. To diversify fully, you may be tempted to own so many issues that you do not have time to follow them all carefully. Or you may buy investments for which accurate information is difficult to obtain. Remember that less can be more. Choose a mutual fund or two instead of a host of individual issues to fill out the gaps in your diversification plan.

Overlooking important assets. Many investors focus their diversification efforts narrowly, excluding assets such as their earning power, their home, and their tax-deferred accounts. But such assets may be the most valuable. If your IRA is stashed in long-term bonds and cash, for example, consider tilting your remaining assets toward growth-oriented investments.

currencies carry the risk that a rising dollar will reduce their value.

Stocks also carry specific risks—those that are unique to a single firm or industry. Poor management or bad luck can dampen earnings or even bankrupt a company. And high-flying growth stocks are particularly vulnerable to earnings disappointments. One good way to reduce such risks is to buy shares that appear undervalued because they are selling at comparatively low price/earnings ratios or above-average yields.

Bonds. Their prices generally fall when interest rates rise. But the extent of the drop depends upon a bond's maturity and the amount of its coupon. Short-term bonds fall only slightly when interest rates move upward, and a high coupon also offers some protection against climbing rates.

A recession usually brings lower interest rates, which boost bond prices. But some issues react negatively to the threat of an economic slowdown. So-called junk bonds, which are rated less than investment grade by Moody's or Standard & Poor's, may lose ground because investors fear that financially weak firms will default and fail to make payments of interest and principal to bondholders on time. Treasury and high-grade corporate bonds gain the most during hard times because income investors seek them out as the safest havens.

Real estate investments. Although they tend to beat inflation over the long haul, they present other hazards. For example, if you own a rental property, you run the risk that you won't find a tenant. A real estate partnership that owns several properties in different regions can reduce such risks through diversification, but it may lose value if tax changes or a sluggish economy drive down property values across the country. And real estate investment trusts and real estate mutual funds fluctuate with the stock market as well as with property values.

Gold and other tangible assets. The price of gold can skyrocket when inflation rises rapidly. Since 1968, the consumer price index has posted nine annual increases of 6% or more. During those years, gold has well rewarded

Asset Allocation

Putting fixed percentages of your capital into different types of investments is a form of diversification called asset allocation. In these charts, Marilyn Capelli, a financial planner in Naperville, Illinois, suggests typical allocations for people at different stages of life. No two advisers are likely to recommend exactly the same divisions, but Capelli's come close to those made by other planners.

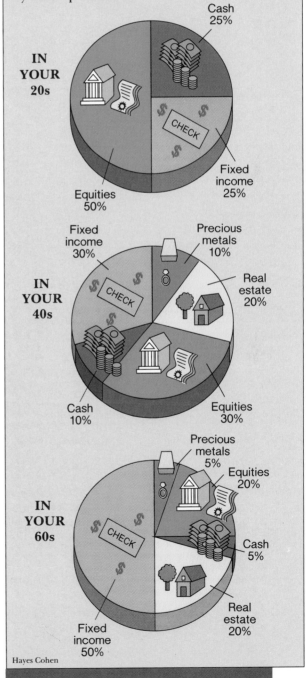

IN YOUR 20s
Cash 25%
Fixed income 25%
Equities 50%

IN YOUR 40s
Fixed income 30%
Precious metals 10%
Real estate 20%
Equities 30%
Cash 10%

IN YOUR 60s
Precious metals 5%
Equities 20%
Cash 5%
Real estate 20%
Fixed income 50%

Hayes Cohen

How Different Kinds of Assets Compare

Returns for almost every type of investment vary considerably from year to year. The table below shows the annual total return for five kinds of assets as well as for an index devised by Bailard Biehl & Kaiser, an investment advisory firm. The index represents a hypothetical portfolio equally divided among the five asset categories. As you can see, the BB&K diversified portfolio index provided steadier gains than U.S. stocks. Further, money invested in the index in 1967 would have grown at an average annual rate of 10.5% during the period, compared to a rate of 9.1% for the S&P 500.

YEAR	S&P 500	Foreign stocks	Long-term bonds	Treasury bills	Real estate	BB&K index
1968	11.1%	31.7%	-0.3%	5.3%	8.1%	11.2%
1969	-8.5	6.8	-5.1	6.5	9.7	1.9
1970	4.0	-10.1	12.1	6.6	10.8	4.7
1971	14.3	30.1	10.6	4.4	9.2	13.7
1972	18.9	37.1	8.1	4.1	7.5	15.1
1973	-14.8	-12.8	2.3	6.9	7.5	-2.2
1974	-26.5	-21.6	0.2	7.9	7.2	-6.6
1975	37.3	37.0	12.3	5.8	5.7	19.6
1976	23.6	3.8	15.6	5.1	9.3	11.5
1977	-7.4	19.4	3.0	5.2	10.5	6.1
1978	6.5	34.3	1.2	7.1	15.9	13.0
1979	18.5	6.2	2.3	10.0	20.6	11.5
1980	32.5	24.4	3.1	11.4	17.9	17.9
1981	-5.0	-1.1	7.2	14.2	16.6	6.4
1982	21.6	-0.8	31.1	10.9	9.3	14.4
1983	22.5	24.6	8.0	8.9	13.3	15.4
1984	6.2	7.9	15.0	9.9	12.9	10.4
1985	31.7	56.7	21.3	7.4	9.8	25.4
1986	18.7	70.0	15.6	6.2	6.3	23.3
1987	5.3	24.6	2.3	5.9	5.0	8.6
1988*	5.7	15.3	3.6	1.5	1.2	5.4

*First quarter. The Bailard Biehl & Kaiser diversified portfolio index reflects the performance of indexes for five types of assets, which are equally weighted. Data are derived from Standard & Poor's 500-stock index, the Morgan Stanley Europe, Australia, Far East stock market index, the Shearson Lehman Hutton government/corporate bond index, yields for 30-day Treasury bills, and the Frank Russell Co. property index.

investors with an average gain of 34%. Gold-mining stocks are more volatile than the metal itself and expose investors to other risks. A South African miners' strike, for example, might boost the price of bullion but cut profits at some mining companies. Gold-related shares also swing with broad stock market moves. In October 1987, mutual funds that invest in gold-mining shares fell 27%, while the price of gold rose 2%.

Other tangibles present their own problems. A commodities fund may soar when inflation takes off—or it may sink if the fund manager has been betting on lower inflation by selling commodities futures short. Collectibles are often illiquid. And while antique armoires or rare stamps may be able to outpace inflation in the long run, prices of specialized items such as baseball cards are largely subject to collec-tors' whims.

While you are examining your assets, don't forget to review your borrowing habits. Higher interest rates will increase your expenses if you hold variable-rate loans such as a mortgage, credit-card debt, or auto loans. And if you invest borrowed money using a margin account or other credit source, higher rates will raise your expenses and lower your net returns.

Once you have identified the risks in your portfolio, you can adjust them to suit your goals and temperament. That might mean reducing your interest-rate risk by selling a few long-term bonds. Then again, you may decide to shoulder new risks in pursuit of higher profits. And if you're wrong? Just make sure that your portfolio is amply diversified so that you can afford an occasional mistake.

Beyond Dollar-Cost Averaging

By keeping you from investing when prices are at a peak, these strategies can boost your returns and cut your risk.

Like alchemists searching for the philosopher's stone, investors are always looking for a system that will transmute their investments into big profits. While no such magic formula exists, fairly sophisticated variations of the familiar technique known as dollar-cost averaging can help you reduce your risk and enhance your chances for above-average capital gains.

As anyone who owned stocks between 1982 and 1987 knows well, there is no substitute for buying shares in the early stages of a bull market and selling them as prices peak. But doing it requires clairvoyance—or incredible luck. Investors who put all of their money into the market at once can never be sure which way prices will go. If, for example, you had invested everything right before the October 1987 crash, you could easily have lost 25% or more on paper in just a couple of days.

The best way to avoid such disasters is to buy shares on the installment plan, a technique that encourages you to buy more shares when prices are low and fewer when prices are high, thereby lowering your average cost.

The table on page 41 shows the results of five common installment strategies. In each case, *Money* followed a system that divided a $200 monthly contribution between a stock index fund that tracks the Standard & Poor's 500-stock index and a money-market fund. Returns were calculated for the period from September 1976 through March 1988. The portfolio values indicate final results for both funds, while average share prices for the stock fund represent risk levels. (The lower the price, the less risky the system.)

In general, three key principles apply to all installment strategies:

● They work best when the market is choppy, without any overall trend, and they can cause your portfolio to lag during an extended bull market.

● They can reduce anxiety and second-guessing. Unambiguous rules tell you when and how much to buy. But they must be followed consistently.

● They can be used with stocks and with bonds. But because brokers' commissions will cut into your returns, installment techniques generally work best with no-load mutual funds.

The simplest system, known as the constant share purchase plan, calls for you to buy a fixed number of shares at regular intervals. For example, instead of buying 500 shares of a fund all at once, you might buy 100 shares each year from now through 1993. This approach lowers the risk of buying all your shares at a high price, but you can usually get better results from more advanced strategies.

The most popular form of installment investing is known as dollar-cost averaging. You simply invest a fixed dollar amount at regular intervals. When prices rise, your money buys fewer shares, and when prices fall, it buys more. As a result, the average cost of each share will be lower than if you used the constant share purchase system. In the example shown in the table on page 41, dollar-cost averaging lowered the average share price by 70 cents while increasing the portfolio value by $1,964 over the constant share purchase method. (You may be using dollar-cost averaging already if you are enrolled in a payroll deduction plan at work.)

Here are three supercharged variations of dollar-cost averaging that can often magnify your profits:

The constant ratio plan. This strategy calls for blending dollar-cost averaging with a formula for adjusting the mix of investments in your portfolio. First, you divide your investments between stocks and more conservative assets according to the amount of risk you are willing

to take. Many professionals today recommend that conservative investors split their money fifty-fifty between a stock fund and a money fund. In that case, you would begin by making equal monthly or quarterly contributions to each. If a big move in stock prices makes the stock fund worth considerably more or less than the money fund, you would transfer money to make them equal again.

The hypothetical example in the table shows the results for a constant ratio plan that adjusts whenever the shares of either fund exceed 55% of the total value of the portfolio. For example, if the shares in the stock fund rise to 55%, the investor shifts cash from the stock fund to the money fund to make them equal again. And if the stock fund drops to 45% of the portfolio—making the money fund 55%—the investor moves money in the opposite direction. The size of monthly contributions, however, remains unchanged.

Say you began the year with $4,000 in the stock fund and $4,000 in the money fund. Four months later, stock prices have increased enough for the stock portfolio to be worth $5,500, while the money fund has grown to $4,500. You would then transfer $500 from the stock fund to the money fund so that you would have $5,000 in each.

In the example in the table, a constant ratio strategy would have produced a portfolio worth $426 more than if you had used simple dollar-cost averaging. As a rule, your trigger should not be higher than a five-percentage-point divergence from the original balance of your portfolio, or you will rarely make an adjustment. With five points, the hypothetical plan required just six adjustments in nearly 12 years.

The variable installment plan. Start by investing equal amounts in a stock fund and a money fund and adjust your contributions to the stock fund so that you invest more money in it if the fund's share price declines. (The balance of your monthly investment goes into the money fund.) One simple way is to put your entire monthly contribution in the stock fund whenever its share price falls a fixed amount—say, 10%. Similarly, you could halve or skip your monthly stock fund investment if

Ways to Cut Your Risk

Dollar-cost averaging and similar strategies can help you avoid investing too much money when prices are near a peak. The tables below compare five hypothetical portfolios to illustrate how such strategies work. In each case, we have invested $28,000 over nearly 12 years, following formulas that split a $200 monthly contribution between Vanguard Index Trust-500 Portfolio, which mirrors the S&P 500 index, and Vanguard Money Market Reserves-Prime Portfolio, a top money fund. We began our calculations with September 1976, the month the Vanguard index fund was started, and we ended with March 1988.

Constant share purchase

Avg. cost per share:	Portfolio value:
$19.82	**$57,874**

▶ Each month, buy the same number of shares in the stock fund (for comparison with the strategies below, 5.4 shares) and invest the remainder in the money fund.

Dollar-cost averaging

Avg. cost per share:	Portfolio value:
$19.12	**$59,838**

▶ Each month, invest $100 in the stock fund and $100 in the money fund.

Constant ratio

Avg. cost per share:	Portfolio value:
$19.23	**$60,264**

▶ Each month, invest $100 in the stock fund and $100 in the money fund.
▶ Whenever the value of your stock fund shares reaches 55% of the total portfolio, shift assets to the money fund to reduce the percentage to 50%.
▶ Do the opposite if the value of the stock fund shares falls to 45% of the portfolio.

Variable installments

Avg. cost per share:	Portfolio value:
$18.75	**$59,344**

▶ Start out by investing $200, divided equally between the two funds.
▶ Thereafter, when the stock fund's share price is below your average cost, allocate more of your monthly $200 to stocks, using the formula described in the story.
▶ When the price moves above your average cost, park more in the money fund.

Leveraged variable installments

Avg. cost per share:	Portfolio value:
$18.66	**$59,902**

▶ Begin by investing $200, divided equally between the two funds.
▶ Thereafter, use a formula, such as the one described in the story, which sharply varies the amount going to the stock fund as its share price rises and falls.

its share price rises by 10%.

A refinement of this approach requires you to keep track of the average cost of your stock fund shares, including those purchased with reinvested dividend and capital-gains distributions. When the fund's current share price is higher than your average cost, you invest less. When it is lower, you increase your contribution. There are several ways to determine the amount to contribute to the fund. One standard method requires you to divide the average cost of your shares by the current price and multiply the result by the amount of your original contribution.

For example, say you started out investing $100 a month in a stock fund, and your shares cost $9 each. If after a month the fund trades at $10 a share, you would figure your second contribution as follows: Divide your average cost ($9) by the fund's current price ($10). Multiply the result (0.9) by your $100 original investment. Your second contribution should be reduced to $90.

For the investment program in the table, the variable installment plan earned $494 less than dollar-cost averaging. The reason: As stock prices rose steadily during the 1982-87 bull market, the variable installment investor would have made smaller and smaller contributions to the stock fund, thereby missing some potential capital gains. That investor would have paid only $18.75 a share on average, however, 37 cents less than with dollar-cost averaging.

The leveraged variable installment plan. This method is a variation on the simple variable plan explained above. It's called leveraged because it increases the extent to which the investor buys more shares when prices fall and fewer when prices rise. While the formula for adjusting the size of your contribution is quite complex, this system can produce the lowest average stock cost—and therefore the lowest risk. Start by deciding how much to vary your contributions. The greater the leverage you use, the lower your average cost and risk will be. But high leverage can also cause you to miss out on big gains in a bull market.

Initially, you should invest equal amounts in a stock fund and a money fund. Then figure the average trading price of the fund over the past 12 months and calculate the percentage difference between that average price and the current price. Multiply the percentage by your leverage factor and adjust your contribution to the stock fund accordingly. A very conservative version of this strategy could use a leverage factor as high as five.

The following example may make the system sound less bewildering. If the average price of the stock fund is $9 over the past 12 months and the current price is $10, then the difference is 10%. You would therefore multiply 10% by your leverage factor of five and reduce your contribution by 50%—from $100 to $50 a month, for instance. In the hypothetical example in the table, which uses a leverage factor of five, the average cost per share is only $18.66, compared with $19.12 for dollar-cost averaging.

If you are an avid do-it-yourselfer, you may want to consider other modifications that some investors make to fine-tune their dollar-cost averaging systems. You could, for example, adjust for inflation by increasing your contributions each year by the percentage gain in the consumer price index. Or you might want to boost your installments as your income rises. If, for instance, you earn $40,000 a year and receive a $4,000 raise, you could increase your monthly contribution proportionately—say, from $200 to $220 a month.

One interesting, but complex, technique is to incorporate elements of market timing into your system. To do this, you would adjust your contributions based on the market's current price/earnings ratio or dividend yields compared with their historic norms. For example, you could increase your installments whenever the P/E of the S&P 500 was below 10 or its dividend yield was above 5%. Conversely, you would reduce your contribution if the P/E of the S&P 500 was above 15 or its yield was below 3.5%.

Most important, before moving on to something more complicated, gain experience with basic dollar-cost averaging or a moderately more advanced system. Or stick with a simple system. But whatever approach you take, regular contributions can make your portfolio grow.

Profiting from Rising Interest Rates

Although higher rates undermine stock and bond prices, you can play it safe and perhaps even profit.

When interest rates crept up nearly a full percentage point last spring, stock prices dipped about 5% as investors began to worry that a slump lay ahead. In particular, they feared a replay of 1987, when hefty rate increases pushed yields of 30-year Treasury bonds above 10% just prior to the stock market crash. The market bounced back in mid-1988, but investors' confidence remained fragile. That skittishness was magnified by economists' forecasts of higher interest rates by early 1989. The reason: A robust economy and rising prices for raw materials would encourage inflation, which causes investors to demand higher yields.

A return to double-digit interest rates—as long as it is short-lived—could create a splendid chance for long-term capital gains from bonds (see the table on page 44). But most of the immediate consequences would likely be bad news for the stock and bond markets. To keep a portfolio safe when rates are rising, experts offer the following advice for moderately conservative investors with a long-term outlook:

Keep a large chunk of your assets in short-term income investments. Some strategists advise you to safeguard at least half of your money in Treasury bills, money-market funds, or short-term bond funds. If you have a large portfolio, you may prefer Treasury bills, currently yielding about 7.5%, which come in denominations of $10,000. You can buy Treasury securities of all kinds through any broker or commission-free from one of the 12

Federal Reserve Banks or 13 branches. (For further information, write for *Buying Treasury Securities,* Federal Reserve Bank of Philadelphia, Public Information/Publications, P.O. Box 66, Philadelphia, PA 19105.)

If you prefer the convenience of mutual funds, or if your portfolio is less than $20,000, favor a money fund or a short-term bond fund. Such funds require initial investments of as little as $250 and usually offer check-writing privileges. Top-performing money funds recently were yielding about 7.3%. You can do even better in taxable short-term bond funds—those that own issues with maturities ranging from two to four years. Investors in the 28% or 33% tax brackets may want to consider a tax-exempt fund instead.

Stay defensive with your stocks. Absent any clear evidence that interest rates are falling, such as a cut in the prime rate that banks charge their best corporate customers, you should keep your stockholdings to a minimum—perhaps only 25% of your total portfolio. The safest shares to own are those of companies in industries that are resistant to an economic slowdown, such as utilities, drugmakers, foods, and beverages. Then, once rates appear to be at a peak, you can start buying stocks again with an eye for bargain-priced blue chips with secure dividends.

Be ready to pounce on long-term bonds. After interest rates peak, the economy will slow and may even go into a full-scale recession. That will cause interest rates to fall substantially. Yields on long-term Treasuries could go as low as 7%, economists say. As the table below shows, if you buy long-term Treasuries when yields are 10%, and yields drop to 7.5% over two years, you would earn mouth-watering interest and capital gains totaling 50%, or 22.5% at an average annual rate.

In addition to long-term Treasuries, you may want to consider zero-coupon bonds, which pay no interest but trade at a steep discount to their eventual redemption value. Long-term municipals may offer even higher returns on an after-tax basis for investors in the top brackets. Top-performing tax-exempt funds, recently paying 5%, offer yields equivalent to a taxable 6.9% for someone in the 28% bracket. And you will still be able to earn tempting capital gains as muni prices rise once rates start downhill.

The Coming Bond Bonanza

Many economists expect long-term interest rates to rise and then fall within the next two years. The table at right shows the annual rate of return you would earn if you bought 30-year Treasury bonds at a high yield and held them until rates dropped.

If you buy T-bonds when yields are . . .	9.5%	9.75%	10.0%	10.25%	10.5%
. . . and hold for two years as rates fall to . . . **9.0%**	11.4%	12.84%	14.1%	16.0%	16.9%
8.5%	13.4	15.3	16.7	18.2	19.5
8.0%	16.6	18.1	19.5	20.9	22.3
7.5%	19.5	21.0	22.5	23.9	25.4
7.0%	22.6	24.1	25.6	27.1	28.6

. . . your annual rate of return will be . . .

How to Avoid Being Ripped Off by a Lousy Broker

In the post-crash era, knowing how to fend off selfish, hard-sell brokers is more important than ever.

Following the advice of a persuasive broker, Kelly Vickrey of Germantown, Tennessee shifted his $221,860 savings from bank certificates of deposit to a brokerage money market account in March 1986. Vickrey believed the move would improve his yield without any additional risk to his principal. Instead, he very nearly got wiped out. His guide, according to charges subsequently brought by both Vickrey and the State of Tennessee Securities Division, was Darryl Myers, a young broker for the investment house of Thomson McKinnon. Within just three months, Vickrey's initial stake shrank to $26,206—some $6,000 less than the $32,490 Myers allegedly earned in commissions on the account. Thomson McKinnon refuses to discuss the case while it is in litigation. Myers, who has since left the brokerage business, could not be reached for comment.

The five-year bull-market party that ended abruptly in October 1987 set the stage for disasters such as Vickrey's. Lured by the prospect of unprecedented profits, millions of first-time investors were drawn into risky products and strategies. Brokers, many of them equally inexperienced, rushed to sign on the new clients and actively trade their accounts, sometimes against the investors' best interests. The result? The number of investor complaints filed against brokers at the Securities and Exchange Commission has jumped 258% since 1982. Moreover, many investors who have reported financial losses might not have lost much money if their brokers had observed proper sales practice rules in the weeks, months, and years preceding the crash.

While the average broker still strives honestly to make money for you as well as for himself, the 20% to 30% drop in commission income since Black Monday has exacerbated the traditional tug-of-war between a broker's good intentions and his own self-interest. As sales pitches build in intensity, so does the need for small investors to stand vigilant against the onslaught. The potential problems range from being given false or misleading information by overzealous salespeople hawking investments unsuitable for your financial goals to outright fraud committed by unscrupulous brokers. Fortunately, there are several defensive tactics you can use from the time you open your account to monitor your broker's actions. And if these precautions fail, the burned investor does have some recourse.

Here is a closer look at the most common problems that investors may suffer at the hands of brokers, illustrated by examples from the saga of investor Kelly Vickrey and accompanied by tips on how best to protect yourself:
Unsuitable Investments. Vickrey charges that shortly after he opened his money market account at Thomson McKinnon, his broker, Myers, suggested trading stock options to generate income. Myers allegedly didn't make clear that he intended to write naked puts and calls, one of the most speculative forms of options trading. Says Vickrey, whose only market

experience was trading $800 worth of L&N Railroad shares in the late 1970s: "I didn't know anything about options, but I trusted Darryl when he said he would leave everything in the money fund unless he could make a guaranteed 7% on a transaction."

Under "know your customer" rules enacted at the turn of the century by major stock exchanges, brokers are required to learn as much as possible about a client's financial goals and resources to assure that their recommendations are suitable. But many brokers do not do that.

To protect yourself, clearly define your goals to your broker in writing when you open your account and update them periodically. If, for example, you cannot tolerate any risk to your principal in exchange for a chance at higher returns, say so explicitly instead of using a vague word such as *safety* to describe your financial needs. Beyond that, steer clear

How To Find A Good Broker

To choose a broker who will work conscientiously to meet your financial goals, take the following steps:
● Get references from people who share your investment philosophy. Good brokers, like good doctors, get most of their business through referrals from satisfied customers.
● Interview several promising candidates by phone. Ask what investments they would recommend to meet your needs. Also pin down the firm's commission rates and investment services. Then meet with the two or three brokers who gave the most satisfactory answers to your questions to determine which one makes you feel most comfortable.
● Before making a final decision, check with your state securities commission office to see whether any disciplinary actions have been taken against each broker.
● Once you have opened an account, do not invest all of your money right away. Start with a small sum and add investments as you become more confident about the broker's performance.

of any broker who tries to sell you an investment before interviewing you at length about your goals, history, and resources.

If you are an inexperienced or conservative investor, do not open a margin or option account. Securities in these types of accounts are usually bought on credit and are among the riskiest ways to invest. Never put your cash into anything you couldn't explain to your Aunt Millie, and always get a second opinion to verify a broker's explanation of an investment or strategy that is new to you.

Improper Transactions. From March through June 1986, Myers allegedly made 166 options trades in Vickrey's account. Vickrey asserts that he never gave the broker the discretionary authority to make these transactions.

An unauthorized transaction is one made without your prior knowledge or permission. An improperly executed trade may be one in which the broker bought instead of sold, made an error in the amount or price of securities you ordered, needlessly delayed executing your order or didn't place it at all. Whether the error was an honest mistake or a deliberate act of fraud, the broker can be compelled under federal securities law to restore your account to its position before the unauthorized or improperly executed trade.

You should never open a discretionary account, which gives a broker the authority to make trades without your prior knowledge or consent, unless you have a long, satisfactory history with him or her. Even then, give the broker discretionary power only to sell, not buy, securities. And always confirm in a letter to your broker (and keep a copy for yourself) any instructions or approvals you give over the phone. A broker who knows that you are keeping scrupulous records about your account is less likely to take liberties.

Churning an Account. From June 2 through June 6, 1986, Myers allegedly earned more than $14,000 in commissions on 58 trades in Vickrey's account. Indeed, after paying the broker's fees, Vickrey would have needed to earn nearly a 60% annualized return just to break even during the three-month period that Myers managed his portfolio.

A broker who boosts his commissions by ex-cessively trading securities in a customer's account is engaging in an abuse known as "churning." No matter how the broker gained control of the investments—whether directly through his powers in a discretionary account or indirectly by influencing an unsophisticated customer—churning is illegal. At the very least, it erodes portfolio profits and, at worst, it results in steep losses.

To detect churning, carefully check both the confirmation slips sent to you after each transaction and your monthly statements. Before mailing your statement, brokers usually rip off and retain the portion that lists all commissions and related fees per trade, with cumulative monthly and year-to-date totals. To aid you in monitoring your costs, ask your broker to send you copies of that section of your records. Contact your broker immediately about any questionable item. If he lays the blame on a mysterious computer error or gives some other unsatisfactory response, check out his story with the branch manager.

If you suspect that your broker is churning, confirm your doubts in two ways. First, divide the commissions you paid by the average net equity in the account to determine the percentage of return needed just to meet expenses. Unless you are an active trader or speculator, 12% or more indicates churning. Second, divide your total purchases by your average net equity. A turnover rate of three or more in an ordinary account spells trouble.

Lies or Omissions. Myers allegedly promised that he would not trade options in Vickrey's account unless he could guarantee a minimum 7% return on the investment. Although the broker, in fact, could not guarantee any profit on uncovered options, according to Vickrey's charges, he proceeded with the transactions anyway.

Any broker who intentionally makes an untrue statement, omits a vital piece of information, or otherwise deceives a client about an investment or the status of his account may be charged with fraud under SEC rules. Unfortunately, recognizing and then proving willful misrepresentation of facts is not easy, particularly if you are not familiar with the securities or market strategies in question. As with other

Making Arbitration Pay Off for You

Proposed Securities and Exchange Commission arbitration reforms, if adopted, may improve investors' odds of recouping unfair losses from brokers. The reforms focus on investors' main gripe that judgements favor the brokerage industry because most hearings are conducted by the stock exchanges' own self-regulatory arms. For example, the new rules would bar securities industry retirees and others with brokerage links from serving as public arbitrators.

The reforms, which an SEC spokesperson says could be adopted as early as this year, would also force brokerage firms to produce documents investors need to substantiate their cases in advance of the hearings. In addition, the reforms would make the hearings' decisions available to other investors facing arbitration, including the award amounts and how each arbitrator voted. As a result, investors' attorneys could drop anyone with a pro-industry bias from subsequent arbitration panels.

Still, the present imperfect system can work for you. Stuart Goldberg, a New York City securities attorney who has won hundreds of cases for investors through arbitration, nearly always chose the process even before the Supreme Court's June 1987 ruling that investors could not sue if they had signed standard brokerage agreements requiring them to submit to arbitration. One reason Goldberg favors arbitration is that cases typically are resolved in nine to twelve months versus several years in the courts—and therefore are less costly than trials. Fees for a $100,000 arbitration are likely to total $25,000, compared with more than $100,000 in the courts.

Currently, however, arbitration success does not come easily, nor is it complete. In 1987, for example, investors won only about 55% of the 1,020 cases handled by the predominant arbitration groups, the National Association of Securities Dealers (NASD) and the New York Stock Exchange. Moreover, the panels rarely assess punitive damages or award investors the full amount they lost.

To improve your chance of being among the winners, bittersweet though the victory may be, here are some tips:

● If your claim is $10,000 or more, hire a litigator with securities arbitration experience. You are likely to be going up against a brokerage's experienced in-house attorney, so you need to be equally well represented. To find a lawyer, contact the local bar association.

● Do what you can to help yourself by choosing the right arbitration forum. The clause in the standard brokerage contract binding you to arbitration also limits you to two or three choices among the 11 panels that conduct such hearings—self-regulatory bodies of the 10 stock exchanges and the American Arbitration Association. You cannot control which panels are specified in the clause, but there are two that you should jump at if they are available to you: the AAA, which is independent of the brokerage industry, and the NASD, which has demonstrated the greatest concern for improving broker-investor relations. If neither are named in your contract clause, you can try to write them in before you sign. The brokerage firm may not accept your amended clause, but it is worth a try.

● Marshal as much written documentation as you can of transactions and conversations with your broker. Investigate the broker's background for a pattern of past complaints by checking his or her record with your state securities commission office. Trace your account at the brokerage firm. You are entitled to copies of documents and correspondence relating to your account and should not be buffaloed by a brokerage firm's claims to the contrary.

● If there is something amiss in your account, do not wait until you suffer losses to complain. While you can press charges up to six years after a dispute occurs, arbitrators will generally find in favor of your broker if his attorney can establish that you were aware of improper activity, yet let it continue without complaint as long as the trades were profitable.

common problems, the best defense against broker fraud is a good offense.

Before putting any money into a security that a broker recommends, ask what might happen under the worst-case scenario, and beware of any deal that sounds like a dream come true. A couple of times a year, or as soon as you suspect a problem, go to your brokerage's office and get a current computer printout of your account. That way you can make sure your broker is not painting you a falsely rosy picture over the phone. Also compare the printout to your monthly statements. Cases of embezzlement have been reported in which brokers siphoned money from clients' accounts for their own use, then concealed the theft by doctoring the monthly statements before they were mailed to their clients.

If these precautions fail to adequately protect you against abusive or fraudulent sales practices, and if efforts to resolve the problem directly with your broker prove fruitless, send a written complaint to his branch manager. Also send a copy of your grievances to the firm's compliance division and ask for a written response from the officer in charge.

If you do not get satisfactory answers after 30 days, write your state securities regulation office to discuss your complaint. Unlike the investment firm's employees, state regulatory officials do not have a vested interest in siding with the broker. As a result, they can assess the merits of your case objectively and advise you about whether and how to proceed to arbitration. (For tips about how to win at arbitration, see page 47.) The North American Securities Administrators Association (800-942-9022), the state regulators' national organization, also offers useful information on resolving broker disputes in its free booklet, *Coping with the Crash: A Step-by-Step Guide to Investor Rights.*

Vickrey, who is awaiting arbitration proceedings through which he hopes to recover his entire $221,860 savings, seems to have learned that lesson the hard way. After Vickrey filed his complaint, Myers transferred to Thomson McKinnon's Denver office, where he was fired in December 1986 after several other investors lodged similar complaints. Myers nonetheless was able to get a job as a broker at a Los Angeles branch office of Shearson Lehman/American Express a few weeks later by falsely claiming on his application form that he had no investor complaints pending against him. Shearson says Myers finally left the firm in June 1987 and his former Thomson McKinnon supervisor reports that he is out of the brokerage business.

An Attractive Alternative for Conservative Investors

Convertibles can reduce your risks.

Stocks? Bonds? To buy or not to buy is the question. But the wisest answer for conservative investors is not to buy either one alone, but both. Convertibles, hybrid securities that combine characteristics of stocks and bonds, are a traditional but timely choice now for investors who want to share in stock market gains, while cushioning themselves against losses. As stock prices sank in the fourth quarter of 1987, for example, convertibles fell four percentage points less than Standard & Poor's 500-stock index did.

Convertibles are bonds or preferred shares that can be converted at the owner's option, usually into common stock of the same company that issued them. Generally, convertibles that are attractive alternatives to stocks trade at prices 5% to 25% above the current value of the common stock into which they could be converted. The reason for this so-called premium over conversion is that such issues usually yield from three to five percentage points more than common stocks do. As a result of their premiums and high yields, typical convertibles rise about three-quarters as much as common shares when the stock market goes up but fall only half as much when the market goes down.

Mutual funds specializing in convertibles offer the simplest way to invest. Or you can get lists of attractive convertibles from brokerages. One basic test of whether a convertible is a better buy than the corresponding common stock is known as the payback period—the length of time it would take for the convertible's extra yield to recoup the cost of the premium. A payback period of five years or less is a good sign. An approximate calculation of this payback period can be made as follows: Say that the convertible bond of XYZ Inc. carries a 7% coupon and matures in 2011, and currently trades at $845 per bond with a yield of 8.3%. The issue sells for about 25% more than the value of the XYZ common into which it could be converted. Since the common yields only 2.1%, the convertible has a 6.2-point yield advantage. This higher yield would compensate the investor for the convertible's 25% premium in three to four years.

At any given time, only a small number of issues pass the payback test. Those with longer payback periods can also be attractive. To select convertibles for your portfolio, you should rely on these guidelines:

Be sure you like the common. Buy a convertible only if you would buy the common stock of the issuer. If the stock does well, the convertible will also do well. But if the stock does poorly, so will the convertible.

Beware of convertibles issued by takeover candidates. A takeover can sometimes force holders to convert before they have received enough extra yield to make up for whatever premium the convertible carries.

Consider high-yield convertibles. Issues with yields comparable to those of conventional bonds often carry high premiums and will gain only a little bit if stocks go up. But they may still be a sound choice if their underlying stocks have substantial appreciation potential.

Avoid low-quality issues. Limit your purchases to convertibles rated B or better by agencies such as Standard & Poor's.

Look for call protection. Some convertibles can be redeemed by their issuers at a specified call date. Check with your broker or a newsletter to see whether an issue is susceptible to an early call. Then make sure that the premium will be recovered or that the stock could have a big gain before a call is likely. That way, you can enjoy profits before your convertible is redeemed.

Dividend Plays: One Less Thing to Worry About

Investors who own shares of a high-yielding stock that one day suddenly trades at five or six times normal volume can relax. Your stock probably has been the target of dividend-recapture trading—a ploy that lets Japanese insurance companies get around a quirk in their country's law. The law requires them to pay distributions to policyholders out of income from the firms' investment portfolios, not from capital gains. So to raise enough money to make payouts, the insurers arrange through big brokerages to buy millions of shares of high-yielding U.S. stocks, hold them just long enough to claim the dividends and then sell them back at a small loss—roughly the amount of the U.S. companies' dividends. In effect, the insurers have converted capital into income that they can pay out. Dividend-recapture trading has gone on for years, but not until the low market volume of recent months was it so noticeable. The strategy may bring your stock a moment of notoriety—especially on slow trading days—but you won't get hurt because the effect on its value is negligible.

Stocks Worth Holding for the Long Haul

Value investing—buying a cheap duckling that can become a swan—pays off for patient investors.

When investors' relentless hunt for emerging growth stocks suddenly ended in the second half of 1983, dashing illusions that glamorous technology shares were a shortcut to wealth, investors discovered that the real prize of the early 1980s was so-called value stocks. From 1980 to 1983, the shares of depressed, ugly-duckling companies outperformed Standard & Poor's 500-stock index by 62%. Today many investment strategists see a similar pattern developing in the wake of the October 1987 stock market crash.

A study published in mid-1988 by Avner Arbel, Steven Carvell, and Erik Postnieks at Cornell University shows that shares with value characteristics declined in price by only 20% to 25% during the market crash, compared with a loss of about 30% for issues that did not meet such criteria. Further, stocks with low price/earnings ratios—a commonly used measure of undervaluation—outperformed the S&P 500 in four of the past six years. Analysts expect the superior performance of undervalued stocks to continue.

The value approach has the finest pedigree of any stock market strategy. Devised half a century ago by two now legendary Columbia University finance professors, Benjamin Graham and David Dodd, value investing concentrates on identifying companies whose shares trade at prices that are substantially below the companies' inherent worth. Such worth is based on the businesses' earnings and the price for which their assets could be sold. Since this approach was first set forth in Graham and Dodd's *Security Analysis* (McGraw-Hill, $49.95), it has been modified many times. But the essential idea remains unchanged: the shares of any financially sound company—even a boring, slow-growing business—are a fine investment if they are cheap enough.

Value investors rely on a variety of criteria aside from low P/Es. Most often, they look for shares that also have high yields and low prices relative to book value (or net worth per share). More advanced measures include a low price relative to cash flow (the actual amount of cash a company generates, which can be considerably higher than its reported earnings) and a high return on equity (a common gauge of profitability). These criteria are discussed at greater length elsewhere in this article.

Individual investors who learn how to calculate such measures can discover promising situations, but it will require hours of work. If you don't want to spend time reading through reams of annual reports, there are many sources that will do the analysis for you. Chief among them is the *Value Line Investment Survey* (711 Third Ave., New York, NY 10017; $495 a year), which is available in many large public libraries and provides information on about 1,700 companies in an easy-to-read format.

You can also pick up promising leads from interviews with money managers in financial publications such as *Barron's*, the *Wall Street*

Journal, and *Money.* Some brokerage firms, such as Smith Barney, A.G. Edwards, and Oppenheimer, also publish research that focuses specifically on stocks that meet various value criteria. In addition, many newsletters use such an approach. Among them: *Standard & Poor's Outlook* (Standard & Poor's, 25 Broadway, New York, NY 10004; weekly, $240 a year), *Generic Stock News* (P.O. Box 6567, Ithaca, NY 14851; monthly, $200 a year), and *Investment Quality Trends* (7440 Girard Ave., La Jolla, CA 92037; biweekly, $225 a year).

If you prefer not to choose individual stocks yourself, there are mutual funds that will provide you with a readymade portfolio. One of the best known is Mutual Shares, which invests in bankrupt companies as well as other depressed issues. In 1987, Mutual Shares was up 6.3%, or one point more than the S&P 500; and for the five years to October 1988, Mutual Shares beat the market with a return of 138% versus 99% for the S&P 500.

Graham was highly suspicious of rosy predictions about a company's profit performance. Instead, he stressed the importance of basing analysis on past results, a principle that is still central to analysis today. If you need encouragement to undertake the value approach, just meditate on the career of Warren Buffet, the chairman of Berkshire Hathaway and one of the most admired disciples of Benjamin Graham. Someone who initially put $10,000 into a private investing partnership Buffet organized in 1956 would have walked away with $300,000 14 years later when the venture was dissolved.

Buffet's spectacular record illustrates an important point about value investing. The big money is made in the long run; often it takes three to five years for investors to recognize that a stock is selling for less than its inherent worth and bid up the price. Just like clothes, stocks go through fashion cycles, and you have to be willing to wait for fashions to change.

In the meantime, your portfolio will benefit from the fact that the prices of undervalued stocks typically hold up better than those of more popular shares. The reason is that value stocks are often so depressed that their prices don't have as far to fall in bad times.

As is true with all investment approaches, value investors should diversify so that if one or two stocks turn out to be duds, your portfolio can still perform well overall. You can also reduce your risk by limiting your purchases to shares of companies that are strong financially. The lower the debt, the better, because debt creates heavy interest expenses that can be a drag on earnings growth. Look for stocks whose debt is no more than 20% of total capital (the sum of long-term debt and shareholders' equity).

Here are some of the other criteria value investors frequently use. Stocks do not have to meet all five to be considered good bargains, however. Most important is a low P/E or a low ratio of price-to-cash flow. If combined with a high return on equity, chances are very good that the stock is attractive on a value basis. Even without a low P/E, a stock can qualify as a buy if it has a low price-to-book ratio or a high net current asset value.

Low P/E ratios. A low earnings multiple shows that investors are not willing to pay very much for each dollar of a company's current earnings—a sure sign that a stock is out of favor and depressed. As a result, value stocks generally have P/Es that are well below those of typical blue chips.

High yields. Because value investors may not realize significant capital appreciation on a given investment for some time, an above-average yield is especially important. A high yield of 5% or more helps support a stock's price if the market turns down. And consistently rising dividends provide your portfolio with a return while you wait for a stock's price to reflect its inherent worth.

Low price-to-book value. A company's book value—its assets minus liabilities, divided by its total number of outstanding shares—gives an indication of what a company's assets are worth, based on historic prices. In a 1973 update on his investment theory, Graham recommended that investors pay no more than 1.2 to 1.5 times book value for a stock. Even though the rapid inflation of the 1970s has made historic prices less meaningful than they once were, many value investors still look for shares with a price that is less than 1.25 times book value, compared with a recent price/book ratio of 1.9 for the S&P 500.

The most conservative value investors, however, apply the more stringent test of net current asset value, which harks back to Graham's original 1934 investment theory. In essence, this approach looks at what you would get if a company were to liquidate and you were the last shareholder in line. In other words, net current assets are what would remain if a company's ongoing business (its plant and equipment, which could be hard to sell on short notice) were reduced to zero and all debts were paid off with short-term assets, such as cash, inventory, and accounts receivable. While it is very hard to find stocks selling around, or below, net asset value, those that are trading at such a level are automatically attractive.

Low price-to-cash flow. Some companies earn quite a bit more in cash each year than they report as earnings. Here's why: To figure earnings, companies deduct such things as depreciation and amortization, which are expenses for bookkeeping purposes but don't require an actual outlay of cash. As a result, many value investors judge price-to-cash-flow ratios to be more reliable than price/earnings ratios. The typical blue chip stock recently had a price-to-cash-flow ratio of 7.5. Many value hunters favor stocks with a ratio of less than 5.

Return on equity. A basic measure of profitability is the amount a company earns on each dollar of a shareholder's investment. This is called return on equity (ROE) and is figured by dividing net income by shareholders' equity. A stock with a high ROE often sports an equally high P/E, but sometimes a company with a high ROE will have a low price/earnings multiple. When that happens, value investors pounce, especially if the P/E is 20% or more below the ROE. Such companies can use their high profitability to finance expansion without having to borrow. Further, fast earnings growth converts into fast dividend growth.

Understanding Annual Reports

A few key items can tell you a lot about the stock.

Every spring, annual reports pile up in shareholders' mailboxes like so much junk mail. In fact, many investors consider these lavishly illustrated documents to be no more than corporate advertising. But you can extract valuable information from them if you focus on the items discussed here. (The annual reports discussed here are for manufacturing companies, but some of the principles apply to other businesses as well.)

In general, you'll want to look for significant changes in these items from year to year. For that reason, if you own or are thinking of buying shares in a company, ask the firm's shareholder relations department to send you annual reports for the three previous years to review along with the current one. The information you can find in an annual report may not always be enough for a definitive conclusion about a stock, but if a company has weak spots, you should be able to detect them so you can ask your broker about them.

Begin with the shareholders' letter, the message from the chairman outlining the company's performance in the past year and its prospects. Compare discussions of the company's plans in past letters with subsequent results. Has earnings growth met the chairman's goals? Have intended acquisitions or expansion projects been carried through? Look for an honest, forthright discussion of factors both good and bad that have affected the company's performance. Be wary of a company whose chairman doesn't acknowledge widely publicized problems.

The table of figures called the balance sheet gives a quick snapshot of the company's assets and liabilities on the last day of its fiscal year. For an important indicator of a company's financial soundness, divide the company's current assets by its current liabilities. (So-called current entries are those with a life of less than a year.) The result is called the current ratio. Most analysts believe that a ratio of 2 to 1 indicates that the company has sufficient assets on hand to meet its immediate debts.

You should also determine whether the company is carrying too much long-term debt. To do that, divide long-term debt by long-term capital, which consists of long-term debt plus shareholders' equity. (You can find both figures on the balance sheet.) A result above 50% may give you pause. That's because the more debt a company has, the less financial cushion it has for bad times, and the less ability it has to borrow for other needs.

Another key item is accounts receivable, listed under current assets. Accounts receivable are payments for sales of products or services that the company expects to get shortly—perhaps in 90 days or so. If receivables are growing faster than sales, which are reported on the accompanying income statement, the company could be having trouble collecting its bills.

Below receivables on the balance sheet you will find current inventories. If inventories are rising faster than sales, the company may be producing more than it can sell. To see whether this is the case, examine how the company's inventory turnover ratio has changed from year to year. You compute this ratio by referring again to the income statement for the revenue figure, then dividing that number by current inventories, which is listed on the balance sheet. A ratio rising from year to year is good news, but a declining one is an indication that the company's products are not moving well.

On the income statement, which lists the company's revenues and expenses, usually for the past three years, you will find figures for net income per share. They can tell you whether the company's earnings have been growing steadily, declining, or swinging erratically. (Many annual reports have a table listing revenues and net income for the past five or 10 years.) You should also compare yearly changes in revenues with those in expenses. If expenses are going up faster than revenues, the company may not be doing an adequate job of holding down costs.

Sometimes companies show earnings increases that are boosted by so-called nonrecurring gains that occur as the result of an unusual action, such as selling a subsidiary. Such gains cannot be counted on to supplement a company's income on a regular basis. Similarly, a nonrecurring loss, such as writing off a failed project, cannot be blamed for a trend of continuing losses. Nonrecurring items should be listed separately on the income statement. To make sure that they are, read the footnotes to the income statement carefully.

Indeed, the footnotes can be the most important part of an annual report. They provide details of the accounting practices the company used in preparing the report. You can pick up hints from footnotes that the company took unusual measures to enhance its profits. A change in accounting procedures can sometimes signal bookkeeping legerdemain. The footnotes will also tell you whether there are any lawsuits or pending liabilities that could affect the company's future.

Finally, check the auditor's statement to make sure that an independent accounting firm has given unqualified approval to the report. Such approval is by no means a guarantee that the company is financially sound, but it does assure that the report complies with generally accepted accounting principles. If the auditor hedges, watch out. Such phrases as "except for" or "subject to" indicate the auditor could not fully approve the company's report, and you may want to steer clear of its stock. Even if the idea of reading a company's annual report makes you drowsy, the information it contains could keep you from making an expensive mistake.

The *Money* All-Weather Funds

Looking for a mutual fund to help glide you through jittery times? These steady performers offer superior returns at acceptable risks.

It is almost an article of faith on Wall Street that mutual fund investors who hope to earn exhilarating profits must lead lives of danger, enduring frightening fluctuations in the value of their assets. The truth is otherwise. Indeed, a handful of mutual funds defy the conventional wisdom and deliver consistently high returns while taking comparatively low risks.

To determine the 10 champions in each of two categories—stock and bond funds—*Money* asked Lipper Analytical Services to rank 322 stock funds and 168 bond funds according to their risk-adjusted performances over the five years to April 30, 1988. (The competitors had to be widely available, accept initial investments of $10,000 or less, and have at least $25 million in assets.) The stock funds that scored highest are listed in the table on page 55. The top risk-adjusted fixed-income funds are presented on page 56.

Although the All-Weathers are solid gainers, you won't necessarily find them at the top of the mutual fund performance rankings that begin on page 185. Their success is measured by a more complex formula. Developed by Stanford University finance professor William Sharpe, it takes into account a fund's volatility—the amount by which each month's returns deviate from the fund's average monthly return—as well as its gains during the five-year test period. Spectacular total returns (yield plus price change) boost a fund's score, but so do steady gains. Thus, the typical All-Weather combines above-average performance with an enduring—and to shareholders, endearing—ability to withstand market setbacks.

Some funds are unsuitable for All-Weather status, regardless of performance. Excluded were global and international funds because their share values swing sharply with currency fluctuations. High-yield bond funds, which invest primarily in low-quality corporate debt, missed the cut because they could be pounded in a recession. Also eliminated were inherently risky sector and gold funds; tax-exempt municipal bond funds, which appeal only to upper-bracket investors; equity income funds that do not invest primarily in stocks; and funds closed to new investors as of June 15, 1988.

The all-stars employ diverse strategies, so the thumbnail sketches that follow should lead you to one that suits your investing style.

Stock Funds

All of the stock funds on the list enjoyed the benefits of portfolio managers who are extraordinarily adept at judging when a risk is worth taking. Michael Price, who manages Mutual Qualified and Mutual Shares, the two top-rated All-Weather stock funds, is a case in point. Price has a well-known penchant for investing in ailing enterprises, including bankrupt and near-bankrupt firms. But he usually limits such investments to bonds so that the funds can claim a share of a company's assets if it fails. Price also invests about half of the two funds' virtually identical holdings in stocks that sell at 40% to 50% discounts from the companies' book value (net worth) per share. Such stocks are often prime takeover bait. Although both funds notched stellar gains during the five-year period, they did so with less volatility than 82% of the funds analyzed.

Third-rated Merrill Lynch Phoenix shops exclusively for stocks and bonds of companies with excessive debt or depressed earnings and waits for the firms to recover or attract other value-oriented investors. "Buying stocks at prices that reflect the bad news about a company is less risky than buying high fliers," says manager Robert Martorelli. The fund's portfolio of under-the-weather companies made it the most volatile of the stock All-Weathers. Even so, it turned in a more even-tempered performance than did 77% of the stock funds surveyed.

Phoenix Balanced Series made its mark with a very different strategy—buying shares of financially fit companies. "We buy companies that are meeting their potential," explains manager Patricia Bannan. She usually keeps 60% or more of the fund's assets in stocks, but

Treasury bonds and cash may dominate the portfolio when stock prices strike her as unrealistically high. In October 1987, for example, stocks accounted for just 40% of the fund's pre-crash holdings. Result: Shareholders suffered only an 8.8% loss during the fourth quarter of 1987, while the Standard & Poor's 500-stock index plopped 22.8%.

Another balanced fund, IDS Mutual, rarely varies its mix of about 60% stocks, 30% bonds, and 10% cash. "I'd rather focus on finding good investments than worry about timing," says Tom Medcalf, who favors neglected stocks with price/earnings ratios of 10 or less and high dividend yields of 4% or more. Those yields, plus income from corporate and government bonds, bolster the fund's total return while Medcalf waits for his out-of-favor picks to realize their potential.

Manager Andrew Richey of Alliance Balanced takes a different approach. He shuns high-yield stocks and buys shares in established companies with strong earnings growth potential and liberal cash flow. To produce the fund's customary 3.5% to 5.5% yield, he invests about a third of his assets in bonds.

Successful market timing and economic forecasting have paid off for shareholders in

Ten Top Stock Funds that Keep Risk in Check

These funds deliver exceptional profits for the risks they take. They are listed in order of their risk-adjusted returns for the five years to April 30, 1988, according to a formula described in the story. Total expenses, which include front-

and back-end loads as well as management and 12-b 1 fees, assume a $1,000 initial investment, a 5% compound annual return for five years and the sale of other fund shares at the end of that time.

	% gain (or loss) to July 1				% compounded annual return (five years to July 1)	Type	Minimum initial investment	Five-year total expenses*	Telephone	
	1988	One year	Three years	Five years					Toll-free (800)	In state
STOCKS										
1 Mutual Qualified	22.4	8.8	73.5	148.2	18.6	G&I	$1,000	$38	553-3014	—
2 Mutual Shares	23.1	9.4	71.0	141.4	18.0	G&I	5,000	39	553-3014	—
3 Mer. Lynch Phoenix	28.4	10.3	72.5	128.4	16.9	G&I	1,000	125	637-7455	—
4 Phoenix Bal. Series	1.0	(4.2)	49.7	104.5	14.6	Bal	1,000	N.A.*	243-4361	—
5 IDS Mutual	9.6	2.3	57.6	106.9	14.8	Bal	2,000	83	328-8300	—
6 Alliance Balanced	16.9	5.1	58.9	121.9	16.3	Bal	250	121	221-5672	—
7 Strong Total Return	10.5	(1.0)	58.9	97.8	13.9	G&I	250	71	368-3863	—
8 Evergreen Total Ret.	14.0	(2.4)	40.2	102.9	14.4	EqI	2,000	56	235-0064	—
9 Fidelity Puritan	14.6	0.5	49.2	107.4	14.9	EqI	1,000	N.A.*	544-6666	617-523-1919 (Mass.)
10 Natl. Total Income	9.4	2.9	51.0	99.3	14.0	EqI	250	N.A.*	223-7757	212-661-3000 (N.Y.)

Types: G&I—Growth and income; Bal—Balanced; EqI—Equity income   *Not available. Fund is not required to report these data until end of its fiscal year.

Strong Total Return. Fund manager Richard Strong quickly shifts assets from stocks and long-term bonds to cash when, say, he sees the Federal Reserve Board squeezing the money supply and chilling economic growth. About half of the fund's assets were in stocks last June, including shares of manufacturing companies that Strong believed would profit from rising exports and fertilizer firms that would gain from the farm belt drought.

Three funds on the All-Weather stock list make current income a primary goal. Evergreen Total Return is known for shrewd choices in undervalued stocks that become takeover targets. But co-managers Nola Maddox Falcone and Stephen Lieber also keep up to half of their portfolio in high-yielding shares such as those of utility and financial services companies. Manager Richard Fentin stashes a lofty 60% to 80% of Fidelity Puritan's assets in high-yield stocks such as bank and utility shares. National Total Income invests about half of its holdings in high-yielding stocks whose prices have lagged the market in recent years. Cash and short-term Treasury issues provide stability, and intermediate corporate bonds help boost the fund's yield.

Bond Funds

As a group, the All-Weather bond funds were no less impressive or diverse than their stock market counterparts—nine of the 10 funds scored gains that placed them among the top 18% of the fixed-income funds analyzed. The lone exception was Vanguard Fixed Income Short-Term Portfolio, which still managed to turn in the top risk-adjusted performance of the fixed-income funds. Manager Ian MacKinnon invests mainly in high-quality corporates with average maturities of two to four years.

To pick up additional income, several All-Weather bond funds maintain marginally higher average maturities than those of MacKinnon's fund. Kemper U.S. Government Securities' average maturity is rarely shorter than five or longer than 12 years. The fund keeps as much as 75% of its portfolio in mortgage-backed securities such as Ginnie Maes. A sister fund, Kemper Income & Capital Preservation, loads up on investment-grade corporates with an average maturity of five to eight years.

Bond Fund of America is divided into five pools of money, with each managed by an

Introducing *Money*'s All-Weather Bond Funds

These 10 fixed-income funds, ranked by five-year risk-adjusted returns to April 30, 1988, have provided high profits at relatively modest risk. As the accompanying article explains, however, some are more volatile than others. All but two invest primarily in high-quality corporate bonds. The exceptions—Kemper U.S. Government and Lord Abbett U.S. Government—specialize in mortgage-backed and Treasury securities, respectively.

	% gain (or loss) to July 1				% compounded annual return (five years to July 1)	Type	Minimum initial investment	Five-year total expenses*	Telephone	
	1988	One year	Three years	Five years					Toll-free (800)	In state
BONDS										
1 Vanguard F.I. S-T	4.1	7.3	28.6	65.2	10.2	STT	$3,000	$19	662-7447	—
2 Kemper U.S. Gov.	4.5	6.3	36.9	78.9	11.8	MBS	1,000	N.A.	621-1048	—
3 Kemper Inc. & Cap.	6.1	7.8	35.6	78.1	11.7	HGC	1,000	N.A.	621-1048	—
4 Bond Fund of Am.	7.2	8.3	40.4	82.1	12.2	HGC	1,000	79	421-9900	714-671-7000 (Calif.)
5 Babson Bond Trust	4.2	6.7	33.1	70.5	10.8	HGC	500	54	422-2766	816-471-5200 (Mo.)
6 American Cap. Corp.	9.0	11.5	41.9	81.6	12.1	HGC	500	85	847-5636	—
7 Axe-Houghton Inc.	5.3	6.2	41.8	84.4	12.4	HGC	1,000	84	431-1030	914-631-8131 (N.Y.)
8 M.L. Corp.-Int.	4.8	7.0	31.4	70.3	10.8	HGC	1,000	96	637-7455	—
9 Lord Abbett U.S.	5.5	8.3	33.4	73.4	11.2	USG	500	N.A.	223-4224	212-848-1800 (N.Y.)
10 IDS Selective	5.7	6.8	39.9	76.2	11.5	HGC	2,000	88	328-8300	—

*Figure represents the total amount an investor would pay on a $1,000 initial investment that compounds at a 5% annual rate and is terminated after five years.
Types: STT—Short-term taxables; HGC—High-grade corporates; MBS—Mortgage-backed securities; USG—U.S. Government bonds.

independent fund manager. Sounds like a recipe for chaos, but the managers are adept at finding bargains among corporate bonds. Edward Martin, manager of the Babson Bond Trust, posted a steady performance by maintaining a portfolio of corporates with a seven- to 12-year average maturity. He shuns market timing and, instead, prefers to prospect for attractive yields and potential capital gains among bonds issued by neglected companies with strong earnings growth potential.

Two funds, American Capital Corporate Bond and Axe-Houghton Income, increase shareholders' current income—and subject them to somewhat greater risk—by holding long-term bonds. American Capital's average maturity ranges from 12 to 17 years, Axe-Houghton's from seven to 20. American Capital's manager David Troth uses his experience as a former stock analyst to avoid securities issued by firms that seem likely takeover targets. Such companies often damage their credit ratings through financial maneuvers such as stock buybacks designed to fend off raiders. Such a weakened credit picture can adversely affect the value of a company's bonds. Axe-Houghton's Robert Manning boosts current income by concentrating on intermediate- and long-term corporates.

By contrast, Merrill Lynch Corporate Bond Fund Intermediate Portfolio provides consistent returns by investing mainly in corporate issues that mature in 10 years or less. Fund manager Martha Reed concentrates on corporates rated BBB or better and adds Treasuries to the portfolio when their yields rise relative to those of corporate issues.

Lord Abbett U.S. Government Securities invests solely in government issues. But fund manager Bob Dow runs the portfolio aggressively, varying his cash holdings to protect shareholders from swings in interest rates. But a run of bad luck could cost shareholders in this comparatively volatile All-Weather. Ray Goodner, who runs IDS Selective, also one of the more volatile All-Weather bond funds, freely moves the fund's assets among different sectors of the bond market, including convertibles, junk bonds, and overseas issues. As with all of the All-Weather Funds, however, those changes are usually to their shareholders' advantage.

CDs Reconsidered

These once dull investments now offer great interest.

When stocks are on the upswing, few investors are entranced by certificates of deposit, which are issued by banks or savings and loans. But CDs' popularity rises when the market is down or the economic outlook uncertain. As stocks surged in the first eight months of 1987, for instance, $12.1 billion flowed out of federally insured savings institutions as depositors withdrew money from CDs and savings accounts. After the market crash, however, investors did an abrupt about-face and poured $27.1 billion into CDs and savings accounts from October 1987 through March 1988.

The appeal of CDs traditionally has been safety. As a result of bank deregulation, however, relatively fat yields have also become a prime attraction. The average CD tends to yield one-quarter to three-quarters of a percentage point more than U.S. Treasuries of comparable maturity—the closest alternative to CDs in terms of safety. As a further enticement to depositors, some banks and thrifts have recently begun issuing CDs that permit partial withdrawals without penalties.

When you buy a CD, you are lending money to an institution for a specific period of time, most commonly 30 days to five years. Generally, the longer you commit your money, the more you will earn on it. For example, the average recent yield on a five-year CD was 8.5%, compared with 8.2% for 2½ years, 7.9% for one year, and 7.6% for six months. Unlike bond interest, which is paid to you periodically, CD interest usually compounds—that is, you earn interest on the interest you have already built up. You receive your principal and all the interest when the CD matures.

Exactly how much you will earn from your CD depends on its effective annual yield, which is the figure you should always use when comparing offers at different institutions. Yield reflects both the quoted interest rate and how frequently interest is compounded. The more frequent the compounding, the higher the yield. The difference won't be enough, however, to justify a lot of shopping around.

Maturity is as important as yield in selecting a CD. If you believe interest rates may soon peak, you would be wise to lock in current high yields as long as possible. But if you think interest rates will rise, you should stick with maturities of less than one year, or with variable-rate certificates whose rates are adjusted every six months or so. That way, you can earn more than you would in a money-market mutual fund yet avoid having your money locked in for long at below-market rates.

An alternative for investors who do not care to gamble on interest-rate moves is to spread your cash among CDs with due dates six months apart. This way some of your money will soon be available to reinvest should rates rise, and some will be locked into what may prove to be superior yields if rates fall.

You can buy CDs for as little as $500 directly from a bank or savings and loan. S&Ls generally offer higher yields than commercial banks do. If you do not mind giving up the convenience of dealing with a local institution, banking by mail may improve your yield by a percentage point or two. Higher-yielding institutions are often in economically depressed areas—or fast-growing ones—and must offer above-average rates to attract deposits.

No matter where you purchase CDs, here are two questions to ask before committing your cash:
● What is the penalty for early withdrawal? The amount of interest you sacrifice is set by each institution and ranges from nothing on partial withdrawals to several months' worth of interest.
● Can you add to your CD balance at some later point? Some banks and thrifts let you put additional money into your CD throughout its life, with the new cash earning interest at the rate you locked in originally. This can be very attractive if current rates are lower than that on your certificate.

For the best combination of high yield, convenience, and liquidity, you can buy your CDs through a broker. So-called brokered CDs sport higher-than-average yields because the firms buy them in volume from banks and S&Ls nationwide for resale to individual investors. The minimum investment is usually $1,000. Often you pay no broker's commission on the transaction (the broker is recompensed by the issuing institution).

There are two ways to cash in a brokered CD before it matures: You may pay the issuing institution's penalty for early withdrawal or your broker can sell your CD for you. If prevailing yields are lower than your CD's, selling could earn you a profit. If current yields are higher, your broker can calculate whether your loss from selling will be less than the early-withdrawal penalty.

Even if you buy through a broker or from an out-of-state institution, your cash is safe, provided you buy only certificates issued by banks and S&Ls that are covered by the Federal Savings and Loan Insurance Corporation (FSLIC) or the Federal Deposit Insurance Corporation (FDIC), which insure balances up to $100,000.

If a bank fails and the FSLIC or FDIC must pay off depositors, local customers are likely to be reimbursed sooner than out-of-staters. So if you have invested by mail or through a broker, your money may be tied up for a few weeks at no interest. But the forfeited interest would not amount to much—perhaps $15 on a $5,000 deposit.

Why Munis Still Make Sense

Despite confusion about the status of municipal bonds, their after-tax yields are hard to resist.

The municipal bond market has been under siege ever since the Tax Reform Act of 1986. First, Congress limited the number and the types of tax-exempts that state and local governments could issue. Then the Supreme Court resoundingly endorsed those restrictions in April 1988, when it ruled that the Constitution does not protect state and local governments against federal taxation of the bond interest they pay.

The resultant confusion among investors has made buying munis a little riskier than in the past. But the potential returns are so exceptional that munis almost certainly deserve a place in your portfolio. Munis still offer the most attractive high-grade yields available for people in top tax brackets. A married couple in the 28% bracket—with a joint 1988 taxable income of $29,750 to $71,900—would earn the equivalent of an 11.1% taxable yield from an 8% municipal bond. Once taxes and inflation have been taken into account, yields on municipals surpassed those on long-term Treasuries in all but two of the past 28 years.

Moreover, new restrictions on tax-exempt financing do not threaten existing bonds at all. In fact, they have prompted state and local authorities to issue new classes of municipals that can reward you more amply than ever. Over the long term, if the volume of new high-quality tax-exempts doesn't keep pace with demand, the prices of existing issues could rise.

Of course, the disarray of the municipal market in recent years has created problems for small investors. Chief among them is a lack of liquidity. Prices for a particular muni issue can vary by more than $20 per $1,000 bond. You should therefore be sure to get more than one quotation from brokers. Further, while $1,000 muni bonds can be bought in amounts as small as $5,000, you may have trouble selling fewer than 25 bonds unless you are willing to accept a reduced price. But if you want to lock in a high yield and hold your bonds until they mature, limited liquidity is not an especially serious drawback.

Once you have decided that investing in munis is right for your portfolio, your next decision is what to buy. Since you will probably hold your bonds for a decade or more, you should stick to high-grade issues—those rated A or better by services such as Standard & Poor's or Moody's. Insured bonds may be worthwhile if they are priced to yield only one-quarter of a percentage point less than comparable uninsured issues. Otherwise, the benefits of insurance are psychological, not financial.

In addition to conventional tax-exempts, there are several special types of munis to consider. The newest of these issues are AMT (alternative minimum tax) bonds. They have sprung from tax law provisions that decree that certain bonds used to finance such private activities as airports and veterans' mortgages, would not be completely tax-exempt. While bondholders do not have to pay ordinary income tax on the bonds, interest from such issues is subject to the alternative minimum tax—a 21% levy on wealthy taxpayers who would otherwise not owe any taxes. Because

AMT bonds are not tax-exempt for everyone, they typically pay a yield around half a percentage point higher than that of comparable ordinary bonds. Thus, for the 99% of all taxpayers who are not subject to the AMT, these bonds could be a good deal.

Two other special kinds of munis are especially appealing for small investors. Those called pre-refunded bonds are, in effect, Treasury issues that pay tax-exempt interest. These bonds are created when an issuer of tax-exempts wants to take advantage of a drop in interest rates. For example, if rates fall, a county government could sell a new bond issue with a lower yield and use part of the proceeds to buy Treasuries and place them in escrow to pay the principal and interest on an old bond issue. Such pre-refunded bonds offer the highest degree of safety that you can get.

Another type, zero-coupon municipals, have existed for six years. But the 1986 tax law made these issues newly popular as a way of funding a child's education. Zero-coupon munis—which pay no periodic interest but assure that a fixed sum will be paid at maturity—enable a child to earn interest and build principal tax-free with a bond that reaches maturity on the day the tuition bill arrives.

The first step in buying individual issues is to ask your broker to check all the provisions that allow for an early call, which permits the issuer to redeem a bond at or slightly above face value before its maturity date. If interest rates fall, an issuer may want to reduce his payout by calling a high-yielding bond and selling new bonds at lower rates. When this happens, holders of the old bonds are deprived of high yields that they thought they had locked in safely.

For investors with less than $25,000 to invest, it may be wisest to purchase a municipal bond fund or a unit trust. Each offers professional bond selection and diversification. Investors with as little as $1,000 who want to be able to withdraw their money before maturity are probably best served by a no-load fund. Those who think long-term may do better with unit trusts—fixed portfolios of municipals are usually available with a $5,000 minimum investment. Sales charges on trusts run 4% to

5% of the initial investment, but annual expenses are only about 0.15% of total assets, more than half a percentage point below those of a typical bond fund. Over a period of seven years or more, the lower annual fee of a trust will more than make up for its initial sales charge. Most important, trusts do not change the composition of their portfolios; unlike funds, they hold bonds until maturity. In addition to enjoying a high current yield, you can therefore count on getting all of your principal back.

Your Guide to Five Vital References

No matter which type of investment you are considering, the reference books vital to your research have confusingly similar names. These thumbnail descriptions should help you sort them out:

Standard & Poor's Corporation Records. Six annual volumes of brief entries on 12,000 stocks. The information includes each company's address and lines of business.

Value Line Investment Survey. Two loose-leaf volumes divided into three sections. The first gives analysts' outlooks for various industries and averages of key financial data. The second: analysts' outlooks for the economy and the stock market. The third: one-page reports on 1,700 companies with data going back 15 years. Updated quarterly.

Standard & Poor's Stock Reports. Twelve volumes of two-page reports on 4,300 stocks containing less analysis than *Value Line.* S&P's data go back 10 years. Updated quarterly.

Moody's Manuals. A series of eight multivolume annuals of which the most useful to stock investors are *Moody's, OTC Industrial* and *OTC Unlisted Manuals.* The manuals offer limited data on 22,000 stocks.

Standard & Poor's Industry Surveys. These two loose-leaf volumes include tables of key financial data on 1,000 companies along with industry averages and analysis. They are updated quarterly.

How to Choose the Right Money Market Fund

Look for more than high yield. Convenience, fees, the quality of the fund's securities, and your tax status are also important to consider.

In the face of uncertainty about the fate of the stock and bond markets, you may be looking for a safe and simple investment. The likeliest choice is a money market fund, which presents minimal risk, provides instant liquidity, and pays a higher yield than you can get in a savings account at a bank. Taxable money funds recently yielded about 7.3%, compared with 5% on average for tax-exempt funds. Even if you prefer investments such as stocks and bonds, you should have an active money fund account as a haven for your cash if you decide to sell on short notice.

A money fund is basically a mutual fund that buys short-term debt securities, such as Treasury bills and corporate debt obligations known as commercial paper. By investing in issues that mature in a few days or months, money funds can be fairly certain that they will not have to sell securities at a loss. As a result, a money fund can nearly guarantee that investors will never lose their principal. In more technical terms, the money fund asserts that it will hold its net asset value—the price at which you buy into or redeem from the fund—at $1 a share. To be permitted to make such a promise, money funds are required by law to invest in securities with maturities of 120 days or less.

If you are willing to take a little more risk, you may want to consider a short-term bond fund—one that buys issues with maturities of one to four years. Such funds typically yield one to two percentage points more than money market funds. And while short-term bond funds can suffer declines in principal value, their losses are much smaller than those of long-term bond funds. If interest rates rise one percentage point, for example, a bond fund with an average maturity of two years would fall less than 2% in price, while a fund with a maturity of more than 20 years could fall 9%.

In selecting the right money market fund, start by considering convenience. Most funds offer check-writing privileges, and many require a minimum investment of only $1,000 (Many also require checks written on the account to meet a minimum amount of, say, $500). If you want to be able to switch among the stock and bond funds in a particular fund family, it will probably make the most sense to choose that family's money market fund. Since the difference in yield between comparable money makret funds is only about half a percentage point, choosing the most convenient fund is likely to cost less than $50 a year in interest for a $10,000 account.

If you have considerably more money to invest, though, you may want to compare funds more carefully to find the best values. To obtain information on a fund, telephone for copies of its prospectus and annual report. In addition, fund data are published weekly in *Donoghue's Money Fund Report* (Box 6640, Holliston, MA 01746; $695 a year, $5 a copy). These are the most important factors investors should consider:

Yields. In choosing a money fund, you should look at more than just its current yield for the past 30 days. You will get a better picture of how well a fund has been managed by checking its 12-month yield, which is based on actual distributions over the past year. With short-term bond funds, you should also look at total return for the period, which reflects any capital gains or losses as well as yield. You should not, however, automatically choose the fund with the very highest past yield or total return. The fund could be inflating its yield by taking greater risks.

Fees. All money funds pay for management costs and other expenses, such as advertising, by deducting them from the yield that a portfolio earns. These amounts are usually expressed as a percentage of the assets in the fund—a figure known as the expense ratio. This ratio, which usually runs 0.7% to 0.8% a year, may seem trivial. But remember that these costs are subtracted from the yield you receive; a fund with a 1% expense ratio will probably yield about half a point less than one with a 0.5% ratio. In fact, differences in expense ratios account for nearly two-thirds of the variation among money fund yields. And funds with expense ratios above 1% often underperform the average for the industry. Funds are required to state their expense ratios in their prospectuses.

Maturity. The longer the average maturity of fixed-income issues, the more they fluctuate in price as interest rates change. The reason is that longer-term securities are locked into a below-average yield for a greater time when interest rates rise. Because of their short maturities, money funds are rarely affected much by changes in interest rates. In fact, only one fund has ever failed to return a full $1 a share

to investors. In 1975, First Multifund extended its average maturity to almost two years to pump up its yield. When interest rates rose suddenly in late 1978, the fund's net asset value dropped to 94 cents. Since money funds today have average maturities of fewer than 120 days, the worst that is likely to happen is that a fund's yield may lag when interest rates rise. But short-term bond funds, which have maturities as long as four years, can actually decline in value.

Quality. In general, the lower the quality of the securities held by a fund, the higher its yield and risk. For example, funds that invest in commercial paper issued by companies with mediocre credit ratings are riskier than funds invested entirely in supersafe U.S. Treasury bills. The actual risk of losing principal in even a poorly rated fund is fairly low, however. Nonetheless, a fund that takes a loss on risky securities could have to reduce its yield. Some money funds are insured against such losses, but because the cost of this protection diminishes a fund's yield by about 0.5% a year, most fund experts consider that insurance not worth the price.

Tax status. Whether you decide to invest in a money fund or a short-term bond fund, you should always check to see whether you would be better off in a tax-free fund. (If you live in a high-tax state, consider double- or triple-tax-free funds that are also exempt from state and local taxes.) To find the equivalent taxable yield, divide the tax-exempt yield by 1 minus your tax rate. For example, if a tax-exempt fund is yielding 4.8% and you are in the 28% tax bracket, divide 4.8% by 0.72 (or 1 minus .28). The result, 6.7%, is the taxable yield you would have to receive to get 4.8% after taxes. If you are in the 15% bracket, you are probably better off in a taxable fund. In the 28% bracket, it could go either way. But if you are in the 33% bracket or live in a high-tax state, a tax-exempt fund may very well put the most money in your pocket after the government takes its cut.

Zero-Coupon Bonds

They can be lovely for savers and lively for speculators.

Imagine an investment that produces wide swings in value in the course of a week but at the same time lets you lock in a predictable rate of return. This seemingly paradoxical investment is a zero-coupon bond, which appeals to conservative investors saving for retirement, parents putting money away for their children's college education, and speculators seeking quick profits by gambling on interest-rate movements.

Zeros, so named because they pay bondholders no interest until maturity, are sold individually by stockbrokers and through mutual funds with portfolios that will mature around the same time. There are zero versions of Treasury, government agency, corporate, and municipal bonds. Their strong points are a high, guaranteed return (if held until maturity) and a low price that is a fraction of the bond's typical $1,000 face value.

Their premier flaw is that you could lose by selling the bonds early. Unloading a zero right after a one-point rise in interest rates might mean accepting a double-digit loss. If interest rates fall, however, bond prices will go up and you could profit by selling before maturity.

Zero-coupon bonds first became widely available in 1981, when Merrill Lynch split U.S. Treasury bonds into their two components—principal and interest coupons—and sold them separately. When you buy a zero, you actually own a bond's interest coupon, reissued as a new security, that will be paid out in a lump sum at maturity. That means there are no semiannual interest payments, as there are with other bonds. The bond's maturity date could be in a few months or as long as 30 years hence. The further away the bond's maturity date, the bigger its discount from face value and thus the lower your purchase price.

Keep in mind that even though a zero does not distribute income until you cash it in, the IRS and some states require you to pay income taxes annually on the interest the bond has accrued during the year. Two exceptions: Municipal zeros and those held in tax-deferred plans such as Individual Retirement Accounts and Keoghs. Your stockbroker or zero-coupon bond fund will send you a form listing the amount on which taxes are due.

Zeros do eliminate a drawback of conventional bonds known as reinvestment risk. If you hold a standard bond and rates fall, you will be stuck with a lower rate when you reinvest the bond's income. Zero-coupon investors avoid this uncertainty since they get their interest only by cashing in their bonds. This lack of reinvestment risk, however, also contributes to a zero's jittery price movements. As interest rates drop, an investor will pay more for a zero with its locked-in rate than for another bond, so the zero price goes up. But when rates rise, the zero's lower rate makes the bond less enticing to investors, and its price sinks.

How much you will shell out for a zero is hard to determine but pivotal. Brokerage firms buy zeros wholesale and resell them to investors at retail prices reflecting their cost of holding the securities in inventory plus a profit. This markup, assessed in lieu of a sales commission, increases the price you pay for zeros and reduces the price you get if you sell.

The best way to avoid overpaying is to comparison shop among several full-service and discount brokers. Ask each how much you must invest for the zero you want, how much your investment will be worth in dollars at maturity, and the effective yield to maturity. The broker with the lowest figure for the first question and the highest for the latter two is offering the best deal.

Be sure to ask whether the bond is callable, which means that its issuer can redeem the security before its due date if, say, market interest rates have declined. If the zero can be called, ask for both its yield to maturity and its yield to call—your guaranteed return if the bond must be redeemed early. Try to buy only non-callable zeros for their guaranteed yields.

When considering corporate or municipal zeros, it is essential to review the financial stability of their issuers. Even when you hold a corporate or muni zero to maturity, your return is certain only if the issuer can pay its debt. Moreover, you could have a tough time selling one of these zeros in the face of bad news about its company or municipality because the market for the bonds is relatively small. The safest are the ones rated triple-A by Moody's or Standard & Poor's.

If you prefer the certainty of Treasuries, there is also the option of no-load mutual funds, called targets, that buy Treasury zeros set to mature in a given year. In December of the target year, the funds liquidate and investors get their share of the bonds' payouts. Before investing, call the fund for a figure representing the expected value of your investment if held to maturity.

You can redeem these fund shares any time at their current market value—but at your peril. Zeros are the most volatile of all bond funds. For example, the Benham Target 2015 Fund was the worst-performing bond fund in the third quarter of 1987 (down 22.9%) when interest rates rose but the best performer a quarter later (up 25.9%) after rates fell.

Zero fund sponsors eliminate markups by buying bonds at wholesale prices, but investors do pay annual fees for management and other fund expenses. So if you are certain you will hold the bonds to maturity, individual Treasury zeros will generally give you a higher return, after expenses, than funds.

Zeros for Every Investment Need

You can use zero-coupon bonds for many purposes, from funding a child's college education to speculating on interest rates. The table shows how zeros grow over time and how changing rates would affect their prices in the short run. Treasuries and most corporate zeros are taxable. But the three corporates in the example below are uniquely tax advantaged.

| | Recent price (per $1,000 bond) | Price if rates change over the next year | | Yield to maturity | At maturity $1,000 invested today will grow to |
		One-percentage-point rise	One-percentage-point drop		
TREASURY ISSUE					
Five-year (maturing 1993)	$671.40	$702.16	$756.19	8.37%	$1,489
10-year (1998)	427.86	428.35	507.60	8.80	2,337
15-year (2003)	269.43	257.89	336.23	9.02	3,712
20-year (2008)	170.30	155.63	223.25	9.11	5,872
30-year (2018)	76.41	63.34	109.56	8.88	13,087
CORPORATE ISSUE					
Exxon Shipping (2012)	130.00	113.72	176.39	8.72	7,692
GMAC (2012)	112.65	98.80	153.82	9.25	8,877
GMAC (2015)	90.25	77.22	126.20	9.22	11,080

Source: Advest Inc.

No-Sweat Ways to Make Money in Property

There are five methods of investing in real estate for $5,000 or less without getting your hands dirty.

In the heady era that ended with the October 1987 crash, mention of real estate as an investment evoked snores or hoots from the bull market geniuses making big bucks in stocks. But when the market collapsed, investors saw how real estate tends to hold its value. On average, stocks fell 20%, while many securities backed by property holdings dropped less than 10% because of the widely held assumption that real estate is a fundamentally sound, hard-asset-based investment.

The right real estate investment can offer steady income, capital gains, and protection from inflation. Moreover, you don't have to be landed gentry to get in. For $5,000 or less, you can choose among five types of investments that leave property management to the pros: real estate investment trusts (REITs), master limited partnerships (MLPs), mutual funds, variable annuities, and limited partnerships. The table on page 67 provides a comparison of these options. A note of caution: As with any investment, those just mentioned offer no guarantee you will make money. You must choose carefully.

If you do invest in real estate, you can probably earn greater profits and tax benefits by buying and managing a rental property on your own. But the money, time, and expertise required are beyond the means of most investors. Besides, investments for armchair real estate moguls have shown impressive performances of late, fueled in part by inves-

tors' expectations of higher inflation and corresponding appreciation in properties. For example, during the first quarter of 1988, REITs with dividends reinvested returned 9.2% on average, while real estate MLPs delivered total returns of about 18%. By contrast, the total return from Standard & Poor's 500-stock index was 5.8% in that period.

Real estate investors, however, can no longer just put money in any deal and expect to make a profit. Before Congress took a wrecking ball to real estate's tax write-offs in 1986, developers and syndicators went wild, throwing up so many new office complexes, apartment buildings, and shopping centers that vacancy rates now stand at record highs in some areas. As a result, most investment advisers recommend that you temper your optimism by devoting only a small slice of your portfolio—about 5% to 20%—to real estate.

The best real estate investments now for small investors are ones that pay regular dividends from rental income. For safety's sake, advisers suggest that you invest mainly in economically strong areas in the Northeast, Mid-Atlantic states, and on the West Coast. Rental apartments in those regions look especially promising, with mid-1988 vacancy rates as low as 4% in Boston, for example, because of strong housing demand. Strategies for investing in each form of real estate follow, from the types most favored by analysts to the ones they like least.

Real Estate Investment Trusts. Known as REITs, these investments can wrap the attractions of real estate into one package. Well-run REITs provide reliable yields, potential for appreciation, professional management, tax benefits and—because REIT shares trade on major stock exchanges—instant liquidity. A REIT pools investors' money to purchase as many as 20 commercial or residential buildings. Then it hires an independent company to manage the properties. A REIT can offer an appealing yield—lately 8% to 12.5%—because it does not pay corporate taxes and is required by law to pass on 95% of its net income to investors. Up to 40% of a REIT's dividend may be treated as a return of your capital, which lets you defer taxes on that part of the dividend until you sell your shares.

Investors probably should plan to hold REITs for at least three to five years to take advantage of property appreciation, which will be reflected in rising share prices. If you want to limit your risk, buy only REITs with yields below 10%. The reason is that double-digit yields could reflect a highly volatile type of real estate or a REIT with heavy leverage—one that borrows more than 60% of the purchase price of its buildings. Also look for REITs specializing in areas with strong, diversified economies and those whose executives own at least 5% of the shares. This information can be obtained from a REIT's latest annual report or—if it's a new issue—its prospectus.

Master Limited Partnerships. Call MLPs the Comeback Kids of the real estate world. Shares of these partnerships, which own or build properties, trade on major stock exchanges. (They are known as *master* limited partnerships because the deals are often consolidations of smaller, nontraded partnerships.) Real estate MLP prices skidded 22.6% in 1987, largely because Congress debated whether to tax MLP earnings twice, like those of regular companies—first as corporate profits and again as dividends—or only once, at the shareholder level. Congress finally decided that real estate MLPs could keep their favorable tax status indefinitely, and the share prices rebounded 14% in the first three months of 1988. Congress also left intact a law allowing up to 100%

of MLP dividends to be considered a return of capital, making them, in effect, tax deferred until you sell your shares.

Yields lately have averaged 12%. Investment advisers say MLPs are best for aggressive investors who can stand some risk, because MLPs have short performance records—most are no more than three years old. Furthermore, those high yields could indirectly increase your tax-preparation bill. MLP shareholders, like other partnership investors, must deal with complex calculations and fill out an extra tax form known as a Schedule E. That can add $100 to $150 per MLP to an accountant's fee.

Real Estate Mutual Funds. Anyone who has never invested in real estate and is bewildered by the alphabet soup of REITs and MLPs might consider one of the fairly new real estate mutual funds. The funds primarily hold shares of REITs and other real-estate-related companies such as builders. Like other mutual funds, these portfolios offer liquidity, professional management, diversification, relatively low sales fees, and small minimum investments. They do not, however, provide tax benefits. Yields recently hovered around 7.5%. The major funds:

● National Real Estate Stock Fund dates to March 1985, making it the oldest of the bunch. Most of this fund's assets are in REITs that buy recession-resistant, inflation-sensitive buildings, such as shopping centers, nursing homes, and life-care facilities. The fund was down 1.6% in the 12 months to October 1988.

● Fidelity Real Estate Fund mostly holds REITs and aims for a high, stable yield from shopping centers and medical facilities. The fund posted a one-year return of 1.5%.

● U.S. Real Estate Fund, the youngest and smallest of the group, was founded in July 1987. It buys REITs that concentrate in specific types of properties, such as psychiatric hospitals and shopping centers, and had a one-year gain of 7.8%.

Real Estate Variable Annuities. If you are setting cash aside for retirement, you might consider putting some of it in a real estate variable annuity. All income and capital gains in an annuity grow tax deferred until you withdraw the money. At last count, three companies offered real estate annuities: IDS, Prudential, and Monarch Capital. Sold by financial planners, stock brokers, and insurance agents for a minimum of $1,000, a real estate annuity invests in one of two ways. Either it resembles a mutual fund, buying REITs as Monarch does, or it purchases property outright, as IDS and Prudential do. A real estate annuity may give you the option of switching from its portfolio to stocks, bonds, and money-market funds offered by the sponsor. Annual fees run about 1.25% to 3% of your investment. Monarch also charges a $30 initial fee.

You can withdraw your money whenever you wish, but the insurance company will levy surrender fees as high as 9%. And if you are under 59½, the Internal Revenue Service will charge a 10% penalty as well as income taxes on your withdrawal. Such costs make a variable annuity appropriate only if you plan to hold it until you retire or until the surrender fees phase out in five to eight years.

Real Estate Limited Partnerships. Sponsors of public real estate partnerships—those registered with the Securities and Exchange Commission—pool money from hundreds of investors and typically buy up to a dozen or so properties, planning to sell them in seven to 10 years. Until that time, investors collect income—typically 5% to 8% a year—mostly from rents.

Yet, real estate partnerships are problem-prone investments. Investors who sell their units before a partnership disbands will usually get back only 50% to 70% of the value of the properties. Up-front fees and sales charges often run to 25%. What's more, most public programs are blind pools, meaning that general partners decide which properties to buy only after investors put up the money. The topper: Many partnerships formed in the early 1980s have delivered little or no income to investors because they bet so heavily on buildings in the overbuilt Sunbelt.

For years, limited partners were willing to accept such drawbacks in exchange for tax write-offs often worth as much as their investments. Then came tax reform, which threatened to do for partnerships what the ice age did for brontosauruses. Investors in programs bought after October 22, 1986 can now deduct losses only against income from so-called passive investments, chiefly other partnerships and rental real estate. The tax changes drove many hucksters out of business, but attractive

A Head-to-Head Comparison of Investments in Real Estate

ARM'S-LENGTH DEALS IN PROPERTY

Type	Liquidity	Minimum investment	Current yield	Typical initial fees and commissions	Extent of tax shelter
Real estate investment trusts (REITs)	High	$500 for 100 shares	6% to 8%	1% to 8% on purchases of up to $5,000	Up to 40% of your dividends may be tax deferred until you sell your shares.
Master limited partnerships (MLPs)	High	$300 for 100 shares	7% to 16%	Same as REITs	Up to 100% of your dividends may be tax deferred until you sell your shares.
Mutual funds	High	$100 to $2,500	7.5%	None to 7¾%	None
Variable annuities	Medium	$1,000	7% to 11%	None or $30	All of the earnings grow tax deferred until you withdraw them.
Moderately leveraged limited partnerships	Low	$2,000 to $5,000	2% to 6%	15% to 25%	Up to 100% of your income

deals are still scarce.

Financial planners and brokers who specialize in partnerships now frequently prefer moderately leveraged concerns that borrow 30% to 60% of the purchase price of their properties. Annual yields are rarely higher than 6% during the early years of a leveraged program because much of the income from properties must be used for loan payments. In the first few years of a partnership, as much as 100% of an investor's income is tax sheltered by the program's depreciation and mortgage deductions. Then, as the size of the cash distributions grow, the tax shelter diminishes. If the properties appreciate steadily, the deal might produce an annual after-tax yield of 8% to 12% before any capital gains.

Do not invest in a partnership until you have studied the sponsor's record, which is set forth in the prospectus. Look for a company that has been buying similar types of properties for at least three years. Also check the results of a sponsor's past partnerships that have sold buildings. A handy yardstick: The average annual return on those deals, including capital gains, should be at least five to seven percentage points higher than that of medium- or long-term Treasury bonds during the same period. Your adviser should be able to supply you with these comparison returns. If not, perhaps you should look for another adviser and a better deal.

Heavy Metal

Gold offers protection against economic calamity but otherwise is a clunky investment.

Ask any financial planner to outline a well-diversified portfolio and odds are that he or she will recommend that 5% to 10% of it be in gold. Good advice? Only if you have realistic expectations about what gold can—and can't—deliver.

If you expect gold to make your fortune, you are headed for disappointment. Too many people remember only that gold went from $35 an ounce in 1970 to $825 an ounce in 1980, and they expect it to shoot up $50 each time there's the slightest hint of inflation or bad news. On the contrary, gold prices have hovered between $300 and $500 in recent years and the metal has been a poor hedge against inflation, recently running about 4.6% a year.

The key to investing in gold, precious-metals experts say, is to understand that it is not an investment in the conventional sense of something you buy hoping it will pay dividends or grow in value. Instead, gold is insurance against economic or political disaster—its price tends to rise on fears of calamity, as the dizzying price appreciation of the 1970s showed. Gold was then a relatively new investment for Americans. Only in 1971 had its price been freed to float on the market, rather than be fixed—as it had been—by the world's central banks. And not until 1975 could Americans legally purchase it in bullion form—coins and bars. But the upward spiral really took off in 1979 when the U.S. inflation rate topped 13%, the unending oil crisis seemed to threaten limitless price hikes and the Soviets invaded Afghanistan. Gold shot to an all-time high of $825 an ounce on January 21, 1980, then it sagged back to $635 just five days later as people began to realize that the world wasn't coming to an end.

That surge actually set the stage for lower prices this decade. When gold topped $800, a lot more companies were encouraged to mine for the metal, and they found it, increasing supply dramatically and driving down prices. Though South Africa, the world's leading producer, is actually mining slightly less gold today than it did in 1979, worldwide production is up over 40%. Several fairly new producers—including New Guinea, which last year was the world's fourth largest—have also jumped into the market. As a result, the future prospects for gold are not particularly bullish, although some analysts predict that the metal's recent price of around $410 an ounce will rise to $600 some time in the next three years. Other forecasters, however, say slack demand will undercut prices during the 1990s—perhaps to $250 an ounce.

Proponents of gold most often tout it as the ultimate hedge against inflation. They like to point out that an ounce of it bought a handsome suit of men's clothes in 1600—and it still would today. But gold's reputation as an inflation-buster has been tarnished in recent years. An annual survey of 14 categories of investments by Salomon Bros. shows that while gold's compound annual rate of return beat the rise in the consumer price index by 6.5 percentage points over the past 20 years, it actually lagged 1.1 points behind the CPI during the past five years. Super-secure bank certificates of deposit or Treasury bills would have been a better hedge against inflation during that time.

What about the argument that gold reduces your portfolio's risk because it performs well when paper assets, such as stocks and bonds, are falling? On that score, gold lives up to its billing so long as you expect it only to hold its value—not rack up stupendous gains—and are prepared for it to drop again when paper assets recover. Gold was at $461 when the stock market crashed in October 1987, for example, and rose to almost $500 by mid-Decmber 1987. But then it headed southward again as investors regained some confidence in the market and the economy.

The bottom line? If you can hold gold for more than 10 years, a modest investment—say 5% or so of your assets—could help you raise cash in a hurry to take advantage of good buys in a bear market or offer a money cache should the U.S. financial system collapse or some other disaster occur. On the other hand, like all forms of insurance, gold entails an opportunity cost: the income you forego by not holding some revenue-producing asset. If that opportunity cost disturbs your peace of mind more than visions of doomsday do, then gold probably isn't the right investment for you.

How to Buy Gold

Here are some tips on buying gold:

Bullion. The metal comes in a variety of sizes ranging from thin wafers up to 32-ounce bars. The most convenient form is probably coins, since they are easiest to store, price, and sell. For one-ounce coins, expect to pay a premium of 5% to 7% over the value of the gold to cover minting, distribution, and commission costs. With half-ounce, quarter-ounce, and tenth-ounce coins, premiums increase by two percentage points for each step down in size. Be sure to get price quotes from at least three reputable dealers. Never buy from a phone salesman. And if you plan to take possession of the metal, ask about shipping charges and a delivery date. If you buy through a bank or broker, you may want the firm to store and insure your coins at a fee of about one-half of 1% of their value.

Gold accounts and certificates. Several banks, brokerages, and coin dealers will sell you a fractional interest in gold bars or coins that they hold. Some give you a certificate of ownership; others just send a monthly statement. When comparing services, ask for a total of all fees, including application or storage charges (one-half of 1% to 1% is standard).

Gold-mining stocks and mutual funds. These stocks, and the funds that invest in them, are probably the worst way to buy gold, since you are buying not the metal but simply a piece of the company that mines it. Mining share prices tend to swing more widely than the price of gold. And share prices are influenced by fluctuations in the stock market and the fortunes of individual mining companies. Funds are slightly less vulnerable to this last danger since they usually invest in 50 or 60 companies at once.

Your Taxes

Thanks to tax reforms initiated in late 1986, the Internal Revenue Service currently can claim no more than 33% of your top-dollar taxable earnings. While that rate may not inspire you to break out in a chorus of "For the IRS Is a Jolly Good Agency," it looks mighty generous compared with the maximum levy of 76% on average over the past 58 years. In fact, the last time the highest rate ducked below today's level was in 1931, when the wealthy were assessed only 25%.

As recently as 1981, being in the top bracket cost you 70%. Even the pre-reform 50% top rate now seems gargantuan by comparison. Leaner tax rates, however, do not necessarily translate into lower tax bills. (For a comparison of who fares best—and worst—under tax reform, see the table on page 73.)

Some of taxpayers' most cherished benefits and deductions are gone, perhaps for good. Among them are the preferential rates afforded long-term capital gains, the sales tax write-off, and the Individual Retirement Account deduction for many households. The sacrosanct mortgage interest deduction survives more or less intact. But any consumer-credit interest and most tax-shelter losses claimed in 1989 qualify for only a 20% write-off, which is scheduled to disappear entirely in 1991. Still, congressional tax experts estimate that most taxpayers enjoyed at least a token tax cut in 1987, the first full year of reform.

Likewise, 1988 provided another slight improvement for most Americans because rates dropped further across all income levels and the personal exemption and standard deduction increased. Unfortunately, with the nation's annual budget deficit hovering around $150 million at last count, Congress probably will tinker with the tax code again soon to find new routes to your pocket.

Almost certainly some income now shielded from the government's clutches will become taxable, most likely beginning in 1990. For example, Capitol cognoscenti expect a greater portion of Social Security benefits to become subject to tax. Also vulnerable are certain tax-exempt company benefits such as employer-paid health insurance. In addition, withdrawals of cash value from single-premium life insurance policies may lose their tax-free status. All of these revenue raisers have ended up in the discard bin before, but they will be dusted off and proposed again.

So make the most of today's low rates while they last. As this chapter will demonstrate, there are still many clever ways to keep more of what you earn, provided that you plan ahead. But don't be surprised if the windfall you expect to find on the bottom line of your 1040 return is barely enough for a down payment on your accountant's bill, swollen by many of the new law's complexities. Worse, his or her fee is probably no longer deductible.

Tax Reform's Rabbit Punch

Forget the promises about simpler forms and lower rates. After the bloodiest tax-filing season in history, many of us lost money—most of us lost faith.

The combination of indecipherable tax forms, convoluted worksheets, and unexplained rules left behind a thick fog of befuddlement when tax reform's first filing season ended last year. The formidable new 1040 delivered the most devastating blow, battering many of the 32 million Americans who itemize deductions, especially investors and borrowers. Even those who didn't owe higher taxes or accountants' fees found themselves more exasperated than ever at the filing process.

How many taxpayers ended up owing more under the new law? The Treasury Department is still compiling statistics revealing tax reform's winners and losers. But there is evidence that the new law significantly altered the ways Americans manage their finances.

Consider, for example, the ways Americans are saving and borrowing. Benefits consultants say that employee investments in 401(k) salary-reduction plans, the best remaining tax-favored game in town, grew about 5% in 1987 to $6.2 billion. Home-equity loans, whose interest remains fully deductible for most borrowers, grew about 80% in 1987 and are continuing to expand at a 25% annual rate, according to the Federal Reserve. Now an estimated 3 million Americans have them. And sales of single-premium life insurance policies, another darling of reform, nearly doubled in 1987 to $9.5 billion. Meanwhile, lost tax advantages helped cut the rate of growth in charitable giving to its lowest level in 12 years. The new tax rules also played a role in deflating limited-partnership sales by close to 40% in the first half of 1988 compared with those 12 months earlier.

Tax preparation fees went up along with tax bills. Among enrolled agents—tax professionals licensed by the IRS—and certified public accountants, fees for completing returns rose by 10% to 30% nationwide. Most practitioners did not substantially increase their hourly rates but charged so much more because the returns took longer to fill out. The overarching reason 1040s took so much longer to complete was the mare's nest of new forms, instructions, and rules. Here are the sections of the 1040 that most addled tax preparers:

Individual Retirement Accounts. As expected, the number of taxpayers making IRA contributions shrank by more than half because of the new restrictions on IRA deductions. Out of all 1040 forms filed, only 10% showed payments to an IRA, compared with 22% the year before. Counting both short and long forms, the number of returns listing IRA contributions dropped to 7% from 15% for the 1986 tax year. Almost all of the taxpayers who did make 1987 IRA contributions were entitled to deduct the full amount. Only 1.2% of all filers, or just over a million taxpayers, sent in the new Form 8606 for nondeductible contributions.

Guess Who's Paying Less?

Don't let those low, low tax rates distract you. It's the bottom line that matters, and most people's won't shrink or grow much because of the 1988 rate cuts.

The sampling of hypothetical taxpayers at right, computed by the accounting firm Grant Thornton, illustrates how various individuals will fare. To isolate the changes attributable to the altered tax code, we kept income and deductible expenses constant for 1986, 1987, and 1988. The write-offs shown are those allowable for 1986.

BETTER OFF

Tax-filing status	Single	Married	Married
Number of exemptions	One	Four	Three
Salary or wage income	$32,000	$45,000	$150,000
Net long-term gain (loss)	0	(3,000)	(3,000)
IRA contribution	0	2,250	2,250
Sales tax deduction	0	1,500	10,000
Consumer interest deduction	0	1,500	5,000
Miscellaneous deduction	0	1,000	3,000
Other deductions	0	9,000	32,500
TAX			
1986	6,111	4,008	29,684
1987	5,505	3,244	30,554
1988	5,254	3,391	27,712

WORSE OFF

Tax-filing status	Single	Married	Married
Number of exemptions	One	Six	Three
Salary or wage income	$55,000	$70,000	$90,000
Net long-term gain	8,000	5,000	15,000
IRA contribution	2,000	4,000	4,000
Sales tax deduction	1,500	2,500	1,500
Consumer interest deduction	1,500	2,500	5,000
Miscellaneous deduction	800	1,500	900
Other deductions	4,000	15,300	11,500
TAX			
1986	13,253	7,955	18,881
1987	14,938	9,309	21,633
1988	14,151	9,293	20,802

In all likelihood, most of the taxpayers who made nondeductible IRA contributions for 1987 won't do so again. That's mainly because Form 8606 required them to go through the arduous exercise of computing their year-end balance in all of their IRA accounts. Even the taxpayers who could write off their full IRA contribution had to cope with an ugly new 17-step worksheet to make sure they were entitled to the deduction.

Miscellaneous deductions. In the past, taxpayers who itemized could take this write-off if they spent so much as a quarter on a newspaper that helped them with their business or investments. But only 13.5% of all long-form filers in 1987 were able to take a miscellaneous deduction. That's because the revised law allows these breaks only to the extent that they exceed 2% of your adjusted gross income. The new threshold and other changes made the miscellaneous deduction a study in byzantine bookkeeping for taxpayers and accountants.

Reimbursed employee business expenses added further confusion. Those costs can be deducted from a taxpayer's gross income without being subject to the 2% limitation because the reimbursements are reported as earnings on W-2 or 1099 forms. But employees who paid for some business expenses themselves while being reimbursed for others had to sort out the two categories. Often, tax preparers say, it was like beachcombing to document the exact reimbursed amounts listed on the W-2 and 1099 forms.

Passive losses. The tax-filing season's most capacious tar pit, tax professionals concur, is the collection of rules governing deductible losses on limited partnerships and closely held companies. Under the new law, investment gains and losses are split into two categories—portfolio (from stocks, bonds, and interest-bearing investments) and passive (from limited partnerships and most rental real estate). The last was the prime target of reform because it allowed many taxpayers to get away without paying any taxes at all. So the law began narrowing the loophole: Only 40% of any losses from passive activities could be deducted for 1988 versus 20% in 1989.

Until the IRS issued 266 pages of regula-tions and 24 pages of instructions and forms on February 19, 1988, tax preparers could only guess whether any given venture qualified as a passive activity. Because the rules were so complex, tax preparers had little time to digest the changes before April 15. Computer services that accounting firms hire to fill in tax returns had to scramble to adjust their software to conform to the new regulations. Most weren't ready until the second week of March. In many cases, returns that already had been completed needed to be redone, adding to the fees that taxpayers owed to their preparers.

The kiddie tax. Accountants report that last year they filled out returns for two to three times as many children as in the past. The

KO'd by Tax Reform

Money readers liked the old tax law far better than the new one. That is the unambiguous message sent by a representative poll of our subscribers taken last June. When asked how they fared generally under the new law, 61% reported that they were worse off, 28% about the same as before, and only 11% better off. Even readers earning less than $50,000 were clearly disenchanted in spite of presidential and congressional promises that the middle class would benefit from the changes. Just 15% of those polled with incomes below $50,000 said they were better off after tax reform, while 49% felt worse off, and 36% felt they came out about the same.

Higher taxes accounted for some, but by no means all, of the dissatisfaction. Of those surveyed, 43% said they owed more as a percentage of their gross income, 25% paid less, and 32% about the same. But the responses differed significantly by income level. Among those with total earnings below $50,000, just 24% paid more, 34% less, and 42% about the same. In contrast, 58% of readers earning more than $50,000 paid more, compared with only 19% who paid less and 24% about the same.

reason is that under tax reform children who are claimed as a dependent on their parents' return can no longer take a personal exemption. As a result, a child with combined employment income and bank interest in excess of only $500 must file a return. In 1986, children had to earn more than $3,560 to qualify as taxpayers.

Another tax change that affects kids requires those under 14 who have investment income in excess of $1,000 to be taxed on those additional earnings at their parents' rate. Last year, only about 300,000 returns—or 0.5% of all 1040s filed — included the perplexing new Form 8615 for making that kiddie tax computation. But many parents who filed for an extension on their returns had to get

one for their children as well. That's because computing the child's tax on Form 8615 required listing the parents' taxable income, which could be figured only after finishing the parents' return. The IRS has already said it will change Form 8615 so that no more than an estimate of the parents' income will have to be listed.

Home mortgage interest. Mercifully, only about 400,000 taxpayers had to suffer through Form 8598, which computes interest deductions on a second mortgage taken out since August 17, 1986. The victims were homeowners with outstanding mortgages in excess of the original cost of their home plus improvements. Their biggest complaint: Nowhere in the instructions to the form's 16-step, multi-column Section 3 does the IRS even attempt to explain what the dizzying computation is supposed to accomplish.

Other interest deductions. Tax preparers had to concentrate extra hard to make sense of new IRS regulations explaining how to distinguish between investment, business, and consumer interest. Because each type of interest is subject to different deductibility restrictions, the IRS now requires documentation of how loan proceeds are spent. Sorting out those records proved to be a major headache when one loan was used for several purposes or when more than one loan was deposited in the same bank account.

The alternative minimum tax. The new AMT, which is intended to ensure that taxpayers who have huge write-offs pay their fair share to the government, added untold extra hours to tax preparation and billings. The AMT is computed separately from the 1040 and applies only if it exceeds your regular tax. But even though no more than a few hundred thousand Americans owed the AMT, about 4.5% of all 1040 filers, or 2.8 million taxpayers, submitted the new AMT Form 6251. The IRS required the form to be sent in if you had passive losses, depreciation, or other write-offs, regardless of whether you ended up subject to the surtax. Because the computation was yet another sanity tester, it added considerably to the filing season's misery quotient.

State tax changes. Twenty-two states and the

Beware of IRS Goofs

Don't panic if you happen to get a notice from the Internal Revenue Service saying you erred on your tax return. Last year the IRS sent out 5 million such notices to taxpayers. But a General Accounting Office report analyzing IRS letters to 718 taxpayers found that 31% contained major mistakes and that another 16% were unclear or incomplete.

A typical example cited by the GAO involved a man who received an IRS request for $1,000 more in taxes without explanation. After asking for a reason, he received an IRS missive saying, in effect, that he goofed in reporting a medical-expense deduction on his tax return. In fact, the extra taxes had originally been assessed because the IRS thought he had failed to report $4,100 in earnings on his 1040. But the taxpayer actually had listed the amount properly as business income and his original remittance was correct.

To convince the IRS that it—not you—is in error, send a copy of the pertinent section of your tax return, any relevant documentation, and a lucid account of how the IRS flubbed. It may take at least three months to settle the issue. But if you are right and persistent, the IRS will almost certainly succumb.

District of Columbia significantly altered their income tax systems in response to the federal changes. As a result, many taxpayers were confused by their new state tax returns and downright dismayed at the bottom line. For example, wealthy investors in New York State (those with adjusted gross income exceeding $100,000) found themselves paying a new 3% surcharge on interest and dividend income.

For those taxpayers who didn't snap under the pressure by April 15, there is still ample chance to do so. Halfway through 1988 the IRS had sent out 5 million notices questioning mistakes it claims taxpayers made on 1987 returns, and already a disproportionate portion of those letters are themselves in error. For example, one Honolulu C.P.A. says four of his clients have received notices of mathematical errors from the IRS and, in each case, the agency was wrong.

Must-Keep Records

If you've ever wondered why doing your taxes has become so complicated, it may help to know that most of the congressmen responsible for making tax law don't even do their own taxes. When *Money* polled members of the two congressional tax-writing panels, the House Ways and Means Committee and the Senate Finance Committee, the results were conclusive: Of the 55 members, 43 hired someone to prepare their tax returns, eight did the job themselves, and four had no comment. Whether or not you do your own taxes, you must now keep detailed records of these three types of tax-tangled activity:

Loan interest. How much you can write off in 1988 depends on which of six categories the loan falls into. The six categories: consumer loans (40% deductible), mortgage loans (usually fully deductible up to the purchase price of your home plus improvement costs), home-equity loans (fully deductible up to $100,000), business loans (fully deductible), brokerage house margin loans (fully deductible to the extent you have net investment income, plus $4,000), and borrowing for passive investments (fully deductible against income from other passive investments; interest expenses from investments bought before October 22, 1986 are 40% deductible against ordinary income). Keep separate checkbooks for each type of loan you take out. If separate checking accounts are more than you can handle, or if the volume of loans is low, note on each check which loan money you are spending.

Partnerships and rental real estate. Tax reform classified losses from those investments as passive—and thus only deductible against passive income—unless you can prove a certain degree of participation. As a rule, you must "materially participate" in a business partnership to use any losses from the venture against ordinary income. That means you must spend at least 500 hours a year working in the business, or 100 hours a year if that is the most time anyone spends on the activity. Keep daily logs and diary or appointment-book entries. Partnership owners should keep copies of the Schedule K-1, investor letters, prospectuses, and financial statements. When properties are sold, you may be able to use documented losses to offset ordinary income.

Losses from rental property qualify only if you make less than $150,000 a year and "actively participate," which is far less demanding than material participation. Keep invoices, receipts, and any other documents that show you help make management decisions.

Individual Retirement Accounts. If you have a mixture of deductible and nondeductible IRAs, keep confirmation statements for each contribution, all year-end statements for each account, all withdrawal confirmations, and copies of Form 8606 on which you report nondeductible IRA deposits. When you begin drawing down your funds, you will need to prove to the IRS what percentage of your savings stems from nondeductible contributions to avoid being taxed twice.

Even the Tax Pros Are Confused

Money asked 50 tax preparers to figure one family's taxes—and got 50 different answers.

Chances are that when you looked at last year's "simplified" 1040 tax packet, you were ready to seek professional help—either from a tax preparer or a mental-health therapist. The tax reform law has added new complexity to the old forms while creating another whole set of befuddling worksheets for you to complete. So if you have any itemized deductions at all, you probably should see a tax practitioner. But beware: The professionals are plenty baffled themselves.

A *Money* examination of 50 tax preparers nationwide shows that the new tax law is causing all sorts of problems for those who make their living filling out tax returns. What's more, an easier test we conducted reveals that the IRS' own taxpayer assistors are alarmingly ignorant about the revised tax code (see the box on page 81).

Last year, *Money* mailed the financial profile of a hypothetical family to the participants in the study, who agreed to prepare the family's tax returns based on the information sent. (They were also encouraged to call us if they needed additional information.) Formulated with the help of Ernst & Whinney's S. Theodore Reiner, senior manager with the accounting firm's Washington, D.C. office, the profile raised complex tax issues relating to the new law, but included no unfair trick questions. Here are the most striking results of the *Money* survey:

● The 50 pros computed 50 different amounts of tax due from the family. Their bottom lines varied by as much as 50%.

● The preparers were uncertain about the nuances of the new tax law. In cases where the law itself is unclear, the pros are making up rules of their own that differ greatly. Because there are an unprecedented number of gray areas, it's more likely than ever that you could end up paying a higher tax bill—or risking an audit—if your tax preparer takes too many chances.

● Tax preparers, even the most expensive ones, were not immune from making careless mathematical mistakes.

● H&R Block outlets were capable of handling a difficult return as skillfully as some Big Eight firms—at a fraction of the cost. While the Block preparers would have charged an average of only $267 to our hypothetical family, the national accounting firm's fees averaged $1,567.

Originally, we sent our hypothetical case to 60 practitioners. Fifteen were chosen from each of four categories: certified public accountants with national offices, who charge anywhere from $50 to $250 an hour; C.P.A.s with local or regional firms, who on average charge slightly lower rates; enrolled agents—independents who have either worked for the IRS as revenue agents for at least five years or passed a two-day IRS test—who charge between $50 and $150 an hour; and H&R Block preparers, who charge $8 to $24 per tax form—which works out to $50 for a typical return.

Fifty of the 60 practitioners sent us completed 1040 forms within two weeks as promised. Seven C.P.A.s with national firms and three H&R Block preparers backed out, in most cases claiming that they didn't have enough time. Because the law is imprecise about several matters pertaining to the hypothetical case, there was no right or wrong bottom-line answer. (No withholding was assumed, for simplicity's sake.) Ernst & Whinney's Reiner, who helped us develop the hypothetical case, anticipated that the typical response would be around $9,000. He was right on the money; the actual average turned out to be $9,105. But the final tax due that the preparers came up with spanned an enormous range, from a low of $7,202 all the way up to $11,881. (Each participant's fee and bottom line is listed in the table on page 79.)

The factor most responsible for the wide variation was the new, more complicated version of the alternative minimum tax. It will affect more taxpayers than in previous years but still less than 1% of all personal returns. The AMT, as it's called, is a tax computed separately from the 1040 form that prevents taxpayers with sizable deductions from paying very little to the government. Many, but not all, of the preparers who came up with a low tax due simply miscalculated the AMT by omitting an important figure.

Five of the preparers who computed an unusually high tax bill did so because they assumed—quite reasonably—that a technical corrections bill containing an important AMT change would become law retroactive to 1987. Because their fees are relatively high, the five could save their clients as much as $700 by eliminating the need for an amended return after the bill passed. In the meantime, however, the hypothetical family would owe a tax that is $1,596 higher than it would be under the law as it now stands. The lesson: If your preparer tells you that you are subject to the AMT, make sure he spells out the costs and benefits of figuring your return under both the current and the corrected rules.

In addition to the AMT, there were three other important reasons for variations in tax calculations. First, some preparers were unfamiliar with the tax code's finer points. A problem in the hypothetical case involving an excess contribution to a 401(k) retirement plan, for example, stumped six participants. Almost half of the practitioners were unfamiliar with new provisions enacted in December 1987 concerning mutual fund expenses and master limited partnership income. The errors in such instances involved small dollar amounts, though similar mistakes on your return could conceivably cost you a lot of money. We did not count as errors cases in which participants made assumptions on their own that justified a different answer. These independent assumptions caused some minor variations in the bottom lines.

Mathematical mistakes or blatant oversights were the second main reason for differing tax calculations. Thirteen of our participants—five local C.P.A.s, three enrolled agents, three Block preparers, and two C.P.A.s with national firms—made errors that could be characterized as blunders. The lesson here is always review each line of your completed return with your preparer. If he seems vague or uncertain about a particular item, have him show you the pertinent tax code provision or regulation. Remember, if you are ever audited, you—not your tax preparer—will be the one subject to back taxes, interest, and penalties.

The final major cause for differing bottom lines is the gaps in the tax law itself. For some situations, there are no clear rules. In our hypothetical cases, the preparers had to cope with such ambiguities to determine the family's interest and miscellaneous deductions. Aggressive preparers tried to save as much tax for the family as they could justify. But in so doing, they increased the risk that the IRS would audit the family's return. Conservative preparers were more inclined to let the family pay higher taxes. Our participants were split fairly evenly between these two philosophies. C.P.A.s with national or local firms tended to be either very aggressive or very conservative. The enrolled agents and H&R Block preparers were apt to be middle of the road.

Not surprisingly, the C.P.A.s, who by and large serve wealthy individuals and corporate clients, charged fees that far exceeded those of the other preparers. The average bill was $1,567 for those at national accounting firms

More Than Ever, the Tax Preparer Makes All the Difference

The 50 tax practitioners—of four types—who completed returns for our hypothetical family came up with different tax totals—and fees. The average tax was $9,105, but the returns ranged from $7,202 to $11,881. The average fee was $779, but it varied from $187 to $2,500.

PRACTITIONER	COMPANY, CITY	TAX DUE	FEE
Barney M. Hardy Jr.	Dallas, Texas	$7,202	$300
Brenda Potts	Carter Young Wolf, Goodlettsville, Tennessee	$7,234	$400
Cyndi Hutchings	H&R Block, Birmingham, Alabama	$7,281	$221
Paul Henrickson	Coopers & Lybrand, Manchester, New Hampshire	$7,926	$1,200
Victor Altamirano	Deloitte Haskins & Sells, Los Angeles, California	$8,123	$2,500
Thomas Jones	Glotzer Jones & Organek, Hartford, Connecticut	$8,147	$975
Nancy L. Nesbitt	San Diego, California	$8,173	$810
David Gray	H&R Block, Des Moines, Iowa	$8,550	$218
Robert I. Karon	Schweitzer Rubin Gottlieb, Minneapolis, Minnesota	$8,579	$905
Chris W. Strand	Laventhol & Horwath, Seattle, Washington	$8,676	$1,250
Linda Kowalkowski	Portland, Oregon	$8,719	$442
Alan D. Westheimer	Pannell Kerr Forster, Houston, Texas	$8,740	$1,711
Henry Nagel	Laventhol & Horwath, Atlanta, Georgia	$8,837	$1,175
Peter Hukki	Metro West Tax Associates, Framingham, Massachusetts	$8,888	$600
Michael Lee Martin	Washington, D.C.	$8,890	$550
Thomas Warner	Tullahoma, Tennessee	$8,895	$710
Sharon-Kay Hill	Beverly, Massachusetts	$8,896	$425
Patricia Burton	Gales Ferry Tax Service, Gales Ferry, Connecticut	$8,897	$510
Martin Inerfield	Coram, New York	$8,926	$400
William J. Cronin	Weyrich Cronin & Sorra, Timonium, Maryland	$8,944	$1,100
Wes Fitzpatrick	Grant Thornton, Portland, Oregon	$8,957	$1,200
Tricia Pulsifer	H&R Block, San Diego, California	$8,972	$245
James O'Grady	Wallingford McDonald Fox, Houston, Texas	$9,060	$1,375
Annette Sietman	Ashcraft-Sietman, Kent, Ohio	$9,089	$700
Scott McCaulou	James D. Beaton, Tempe, Arizona	$9,102	$654
Jay M. Lieberman	Milwaukee, Wisconsin	$9,105	$575
Susan Klashak	H&R Block, Lakewood, Colorado	$9,126	$258
Louise Hanna	H&R Block, Santa Fe, New Mexico	$9,151	$224
Linda Gilmore	Blackwell Poole, Hapeville, Georgia	$9,156	$550
Alex Yemenidjian	Parks Palmer Turner, Los Angeles, California	$9,191	$1,600
Kay Gagna	Folsom, California	$9,196	$870
Jim Keeley	H&R Block, Dearborn, Michigan	$9,224	$187
Samuel Tannebaum	Tannebaum Bindler, Dallas, Texas	$9,226	$1,600
Nancy Lewis	H&R Block, Duluth, Minnesota	$9,271	$232
Anita Gibson	H&R Block, Chesapeake, Ohio	$9,273	$201
Edward Rishebarger	Burnside & Rishebarger, San Antonio, Texas	$9,299	$885
Judy Frahm	H&R Block, Wauwatosa, Wisconsin	$9,302	$277
Kathleen Dix	H&R Block, Falls Church, Virginia	$9,334	$512
Pamela S. Lambert	Muncie, Indiana	$9,363	$293
Jean Longyear	H&R Block, Portland, Maine	$9,409	$368
Joan Nelson	H&R Block, Chicago, Illinois	$9,434	$255
Joseph Graif	Russell Evans & Thompson, Herndon, Virginia	$9,456	$1,000
Dale B. Demyanick	Lathan Lumsden McCormick, Buffalo, New York	$9,580	$1,000
Marjorie J. Joder	Naples, Florida	$9,747	$450
J. Carl Dornan	McGladrey Hendrickson & Pullen, Phoenix, Arizona	$10,126	$900
William T. Diss	Arthur Young, Denver, Colorado	$10,497	$2,000
Mary McGuire	Brooklyn, New York	$10,529	$675
David J. Silverman	New York, New York	$10,738	$1,000
Barbara Pope	Price Waterhouse, Chicago, Illinois	$10,935	$1,500
Bill McEntire	Sol Schwartz & Associates, San Antonio, Texas	$11,881	$975

and $966 for the local C.P.A.s. In contrast, enrolled agents and H&R Block preparers, who cater to taxpayers of modest means, charged an average of $582 and $266, respectively. The average tax bill that they calculated for the family was slightly lower than the amount that the C.P.A.s computed: $9,076 for the enrolled agents and $9,027 for the H&R Block preparers, compared with $9,086 for the national C.P.A.s and $9,205 for the local ones.

One reason for their high fees is that C.P.A. firms generally offer much more sophisticated year-round tax-planning services. In fact, many C.P.A.s who participated sent along tax-planning tips for the hypothetical family with their tax returns, even though we didn't ask for any. In some cases, their ideas would have saved the family more than the $2,500 that the most expensive C.P.A. charged. No enrolled agent or Block preparer included planning points.

The performance of the relatively inexpensive H&R Block preparers was quite good. Considering that the hypothetical family's finances were far more complex than those of the typical Block client, the chain provided excellent value. Many of the Block participants consulted the firm's eight-person troubleshooting team in its home office in Kansas City to ask about particular changes in the law, a step that preparers in branch offices often take if a client has a complicated problem.

Some of the most interesting results of our test pertain to the specifics of our hypothetical case. The profile we sent describes the Johnsons, a couple earning a combined salary of $100,000 with three children, each of whom earned enough in 1987 to be subject to tax. The family's investments included stocks, corporate and municipal bonds, mutual funds, limited partnerships, and U.S. Savings Bonds and Treasury bills. The Johnsons moved during the year and kept a second home, which they rented out part of the time. To complicate things further, they also took out a second mortgage on the second home. Here, from the top of the tax return to the bottom, is a summary of how the preparers computed the Johnson family's taxes:

Salaries, interest, and dividends. Aside from a couple of mathematical errors, the practitioners generally had little trouble with this section. One exception: Six preparers failed to report as taxable interest $125 that was earned on an excess 401(k) contribution the wife made. Several others also didn't count the money but made assumptions on their own that justified the omission.

Capital gains. On this line, 20 practitioners incorrectly counted $400 in mutual fund fees as taxable income. They would have been correct before December 1987, but since then Congress has passed a bill saying that such so-called phantom income should not be counted as income in 1987.

Losses from limited partnerships. Another 21 of our participants, some of whom knew about the mutual fund fee change, missed a different provision in the December tax bill. They were not aware that tax-shelter losses cannot be used to offset fully the income from a master limited partnership, a type of partnership that is publicly traded like a stock—a fact that some of our practitioners didn't know.

State and local taxes. Here, only a couple of preparers made an error. Nevertheless, the responses differed. Forty-four of our participants aggressively followed a 1983 appellate court ruling to determine the deduction, while six adhered to more conservative IRS rules. The issue concerned the amount of property-tax expense on the family's second home that could be deducted on Schedule A, their itemized deduction form. The IRS and the court disagree about the proper way of allocating expenses between personal and rental use when a second home is rented out part of the time. Using the court ruling formula added $150 to the Johnsons' personal property tax write-off compared with the IRS approach.

Interest deductions. For this write-off we received 49 different answers. The preparers essentially had no guidelines because the IRS hasn't yet written final regulations explaining how to deduct interest on a second mortgage on a second home that is leased out part of the year. Because the second mortgage was used for personal expenses and exceeded the original cost of the property, not all the mortgage interest was deductible. The most aggressive of our participants ended up writing off a total $21,022 in interest, while the most conservative deducted only $17,320. Most of the responses ranged between $18,100 and $18,900. **Miscellaneous deductions.** Here, 38 preparers deducted a conservative amount while 12 were more aggressive. The controversy related to a four-year subscription to a trade publication that cost $200. Following IRS regulations, the conservative practitioners deducted only one-fourth of the $200. The others wrote off the full amount, explaining that there's no law actually prohibiting the $200 write-off. In an audit, the extra $150 would most likely be disallowed, which would leave it up to the John-

sons and their preparer to decide whether to take their case to tax court. Considering the small amount, they would probably just pay up.

These results are anything but reassuring. Moreover, they provide a graphic warning to all taxpayers: Don't sign your return until you have carefully scrutinized every line. That's true whether you filled out the forms yourself or hired the most expensive accountant in town. But don't hesitate to hire someone to do the job for you. Despite the problems they had with our hypothetical case, the majority of the pros proved that they can save taxpayers a lot of anguish, and maybe even a fair amount of money.

Calling the IRS Doesn't Mean You'll Get the Right Answers

When the General Accounting Office examined the IRS telephone assistance program in 1987, it found that the agency answered only 79% of the GAO's questions correctly. The IRS vowed to do better and launched a major public relations campaign promising to "put the service back in The Service."

It's a nice thought. But a *Money* survey conducted last year—using easier questions than those we asked of the tax practitioners—suggests that the IRS "helpers" have gotten *worse*. In fact, the assistors were right only slightly more than half the time. Forty percent of those we queried, for example, didn't even know that the IRS had waived the penalty on tax underpayments for workers who had too little withheld from their paychecks in 1987. Maybe the IRS should call H&R Block.

Money placed a total of 100 calls to IRS assistors. Each helper was asked one of 10 questions, prepared with the help of Ernst & Whinney, and each question was posed to 10 different assistors. The results were appalling. Overall, only 55 responses were correct and 45

were inaccurate. In four cases, the assistors said that additional research was needed and that a written response would be sent within eight working days. All four written answers were wrong.

Spokesperson Johnelle Hunter defends the IRS by saying that *Money's* questions were "not typical." Larry Endy, the director of the GAO's study, says the IRS made the same claim last year. Says he: "We asked questions that we thought the IRS people should be able to answer whether they received them 10 times or a million times."

In the wake of the 1987 GAO report, the IRS hired 1,000 more assistors, bringing the total to 4,500. The service also expanded its training sessions for telephone representatives and required its supervisors to monitor more phone calls. In addition, to solve the persistent problem of constant busy signals, the number of phone lines was expanded by 30%. Unfortunately, despite those efforts, IRS helpers remained woefully ill-informed about the new tax law.

Smart Tax-Trimming Tactics

Write-offs are rare. But don't get mad; get busy. You have entered the age of mandatory tax planning.

If you thought it was safe to forget about taxes for awhile after the April 15 filing deadline, you had better give your accountant a call. The drama of filing your 1987 and 1988 returns was only the opening act of tax reform. While the deductions that once made itemizing worth the trouble are dead or dying (remember the sales tax write-off, unfettered interest expense deductions, fully deductible miscellaneous expenses?), a charmingly low and seemingly simple two-tier rate structure has taken their place. Single filers who earn up to $17,850 and married couples filing jointly and making up to $29,750 fall into the 15% bracket—based on 1988 income levels, which will be increased in subsequent years by indexing to the annual inflation rate. Above those amounts, the rate rises to 28%.

Low? Yes. Simple? Forget it. A five percentage-point surtax on income from $43,150 to $89,560 for individuals and $71,900 to $149,250 for joint filers makes the actual top bracket for them 33%. The purpose is to deny them the advantage of the 15% rate, which they would otherwise be able to benefit from on the lowest portion of their income. The more you have subject to the 33% marginal rate, the closer your effective rate (that percentage of your total income you pay in taxes) moves to a flat 28%. Beyond the $89,560 for singles and $149,250 for marrieds, your personal exemptions and any exemptions for dependents will be phased out. Yet no one pays an effective rate higher than 28%. So much for simplicity.

What there will be more of this year are new rules, intended to clarify the law, that do the exact opposite. This is why record keeping has been upgraded from a niggling chore to a key element of tax planning. The challenge you face is to cut through the confusion and to adjust your strategies to ensure that you pay no more taxes than the law prescribes. Doing so will give you the confidence to take the offensive—almost always the best tax-trimming tactic—using the following guidelines:

Take advantage of the lowest tax rates you will ever see. The top bracket's drop from 38.5% in 1987 to today's 33% may sound like a bit of a cheat to those taxpayers who had not read the fine print about a surtax and were expecting the new ceiling to be a more enticing 28%. On the other hand, the top rate is now at its lowest since 1931. A near consensus among accountants and economists holds that the bulging budget deficit will force Congress to raise revenues, and the most likely option is an increase in income taxes. Although few experts are betting that new taxes will actually take effect in 1989, legislation may be drafted and even passed this year. So tax advisers recommend pulling income, such as retirement distributions and deferred compensation, into 1989 to take advantage of the last of the low rates.

How exactly to adjust your income and deductions depends on your own financial profile. The main goal is to stay out of the 33% bracket whenever possible. For example, if you are nearing the upper limit where 28% kicks back in, you might elect to receive a bonus in December rather than January to push yourself over the top. Self-employed people could collect receivables this year rather than in 1990. Or if your income promises to rise enough next year to push you into the 33%

bracket, accelerate some of it into 1989 to be sure you stay in the 28% bracket.

Begin withdrawals from your retirement savings if you have reached age 59½. If you have a tax-sheltered Keogh, IRA, or 401(k) plan, consider taking some money out now. If you

If You Thought the 1040 Was a Mess, You Better Hope You Won't Owe a Tax Penalty

With the exception of being audited, the worse plight to befall a taxpayer is a notice from the Internal Revenue Service saying he owes more taxes plus penalties. Offenses range from failing to provide a valid Social Security number (penalty: $5) to criminal fraud (penalty: up to five years in prison). And the experience can be a Kafkaesque nightmare even for seemingly inconsequential offenses. Tax experts and a growing number of lawmakers think many of the IRS' penalties are unfair and unnecessarily complex. The system's most serious flaws:

Erroneous fines. In 1986, the IRS levied 11.6 million penalties on individual taxpayers, totaling nearly $2.5 billion. But the agency later nullified $890 million of that amount, or an alarmingly large 36%. Those figures suggest that the IRS is either being overzealous or inappropriately assessing penalties, perhaps using them as bargaining tools in an audit.

Moreover, because computers now assess about 90% of all penalties, a notice may be mailed before a taxpayer has a chance to explain a valid deficiency or discrepancy. Take the 25% penalty for substantial understatement of a tax liability. It applies if you under-report your tax liability by 10% or $5,000, whichever is greater. When the computer detects the discrepancy, the IRS automatically imposes the penalty. But by law, the fine does not apply if a taxpayer can show that his calculation was based on a reasonable interpretation of the tax code. Citing any legitimate support for your interpretation, such as a related tax court ruling, may be an adequate defense.

Disproportionate fines. The penalty sometimes far exceeds the offense because fines often are computed in quirky ways. Suppose the IRS determines that you owe an additional $2,000 in taxes and that $50 of your underpayment is because of your negligence. In that case, the 5% negligence fine and interest will apply to the entire $2,000, not just the $50. In addition, sometimes penalties overlap, resulting in several fines for the same mistake. Let's say a taxpayer erroneously overestimates the value of business property and takes too large a depreciation deduction. The penalty is a maximum of 30% of the extra taxes owed because of the error. But if the IRS also says he was negligent, the 5% negligence penalty and interest would be assessed on the same amount. So a $5,000 underpayment could carry, in effect, a 35% penalty, which when combined with interest, could total another $4,000. That's a hefty price to pay for one error.

Confusing legal guidelines. Some 13 different standards now determine whether a taxpayer is liable for various penalties. In many cases, those guidelines are ambiguous. For example, taxpayers charged with certain negligence penalties must show that they did not "carelessly, recklessly, or intentionally disregard rules and regulations," while others fined for overstating the value of business property must show that there was a "reasonable basis" for their figures, that they were made in good faith, and that there was a "reasonable attempt to comply" with the law. Because few taxpayers know which standards apply to them, even the most well-intentioned can end up penalized. So if the IRS should throw a penalty flag your way unfairly, by all means, fight back!

are younger than 59½, however, dipping into such accounts may not be worth it because you would have to pay a 10% penalty on early withdrawals. How much to take out also requires some caution. The tax code imposed a 15% penalty on distributions from retirement funds of more than $150,000 a year, so time your withdrawals to stay within that amount.

Cut back on your debt. Tax reform is cruelly shrinking the rewards of leverage in two ways: First, interest expenses from consumer loans, such as credit cards, car loans, and any other personal debt, were only 40% deductible in 1988 (they fall to a meager 20% in 1989, then 10% in 1990). Second, a drop in your tax rate makes any deductions less valuable. To ease the pinch, pay off your high-interest debts as quickly as possible. Credit-card loans, which averaged 18.8% in mid-1988, should be among the first to go.

Make the most of home-equity loans—but do so wisely. Borrowing against the value of your house is the only debt that remains fully deductible no matter where you spend it. In fact, taking out a home-equity loan is more tempting than ever. The Tax Reform Act of 1986 allowed you to deduct interest on new loans as long as your total debt did not exceed the purchase price of your home plus any improvements. Thanks to a change in the Revenue Act of 1987, you can now deduct the interest on home-equity loans of up to $100,000, regardless of the purchase price or your outstanding first mortgage. The catch, of course, is that if you default on your loan payments, you could lose your home.

Bunch your medical and miscellaneous expenses. Medical expenses are deductible to the extent that they exceed 7.5% of your adjusted gross income (AGI). If your income is $30,000, for instance, you cannot deduct the first $2,250 in medical expenses. To reach the 7.5% floor, opt to have elective surgery or braces for the kids in a year when your health-care needs are going to be high. The same goes for miscellaneous deductions, which must equal 2% of your AGI before you can begin deducting them. These include tax preparation costs, investment-related expenses, safe-deposit-box fees and unreimbursed business expenses.

Put retirement savings in a 401(k) or Keogh. The 401(k) emerged from tax reform as the most tax-favored retirement plan for wage earners, so much so that if your company offers one, you should make it your top priority for contributions before all other savings and investments. The tax boon is twofold: Your contributions are pretax and all earnings grow tax deferred. Some lucky employees also get matching contributions from their company. In 1988 you could put up to $7,313 into a 401(k), or 25% of your pay, whichever is less. (The maximum dollar amount is annually indexed to inflation.) Don't plan to use the money until you are 59½, however. Withdrawals made before that age are subject to a 10% penalty. If you receive any self-employment income, such as freelance or moonlighting pay, do not pass up the opportunity to open a Keogh. These retirement plans are like super-IRAs that let you contribute as much as 20% of any self-employment income or $30,000, whichever is less. All contributions are fully tax deductible and grow free of taxes.

Open an IRA if you can deduct the contribution. For retirement savings, a deductible IRA is the best choice if you don't have access to a 401(k) or don't qualify for a Keogh. The maximum contribution is only $2,000, but taxes are deferred on all earnings. Under the rules of tax reform, contributions to an IRA are fully deductible if you are not covered by a pension plan, are single and earning less than $25,000, or are a married couple filing jointly and earning less than $40,000. Partial deductions are allowed for singles earning $25,000 to $35,000, and couples earning $40,000 to $50,000. Without the write-off, an IRA makes sense only if you have 10 years or more before retirement to let the tax-deferred earnings compound. Otherwise, the years of record keeping required to prove to the IRS which IRA dollars are still untaxed are not worth the pain.

Consider single-premium deferred annuities for additional retirement savings. For a minimum of $1,500, insurance companies sell annuities that act much like nondeductible IRAs. In fact, annuities allow you to put an unlimited amount away without the record-keeping burden of IRAs. All your money grows tax-free, an enticement that deserves attention if you have money to stash for retirement but have no other tax-deferred savings options. As with other retirement investments, the IRS collects a 10% penalty if you make a withdrawal before age 59½. One other factor may soon help make annuities more attractive: the potential fadeout of single-premium life insurance's dazzling star. Not only does your money grow tax deferred in single-premium policies, but policy owners can also borrow against the cash value at a low interest rate without paying taxes on the loan proceeds. Because the loan can be paid back out of the death benefit, policy owners essentially get tax-free access to their earnings.

Trouble is, Congress seems determined to close off this loophole by fully taxing such life-insurance loans. So unless you need the insurance or want to use the loan option—and are comfortable with the high risk that Congress will tax the proceeds and levy a 10% penalty—don't consider investing in a single-premium policy.

Use capital losses to cut taxes on capital gains. Reform erased the preferential tax rates for long-term capital gains. Yet, losses can still absorb capital gains dollar for dollar. If you expect to take a capital gain this year, consider unloading a losing investment to offset the gain. And you can use as much as $3,000 in capital losses to offset ordinary income each year.

Switch from a taxable to a tax-free money market fund if you are in the 33% bracket. Even with the fall in tax rates, tax-free money market funds can offer better returns than taxable money funds. At a recent top yield of nearly 5%, a tax-free fund makes sense for people in the 33% bracket. And if you live in a high-tax state, such as California or New York, money-market funds whose yields are exempt from federal, state, and local taxes can offer even higher returns.

Choose investments for your child's education that will avoid the kiddie tax. Some parents have learned the hard way that children under age 14 must pay taxes at the parents' rate on income from investments over $1,000.

To avoid reform's kiddie tax, buy only investments that pay no interest until maturity—ideally after the child turns 14—such as Series EE U.S. Savings Bonds or zero-coupon municipal bonds. Tax-free bonds and bond funds are other choices. Growth stocks unlikely to pay more than $1,000 in dividends are a good option, too. No taxes are due on any capital gains until you sell the stock. Or think about employing your child if you own a business. Income is taxed at the child's rate and you need not pay Social Security tax until the child turns 18.

If your income is less than $100,000 a year, consider rental real estate. While stripping away the rich write-offs in real estate, tax reform left behind a nugget for middle-income investors. Rental properties can produce up to $25,000 in losses that can be used to offset ordinary income for investors with an adjusted gross income of $100,000 or less. The $25,000 phases out for incomes up to $150,000. To qualify, you must demonstrate "active" participation by owning at least 10% of the investment and being involved in management decisions such as approving new tenants or deciding on rental terms. Otherwise, rental real estate losses can offset income only from other passive investments.

Don't pay a tax preparer for a simple return. With so few deductions intact after reform, paying someone to fill out a straightforward return is unlikely to pay back in tax savings. H&R Block collects about $50 for preparing a no-frills 1040. Accountants often charge that much for the first 30 minutes, exacting fees of $600 or more for filling out an itemized but essentially uncomplicated 1040. The charge then falls into your bin of miscellaneous expenses, deductible only above the 2% floor. Seriously consider getting help, however, if you own limited partnerships, are withdrawing from retirement plans, have taken out several types of loans, own vacation or rental property, have sold property on installment, or own a portfolio worth more than $100,000. Each deserves expert advice not only to save taxes but also to avoid noncompliance penalties. You might decide that the peace of mind alone is worth the cost.

How To Avoid Being Hit by an Audit

In the past, most taxpayers had little reason to worry about being audited by the Internal Revenue Service because it focused its efforts on the relatively small number of wealthy people claiming huge write-offs from tax shelters. But now that tax reform has deprived the agency of that juicy target, which triggered about a third of all audits before the law changed, the IRS is shifting its attention to unusually large deductions of any kind. In addition, the tax law's confusing new set of forms invites errors. As a result, though once again only about 1% of all returns will get audited, the chances of a typical taxpayer being nailed have increased dramatically.

By knowing which write-offs are most likely to spit your return out of the service's computer and onto an ambitious agent's desk, you can protect yourself by limiting dicey deductions to amounts that you can document. For obvious reasons, the agency refuses to divulge its new secret formula for nabbing tax cheats. But tax experts and former IRS officers offer these educated guesses about how the new system will work. Some potential red flags are obvious. For one thing, you can be sure that the IRS is going to focus on those deductions that require you to fill out their complex new tax forms. That's because a lot of mistakes will be made in calculating those write-offs, and they'll be easy for the IRS to spot.

The items that you should take special care to compute correctly are listed here in descending order of their likelihood to trigger an audit by the IRS:

Passive income and losses. Despite the prohibition on write-offs from new tax shelters, you can still deduct 40% of the 1988 tax losses generated by old shelters against regular earnings. Those losses can be written off in full, however, against so-called passive income. The IRS will be on the lookout for taxpayers who have leftover shelter deductions and try to claim the larger write-off by wrongly labeling income as passive when it's not. To avoid problems, strictly follow the rules about passive income.

Only businesses that you are not actively involved in, such as a limited partnership in which you have no voting rights, qualify as passive-income sources. But publicly traded master limited partnerships and businesses in which you have decision-making power don't qualify as passive. To make matters worse, the form for passive losses, No. 8582, is a mind boggler that would challenge Einstein.

Interest deductions. Of all loans, those used for investment and business purposes are most likely to be audit bait. The reason is that new IRS regulations for calculating interest write-offs on those loans are so complex that only professional tax practitioners can begin to understand them. The IRS will also be looking closely for errors on its form, No. 8598, which you must fill out if your home mortgage exceeds the original cost of your residence, plus any improvements. It's probably best to hire an accountant to do these difficult computations for you.

IRA contributions. Taxpayers who are confused about the new restrictions on IRA (Individual Retirement Account) write-offs may unwittingly take a deduction to which they are not entitled. To see if you can rightfully claim an IRA deduction, carefully complete the worksheet provided in your 1040 instruction packet. If you determine that any or all of your IRA contribution is not deductible, you must fill out a another form, No. 8606.

Investment income to a child. Under the revised tax code, any unearned income in excess of $1,000 received by a child under 14 will be taxed at the parent's rate. Mistakes in filling out the corresponding form, No. 8615, will flag your return.

In addition to these items, the IRS will be closely watching the old standbys. The agency will pay particular attention to large employee expense deductions, such as write-offs for home offices and business travel. Other well scrutinized write-offs include charitable contributions of property, casualty and theft losses, and bad debts.

Are Individual Retirement Accounts Still a Good Idea?

If your IRA contribution is no longer tax deductible, you probably should not make it.

Should you still invest in an IRA? Banks, mutual funds, and other financial institutions would like you to think so as the April 15 deadline approaches for making contributions to Individual Retirement Accounts. But millions of Americans are not listening because tax law changes virtually eliminated the IRA as an effective tool in tax and retirement planning in many cases.

The main problem is that Congress axed the full deduction for contributions by middle- and upper-income taxpayers in 1987. In their zeal to raise revenues, lawmakers cut in half the number of people who qualify for the full deduction, from the 16 million who were expected to take an IRA write-off under the old rules to 8 million today. Congress additionally burdened people who make contributions to nondeductible IRAs with a lifelong snarl of paperwork. Then, too, 1988's lower tax rates dilute the remaining nondeductible IRA benefit: tax-deferred compounding of investment earnings—an advantage that could be wiped out entirely if tax rates rise by the time you start withdrawing your funds.

If you are among those who still qualify for the deduction, putting the maximum $2,000 in an IRA—plus $250 in a nonworking spouse's account—may make sense. You get a tax-sheltered investment return for your retirement as well as more cash in your pocket from tax savings—$560 if you are in the 28% bracket. Those who now qualify for the full deduction

include couples filing jointly with adjusted gross incomes of less than $40,000; singles with incomes of less than $25,000; and anyone who is not covered by a pension, profit-sharing, or other tax-advantaged retirement plan, including simplified employee pensions and Keoghs. Partial deductions are allowed for couples earning between $40,000 and $50,000 or singles earning between $25,000 and $35,000. Their write-off drops $10 for every $50 they earn above $40,000 if married or $25,000 if single.

Whether the twin advantages—a current write-off and tax-deferred earnings—are sufficient to make a partially deductible, or even a fully deductible, IRA worthwhile depends on how soon you may need the money. If you take it out of your IRA before age 59½, you will have to pay a 10% penalty plus income tax on the withdrawal. When those factors are taken into account, a person taxed at the maximum 33% who contributes $2,000 annually to a deductible IRA earning 8% would have to leave his money untouched for more than 11 years to beat the return he would have earned in a taxable investment at 8%. The break-even point for taxpayers in the 28% bracket is 12 years. The bottom line? Even if you can take the full deduction, an IRA is sensible only if you are sure that you won't need to tap it for at least a decade.

But if your IRA contributions are not deductible, the case against making them can be overwhelming, unless you're within 10 years of retirement. Without the write-off, the real cost of your contribution rises sharply to an after-tax $2,560 if you put in $2,000 and are in the 28% bracket. Combined with the new lower tax rates, this higher real cost lengthens the time required for tax-deferred compounding to offset taxes and penalties on early withdrawals. A taxpayer in the old top bracket of 50% who put $2,000 yearly into an IRA earning 8% would have had to leave his money untouched for 10 years before age 59½ to equal the return in a taxable investment yielding the same 8%. But that taxpayer now must leave his money untouched for nearly two decades to match the return from a comparable taxable investment.

Another disincentive is the load of record keeping that now accompanies nondeductible IRA contributions. Each year you must fill out a new IRS tax form—No. 8606—to keep track of your deductible and nondeductible contributions. These forms must be saved for the life of your IRA. The information on them will determine the tax on your withdrawals when you begin taking money out of your account. The nondeductible contributions will not be taxed upon withdrawal; the deductible contributions, plus all earnings in your IRAs, will be taxed at your regular income tax rate.

Furthermore, your bookkeeping headaches don't end once your withdrawals begin. Consider this migraine-maker: Every time you take money out of your IRA, you must calculate the proportion of nondeductible to deductible contributions and earnings in *all* of your accounts combined. Your withdrawal must then contain this proportion of nondeductible contributions and will be taxed accordingly. Say that your combined IRAs total $20,000—$2,000 or 10% of which represents nondeductible contributions. The other $18,000, or 90%, represents deductible contributions plus earnings. If you withdraw $1,000, you will owe taxes on 90% of that amount, or $900.

Some financial advisers argue that the disadvantages of nondeductible IRAs are outweighed by the benefits of tax-deferred compounding of earnings in your account over the long term. But James B. Cloonan,

president of the American Association of Individual Investors, a nonprofit educational organization, disagrees. He calculates that deferring taxes on an investment for 15 to 25 years is equivalent to earning an additional percentage point of annual yield. But you could lose that extra yield if your tax rate when you retire is higher than it is today. Cloonan believes the current 33% top rate is probably the lowest maximum we'll see for a long time. So the yield advantage is almost certain to disappear.

Fortunately, there are attractive alternatives to nondeductible IRA contributions. Topping the list are tax-advantaged, company-sponsored savings plans such as the 401(k). In fact, in most respects a 401(k) is actually superior to an IRA, even the fully deductible kind, because a typical 401(k) allowed you to put away up to a maximum of $7,313 in 1988. If your company doesn't offer a savings plan, top-rated tax-exempt municipal bonds and muni-bond funds, both recently yielding about 7.5%, also can serve well as IRA alternatives.

An IRA Checklist

Consider putting money in an IRA if:
- You are among those whose contributions are fully deductible—couples filing jointly with gross income of less than $40,000, singles who make less than $25,000, or anyone who is not covered by a pension, profit-sharing, or other tax-advantaged retirement plan.
- You qualify for a partial deduction and are sure that you will not need the money in your IRA before age 59½.

Contributing to an IRA is probably not worthwhile if:
- You are ineligible for a deduction, especially if you think that your tax rate when you retire will be higher than now.
- You can use other tax-favored retirement savings plans such as a 401(k).
- You don't want to worry about the lifelong burden of paperwork required to document a nondeductible or partially deductible IRA for the IRS.

All You Need to Know About Annuities

Single-premium deferred annuities offer attractive tax-sheltered yields. But watch out for empty promises.

If annuities were Isuzus, they would open hyperbolic new vistas to the little cars' mendacious TV pitchman. At first glance, single-premium deferred annuities seem to deliver everything risk-averse investors crave: an attractive fixed rate of return, recently as high as 10%; a guarantee that your investment will not be zapped by plunging stock or bond prices; and a shelter in which every dollar of your earnings compounds free of taxes until you make withdrawals. Trumpeting these advantages, an army of insurance agents, financial planners, and stock brokers sold an estimated $10.4 billion of single-premium deferred annuities in 1987. Some companies reported sales increases of more than 60%.

What they are selling is a vessel into which you pour one payment ranging from $1,000 to $500,000 or more for retirement. There is no immediate payout and no definite date for payouts to start. You decide years later whether to use the money and its earnings for lifetime annuity income or to withdraw it all at once. (For a quick fix on annuity jargon, see page 91.)

Unfortunately, some of the highly touted guarantees are about as ironclad as campaign promises. Those secure high rates of return, for example, typically vanish after one year. While marketing brochures stress that your annuity account's balance won't drop if the stock or bond market does, the sales literature glosses over the stiff tax penalties and early-withdrawal fees that can drain your assets as severely as another Wall Street crash. Furthermore, some annuities generate their enticing rates from junk bonds—high-yield, high-risk corporate issues that are most vulnerable to default should hard times befall the firm or the economy.

Annuities, like Individual Retirement Accounts, are often pitched as tax shelters. But, in fact, both work best as ways of stockpiling retirement money. The difference is that you are limited to yearly contributions of $2,000 to your IRA, while there is practically no limit on how much you can sock away in an annuity.

Thus, the ideal candidate for an annuity is someone who wants to put aside a lot of money as soon as possible and be able to use it years later to grind out monthly income. But various penalties and restrictions make annuities ill suited to investors who are just looking to shelter investment earnings at a high rate of return. Don't confuse a tax-sheltered return with the *tax-free* return on municipal bonds, which lately paid a 7.5% after-tax return. Since you must eventually pay taxes on the earnings in an annuity, the after-tax return on a plan paying 8% for 10 years could fall as low as 6.3%—only a little bit more than that of a comparable taxable investment, such as a bank certificate of deposit. To reap even this modest reward of tax deferral, you must not dip into your investment before age 59½. If you withdraw your funds earlier, a 10% penalty on all your earnings, on top of regular income taxes, will ordinarily wipe out most or all of the benefit of tax deferral.

The theory behind single-premium annuities is simple and reassuring. An insurance company invests your money in its portfolio of bonds, mortgages, stocks, and real estate and assumes full market risk. You are guaranteed a set rate of return for a specific period, usually one year but sometimes as long as five years. After that, the company declares a new interest rate each year. When you are ready to start drawing on the account, you can postpone the tax bite by annuitizing—that is, converting the balance into a monthly income stream. At that point, the portion of payout representing the growth of your original investment is taxable.

Annuities bristle with hidden and undis-closed costs that make comparison shopping tricky. The tallest tariffs are company-imposed surrender charges for early withdrawal; these penalties usually kick in if you tap more than 10% of your account value in a year. Typically, these charges start at 6% to 8% for the first year or two and then decline by a point or so each year until they disappear. But some companies' penalties are absolutely draconian. In 1987, Guarantee Security Life of Jacksonville hit investors with surrender charges as high as 15%, for example, and the widely sold annuities of Federal Kemper Life in Long Grove, Illinois had a non-declining surrender charge of 6%. By contrast, withdrawals from annuities sold through the mail by USAA Life in San Antonio were subject to only a 4% charge, plus $25, in the first three years. After that, you paid just $25 for each withdrawal.

Ten High-Yielding Plans Worth a Look

SINGLE-PREMIUM DEFERRED ANNUITIES

	Annuity name	Minimum investment	Current rate	Years guaranteed	Guaranteed minimum rate: initial (long term)	Maximum surrender charge	When the surrender charge expires	Bailout option if rates drop sharply
Allstate Northbrook, Illinois	SPDA	$7,500	8.25%	1	4.0%	5%	8th year	No
First Capital Life La Jolla, California	Pilgrim Capital Foundation	5,000	8.25	2	4.0	7	6th year	No
Jackson National Life Lansing	Max Plan	1,000	8.75	1	5.0	6	7th year	No
Lincoln Benefit Life Lincoln, Nebraska	The One	5,000	8.25	3	5.0	7	8th year	Yes
Lincoln National Pension Fort Wayne	SPDA	5,000	8.25	1	4.0	7	8th year	No
Metropolitan Life New York City	Asset Builder I	10,000	8.25	1	5.0 (4.0)	7	8th year	No
Transamerica Occidental Life Los Angeles	Capital Accumulator	2,500	8.40	1	6.5 (3.5)	8	9th year	Yes
Travelers Insurance Hartford	T-Flex	1,000	8.25	1	3.5	7	6th year	No
USAA Life and Annuity San Antonio	SPDA	10,000	8.80	1	4.0	4% + $25	4th year	No
Washington National Life Evanston, Illinois	WN Plan I	1,000	8.45	5	4.0	5	6th year	No

Sales brochures seldom reveal how seriously taxes and surrender charges can erode the return on your investment. A bar chart in a brochure of Keystone Provident Life of Boston shows that $100,000 invested in its annuity and earning 8.5% for 10 years would grow to $226,098, while the same amount in a taxable investment yielding 8.5% would be worth $181,122. The annuity is a clear winner—except there's no way you could put your hands on the full $226,098. Income tax for those in the 28% bracket would siphon off $35,307. If you were under 59½, the 10% tax penalty would take another $12,610. That leaves $178,181—or less than you would net from the taxable investment.

For greater flexibility in cashing out, seek an annuity with a more favorable escape clause, called a bailout provision. Some insurers agree to waive surrender fees if the renewal yield falls one percentage point or more below the rate initially guaranteed. Others give you the right to exit without penalty when the initial guarantee expires, which enables you to switch profitably to a competitor's annuity paying a higher rate. Note that you can also escape taxes through something called a 1035 exchange, which is similar to a tax-free rollover of an IRA.

Even if you don't have to pull out early, your return in an annuity can suffer from sales charges and administrative expenses. While these charges are seldom collected up front, agents nevertheless earn commissions of 3% to 7% of your original investment (some insurers pay them as much as 10%). The money comes from the proceeds of high surrender fees or from your portfolio earnings. Before you buy an annuity, don't be embarrassed to ask the agent what commission he will earn on the sale. If he balks, go to another agent. At least one company, USAA Life, operates without a sales force and offers true no-load annuities.

Translating Annuity Speak

Insurance jargon can stop an annuity shopper cold. Here are some important terms you need to know:

Immediate annuity. A contract issued by an insurance company that pays monthly income, usually for life, in return for a large, nonrefundable amount of cash. The amount of income depends on the age and sex of the recipient, as well as the number of dollars put in.

Deferred annuity. A contract in which investment earnings accumulate tax deferred until you convert the annuity to life income or withdraw the money.

Fixed annuity. A deferred annuity that pays a fixed rate of return for a specified period, usually one to five years. The company then adjusts the rate yearly.

Variable annuity. The return varies from day to day with the performance of mutual-fund-like portfolios chosen by the investor. An expense ration of at least 1.5% a year comes out of your assets, which in most variable annuities are guaranteed not to fall in value below the amount paid in.

Surrender charge. A penalty imposed by the company for withdrawing more than 10% or so of your accumulated investment in one year. This charge usually starts at 6% to 8% and declines yearly until it vanishes after seven years.

Bailout provision. An option in many contracts that lets you withdraw all of your money without penalty if the rate of return drops by a certain amount, typically one percentage point, from the initially guaranteed rate.

1035 exchange. Moving money from one annuity to another without losing the tax deferral—just like an IRA rollover.

Market-value adjustment. A charge against the accumulated value of a fixed annuity if you make withdrawals when interest is on the rise. The adjustment would also raise the cash-in value if rates drop.

Commissions can influence which annuity a salesman recommends. For example, a financial planner who stands to earn $9,000 selling a $100,000 Guarantee Security single-premium annuity or a mere $2,500 for pushing a John Hancock annuity might lean toward the one with the higher reward. And brokerage houses such as Merrill Lynch, Dean Witter, and Prudential-Bache entice their brokers to push the annuities of affiliated insurance companies by offering slightly higher commissions for selling the house brand. Insurance companies also lure salesmen with free travel and vacation packages.

The biggest challenge for shoppers is choosing an annuity that consistently will pay a competitive interest rate. All annuities guarantee a rate for the life of the plan, but it is a trifling 3% to 5%. To sell their plans lately, insurers have been promoting one-year rates of 8% to 10%. When the initially guaranteed rate expires, your renewal rate will be whatever the insurer decrees. In setting it, most companies look to the current and forecast yields on their investment portfolio and rival instruments such as CDs. But companies also know they don't necessarily have to be competitive in renewals, because some investors don't keep track of their rates. To avoid getting trapped in an annuity with a lagging return, ask the salesman for a history of the company's rate renewals. A competent salesman who regularly deals with one or two different companies should be able to produce at least a partial record. In 1984, for example, Transamerica Occidental Life guaranteed new buyers a 10.7% one-year rate. Renewals have not dropped below 9.7%.

High rates also require some scrutiny; they could be a sign of a high-risk investment strategy that could lead to the financial failure of the insurance company. The 9.5% rate recently offered by American Investors Life in Topeka is backed by a bond portfolio, one-fifth of which is in lower quality bonds. Another large insurer with perennially high rates, Executive Life of California, keeps two-thirds of its bondholdings in low-grade issues. In general, avoid companies with more than 20% of their bond portfolio in issues rated BB or lower. You can size up an insurer's portfolio in *Best's Insurance Reports* which is available in the business section of major libraries.

This fact-crammed reference also rates the company's overall financial stability. Just six years ago, one major annuity issuer, Baldwin United, filed for bankruptcy, jeopardizing $3.4 billion in annuities held by 165,000 investors. The annuity holders didn't lose their principal, but many were unable to touch it for several years and wound up getting lower yields than they were promised.

To assure the safety of your investment, stick to companies that are rated A+ (superior) or A (excellent) by Best. Since these ratings can change, you should check periodically to make sure your company has not been downgraded—Baldwin United was once an A+. If its rating does slip, you might consider a tax-free exchange to another annuity, even if it means paying a surrender charge.

One more caveat: Be sure to look up the rating of the actual issuer of the annuity, not an affiliated company. For example, a Merrill Lynch brochure for its Tandem annuity notes that the Tandem Insurance Group is a joint venture of Merrill Lynch and Equitable Life, a company with an A+ rating. But Equitable does not guarantee the Tandem annuities. And Tandem itself not only has no rating but was targeted in 1987 for regulatory attention by National Association of Insurance Commissioners. While this does not mean that Tandem's financial condition is shaky, it does suggest that anyone considering a relationship with a targeted company should exercise due caution.

Thirty-nine states have guaranty funds that offer annuity investors some protection against bankruptcies. But state guaranty funds maintain no pool of money in reserve. If an insurer goes bust, the state fund assesses charges against other insurance companies in the state to cover the losses. This can make reimbursement far slower than for failed banks.

The questions of solvency, rate guarantees, and surrender charges that preoccupy you when you are shopping for an annuity give way to other concerns as you near retirement. Then the major question becomes when and how you should start drawing from your account. Annuities provide a great deal of flexibility. You can take a lump sum and pay taxes immediately or you can choose one of several life-income options. Among the alternatives: a straight life annuity, which pays a fixed monthly benefit for the rest of your life; a period-certain plan, which pays you for life but continues paying your beneficiary if you die before a set number of years; and a joint and survivor annuity, which promises a monthly check as long as you or your beneficiary lives.

Built into almost all annuity contracts at purchase are guaranteed payout rates based on ages and benefit options. But these guarantees are so low they are largely irrelevant. Instead, when you are ready to annuitize, compare the *current* payment rates being offered by your company with those of others and roll over your money if the differences are substantial. Last year, for example, a 65-year-old man who had amassed $233,048 in a Northwestern Mutual Life annuity could have converted it to a monthly lifetime income of $2,268. The same account balance at Family Life, a Merrill Lynch subsidiary, would have generated just $2,072 a month.

Given such wide disparities in rates, you should never automatically take the annuitization deal offered by your present company. By doing a little shopping around, you could easily increase your monthly income by more than 10%.

Questions to Ask Before You Buy

Knowing the right answers can save you thousands of dollars when you deal with an annuity sales agent:

1. What kind of return will I get after my initial rate expires?

No agent can guarantee a continuous string of high renewal rates, but a competent agent should be able to provide you with a three-to-five-year history for specific annuity contracts. If not, take the sale to one who can.

2. What penalties will the company impose on withdrawals?

The agent should explain surrender charges in detail (as well as the federal income taxes and penalties on withdrawals). Any worthwhile plan should allow annuity holders to take out 10% of their account balance each year without charge. Surrender charges on larger withdrawals should start no higher than 8% and should disappear by the eighth year.

3. Is there a way to get all my money out without paying the company's penalty?

The agent should explain the bailout provision in detail if his annuity has one. This is a highly desirable escape clause in which, typically, the insurance company agrees to waive all surrender charges if its renewal rate falls one or more percentage points below the guaranteed initial rate. Avoid annuities that have no bailout but do have high surrender charges. The reason: If the insurer decides to keep renewal rates low, you will pay dearly to liberate your money.

4. How do I know my investment is secure?

The salesman should respond by citing the company's rating from A.M. Best Company. Limit your field to top-tier, financially solid insurance companies with a Best rating of at least A and preferably A+. Also scan the Investment Data section of *Best's Insurance Report* to see how heavily the insurer relies on noninvestment-grade bonds, which are better known as junk bonds. Avoid companies that keep more than 20% of their holdings in junk bonds.

5. Will the salesman's commission affect his recommendation?

The answer you get will almost always be no. Follow up by requesting disclosure of the commission on each plan you are offered. Even though you don't pay a sales fee directly, most insurers compensate their representatives with an up-front commission that ranges from 3% to 7%—and sometimes as much as 10%—of the premium. Spreads that huge can easily tempt a salesman to push an annuity that's better for him than for you.

Your Home

Since the days of settlers who headed west to bust the sod and build a log cabin, owning your own home has been perceived as a reward for thrift and industry and a cornerstone of American affluence. Housing also has been the best investment most of us could make over the past decade or two. For much of that period, "buy as much house as you can afford" served as a golden rule for home buyers, who commonly put 10% down and quickly recouped their investment with the first 10% rise in the value of their property.

Subsequent appreciation magically multiplied homeowners' equity— market price minus one's outstanding mortgage—enabling many middle-class families to trade up to progressively larger abodes (and mortgages) or to borrow freely against their home's increasing value to finance cars, boats, and other trappings of the good life.

In the past year or so, however, a fundamental erosion of real estate prices has undermined the consensus regarding housing as a can't-lose investment. Softer prices seeped into the national fabric well before the mid-1988 upturn in mortgage rates. The National Association of Realtors reports that house prices fell in 30 of 61 markets nationwide in the first quarter of 1988 compared with the previous quarter. Foreclosures also have been rising in many regions. A National Association of Home Builders' survey of 259 banks and thrifts in 24 states found that the foreclosure rate jumped 41.6% from June 1987 to June 1988, including both residential and commercial properties.

The pervasiveness of this slump is unsettling. House-price deflation, once written off as a quirk of boom-and-bust overbuilding in Texas and other oil-patch states, has quietly become a national trend. If the trend persists, its impact on Americans' financial well-being could be profound.

For most homeowners, this new reality means they must face the possibility that their equity could go down—or perhaps has gone down—without their realizing it. The prospect could force many families to retrench and rethink their basic financial plans. At worst, homeowners who have built up little equity may one day owe their mortgage holder more than their house is worth. Older couples, ready to trade down to a smaller house or retirement condo, may end up with a meager cash cushion for their declining years. And those in the middle who are counting on taking out a second mortgage to finance their children's college education may have to reassess their options. This chapter describes some of the steps you can take to reduce your exposure to—or take advantage of—these uncertainties. Included is advice on how to determine whether the market in your area is strong or weak, how to sell a house if prices are soft, and where bargain hunters can get the best deals on properties and mortgages.

Selecting the Best Mortgage

These days you need a scorecard to sort out the gimmicks from the good deals.

The faithful fixed-rate, no-frills, 30-year mortgage is back in style. Yet banks and mortgage companies continue to churn out a multitude of choices, one or another of which might match up better with some people's needs.

The loan that has lost the most ground lately is the adjustable-rate mortgage (ARM), whose interest rate changes at regular intervals in step with a designated interest index. Only about 25% of home loans being written these days are ARMs, compared with 65% in October 1987. One reason is the narrowing of the rate gap between the low first-year interest cost of a 30-year ARM and today's fixed-rate mortgage. While more than three percentage points once separated the two rates, the difference was recently 2.6 points—typically 8.2% versus 10.8%. That differential doesn't look like much of an edge in any ARM with a yearly rate adjustment. The first fact about this type of loan is that the rate is marked up two points on its first anniversary unless rates in general fall.

Even so, an ARM could cost you less if you don't expect to own the house more than about five years. Or you might want to consider the trendy new convertible mortgages, designed for folks who worry about marrying themselves to a mortgage contract for better or worse, interest-wise. Convertibles give you a chance in the early years to switch from a variable to a fixed rate or from the original fixed rate to a lower rate if one comes along. Still another alternative is an accelerated, biweekly payment plan, which slashes your interest cost. Here is the rundown on new mortgages, starting with the popular fixed-rate loans.

The biweekly mortgage. You pay half the monthly payment on a fixed-rate mortgage every two weeks. That's 26 payments a year, or 13 monthly payments, so you're really shortening the term of the loan and reducing the interest cost a bit each month. The result on a $100,000, 30-year mortgage at 10%, for example, is that you can retire your mortgage in just under 21 years and save $78,359 in interest, before taxes.

As an additional sweetener, some banks charge slightly lower rates for biweeklies. In exchange, however, banks almost always tie biweeklies to an automatic payment plan. You open a money-market account, from which the bank extracts the payments. If you have insufficient funds on deposit, you are slapped with an overdraft charge that may range from $9 to $22.

Convertible ARMs. Conversion was the star feature in ARMs during last spring's house-hunting season. Like most ARMs, the convertibles usually have a 30-year term and permit rate adjustments once a year. As with rate-reduction mortgages, the conversion privilege is short-lived and usually costs $250 or so to invoke. The initial interest rate on a convertible ARM may vary according to the terms and so may up-front charges such as points—each point equaling 1% of the amount borrowed. In addition, the new fixed rate runs about half a point higher than the national average 30-year rate.

Lenders are writing a symphony of variations on this conversion theme. The more flexible the schedule, the more advantageous it is to the borrower.

Whatever type of mortgage you choose, the amount you can borrow depends on your income and other debts. It all boils down to the monthly carrying cost as a percentage of your income. Personal variables such as your tax bracket, closing costs, and points, and how long you expect to stay in the house should be factored into your choice of a mortgage. Also, check out all of the following terms and conditions:

Good-faith estimate. Lenders must give you this statement of all mortgage origination costs, including application-processing fees ($200 to $400), appraisal fees, and points, within three days after you sign an application. But don't wait that long. Ask for the estimate before you apply.

Late-payment charges. Most lenders penalize borrowers for missing a monthly payment deadline. In states where there is a statutory grace period, no penalty can be levied unless you are delinquent for one or two weeks. The charge varies from 2% to 10% of the unpaid amount.

Prepayment penalty. Lenders sometimes charge extra if you pay off part of your loan ahead of schedule. This charge usually equals 2% of the amount prepaid. Avoid mortgages with prepayment clauses that extend past the third year.

Assumption. A mortgage with an attractively low rate can help you when you put your house on the market, but only if your loan contract permits acceptable buyers to take over, or assume, the debt. Most fixed-rate mortgages these days are not assumable, but ARMs usually are. If your lender reserves the right to raise the interest rate, the right of assumption loses some value.

ARMs disclosure. All details about the frequency of rate adjustments and the limits, or caps, on rate boosts must be disclosed at the time of application. The cap is usually about 2% a year and 6% over the life of the loan. You should also get full disclosure of any conversion rights and fees, which may range from a flat $250 to $1,000 plus points. Above all, make sure you understand the basis for rate adjustments. The lender usually pegs them 2.5 to three points above some published index, most commonly the one-year Treasury rate.

Kickbacks and referrals. A worrisome problem today is the practice by some lenders of giving kickbacks to real estate agents or others who refer house buyers to them. While kickbacks are probably not widespread, their very existence undermines the recommendations of all brokers. Some so-called loan finders charge fees for finding you a supposedly favorable mortgage. Your best protection against being misled or bilked is to check out the market yourself, getting quotes from four or five lenders.

Deciding Whether to Buy or Rent

From the late 1970s through the mid-1980s, the decision to buy was simple. House prices were streaking up so fast—rising more than 50% a year for some properties in hot markets such as New York City and Orange County, California that it made sense to buy almost anything with a roof on it. No matter how much you overextended yourself, appreciation would bail you out.

Today, though, house prices are rising only 5% a year on average. And in many areas, prices have actually declined. In Houston, for instance, home values have plunged as much as 40% since 1983 because of falling oil prices. Even in markets that are generally strong, such as Greenwich, Connecticut, prices for some types of houses dropped as much as 10% in the first four months of 1988.

If you are considering buying a house, be sure to play by the current market rules:

● Don't overextend yourself. The total cost of owning (see the box at right) shouldn't consume more than 40% of your monthly net income. The National Association of Realtors says you need an annual household income of $30,000 for a mortage on a $95,000 house, $40,000 for a $126,500 house, $50,000 for a $158,000 house and $60,000 for a $190,000 house.

● Comparison shop. Even if you can afford to buy a house, you may come out ahead by renting. As the map at right shows, the differences between the costs of buying and renting can vary in different parts of the country and from neighborhood to neighborhood.

● Think twice about buying if you plan to move soon. By tying up money in a down payment and closing costs, you are foregoing interest that you could be earning. If your home doesn't appreciate at least 10% to 15% over four years, you would have been better off renting as long as your rent was no more than the monthly cost of owning.

Nevertheless, if you buy for the long term—four years or more—a house is still one of the best investments you can make. Just try to enjoy yourself as you paint, mow the lawn, and tile the bathroom.

Is Renting Right for You?

This quiz will help you decide whether to rent or own:

1. How much has the price of a typical house in your area increased in the past five years? If less than 20%, score five points. ____

2. Do you plan to move within four years? If so, score five points. ____

3. Do you have ready assets for a down payment and closing expenses worth at least 25% of the price of a typical house in your neighborhood? If not, score three points. ____

4. Are you willing to devote time to repair the plumbing, weed the lawn, grout bathroom tiles and similar homeowner headaches? If not, score one point. ____

5. Will you be in the 15% tax bracket in 1988? If yes, score two points. ____

6. Do you contribute at least 10% of your income each year to tax-deferred savings plans such as 401(k)s and Keoghs to compensate for the lack of a mortgage deduction? If yes, score one point. ____

7. Are attractive, inexpensive rentals available in your area? If yes, score two points. ____

8. Is your credit so good that you could borrow $20,000 without using a house as collateral? If yes, score one point. ____

9. Is your annual income less than 32% of the purchase price of the kind of house you want? If yes, score three points. ____

10. Add up all your entries. ____

If you score nine or less, it may be time to buy a home; 10 or more suggests that you should probably be renting.

Closing Costs

Usually your mortgage lender prefers a down payment of 20% of the purchase price. But the bucks don't stop there. Figure on paying another 4% to 6% of the mortgage value up front for closing costs. If you buy a $150,000 house with a $120,000 mortgage, for example, your closing costs could amount to $5,000 to $7,200. Here's a typical breakdown:

Loan origination and points	$2,500
Fees (appraisal, inspection, insurance application, settlement, attorney)	800
Abstract and survey	300
Tax and insurance	1,400
Total	$5,000

What a Mortgage Costs

When you contemplate buying a home, remember that the actual cost of a mortgage is higher than the monthly payments. To start with, you forego interest on the money that goes toward the down payment, which is called an opportunity cost. Further, you pay maintenance expenses and property tax. These costs are partially offset, however, by the tax benefit of interest deductions.

The table shows how the costs and tax benefits balance out for someone in the 28% tax bracket who buys a $150,000 house with 20% down and closing costs of $5,000. The figures compare three different types of mortgages—each five years old—with the approximate cost of renting a similar property. Current mortgage rates are used, and the opportunity cost is based on an annual interest rate of 7%.

	30-year mortgage, 10% fixed	15-year mortgage, 9.5% fixed	30-year ARM, now 9%	Rental
Monthly payment	$1,053	$1,253	$972	$1,100
Opportunity cost	278	278	278	N.A.
Tax benefits	−271	−216	−243	N.A.
Maintenance + property tax	280	280	280	N.A.
Total	**1,340**	**1,595**	**1,287**	**1,100**

Warren Isensee

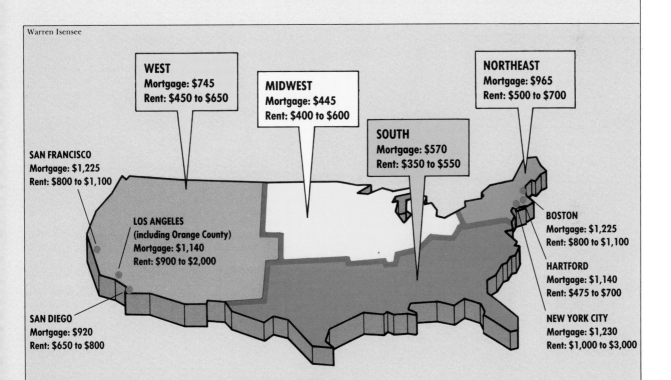

WEST
Mortgage: $745
Rent: $450 to $650

MIDWEST
Mortgage: $445
Rent: $400 to $600

NORTHEAST
Mortgage: $965
Rent: $500 to $700

SAN FRANCISCO
Mortgage: $1,225
Rent: $800 to $1,100

SOUTH
Mortgage: $570
Rent: $350 to $550

LOS ANGELES
(including Orange County)
Mortgage: $1,140
Rent: $900 to $2,000

BOSTON
Mortgage: $1,225
Rent: $800 to $1,100

HARTFORD
Mortgage: $1,140
Rent: $475 to $700

SAN DIEGO
Mortgage: $920
Rent: $650 to $800

NEW YORK CITY
Mortgage: $1,230
Rent: $1,000 to $3,000

Buy in New York, but Rent in San Diego

To a large extent, your decision to buy a home or to rent will depend on how prices and rentals compare in your own area. Naturally, costs vary from neighborhood to neighborhood, as well as from region to region. The map above shows how typical monthly mortgage payments for a one-family house or large apartment compare with rental costs for a similar property in four regions of the country and the six most expensive metropolitan areas. As you can see, in New York City it is often cheaper to buy, but it may make more sense to rent in many other parts of the country. Of course, as a renter you would not profit from any rise in housing prices.

How Big a Mortgage Can You Afford?

Before approving any mortgage, lenders decide how large a monthly payment you can afford. By filling out this worksheet, you can determine that amount—and whether it covers the loan you want.

First, gather the following facts about the house, the mortgage and yourself:

1. Price of the house ____
2. Down payment ____
3. Mortgage loan (line 1 ____ minus line 2)
4. Interest rate and ____ term of the loan

If it is an adjustable-rate mortgage:

5. Highest rate increase ____ permitted in any one year
6. Highest rate increase ____ permitted over the life of the loan
7. Monthly real estate ____ tax (annual tax divided by 12)
8. Estimated monthly ____ home-owners insurance premium
9. Your total monthly ____ payments on all current loans
10. Your monthly income before tax deductions ____

Next, figure the largest monthly payment acceptable to most lenders.

For a mortgage only:

11. Multiply line 10 by ____ 0.28, then subtract the sum of lines 7 and 8

For all your debts:

12. Multiply line 10 by ____ 0.36, then subtract the sum of lines 7, 8, and 9

13. Your payment limit ____ is the larger of lines 11 and 12

Then use the accompanying table to figure the monthly payment on the mortgage needed to finance the house you want to buy.

With a fixed-rate mortgage:

14. In the first column ____ of the table, go to the interest rate that you entered on line 4 and across to the term of the loan, also on line 4. Figure the monthly payment for the size loan you entered on line 3 above.

With an adjustable-rate mortgage:

15. First-year monthly ____ payment (use the rate and term on line 4)
16. Highest possible second-year monthly ____ payment (use the rate on line 4 plus the increase on line 5)
17. Highest possible ____ monthly payment over the life of the loan (use the rate on line 4 plus the increase on line 6)

If the maximum second-year payment for an adjustable-rate mortgage (on line 16) is no larger than your limit on line 13, you can probably afford the loan. But weigh as well the worst-case possibility (on line 17). How soon could the rate reach the ceiling set on line 6? Is your income likely to rise enough by then to keep up with the payments?

Payment Table

Look down the interest-rate column for the rate quoted by your lender, then across that row to the column for your mortgage term (15 or 30 years). The monthly payment shown at the intersection of the two lines is for each $1,000 borrowed. Divide your loan amount by 1,000 and multiply the result by the payment per $1,000. For example, if you need to borrow $100,000 for 30 years at 10%, go across the 10% row to the 30-year column. The payment shown is $8.78 per $1,000. Your monthly payment is $878, $8.78 times 100.

Interest rate	Monthly payments per $1,000 borrowed	
	15 years	30 years
7.00%	$8.99	$6.65
7.25	9.13	6.82
7.50	9.27	6.99
7.75	9.41	7.16
8.00	9.56	7.34
8.25	9.70	7.51
8.50	9.85	7.69
8.75	9.99	7.87
9.00	10.14	8.05
9.25	10.29	8.23
9.50	10.44	8.41
9.75	10.59	8.59
10.00	10.75	8.78
10.25	10.90	8.97
10.50	11.06	9.15
10.75	11.21	9.34
11.00	11.37	9.53
11.25	11.53	9.72
11.50	11.69	9.91
11.75	11.85	10.10
12.00	12.01	10.29
12.25	12.17	10.48
12.50	12.33	10.68
12.75	12.49	10.87

Selling Your Home in a Soft Market

There are important things to do before the "for sale" sign goes up.

You didn't need a super-salesman to sell your house a few years ago. In 1985 and 1986, the robust economy and falling mortgage rates spurred more than a 10% annual jump in the number of homes sold and an 11% two-year increase in median prices. But sales in many areas slowed last year as rising interest rates and the aftershocks of the stock market crash forced many prospective home buyers out of the market. With mortgage rates recently near double digits and the threat of recession hanging over the economy, sellers face tough times. The National Association of Realtors expected resale volume to drop 8% in 1988 to 3.2 million homes and median prices to rise only 4.6% (to $89,000), compared with a 6% price climb in 1987.

Selling your house in a sluggish market requires hard work before you put out a "for sale" sign. To get top dollar, you want a speedy sale. That means making sure your house is attractive to buyers before it goes on the market; otherwise, you may be forced to lower the price. Among the steps that you might take:

List your house with a knowledgeable local broker who will market it aggressively. You may be tempted to sell your home yourself, thereby saving the customary 6% broker's commission. But a soft market is precisely when you most need professional help. Interview at least four brokers before signing a contract, paying particular attention to their marketing strategies. Make sure the broker you choose plans to advertise your house through a multiple-listing service, which alerts every agent in the area that it is for sale. The more potential buyers who see your home, the better your chances of selling it at an acceptable price. Inquire about the broker's willingness to pursue other means of finding buyers, such as asking large local firms for the names of recently transferred employees who may be house hunting.

Once you have selected a broker, don't haggle over the commission, which is the broker's only incentive to work hard for you. In fact, if housing sales are particularly slow in your area and you are in a hurry, you might consider offering a higher-than-average commission. A 7% commission on a $150,000 house, for example, would cost you $10,500, or $1,500 more than a 6% commission. But the promise of extra money might stimulate the broker to push your house harder, resulting in a faster sale at a better price.

Set a reasonable price. Your asking price is the most important decision—even more important than location. If you try to test the market and set too high a price, you may never sell your house.

Use recent selling prices of comparable homes in your neighborhood as a guide. Some brokers suggest adding a 5% to 10% negotiating cushion to your asking price, but too high a price could scare away potential buyers. In fact, not adding that cushion might even work in your favor. That way, when negotiating with a buyer, you could prove that the house is priced in line with the market.

Make necessary repairs and improvements before you put your home on the market. A house in need of major repairs will not attract buyers. If the roof leaks, fix it; if the plumbing is antiquated, be sure it is in working order. Major remodeling, however, rarely pays off. Exceptions are projects that add real value to your home. For example, if your house has only one full bathroom, the $5,000-or-so cost of adding another one can easily be recouped in the sale price. A two-bathroom house usually sells a lot faster than a single-bath home.

Otherwise, concentrate on cosmetic changes to enhance your home's looks. A fresh coat of paint—inside and out—can work wonders. At the very least, spruce up the trim and sashes. Also repair drooping gutters and damaged window screens. One inexpensive tip is to brighten your home by using higher-watt light

Reading Your Home Market

How To Tell Whether Your Area is Getting Strong:
- Local employment is rising 3% or more annually.
- A stable or shrinking number of houses are up for sale.
- The area enjoys significant upgrading or expansion of retail business.
- There's extensive highway development or a new airport. Improved transportation often brings growth to an area.
- Major land purchases are being made by expanding or relocating corporations or wealthy investor-developers.
- Many of the new houses being built are obviously of high quality.
- There's a high percentage of owner-occupied housing in the neighborhood.

What To Do:
- Buy all the land you can, even if it comes with less house than you want. You can always expand the house when you have more cash, but the increasingly more valuable land may eventually move beyond your reach.
- Get the longest-term mortgage you can if you need to hold down monthly payments in order to buy in the neighborhood.
- Go shopping in November and December, when there are fewer competing buyers to drive up prices.
- Settle for a longer commute to get more house for your money.
- Make a serious offer on an unfinished house or consider taking on a handyman's special.

How To Tell Whether Your Area is Getting Soft:
- The average selling time for houses has lengthened by 30% or more.
- There's a widening gap between asking prices and final selling prices.
- The number of residential foreclosures is rising.
- The vacancy rate in office buildings and other commercial real estate is increasing.
- There's a decline in the number of building permits issued. Such a drop in permits means fewer housing starts, which signals that builders believe they won't profit in the market.
- Note who is selling houses. It's a bad sign if a bank is selling; it probably means the owner or developer lost it.

What To Do:
- If you can, relax and ride out the downturn. If you must sell, get appraisals from three brokers and don't be greedy.
- Try to sell your house quickly. Determine the average selling time in your neighborhood, then add two months for closing time; estimate your mortgage, taxes, and utility costs for that period and then lop that grand total off your asking price.
- If your income is secure, look to trade up to a fancier house or move to a more desirable neighborhood.
- Bid about 10% below what similar houses in the neighborhood have sold for recently and bargain hard from there.

bulbs in existing fixtures. Before you let anyone in the front door, clear out cluttered closets. Neat closets look larger than messy ones—and big closets are attractive selling points.

Consider creative financing. If your house is languishing on the market, offering financial incentives to prospective buyers may help clinch a sale. Rather than lowering your asking price, think about offering the buyer a cash rebate of $1,000 to $5,000. A price reduction saves the buyers money on their future mortgage payments but does not help much with immediate expenses, such as decorating the house.

Helping the buyer with the costs of a mortgage can also smooth the way to a deal. You might, for example, offer to pay the buyer's points—the up-front fee charged by the lender. Sellers can also help finance the mortgage itself, but do so only as a last resort. Few sellers can assess the creditworthiness of a buyer as well as a bank can, raising the risk of default.

The Plentiful Pickings in Vacation Condos

Prices are super soft, so you can bargain hard for your place in the sun.

Welcome to the buyer's market in vacation condominiums. In recent years, the effects of tax reform have forced out many investors who previously bought residential properties more for tax than for human shelter. The stock market's Black Monday simply hastened the exodus. The result is that prices in mid-1988 were off 10% to 40% or more from their early 1980s highs in places where the skies are sunny (Palm Springs, California), the powder is deep (Vail, Colorado) and the surf is close at hand (Kiawah Island, South Carolina). Even in many spots where second-home prices continue to bubble, condos often lag behind.

Most of the blame goes to tax reform. Before 1987, if you bought a second home primarily for investment and restricted your personal use to fewer than 14 days a year, you could write off tax losses on the place—depreciation, mortgage interest, real estate taxes and operating expenses exceeding rental income—against your ordinary income. Under the new rules, such losses can usually be deducted only against "passive" income from limited partnerships or other rental properties. There is one major loophole: If your adjusted gross income is $100,000 or less and you actively manage your holdings, you can still claim up to $25,000 in passive losses against your salary. With the top marginal income tax rate slashed from 50% to 33%, however, the value of write-offs is vastly diminished.

As a result, most real estate analysts agree that any decision should ultimately be based on how you and your family like to relax—and where. What follows is a regional roundup of the most intriguing possibilities, plus some tips on how to get the bargain of your choice.

The Northeast. Second-home prices remain generally firm in this densely populated and economically overachieving area. Some of the best condo deals lie in New Hampshire's Lake Winnipesaukee region and in Ocean and Monmouth counties along New Jersey's coast. For instance, prices of two-bedroom nonwaterfront condos near Weirs Beach and Laconia, New Hampshire started at around $100,000 in mid-1988, or roughly 8% less than the asking prices 12 months earlier. And a block or so from the Atlantic Ocean in Point Pleasant Beach, New Jersey, neat, traditional-style one-bedrooms were selling for $95,000—a 5% to 15% markdown from the year before.

The South. Dixie resort condos suffer from energy price woes, overbuilding, and sputtering local economies. On Hilton Head Island, South Carolina, prices have dropped 15% on average since 1985. Typical cost of a two-bedroom-and-bath condo a 10-minute walk from the beach: $110,000. On tony Kiawah Island off Charleston, gracefully designed luxury condos nestle among cypresses or perch atop bluffs. One-bedrooms, a minute's stroll from the Atlantic, fetched $110,000, versus $160,000 the year before.

More bargains line the Gulf Coast, where many condominiums at popular retreats such as Gulf Shores, Alabama, and Destin, Florida sell for 20% to 30% less than in 1985. Farther south in Florida, prices are nearly as flabby. Brokers say East Coast units in Dade and Broward counties harbor particularly good deals. In Clearwater, for example, the asking price of a two-bedroom unit on the Gulf of Mexico was $209,000, down from $250,000 in 1983.

The Midwest. You can fish, golf, swim, or cool off with an icy six-pack at Missouri's languid Lake of the Ozarks, where prices have dropped 5% to 25% since 1986 because of overbuilding. Attractive two-bedroom waterfront units were selling for $70,000 there.

The Rockies. For most of this decade, the real estate market in Colorado's ski country has been painfully flat or headed downhill. The oil price collapse is the chief leveler. The choicest deals are in Vail and in Park City, Utah, which are less prestigious and more overbuilt than top-of-the-line Aspen. At Park City, two-bedroom units a few blocks from the lifts were offered at $125,000, all the way down from

$225,000 in 1985. More reasonable still are the buys in northwestern Montana, where the depressed agriculture and lumber industries sent the region reeling. At unspoiled retreats such as Whitefish Lake, Flathead Lake, and Big Mountain, a fire sale is in progress. At Big Mountain, for instance, a four-bedroom condo was priced at $86,000, down from $125,000 in 1985.

The Far West. Oregon's majestic Mount Hood caps a vacation culture that thrives on winter skiing, summer hiking, and white-water rafting in the Deschutes River. Yet, condo prices in the region have come down 30% since 1980 as a consequence of rising interest rates, tax reform, and a depressed timber economy. Two thousand miles south, on the floor of the Coachella Valley, lies Palm Springs, California. Mayor Sonny Bono's bailiwick, which boasts 76 area golf courses, has been widely overbuilt. Real estate prices have fallen as much as 30% since 1980, and desirable two-bedrooms were selling for as little as $112,500.

Before you buy anywhere, keep in mind that a condo bargain is not always a good value. Here is how to ensure that you get both:

● Go for the best location you can afford. The closer to the lake, for instance, the easier the sell.

● Check out the developer's reputation. A thoughtfully planned, well-maintained complex will hold its value better.

● Haggle. Some experts suggest offering a miserly 60% of a condo's asking price as a starting figure.

● Also consider buying at auction. Most big-city newspapers carry an auction page in their Sunday editions. Look among the classified ads for such major auction houses as Hudson & Marshall, Sheldon Good & Co., and JBS Associates. The biggest markets are Florida's Gold Coast, Texas' Padre Island, and coastal South Carolina. Always be sure to check out the building, the developer, and the location first. Usually, auctioneers set a predetermined time for inspecting condos—say, a couple of days in advance. In addition, scrutinize the closing records (available at the local courthouse) to see how much any similar units sold for a year ago; then bid no more than that.

Knowing When to Do It Yourself

The dilemma facing homeowners is whether to save money or precious leisure time.

To do or not to do? Deciding when to hire workers for a job and when to try it yourself is one of the trickiest—but potentially most rewarding—aspects of home remodeling. The trick is to find jobs you can handle competently in a reasonable time. The reward is the greatly reduced cost, since about 40% of professional remodeling cost is labor and 23% is overhead and profit.

The main advantage of hiring a professional, of course, is that your workload can be lightened to a single chore—writing the check. And, often, a professional will do a better job in less time than you can. Still, professionals may not devote the same loving care to your property that you would. And many of them overbook; workers show up one day to start your job and then disappear for a week to meet obligations elsewhere. (For suggestions on how to deal with contractors, see the box on page 106.)

Doing it yourself, on the other hand, has its own headaches. Most projects take longer than you expect. The quality of workmanship depends on your own patience and skill. And then there's that great imponderable: the value of your leisure time. For example, if you're a professional who can earn more per hour than you'd pay the contractor, you might be better off sticking to what you're trained to do.

When it comes to deciding which projects make the most sense for you, you should first pick a job that you enjoy doing—if you don't like the work, odds are you will do it poorly.

Then get some bids from professionals. Calculate how much you would spend on materials if you did the work yourself and how long it would take you. Finally, use these estimates to figure your savings per hour of effort—a good measure of your immediate payback—and also how much value it will add to your home. Be realistic about your own skills, though. You might save $1,000 by doing it yourself, only to have a prospective home buyer knock $2,000 off your asking price to cover the cost of tearing out your sloppy workmanship. (For examples of projects that typically have a good return, see the table on page 107.)

Beginner's projects that require more patience than skill can have a remarkably high return if they save a tradesman's house call. Fixing a leaky faucet, for example, is small change in every respect, but the cost of a licensed plumber, typically $50 to $100 an hour, is not. Most of the time, the faucet needs only a new rubber washer anyway, and replacing it requires only a $5 kit from the hardware store, an adjustable wrench, a screwdriver, and about an hour of labor.

Minor electrical jobs are also within reach of most amateurs. Replacing a doorbell chime or a dimmer switch, for instance, takes an hour or so, costs less than $15 in gear, and saves the cost of an electrician's visit—about $100. More ambitious projects, such as painting or retiling, can pay off if you are willing to spend more than one full weekend working at home. The most common error for do-it-yourselfers is that they get 95% of the job done and then they're too tired for the last 5% that makes it look great.

Professional painters would charge between $200 and $400 to put two coats of paint on the walls and ceiling of a 15-foot by 20-foot dining or living room, for example, but they would finish the job in a day. A rank amateur would probably require two days—one to prepare the walls and one to paint them—but would spend only about $75 for paint and supplies.

Laying new ceramic tile (cost: $3 to $6 a square foot) is a little more complicated. Sometimes you can put down a layer of adhesive and place the tiles directly over an existing vinyl or linoleum floor. Other times the floor is too uneven, and you must chisel up the old covering to expose the concrete underneath or lay down a thin layer of concrete for a foundation (probably not a job for beginners). You will need to rent a tile-cutting tool for about $5 a day, then spend some time practicing with it to get clean, straight cuts. But with all the labor that is involved, your savings can be substantial: $6 or so per square foot.

Big jobs entail the most effort but yield equivalent savings. One popular project is to add an outdoor deck to your home. A builder would charge $3,000 to $5,000 for a 200-square-foot platform suitable for long summer evenings of mint juleps and insect repellent. But you can buy the materials and build a custom model for about $1,000 or pay $400 to $700 for a prefabricated kit. In most communities, you will need to submit your plan in advance to the local building authority and pay about $50 to $150 for a permit. Later, the deck must pass an official inspection.

Taking a sledgehammer to your house—that is, gutting a room or ripping out a back porch before a major renovation—can also be profitable, not to mention cathartic, and can shave $1,000 off the project cost. The tools you would require are simple: a crowbar ($4) and sledgehammer ($10) usually suffice. The only caution is to check your building plans to make sure you aren't removing something critical to the rest of the house, like a load-bearing joist. Paying to replace a support destroyed by mistake could be more costly than hiring someone to do the original job correctly.

Knocking down and clearing away an 8-foot by 14-foot wall would probably take two desk jockeys about a day, including hauling off the debris (or, you can pay someone $50 to haul it). If you leave the job to your contractor, the cost would be about $130.

There are some jobs—anything complicated involving electricity or plumbing, for example—that are usually best left in the hands of experts. Don't even think about running natural gas lines or connecting to city sewage. Also better for professionals are jobs that require skilled craftsmanship: detailed interior woodwork, fine cabinetry, fancy tiling, carpeting, and wood flooring, to name a handful.

Tips for Dealing with Contractors

Get bids from at least two or three and pick one you like who has been in business locally for several years. Check with past customers and the Better Business Bureau. Then insist on a written, signed contract including:

● A fixed price not based on hours.

● Detailed plans with specifics about materials, appliances, etc.

● A reasonable payment schedule (30% each at start, middle, and end is common, with 10% upon final okay).

● Start-up, completion dates and, if possible, a fee for lateness.

● A guarantee that the contractor carries workers' compensation insurance and also liability insurance.

● A promise that you will get a *release of liens* before final payment so that subcontractors can't sue you if the contractor fails to pay them.

Some Do-it-yourself Projects that Are Worth Your Time

Project	Cost if done by professional	Cost of materials if you do it yourself	How long it will take (hours)	Total amount you will save	Your savings per hour	Total value added to the house	Comments
SMALL JOBS							
Caulking leaks around your house	$200	$35	5	$165	$33	—	Though the tax credit for energy-savings is gone, this half-day job can still weatherproof your home and cut utility bills by 15%.
Painting a 15-ft.-by-20-ft. room	$400	$75	16	$325	$20	—	Unless your walls are in pristine shape, plan to spend as much time preparing them (patching and sanding) as you do applying paint.
Putting in a dimmer switch	$100	$15	1.5	$85	$57	—	Avoiding the cost of an electrician's house call makes this—or similar jobs, like replacing an outlet—the biggest money saver listed here.
Fixing a leaky faucet	$75	$5	2	$70	$35	—	You escape the expense of a professional plumber; but be sure to turn off the water under the sink first, or you'll get a rude reminder later.
MEDIUM JOBS							
Wallpapering a 15-ft.-by-20-ft. room	$800	$300	16	$500	$31	—	Enlist a helper for this task: four hands are better than two on a gooey strip of wallpaper. Also, errors are most easily traced to an accomplice.
Painting 10 outdoor windows	$300	$50	10	$250	$25	—	Doors, trimwork, shutters and the picket fence always take longer to paint than you ever dreamed possible, which is why your per-hour savings add up.
Stripping the paint from kitchen cabinetry	$750	$150	75	$600	$8	—	Only if the cabinets are worth keeping, since the per-hour savings from this job is rather low.
Tiling and grouting a 6-ft.-by-10-ft. bathroom floor	$600	$150	16	$450	$28	—	Easy and inexpensive but with a potential for dramatic effect, this job goes best when you can detour the family to a second bathroom.
BIG JOBS							
Demolishing a 12-ft.-by-15-ft. enclosed porch	$1,500	$400	24	$1,100	$46	—	Be sure to check the blueprints before swinging that sledge so you don't remove a load-bearing joist.
Laying ceramic tile on a 12-ft.-by-14-ft. kitchen floor	$1,700	$400	24	$1,300	$54	$1,500	Easiest if the existing floor has a concrete foundation; otherwise you may need to lay some concrete in first.
Building a 14-ft.-by-16-ft. deck	$4,000	$1,000	80	$3,000	$38	$3,500	Stick with pressure-treated lumber. And, for the sake of your family, resolve now to stop bragging after a month or so.
Finishing a 16-ft.-by-14-ft. addition	$4,000	$2,000	200	$2,000	$10	$4,000	Let the pros build the foundation, frame and roof; you can finish the interior, but you'll need almost every summer weekend and maybe some vacation too.

Home Is Where the Office Is

Better gear and changing life-styles are making working at home more popular and profitable.

More and more people are realizing that you don't have to be self-employed for a home office to make sense. The American Home Business Association estimates that 27 million of us labor from home at least part of the time, up from 23 million in 1983. Whether you are selling widgets, bringing work home in a briefcase, or just trying to get a better grip on your personal finances, the right type of home office can help you meet your goals.

Personal computers, especially the venerable IBM PC and Apple's Macintosh, led the home-office revolution. Silicon Valley marketers discovered that the computer's real value was not for balancing checkbooks or playing Donkey Kong but for bringing the workplace into the home. Today you can crunch numbers, keep address files, tap into remote computers, even publish your own book—all with Fido at your feet. The simplest telephones come with features such as speed dialing and automatic redial. If you can forward your calls from the office, no one even has to know you are at home. Personal copiers bring office-quality copying to your living room. And the new darling of the technology market, the $1,000 home fax machine, enables you to zip documents anywhere in the world for just the price of a phone call.

While technology has made the home office increasingly viable, the changing needs of workers have made it necessary. For example, two-income families can more easily maintain their professional lives while raising children. Indeed, a survey by a New York City-based research firm Link Resources, found that two out of three home workers are in dual-career households and more than half have kids under 18 at home. Those who toil at home cite other benefits as well, notably increased productivity and independence.

You don't have to earn wages to set up a home office, of course. The business of running a household and managing investments can be reason enough. The trick is to choose the right equipment and space. Here are some suggestions:

Before you set up your home office, check the local zoning regulations to make sure you won't encounter problems from the city. Next, select a space to work in. If you want a tax deduction, devote a well-defined area solely to the office (see the box on page 109). Then lay in some reliable equipment; your choices will depend on your tasks. A good phone, a second phone line (or call-waiting service), and an answering machine are essential if your business depends on making or taking calls. You probably will also want a computer or dedicated word processor. Besides generating letters, reports, financial analyses and the like, the computer can organize your life with an inexpensive desk manager that serves as your appointment book, address book, notepad, calendar, calculator, and even alarm clock to get you up in the morning.

If you buy expensive hardware, make sure it's insured. Most homeowner policies don't cover items used for business, so ask your insurance agent about an incidental business rider or a small-business policy. It might also be wise to inquire about liability coverage if you bring clients to your home, since if one of them falls and breaks a leg, your home policy won't pay.

In spite of the many joys of working at home, perhaps in your bathrobe or on your sun deck, there are disadvantages. Some people won't take you as seriously as you would like, so train your kids not to answer the phone or to do so in a businesslike way. You will also need discipline—both to get down to business in the morning and to stop at night. A more personal consideration, but not one to take lightly: Many work-at-home people feel severely isolated when they first cut loose from a big office. You will need to cultivate the habit of arranging lunches, visiting clients, and keeping in touch with the grapevine. And make sure the address on your stationery, cards, and envelopes does not betray the fact that your office doubles as your residence.

Tax Breaks from Your Home Office

Besides affording a comfortable place to work, your home office can save you a bundle on taxes—provided you plan carefully to meet the Internal Revenue Service's recently toughened-up requirements.

The IRS allows deductions for a home office only if you use it exclusively and regularly for business. "Exclusively" means that the area— whether it be a single desk, a room, or an entire floor—is used only for work and for nothing else. You cannot sleep or watch TV there, unless those are required by your job. "Regularly" is loosely defined but probably means you labor there about three to four times a week for 10 to 12 hours in total. And "business" means you must have shown a net profit in at least three of the last five years, or else it will be considered a hobby.

If you are running your own company from home, you most likely meet those standards. But what if you are just bringing work home from the office? You may still be able to write off your expenses if your job requires you to do this—and if you can show the IRS a memo from the boss stating so.

Once you pass the tests for a write-off, calculate—either by square footage or number of rooms — what fraction of your home the office occupies. You can then deduct that fraction of household expenses, such as mortgage interest and property taxes (these are deductible anyway, of course, but you have to assign a portion of them to your business in order to take the other write-offs). Do the same for rent, utilities, major repairs, maid service, trash collection, and the like. You can even depreciate the space allotted to your office. Such household deductions are allowed only up to the amount of net income you earn from your home business. But should your losses exceed your gains in any particular year, you may carry them forward to future years in which you earn enough at home to balance them.

Office equipment can be another source of tax breaks. And since hardware is considered a direct business expense (unlike household costs, which are indirect), a loss here can be used to offset any income. If you run your own business, you can deduct up to $10,000 a year for a computer or copier or depreciate them over five years.

Be warned, though, that should you ever sell your home, the office could become a liability. Normally you can avoid capital-gains tax on the profit from a sale by rolling it into the purchase of your next house. But if you take home-office deductions that year, you are required to pay capital-gains tax on a fraction of the profit equal to the proportion of household expenses you deduct. To avoid this, simply convert the office back to personal use before the year of sale.

Finally, since home-office deductions may flag your return for an audit, be sure to consult a tax professional, keep scrupulous records, and follow the law to the letter.

Family Matters

A family's life cycle is marked by certain predictable events with financial consequences. These include such things as insuring against a spouse's untimely death or disability, saving for your children's college education, providing for financial emergencies, and even negotiating a divorce and adjusting to the new realities of being a single parent.

One of the biggest anxieties confronting parents is how best to plan for their children's education. Meeting the ever-increasing cost of higher education demands greater ingenuity on your part because tax reform has made it more difficult to save or borrow to pay for college. For example, "How to Slash Your College Debts" assesses a variety of clever no-debt and low-debt techniques—and the trade-offs that accompany them—for financing your child's diploma.

For advice on selecting the best school and enhancing your aspiring scholar's chances of getting into it, study "What Colleges Don't Tell You—but Should" and "Guides to the Admissions Maze," which look at the merits of consultants who, for a fee, steer your child to the right college.

Another perplexing question for families is how much insurance they really need and where to obtain the best deals on coverage. Adequately insured or not, most of us have a penchant for overpaying for protection against financial catastrophe. "Cutting the Cost of Your Coverage" gives guidelines for figuring out what your family requires—in terms of life, health, disability, auto, homeowners and personal liability policies—plus the names of insurers that consistently offer competitive prices and good service.

Your health insurance plan deserves special attention. More and more employees are being asked—perhaps even pressured—by their companies to join health maintenance organizations (HMOs) that provide comprehensive care at a fixed monthly rate. But with three in four HMOs posting losses, you may be hard put to pick a healthy one. "Is an HMO Right for You?" tells you how to take the pulse of the plan chosen by your employer.

Recovery from the trauma of a divorce or the death of a spouse is often hindered by unexpected financial complications. Yet the odds of suddenly becoming single are high. A person who marries today has a fifty-fifty chance of getting divorced, and a wife faces a 70 percent probability that she will be a widow. "Dealing with a Divorce" leads husbands and wives through the labyrinth of new state laws that make issues of property, alimony, and child support more complex than ever. And "Coping with a Spouse's Death" will help you prepare for the worst. Survivors face tasks and decisions that would be trying in the best of times. But there are steps that can be taken to minimize the financial anguish.

What Colleges Don't Tell You—but Should

It's a big investment. But do you know enough about what you are buying?

Every year, colleges publish viewbooks teeming with four-color pictures of lawns, lakes, and lolling students. Some facts are available, too, such as home states of students and the number of volumes in the library. There's even a movement under way to require colleges to reveal on-campus crime statistics. Yet few of these facts aid candidates and parents in comparing similar colleges. Indeed, most people have more useful information about buying used cars than they do about a service that can cost up to $75,000 over four years.

What kind of information might be useful to parents and students? Here is a list of questions you might begin with. If the applicant is shy about aggressive grilling, parents should feel free to pose such questions to admissions officers by mail or by phone, or even during campus visits. Be warned that only some of them will be answered. But be assured that considering the cost in time and money involved, all of them should be.

What are the admissions standards for different groups? The most selective private colleges build classes composed of scholars, minorities, offspring of alumni, athletes, development cases (those whose parents are wealthy), students with a specific academic expertise, and youngsters with special creative talents. Standards vary not only by group but also by separate schools—arts and sciences, engineering, and business, say—at the same university. To give candidates an estimate of their chances, colleges should provide information about the number of applicants in each group and for each school, the number that was admitted, and the average Standard Aptitude Test score within each. At one Ivy League university, for instance, the combined SAT average for the freshman class several years ago was 1350. But in the engineering school, the SAT average was 1380; for Asian-Americans, 1350; for children of alumni, 1280; for athletes, 1240; for development cases, 1220; for blacks, 1200; and for Hispanics, 1180. Admissions officers will likely be willing to provide SAT breakdowns by schools within a university but not for types of student. The contentious fallout from the release of such sensitive data could be considerable. But ask anyway; you may get a straight answer.

What are your specific admissions policies? Most college catalogues say something such as: "Incomparable College is looking for highly motivated, intellectually curious students who want to pursue a rigorous program of studies."

It will not be easy to get any college to be more direct. For one thing, it is difficult to write an admissions-policy statement without offending someone. For another, without written guidelines, the college administration can change the composition of the classes depending upon the needs of the hour. After bitter internal debate that spilled over into the newspapers, for instance, Trinity University in San Antonio last year shifted from a "need blind" admissions policy to one of "parents' ability to pay."

Yet many admissions offices employ rating systems that might be useful to candidates. Princeton, for example, uses a one-to-five system, with candidates rated separately for academics and nonacademics. Ask admissions officers to tell you which credentials will weigh more heavily. This will give the candidates something to shoot for.

What is your graduation rate? This is a rough measure of consumer satisfaction with the institution. Only 47% of those who start college eventually earn a degree from any school. Be skeptical if a private college lost more than 15% and a public college over 25% of a class in the first two years; you should also be con-

cerned if the independent college did not graduate 75% of a class and if the public institution did not graduate 60%. It would be interesting for colleges to publish charts showing what percentage of each class flunked out, was dismissed for disciplinary reasons, left for financial reasons, transferred to other institutions, or simply departed.

What is the real success rate of the college's graduates in postgraduate admissions? It's one thing to say that X% of a particular class goes on to law school and Y% goes on to medical school, but a more helpful measure of the intellectual development of the student body would be statistics on how many applied but were not admitted anywhere and the ranges and median scores of all the undergraduates who took the various standardized tests for graduate schools.

How much do undergraduates use the library? Most colleges boast only about the number of volumes there. Other leading indicators: What percentage of the undergraduate student body can the library's seating accommodate at any one time? Are any carrels assigned to undergraduates and, if so, what percentage of the senior class has them? What is the average number of books checked out a year by each undergraduate?

How ambitious are your computer facilities? Because computers will play a significant role in the professional and personal lives of today's students, it is helpful to know what the institutions are doing to make them available to undergraduates. Are students required to have personal computers? Are they given reasonable access to the school's mainframe with terminals placed strategically around the campus? Colleges could easily publish a terminal-student ratio. At Duke, where there are only 420 terminals to some 6,000 undergraduates, the university administration says it wants to right the imbalance.

How accessible are the athletic and recreational facilities? College viewbooks are as full of pictures of impressive indoor and outdoor sports centers as they are silent about the amount of time these Taj Mahals are available to the nonintercollegiate athlete. All you need is a listing of all the facilities and the hours when the usage was restricted for intercollegiate teams, for intramural programs, and for recreational use. All too often, 95% of the undergraduates get to use the best facilities only as spectators.

Do students get to take the courses they want? It is common for undergraduates to select courses only to find them already closed out. It isn't easy to fathom how the colleges have been able to get away with this practice when tuition costs require such great sacrifices by families. There may be good reason for limiting some classes, especially when there is restricted lab space. But many of the class-size limits appear to be arbitrarily imposed by individual faculty members. Colleges should publish a list of courses that have limited enrollments, identifying both the number of students who requested those classes and the number who actually enrolled. If colleges were required to do this, the number of limited-enrollment courses might drop dramatically.

Do undergraduates get a chance to study with seasoned professors? Faculties are ranked as follows: professors, associate professors, assistant professors, instructors, and teaching assistants. Applicants and their parents should not be reluctant to inquire about the average amount of weekly time those at each rank devote to teaching undergraduates. While most colleges profess to being committed to undergraduate education, actual evidence of the extent of that commitment is difficult to find. If a youngster sees that full professors at one institution spend nine hours a week teaching while their counterparts at another teach only four, the candidate might legitimately question the amount of attention he or she is likely to receive at the latter school. At the University of Pennsylvania, admissions officers are willing to provide such data. Fewer than 10% of Penn's introductory undergraduate courses are taught by teaching assistants, for example, and most of those are science labs.

Students are attracted to many major universities by the reputations of superstar faculty members. Those who are not expected to teach undergraduates should be so designated in the catalogue. Colleges should list not only those on their faculty who have been recognized for outstanding work but also the courses they teach—if any. A famous professor's mere presence on campus is no help to a student and cold comfort to a family whose home may be in hock in the elusive pursuit of higher education.

Guides to the Admissions Maze

Fierce competition to get in has created a new kind of professional—the independent consultant who can lead your child to the right college.

The thick envelope, please, not the thin. That was the teenager's fervent prayer in April 1988, as the most competitive college-acceptance season in history came to its calamitous close. Despite a steady decline in the absolute number of 17-year-olds, a greater percentage of them appeared to be bidding for a high-quality bachelor's degree than ever before. In came the paper flood, as many students tried to multiply their chances by applying to not a handful but a hatful of schools. Out went a countertide of thin envelopes containing cheerless rejections and confirming the grimmest rumors: Top colleges were turning away valedictorians, varsity athletes, and Scholastic Aptitude Test stars at a rate that could shock any proud parent. All told, more high school seniors were turned down by more colleges than in any spring ever.

Enter the independent college consultant, right on cue and bristling with bright ideas. For fees ranging from $50 an hour to as high as $2,500 for a full-service package, these specialists try to see their teen clients through more thick than thin. They offer guidance in matching the student to a group of prospective colleges and then advise on all aspects of the application process, particularly essays and interviews. More than 200 independents, twice as many as in 1980, are selling their services, mostly in big cities and their affluent suburbs. They can supplement, or supplant, the efforts of your high school college guidance counselor. (Officially, the independents prefer to be called consultants to differentiate themselves from psychological counselors.)

Many of these for-hire advisers are themselves former guidance counselors or college admissions officers who have jumped the fence to the private sector. In fact, the best of them usually come from either of those backgrounds, which provide a broad knowledge of the college admissions process and an invaluable feel for the differences among colleges. As with any new and mostly unpoliced profession, quality can vary markedly among practitioners.

The consultants' major selling point is the specialized attention they can offer—and that is tough to find in a busy school setting. At public high schools, especially, a single guidance counselor may be expected to oversee the college plans of hundreds of students while holding down other duties as a teacher or team coach. Even some private schools have overburdened staffs; or your child may not get along with the school's counselor. Public or prep school, many students could benefit from a second professional opinion about their college strategy.

The price of independent help depends on your needs and budget. If you and your child believe that you have settled on the ideal colleges to besiege, you may require only one or two consultations. Hourly rates run from $50 to $125. Or you may want to spring for a full package of services that may last for a year or more and cost from $400 to $2,500.

The Complete Treatment

The consultant starts a full-service job by matching your child's and your family's expectations against the high school transcript and standardized-test scores. He or she may also coach your child on improving those scores or make a referral to a test-coaching course.

Independent consultants can earn their pay just by bringing the family's expectations down to earth from the start. For example, they might gently inform families that if a student's SAT scores are lower than what Harvard expects, the odds on getting in may be too long. The consultant goes on from there to identify a group of colleges where the student would thrive and then helps the teenager prove the point to those schools.

The prospective choices fall along an admissions-difficulty spectrum from reach to cinch. The theory is that at least your child gets in somewhere and at best may land a better school than expected. Then the family takes over, researching the schools on the list. This can involve everything from reading the best college guides to visiting the schools. You should narrow your choices to six or so schools; that's widely recommended as the most manageable number to apply to. Count on application fees ranging from $15 to $50.

Consultants can help your child fill out the application forms, solicit recommendations from teachers, and prepare for the admissions interviews. The application essay, which has been known to vault otherwise listless applicants over the gate to a selective school, comes in for close scrutiny. First-rate consultants brainstorm ideas and review drafts but never ghost or edit the essay.

During the spring when the acceptance letters arrive, consultants are still on call. They advise how to proceed if, say, a first choice puts your child on the waiting list or—the dreaded doomsday scenario—every one of his applications was spurned. Likely advice to the wait-listed: Restate your earnest desire to attend the school in a letter with an updated transcript of your senior year grades and another recommendation. For the abject rejectee, a well-connected college consultant can call schools that are not ultracompetitive this year to see whether they would entertain a late application.

Generally, schools do not see outside counselors as unwanted competition. For parents, no matter how capable the independent is, the school counselor is the indispensable one. He or she must collect all required transcripts and necessary recommendations and forward them to the colleges. In fact, some school counselors argue persuasively that they can represent your child more accurately than an outsider in cases in which they have known the family for years.

Independents respond that generally their one-on-one service is a better assurance of effective follow-through. For example, one consultant called the University of Wisconsin on behalf of a client who had been rejected. The reason given was that Wisconsin wouldn't consider any applicant not in the top half of his or her class, and this student was just barely out of the running. The consultant explained that her client had taken an unusually exacting course load at a high-standards school. Result: Wisconsin accepted the student.

Since the admissions game is likely to grow even more competitive in coming years, you will be wise to choose a consultant almost as carefully as a college. Ask other parents for referrals or call the admissions office at the top college in your area. A fairly trustworthy credential is membership in the National Association of College Admission Counselors (phone 703-836-2222) or the Independent Educational Consultants Association (508-477-2127), both of which set some standards. Many excellent advisers, however, choose not to belong.

In interviewing an adviser, ask how many colleges he or she visited last year. (The answer should be at least 25. Attendance at local college fairs does not count.) Get references from previous clients, and call them to see whether they were satisfied.

How to Slash Your College Debts

Today's tuition almost demands that parents and students borrow. Here are ways to lighten your burden.

Take out your No. 2 pencil, please, and answer this question: *A senior graduating from a private college last year was this much in debt, on average: (A) zero, (B) $2,000, (C) $9,750.*

If you answered (C), you are both correct and painfully aware that the typical four-year cost of tuition, room and board, personal expenses, and transportation at a private college is now $48,000. But if you answered (A), you may be among the few Americans who mas-

tered strategies that can reduce the burden of college loans drastically and sometimes totally. Plenty of debt-cutting tools are available to families, and the supply grows by the semester. To produce a low or no-debt degree:

Bargain hard for the least expensive forms of financial aid. Make your first offensive move when mailing in your application for admission. If you do not see what you want in the way of financial aid at a college, ask for it. Do not assume you will be rejected; even families with six-figure incomes can sometimes qualify for low-cost loans and grants.

Once a child is accepted at a college, the financial aid office will send an aid package describing school grants, loans, and campus work-study programs. Negotiate with the aid officer to substitute grants and work-study for loans. Duke University, Swarthmore College, and others have started student loan-replacement programs. Swarthmore (total cost last year: $15,650) guarantees that students on aid need not borrow more than $2,250 a year. Duke replaces loans of as much as $2,000 a year for needy North Carolina and South Carolina residents.

You can also play off one school against another for better financing deals, says Kalman Chany, who runs Campus Consultants, a college financial planning firm in New York City. Two years ago, a client's son was accepted at both Macalester College in St. Paul and Bennington College in Vermont. Bennington's aid package was more generous, but the student's first choice was Macalester. So his father alerted a Macalester financial aid officer, and the college upped its grant by $1,000 and added $1,500 in work-study. Father and son grabbed Macalester's offer.

Lock in tuition at the freshman rate. With 1988 tuition increases estimated at 6% and a roughly 45% rise since 1980 (adjusted for inflation), a tuition freeze could save you thousands of dollars. Guaranteed-tuition plans come in two versions. At schools such as Luther College in Decorah, Iowa, the freshman rate can be fixed through senior year for a fee, but tuition is still paid annually. Luther charges $950 for this privilege. The other type of plan lets a student lock in the freshman rate by paying all four years up front, as is the case at College of New Rochelle in New York and George Washington University in Washington, D.C. Colleges offering such plans will usually refund most of your unused tuition money if you drop out.

Do some math before committing to a prepayment plan. You will not save money when the cash used for future tuition can earn a higher rate if invested elsewhere. You may

also lack the cash to pay four years' worth of tuition at once.

Shop for tuition breaks. Many schools offer tuition discounts of one form or another. The most common variety is available to students over age 25. If you are in your mid-twenties or older, knock 25% off the $7,200 tuition at Coe College in Cedar Rapids, Iowa. Alumni children of any age can often tug the old school tie. At Upsala College in East Orange, New Jersey, for example, these students get a $250 scholarship. Columbia Christian College in Portland, Oregon lets a student subtract 10% from his $4,433 tuition if he influences another to enroll.

You can sometimes save when you cross state lines. Public colleges often charge out-of-staters at least triple the tuition for state residents. But a network of 56 institutions in Colorado, Nevada, Wyoming, and seven other western states bumps up tuition only 50% for some students from the region. (Arizona, California, Oregon, and Washington do not participate in this program.) Such deals are not exclusive to public education. Morningside College in Sioux City, Iowa offers free room and board (worth $2,230 last year) to top students from outside Iowa and its six bordering states.

Do the college hop. Enroll at a community college or another inexpensive institution, save money, study hard, and then transfer to a high-priced school. Then collect the prestige diploma for about half or two-thirds what it would otherwise have cost. The only catch is that your academic performance must be stellar. Last year, at superselective Stanford University, just 6% of 1,457 transfer applicants were admitted. In their quest for the upwardly mobile, however, the classiest schools are scouting community colleges and other less-selective institutions for star pupils.

Go military. The armed forces are making a comeback on campus for financial if not political reasons. Among the best deals: Reserve Officers Training Corps scholarships sponsored by the U.S. Army, Navy, and Air Force and offered by more than 2,300 colleges. These deals can pay full tuition for two to four years plus other benefits such as books, lab fees, and a $100 monthly stipend. In exchange, you must serve a minimum of eight years after graduation on active duty or in the Reserves—or a combination of the two. The Reserves require four to five months of initial training full time plus one weekend a month and two summer weeks. There are 30,000 applicants for every one of the 5,700 four-year scholarships.

The Army National Guard deserves a 21-gun salute, too. Join while you are in school and pledge a hitch of six years' worth of weekends and summer weeks in exchange for benefits including up to $9,000 of federal loan forgiveness and a monthly stipend of as much as $140. Also, in many states, Guard soldiers can get free tuition or tuition breaks at public colleges.

Have you seen the Army ads in which a college boy and a girl turn out to be veterans? Here's how it works: You can enlist before you enroll in college and earmark $1,200 from your annual Army pay for tuition. Then, after a two-year tour of duty, you collect up to $9,000 from the G.I. bill, plus as much as $8,000 from the Army College Fund if you have served in certain special jobs in, for example, the infantry. Federal budget cuts, however, have forced the Army to begin reducing tuition assistance for enlisted personnel and officers who take off-duty college classes while in uniform.

Being a veteran can help a student qualify for additional financial aid. When a vet applies to a college, the aid process classifies him or her as an independent student. Aid eligibility is then based on the student's income and assets, which presumably are more limited than his parents'.

Serve the community and save. Students on aid sometimes feel obliged to go for high-paying part-time jobs rather than do volunteer or social-service work. Many colleges are attacking this problem with cash. At the University of Rochester, where last year's total cost was a staggering $16,054, two dozen students on aid won additional scholarships of $2,500 a year in a community-oriented program called Reach. For example, a junior psychology major who hopes to become a doctor works 20 hours a

week with abused and neglected children at a local community center. Reach will cover his $2,500 student loan—and subsidize his wages of $5 an hour. He will graduate this year only $7,000 in debt from one of the priciest schools in the U.S.

Capitalize on the teacher shortage. California, Florida, New York, and more than 30 other states sponsor loan-forgiveness programs for future teachers, especially of science, math, and foreign languages. Students can come from out of state. In Florida, juniors and seniors can borrow $4,000 a year if they attend Florida schools that the state approves, and after graduation they won't owe a penny if they teach in the state's public schools for four years. The repayment period can be halved to two years by teaching in a targeted school, usually an inner-city or rural one. Also check out aid to future teachers at schools such as Hampden-Sydney College in Virginia and Trinity University in San Antonio.

Get a job. Visit your student employment office—a new power center on many campuses that can help slice a huge chunk out of your debt. At the University of Minnesota, the office acts as broker for a giant work force of 14,000 students in part-time campus jobs that typically pay up to $6.25 an hour. The employment office is also the contact point for the hundreds of private companies that are stepping up their hiring of collegiate part-timers. A longtime recruiter is United Parcel Service, with some 75,000 students in positions from package sorter to supervisor. The starting UPS hourly wage is $8.

An old favorite is to go co-op. More than 1,000 schools sponsor cooperative education programs, up from 300 in 1972. Students sign up for paid jobs related to their field of study, usually alternating semesters between classroom and workplace. Most programs last four years. Last year co-op students earned an average of $7,000, according to the National Commission for Cooperative Education.

Beginning this fall, however, working your way through school could reduce other forms of aid. Previously, financial aid officers usually had to add $700 a year ($900 for upperclassmen) of a student's earnings to his family's income when determining how much aid the family could get. Under the new rules, a student is expected to add in 70% of his after-tax earnings if they exceed that threshold. In other words, if you will earn $4,000 from a summer job, your expected contribution to your education will be $2,800, not $700 or $900. This new reckoning could dock you in aid. But, of course, the more money you earn from a part-time job, the less you need to borrow.

Unbundle your college costs. Pick and choose what you will pay for, if possible. The classic technique is to avoid paying for college room and board and fend for yourself more cheaply off campus. Now you may find opportunities for tuition savings, too. The University of Detroit, for example, has begun charging undergrads according to curriculum with a system

known as differential pricing. The school's theory: You should pay for the true cost of the education you get. For instance, a University of Detroit liberal arts student pays $6,900 in tuition while an architecture student owes $7,700. Other schools that permit customized tuition include Columbia University in New York City, DePaul University in Chicago, and Valparaiso University in Indiana.

Attend off-peak. Like airlines discounting fares on their emptier flights, many colleges offer cut-rate tuitions at times when demand is light or their costs are less. Evening classes for sociology and business majors are nearly 70% below day tuition at Furman University in Greenville, South Carolina. At Drury College in Springfield, Missouri, night courses can save you roughly 50% per credit hour. Also, many colleges are cheaper during the summer.

Save at Least $143 a Month for Your Baby's College

The earlier you start a college fund for a child, the better off you will be. The table shows how much you would have to save each month, starting when children are different ages, to pay the entire cost of a B.A. in the future; the portfolio strategy column tells the best way to invest those savings. The table is

based on the current annual cost of tuition, room and board, and other expenses at the average public ($5,800), private ($12,000) and Ivy League ($18,500) schools. The figures assume that college costs will rise a steep but steady 6% a year and that your investments will earn 7% annually.

	Public college	Private college	Ivy League college	Portfolio strategy
Newborn	$143	$296	$457	Start with growth stocks and growth mutual funds that you will hold for at least a decade.
Age 3	$158	$328	$506	Add zero-coupon Treasury bonds that will mature during your child's college years.
Age 6	$180	$372	$575	Diversify with conservative funds and stocks such as utilities. Buy Series EE Savings Bonds. Also, buy a single-premium life insurance policy that you can borrow against.
Age 9	$212	$439	$678	
Age 12	$266	$551	$850	Gradually sell stocks and stock funds. Buy fixed-income investments such as certificates of deposit and money funds so that you will have ready money for bursar's bills.
Age 15	$374	$774	$1,195	

Dealing with a Divorce

The shock can be compounded by financial stress—unless you prepare first.

Divorce can mean more than emotional hardship. In most cases, ex-couples find they need to rebuild shattered finances as well as their lives. The cost can be high for both parties, including legal fees and the expense of maintaining separate households. And while no-fault divorce laws in some states have eliminated the need to prove that one partner has misbehaved, questions of property and support have become trickier than ever.

The cost of your divorce will depend upon the kind of lawyer you retain and how much time he has to put into your case. The meters of most lawyers tick at $150 to $250 an hour. At a nationwide legal clinic such as Jacoby & Meyers, a simple uncontested divorce will cost about $500; a divorce with complex property arrangements can run to $3,000 or more for each spouse.

You may be able to avoid lawyers entirely by using one of the do-it-yourself divorce kits found at many bookstores. They usually provide sample settlement agreements and tell you how to file petitions and other documents. But such kits probably are suitable for those couples who have been married fewer than five years, have no children, and have less than $50,000 in assets.

If you don't meet the do-it-yourself criteria, you most likely will need the help of a lawyer to arrange the division of property, custody, and support set forth in the settlement agreement. This agreement must be reviewed by the court, which will generally approve it if it conforms to state law and produces a fair result.

(For a review of the idiosyncrasies of state laws, see the listing beginning on page 122.) A competent attorney should know what you can expect to get in your state and—sometimes aided by an accountant—may be able to help you and your spouse structure a settlement that would save money on taxes. (For a guide to divorce under the new federal tax law, see page 125.)

You and your soon-to-be ex can limit the amount of legal talent you pay for by avoiding contentiousness. Clients must pay for time their lawyers spend haggling on their behalf, and if no agreement is reached, the couple will have to wage an expensive court battle. Thus, you and your spouse should attempt to settle as many issues as possible on your own before bringing the legal team into the fray. You can cut legal bills further by trying divorce mediation, a relatively new, nonadversarial procedure. In mediation, a neutral party helps the husband and wife work out an agreement that is later taken to their respective attorneys, who review it and translate it into legalese. Trained mediators charge between $50 and $150 an hour for six to eight one- or two-hour sessions. You should be able to find a qualified mediator by getting in touch with the American Arbitration Association, which has offices in 33 cities. A referral costs $125. In California and in some other places, judges will refer you to court mediators to help resolve custody and visitation disputes. There is usually no charge for mediation in those instances.

Where you live will have considerable

influence on the shape of your divorce. In some states, each spouse's entitlement is spelled out in statute, and agreements should be structured accordingly. In other states, legal precedent is your only guide to drawing up an agreement that will pass muster with the court. Judges have a great deal of latitude in interpreting the law, especially in states where there are few governing statutes. In such states it is particularly important for you to arrive at a settlement with your spouse; without one, a judge may impose a compromise whose terms you object to completely.

Only one state, Mississippi, sorts out property according to title—that is, whoever has his or her name on the asset generally gets to keep it. In California and eight other so-called community property states, assets are supposed to be divided fifty-fifty. Most states have adopted instead the equitable-distribution formula to split assets. Such states require a fair—though not necessarily equal—division of marital property. Fairness is determined by a number of factors, including the length of the marriage, the financial contribution each partner has made, the age of the two parties, and their ability to earn money on their own. Most states exclude from division any property acquired before the marriage and bequests and gifts made specifically to one of the partners.

Unfortunately for women, laws requiring equitable distribution have been anything but fair for full-time homemakers who cannot prove that they have contributed, say, 50% of the down payment and the mortgage payments on the house. To correct that imbalance, many states have begun giving weight in dividing property to so-called nonmonetary homemaker contributions—in other words, the labor of running a household and raising children. In some states, women and their lawyers have been able to claim what's known as career assets, which may include a cut of a spouse's business, retirement plan, or professional degree.

A settlement may also have to make a provision for alimony—invariably for the wife—and child support. Generally, both parents are expected to share in paying child support in accordance with their ability and means. Each state, though, has its own complex formula for determining who pays what. The settlement agreement should determine which parent pays for camp, private schooling, travel between the two parents, and other extras. As a rule, child support stops when a child reaches the age of 18 (in some states 21). But if both parents are college graduates, a court may require the wealthier parent to pay the expense of the kids' higher education.

In recent years, courts have become rather stingy in granting alimony. Once upon a time, ex-wives could look forward to years of steady payments until they remarried or died—and in some states and under certain circumstances, they still can. But these days alimony seldom lasts longer than five years, and wives who are young, healthy, and weren't married five to 10 years usually don't get alimony at all. Some states allow so-called rehabilitative alimony, however, to spouses who don't meet the criteria for ordinary alimony. Rehabilitative alimony is paid until the nonworking spouse can support herself, though not necessarily in the style to which she was accustomed. The court may order it paid only until the nonworking spouse gets specific training or else finds a job.

Any wife who does get traditional-style alimony should try to have her lawyer include an income escalator in the settlement agreement. That would entitle the wife to a share in her former husband's future raises. The settlement agreement should also require the person paying alimony to take out life and disability insurance so that income will continue no matter what. An agreement can require one partner to provide health and life insurance to cover the former spouse and kids. Under federal law, health and life coverage provided by your spouse's employer may be continued at group rates for up to 36 months after a divorce, regardless of whether you or your spouse pays for it. The law doesn't apply if you are covered by another group plan.

Finally, divorced people should avoid spending all of their settlement money on living expenses. Instead, they should reserve some assets for a future objective—buying a house, educating the kids, or even going back to school themselves.

When a Marriage Ends

Confusion about how to proceed when spouses call it quits can add to the pain of divorce. The following checklist, devised with the help of lawyers, financial planners, and family counselors, can ease the transition to single life.

While you and your partner are just thinking about a divorce:

● Start putting away savings in an account of your own. This will give you ready cash in the event that your spouse suddenly stops contributing to household bills.

● If you do not already have credit in your own name, get it. Apply for credit cards, and, if necessary, have a friend or relative other than your spouse cosign a small bank loan.

● Make an inventory of all separately and jointly owned assets, including investments, cars, and furniture. This tally, along with an enumeration of outstanding debts, may be necessary to determine a division of property. Have your bank verify a list of the contents of any joint safe-deposit box.

Once you have decided to get a divorce:

● Notify banks and brokerages where you and your spouse have joint accounts of your intent to divorce. Ask that no brokerage transactions be carried out without the written approval of both you and your spouse.

● Close out joint charge accounts, or, if you wish to keep the accounts open, notify the creditors in writing that you will no longer be responsible for your spouse's purchases.

● Try to negotiate an agreement with your spouse on the division of assets, child support, and visitation rights. If you want child support or alimony, work out a budget of your monthly and yearly expenses that your lawyer can use to make your case.

● Collect the names of experienced divorce lawyers from friends, the state or county bar association, or other attorneys. Interview at least two candidates. By all means, question them about their fees.

After the divorce decree becomes final:

● If you haven't already done so, rewrite your will to name an heir other than your spouse.

● Review your health, life, and disability insurance coverage. Change the beneficiaries on policies you own unless your settlement requires you to continue to protect your ex. Replace any needed protection you have lost.

A State-by-State Guide to Today's Divorce Laws

What follows is a look at the idiosyncrasies of divorce statutes and case law in the 50 states. Initials denote whether a state goes by equitable distribution (ED), community property (CP), or title (T) in dividing marital assets.

Alabama (ED) Property acquired by one partner before marriage regularly used by both partners during marriage may be divided. Marital misconduct may bar alimony. A spouse may be forced to pay for a child's private schooling.

Alaska (ED) The court may award property acquired before marriage by one partner to the other. A spouse's nonmonetary contribution to a family business may be weighed in dividing property.

Arizona (CP) A spouse may be compensated for financing a mate's professional education. Alimony may fluctuate with the payer's income.

Arkansas (ED) A homemaker's nonmonetary contribution may be considered when dividing property. Marital misconduct may affect the settlement. Alimony may not automatically be cut off upon remarriage.

California (CP) A spouse can receive property in compensation for financing a partner's professional degree. Cohabitation ends or modifies alimony.

Colorado (ED) Property division is decided first, and that determines whether alimony is granted. An increase in the value of separate assets may be considered marital property subject to division. Rehabilitative alimony may be awarded.

Connecticut (ED) Marital misconduct is considered in the division of property. A parent cannot be required later to contribute to the college education of an adult child unless the obligation is spelled out in the initial divorce decree.

Delaware (ED) A gift or inheritance received by one partner during marriage may be considered joint property. A homemaker's contribution may be considered in property division. Alimony is limited to two years if a couple was married less than 20 years.

Florida (ED) Courts have wide discretion over distribution of property. Homemaker contributions and marital misconduct are considered in property division. Rehabilitative alimony is generally awarded for marriages of short duration.

Georgia (ED) Only dependent spouses can collect alimony. Marital misconduct can bar alimony.

Hawaii (ED) The division of joint and separate property such as retirement benefits, gifts and bequests is left up to the court.

Idaho (CP) Marital misconduct may reduce or elim-inate the guilty party's share of the community property. Otherwise, division should be roughly equal.

Illinois (ED) Courts usually prefer to settle spousal claims through property division rather than alimony. Homemaker contributions may be considered in division of property.

Indiana (ED) The court may award property for financial contribution toward a spouse's higher education. Rehabilitative alimony is usually awarded for only three years.

Iowa (ED) Homemaker contributions are considered in division of property. A court may order either spouse to set aside property for a child. Child support may be tied to the consumer price index. A parent may be required to pay college expenses until the child is 22.

Kansas (ED) Property acquired by either party before or during marriage, including gifts and bequests, is subject to division. Spousal support may be awarded initially for no longer than 121 months, although extensions of up to 121 months may be granted.

Kentucky (ED) A professional degree is not marital property. Unless the court specifically reserves the power to modify alimony, it cannot be changed at a later date.

Louisiana (CP) Marital misconduct may bar alimony. A partner without fault and without sufficient means for support may be granted alimony, but only up to one-third of ex-spouse's income.

Maine (ED) Court has wide discretion in setting alimony awards. Homemaker contributions can be considered in division of property.

Maryland (ED) Homemaker contributions may be considered in property division. Cohabitation ends or modifies alimony. Recipients may have to share military pensions or other retirement benefits with the ex-spouse.

Massachusetts (ED) Division of property is left to the court and may include assets acquired before marriage. A court may order either parent to educate child until 21 years of age.

Michigan (ED) Courts may divide property acquired before marriage, including gifts and bequests. Marital misconduct is a factor in determining alimony. Child support may fluctuate with the payer's income.

Minnesota (ED) Homemaker sacrifices such as foregone job earnings and experience may affect settlements. A spouse may be compensated for financing a professional education. Courts may grant rehabilitative alimony.

Mississippi (T) Legal title to property does not change after divorce; thus, one spouse cannot force the sale of an asset such as the family home that is owned in joint tenancy.

Missouri (ED) Homemaker contributions in a

long marriage may be considered equal to those of a breadwinner. Both partners may have a claim on income that is produced by separate property.

Montana (ED) All property, including inheritance, gifts, and assets acquired before marriage, are subject to division. Homemaker contributions may be considered in property division.

Nebraska (ED) A spouse may be compensated with property for contributing to the other's professional degree. Retirement benefits may be considered marital assets.

Nevada (CP) The court has wide discretion over alimony awards. An alimony award may take into account any nonvested retirement benefits.

New Hampshire (ED) Marital misconduct may be considered in awarding alimony and dividing joint and separate property. Rehabilitative alimony is usually granted in cases where there are no children or where children have reached age 18. The court can order a parent to finance a child's college education.

New Jersey (ED) Division of property and spousal support is left up to the court. A spouse may be compensated for financing professional education with so-called reimbursement alimony.

New Mexico (CP) Unvested retirement benefits may be divided. Alimony awards are left to the discretion of the court, but the

previous standard of living of the dependent spouse is an important factor.

New York (ED) The supporting parent's duty to provide a college education for children may extend only to state schools or universities. A spouse may be compensated with alimony or property for financing a professional degree.

North Carolina (ED) A spouse may be compensated for financing a professional degree with a property award. If spouses have sexual intercourse with each other after execution of a separation agreement, they may void the contract. Alimony may not be payable to an adulterer.

North Dakota (ED) The court may consider marital misconduct when determining alimony awards and property division. Property may be distributed regardless of its ownership. Alimony is left up to the court.

Ohio (ED) Courts have wide discretion in dividing property acquired during marriage. A spouse may be compensated with property and alimony for financing a professional education. Cohabitation usually ends or modifies alimony.

Oklahoma (ED) Property held by either spouse prior to the marriage is not subject to division. Spouse may be entitled to some share of an ex-mate's earnings in exchange for financing a professional degree.

Oregon (ED) A dependent spouse's need to im-

prove earning capacity is considered in determining alimony. Alimony may be terminated after 10 years if the recipient makes no effort to become self-supporting. Child support may stop if a minor marries, supports himself, or leaves school.

Pennsylvania (ED) Homemaker contributions are taken into account in alimony awards and property division. Marital misconduct is considered in alimony awards.

Rhode Island (ED) Marital misconduct is considered by the court when awarding alimony or dividing property. Rehabilitative alimony is available. Adultery may bar alimony.

South Carolina (ED) Courts give weight to title when dividing property. Marital misconduct may bar alimony.

South Dakota (ED) Property acquired before marriage may be subject to division. Rehabilitative alimony is awarded.

Tennessee (ED) A settlement may compensate a spouse for financing a professional degree or for a homemaker contribution. Courts prefer to award only rehabilitative alimony.

Texas (CP) Alimony does not exist. The court may order both parents to support a child until the age of 18.

Utah (ED) Retirement benefits may be divisible marital assets. If the spouse paying alimony can prove an ex-mate cohabits and has sexual intercourse with a person of the opposite sex, then the alimony automatically terminates.

Vermont (ED) A spouse may be compensated with property for financing a professional degree. Homemaker contributions may be considered in division of property. Courts may award rehabilitative alimony.

Virginia (ED) Vested and nonvested pensions and profit sharing may be considered divisible joint assets. Adulterous spouses may receive permanent alimony. Courts have discretion to

order support until a child reaches 19 or graduates from high school, whichever comes first.

Washington (CP) Retirement benefits may be subject to division. Homemaker contributions are weighed in making alimony awards.

West Virginia (ED) The court may consider the value of the labor performed in a family business when dividing property. An adulterous spouse may not receive any alimony.

Wisconsin (CP) A spouse's separate inheritances or gifts may be

awarded to the other to prevent hardship. Homemaker contributions are weighed in dividing property. A spouse may be compensated with property and alimony for financing a professional degree. But cohabitation with a member of the opposite sex could lower any alimony payments.

Wyoming (ED) Property awards are favored over alimony. The court may order part of child support payable to a court appointed trustee who will invest the money and apply income toward support of the child.

Splitting Up the Tax Bill

To carve up family assets and income fairly, you have to know their true worth *after* taxes. Here's how it all sorts out:

Alimony. It is deductible for the person who pays and taxable to the recipient. New tax rules make it easier to reclassify a property settlement as alimony. It is usually in a divorcing couple's interest to do that, since a property settlement generates no tax deduction.

Starting in 1984, to claim $10,000 or more in alimony in a given year, you had to be obligated under your settlement to pay that amount every year for six years. Under the 1986 law, though, payments need continue for only three years and can decline by as much as $15,000 a year. Those who divorced under the old 1984 rules may elect to be covered by the current law.

Property settlements. Before 1985, transfer of property in a divorce was treated as a sale. Now, however, exchanges are treated as gifts, and neither party pays taxes upon divorce. But the taxes will have to be paid eventually making a highly appreciated asset worth less than the recipient might think. If Dee Diddle sells the stock a year after her divorce, she will have

to pay taxes on any profits over the original price. But if Dee had pressed for the family home instead of the stock, she could have cut her taxes when she sold by rolling the profits over into a new house within two years, or perhaps by taking advantage of the $125,000 capital-gains exclusion for those over age 55.

Child support. This is neither deductible for the person who pays nor taxable to the person who receives it. The IRS will be watching for child support masked as alimony. If it is determined that money called alimony is really intended to support a child, the deduction will be lost. Therefore, alimony should not be lumped with child support in a settlement agreement.

Exemptions for the kids used to be taken routinely by the parent in the higher bracket, even if he or she didn't have custody. As long as that partner paid more than 50% of a child's support or the former spouse signed a waiver, he or she could qualify for the exemption. Now, however, the parent in the lower bracket may be the only one who can take the exemptions. Reason: Dependents' exemptions were phased out in 1988 for single taxpayers with incomes of more than $89,560.

Coping with a Spouse's Death

You can take steps to minimize the financial pain.

The death of a spouse deals an especially severe financial blow when a family loses a breadwinner. Even when a family's standard of living isn't threatened by a spouse's death, the survivor must contend with financial tasks and decisions that would be difficult in the best of times. There are, however, steps that can be taken—while both partners are alive as well as after one is gone—that may limit the financial headaches.

A routine analysis of life insurance needs, which any financial planner or insurance agent can perform, should determine whether your family has adequate protection. Such an analysis uses a couple's current budget to calculate the income a surviving spouse would need to live on. In addition to having enough insurance, it is essential that both spouses develop proficiency in handling the family finances. Both husbands and wives should know how much it costs to run their household, how much they owe, how their money is invested, and where to find important documents.

Planning will help, but nothing can prepare you for the emotional shock of your spouse's death. Judith Brown and Christina Baldwin, authors of *Second Start* (Fireside/Simon & Schuster, $7.95), warn new widows to expect to have difficulty concentrating, being objective, and visualizing long-term goals. Thus, if circumstances allow, try to postpone important financial decisions for six months to a year.

In the meantime, focus only on the details that require immediate attention. For example, debts the two of you assumed jointly, such as your mortgage, are now your sole responsi-

bility. If you fail to pay, it could affect your credit rating. In the first weeks of widowhood, you should ask your attorney to start the process of probating your spouse's will. Get in touch with your insurance agent, your spouse's employer, and your local Social Security office to claim any death benefits. (For more on what to do, see the box on page 127.) You also may be entitled to money from less obvious sources. For example, you might be able to claim life insurance benefits from a spouse's union or fraternal organization. Some of your spouse's debts, including the mortgage, auto loan, and credit-card balances, may include an insurance rider that pays off the loan at death.

If you have trouble locating important documents, look for clues by going through your spouse's checkbook. An entry made out to a lawyer, for example, may guide you to your spouse's will; the lawyer may have it on file. Investment assets you may not have been aware of would show up on your spouse's most recent tax return if they produced any income. If you suspect that your spouse may have life insurance policies that you can't find, you can write the American Council of Life Insurance (Policy Search, ACLI, 1001 Pennsylvania Ave. N.W., Washington, D.C. 20004), including a self-addressed, stamped envelope, and request that member companies search their files. The service, which should take six weeks, is free.

Among the complicated financial questions you should postpone is whether to sell your house. Grown children may urge you to relocate near them, or you may feel that your house is just too big or too full of painful memories. But experts say stay put for at least six months. You shouldn't make permanent decisions about what is probably your most valuable asset until the emotional roller-coaster ride is over.

You should be able to collect your inheritance in four months to three years and, in most cases, life insurance proceeds will roll in within a month. Park any excess cash you receive in the bank for at least six months. That might not be as easy as it sounds; you can expect to be bombarded with advice on how to invest the money. Be on your guard for scam artists. In a typical ploy, a salesman phones asking for your spouse and then, on hearing that your spouse is deceased, claims that before he died he was planning to invest in whatever it is the salesman is hawking.

Just as insidious as outright fraud is incompetent advice from friends and relatives. They may tout some investment that may have done well for them but that is completely inappropriate for you. Financial planners sometimes suggest one way to lock away an insurance payout is to split it among four bank certificates of deposit maturing in three, six, nine, and 12 months. As each certificate comes due, you can roll it over or make a more permanent investment. The gradual roll-out will encourage you to diversify and prevent you from acting impulsively. Meanwhile, you can tell people, "Thanks for your advice, but my money is tied up right now."

One reason widows are often so susceptible

When a Spouse Dies

After a partner's death, the widowed spouse must attend to numerous financial details, including these principal ones.

In the first days after the death:
● Try to find directions for the funeral. They may be in the will or a separate letter.
● Order a dozen certified copies of the death certificate from the county clerk's office or the funeral director. Cost: about $5 each. You will need them to claim death benefits and Social Security and to retitle joint assets.
● Have someone stay at home during the funeral. Burglars read obituaries to learn when a house will be unoccupied.

Within the first two weeks:
● Have your attorney review the will and file it in probate court.
● Collect the documents needed to claim death benefits and to value the estate. These include bank, employee-benefits, and brokerage statements, your marriage certificate and both of your birth certificates.
● Apply for death benefits. Call your insurance agent, your spouse's employer, and your local Social Security office.

Within the first month:
● Keep a record of your cash flow. This will help determine where you stand financially.
● As insurance and other benefits come in, set aside the money in short-term bank certificates of deposit. That will buy you time to think about the best way to invest the money for the long term.

Within the first six months:
● Review your own will and change beneficiary designations on insurance policies or retirement plans that name your spouse. Also change names on joint billing accounts or credit cards.
● If you are executor or administrator of the estate, notify creditors and satisfy debts. Be careful: Sending phony debt notices is a favorite con game. Check bills and refer suspicious claims to your lawyer.

Between six months and a year:
● If you are executor or administrator you must pay any taxes the estate owes. File federal estate taxes within nine months of the death if the estate is larger than $600,000. You must also pay the estate's income taxes, due April 15, every year the estate is open.
● Start to plan for your future. Begin to make decisions you have postponed, including whether to sell your home and how to invest your inheritance.

to bad advice is that they fear they don't have enough money to support themselves. Some, of course, do not, and they may have to join the work force or scale down their standard of living. But often, a widow or widower is simply too distraught or financially inexperienced to evaluate his or her circumstances objectively. The solution is to track your outgo for four to six months. Compare that with your income from all sources and you will know whether to cut back or breathe easily.

After six months to a year, you can begin to set long-term goals and make the financial decisions that will help you achieve them: whether to move, how to invest insurance proceeds, and how to readjust an inherited portfolio. It is also time to review your will and re-examine your insurance needs.

If you weren't working when your spouse died, think about getting a job. Be realistic, though. If you have dreams about starting your own business with your inheritance, note that two-thirds of small businesses fail within five years. On the other hand, getting back into the world is probably the best therapy—emotionally, socially, and financially.

Power of Attorney

The day may come when you need to give others authority to handle your money.

A power of attorney is a legal document naming another person to act in your behalf in the event that you are temporarily out of reach or become mentally incompetent. Drawing up a power of attorney should be part of the estate plan of almost anyone. If you have not given someone power of attorney and you become incapacitated, your next of kin must get permission from probate court to act as your conservator or guardian. This can cost at least $300 to $500 in legal fees and take as long as three months.

There are different types of powers of attorney. Each is a two- or three-page document for which lawyers charge $35 to $100. Sometimes it is wise to set up a trust as well.

General power of attorney. This version lets you name another person to act as your agent in business or financial matters when you know you will be away. It becomes void, however, if you are incapacitated. So it is useless as a precaution against most of life's unpredictable setbacks.

Durable power of attorney. This is the form you should use to make provision for the possibility of serious illness, disappearance, or even kidnapping. It is usually signed when you write your will, but it takes effect immediately. It is called durable because it remains operative as long as you live, unless you revoke it. The person you designate can sign checks against your accounts, sell and buy securities and real estate, even run your business.

You don't ordinarily file the durable power document with a court. You just give it to the person to whom you have assigned the power or instruct your lawyer to do that if you become disabled. Those most often named are trusted relatives or friends or the family lawyer. Make sure to inform the person you wish to designate. If he or she should turn out later to be unwilling to act in your behalf, the whole issue will be thrown into court. You can protect yourself by choosing a backup person just in case your first choice becomes incapacitated.

Whomever you choose, there is at least a

theoretical risk that the power will be abused. In the worst case, a concerned friend or relative, seeing your assets squandered, could only go to probate court and ask to be named your conservator. One acceptable safeguard is to have the lawyer assign durable power of attorney jointly to two people in such a way that neither can act alone.

Although the laws governing use of the durable power of attorney vary slightly from state to state, all but Georgia, Louisiana, Oklahoma, and Wyoming recognize it. Banks and brokerages, however, may be less cooperative. In practice, most honor a durable power of attorney. But some require you to execute their own separate power-of-attorney forms before they will let others transact business for you or admit them to your safe-deposit box.

Springing power of attorney. This version of the durable power of attorney is so named because, as a safeguard against someone misusing the power, it springs into effect only if you are incapacitated. The person you designate cannot use it without a physician's statement attesting that you are out of commission. The springing power of attorney is also recognized in most states. While it may ease the mind of an elderly mother who is worried that her prodigal son will abscond with the family fortune, most lawyers consider it a less desirable instrument than an immediate power because the springing power of attorney may be less acceptable at financial institutions. A bank or brokerage, for example, might refuse to accept a physician's statement that you are incapacitated unless it is ordered to by a judge.

In some circumstances, it is advisable to combine a durable power of attorney with a living trust. Some examples: If your wealth is substantial enough to warrant professional management, if you are the key person in a family business, or if you have no spouse or child who would be capable of managing your affairs. Banks and brokerage houses, long familiar with trusts, feel on surer ground with them than they do dealing with a power of attorney alone.

You may immediately endow a living trust with your assets, or you may leave it empty but assign someone durable power of attorney with instructions to pour all your money into it if you are declared incompetent. Meanwhile, you can control its assets by specifying that the trust is revocable. You can receive the income from the trust, which will be taxable to you, and when you die the assets will pass to your heirs without going through probate.

The main advantage, though, is that you can name a secondary trustee, such as a bank or trust company, to assume investment responsibilities if you can no longer handle them. The lawyer's bill for setting up this kind of trust will run as high as $1,000. Furthermore, big banks often will not consider being trustees for amounts under $300,000. Their fee is usually 1% of the assets a year.

Trusts and durable powers of attorney should be reviewed and updated, along with your will, every five years or so. The documents themselves, if not given to the person designated to handle your financial affairs, should be filed with your personal papers. Also store a copy in your safe-deposit box, making sure your designated agent or trustee has a power of attorney to open the box.

Key Legal Terms

You may come across the following when you draw up durable power of attorney, set up a living trust, or appear before a probate court:

Agent: The person or institution to whom you give the power of attorney, also called the attorney-in-fact.

Competency hearing: Held before the probate court, it establishes whether an individual is incompetent to manage his or her affairs.

Inter vivos trust: Known also as a living trust, it can become a repository for the assets of a disabled person, and a trustee can be named to manage those assets.

Principal: The person who grants his or her power of attorney to the agent.

Probate court: The state court that decides estate matters and approves conservatorships or guardianships. In some states it is called surrogate's court.

Is an HMO Right for You?

Your company may ask you to join one. But with three in four posting losses, a healthy HMO could be hard to find.

Last year, 40 pediatricians and 35 family practitioners, disgruntled over their fees, pulled out of North Carolina's largest health maintenance organization (HMO), the 16,206-member Raleigh Blue Cross Personal Care Plan. The increasing incidence of such service brownouts has dimmed the once bright promise of HMOs—comprehensive medical care at a fixed and affordable monthly rate. At the heart of the matter is the failing financial health of these organizations. Nearly three-quarters of them are operating at a loss. In 1987, at least 16 of the 662 plans in operation merged with sturdier ones or closed outright. Some subscribers are being forced out of their HMOs by punishing rate increases levied to staunch the flow of red ink.

Insurance experts and state regulators see more shake-outs in the future in cities such as Denver, Minneapolis, New Orleans, Raleigh/ Durham, and St. Louis, where competition for HMO subscribers has suppressed premiums to below the cost of care.

Although only 13% of Americans hold memberships, the consequences of the HMO's problems are more insidious than you might think. Employers, goaded by insurers who are worried about exploding health-care costs, have been turning more and more to HMOs and similar restricted-service options and away from traditional free-choice plans that let you pick your own doctor.

Between 1984 and 1987, for instance, free-choice plans dropped from 96% to 40% of insurers' group business, according to Health Insurance Association of America, a trade group of health insurers. Faced with insurance rate increases averaging 20% a year, employees have been switching to HMOs. Over the next year or so, according to analysts, total HMO enrollment of nearly 30 million people—96% of them under company plans— will rise by 10% while the number of plans shrinks by an equal 10%.

With all the drawbacks, are HMOs still worth the trouble? The answer is, ultimately, yes; at the moment, maybe. The concept is undeniably attractive. By paying hospitals and doctors under yearly contracts, rather than by fees per patient, HMOs can provide economical health care. In return for this service, you agree to give up only one thing—your unlimited choice of doctors.

HMOs can save you money—up to 28%, in fact—compared with traditional health insurance. Monthly premiums at an HMO average $232 for families and $87 for individuals. That's about the same as standard insurance. The difference is that HMOs cover virtually all medical costs. Insurance almost always has deductibles and requires you to pay a percentage, generally 20%, of most bills.

These cost comparisons, however, gloss over certain complications. In order to contain costs, HMOs may make you wait longer for an appointment with a doctor, discourage you from entering a hospital, and limit the number of tests and other services you receive. Not everyone is happy with a system of medicine with limits. If you object to anything less than lavish health service, an HMO isn't for you.

Yet, it is far from an all-or-nothing choice. The original HMOs, and those that still tend to be the most successful, employ only salaried staff doctors who work together under one roof. Later came the independent practice association, which is now the format of the majority of plans. In this type of HMO, doctors in private practice agree to treat some HMO members in their offices along with their regular fee-paying patients. The catch is that doctors in private practice have less incentive to control costs, since their reimbursement from HMOs is usually a small portion of their income.

Until the mid-1980s, failures to contain costs and control doctors were covered by rising revenues from new members. Then, as the market became saturated, the losses began to mount with no prospect of subsiding soon. At worst, this means that subscribers lose insurance coverage when their HMO goes bankrupt. Federal law provides the subscribers with the slimmest protection: Newly defunct HMOs must continue to provide coverage for one month (six months for Medicare recipients). After that, patients must transfer to other insurance. And coverage can be interrupted for months before a switch is completed.

Government supervision hasn't been much help either. About half of all HMOs have qualified with the Health Care Financing Administration, which administers Medicare, to take Medicare patients. Such an HMO is expected to follow a list of rules. For instance, it must carry insurance in case of insolvency to cover subscribers' outstanding medical bills and the cost of completing treatment that is already in progress. The HMO must also include clauses in its contracts with doctors and hospitals proscribing them from seeking payments directly from patients if the HMO cannot pay its bills.

No one knows how many federally qualified HMOs live up even to these standards because the number of government auditors is too small to guarantee compliance. Indeed, stories abound of impatient doctors and hospitals dunning patients for money owed by their HMOs. And the biggest HMO failure of all time—that of the International Medical Cen-

ters in Florida in 1987—involved a federally qualified chain. The 170,000 members of the bankrupt HMO went back on Medicare or, with government help, found new HMOs to join.

HMOs that don't qualify for Medicare patients are subject only to state supervision. Every state but Alaska, Hawaii, Oregon, and Wisconsin has laws that call vaguely for a sound financial plan as a prerequisite for the approval of a new HMO. Unfortunately, many of the regulators' assumptions about what it takes to maintain services—and, therefore, solvency—have been confounded by massive losses and zooming medical costs. Yet, only five states (Alabama, Illinois, North Dakota, Utah, and Wisconsin) have established guaranty funds to pay the outstanding obligations of a closed-down HMO, assuring that patients will not be dunned for bills. Even this has caused an outcry among HMOs, which would be assessed to contribute to the funds. Their objections are that well-run plans would wind up subsidizing the mistakes of poorly run ones.

It is anyone's guess when HMOs will be up and about again. In the meantime, setbacks of varying size are bound to continue, bringing inconvenience and expense to many people. For example, the Honeywell Corporation in Minneapolis abruptly discontinued its nine-year-old HMO option in 1987. The company cited its inability to get accurate data from the HMOs on how premium money was spent. Employees whose health bills were fully covered under the HMO option now have no choice but to pay 20% of medical bills up to a maximum of $1,000 for their own expenses and up to $3,000 for family members.

Though no subscriber is immune to trouble when an HMO gets into financial difficulty, individuals and the elderly are particularly vulnerable. Some 18% of the 161 HMOs that accepted Medicare subscribers in 1986 decided that government reimbursement was inadequate and refused to sign up these older members again in 1987. That forced 53,000 of them to find new HMOs or return to their more expensive and less comprehensive regular Medicare coverage.

Cutting the Cost of Your Coverage

How much insurance is enough?

Mastering the insurance market is like committing the intricacies of the city bus system to memory. It can be useful, but not something you would advertise at cocktail parties. But even though picking the right insurance policy may be a tedious task, unless you at least become familiar with some basics, you may risk exposing yourself to financial catastrophe. The first step is discerning how much insurance you need. When you buy a policy, you are paying the insurer to assume the risk that disaster will strike. If you can afford to cover at least part of the risk on your own, you don't need as much insurance.

The guidelines at right will help you figure what coverage your family requires. Parents need be especially careful, for example, to buy adequate life insurance for the sake of their children, while retirees may want to buy extra life insurance to protect the surviving spouse. Self-employed people should budget at least $1,000 annually—more if you have children—for a sturdy shield of health insurance.

Once you know how much you need, it's time to go shopping. Try to talk to at least four companies. This is where the chore gets ugly, because insurance agents are reluctant to disclose policy information over the phone. When the Consumer Federation of America, a consumer interest lobbying group in Washington, D.C., called 206 agents in late 1986 and asked them to send cost comparison figures, only 11% came through with the material.

A good place to start is with the following companies which consistently offer good service and competitive prices, according to the National Insurance Consumer Organization in Alexandria, Virginia: USAA Life of San Antonio, Texas for life insurance; Blue Cross/Blue Shield for health; Northwestern Mutual of Milwaukee for disability; and State Farm of Bloomington, Illinois for auto, homeowners and umbrella liability insurance.

One way to simplify the process is to seek independent agents. Common in the property and casualty markets (auto and homeowners insurance), such agents typically represent at least three companies. "You can go to one of them and say, 'Here is how much insurance I need. Now what can you offer me?' Then they will show you at least a few policies," says David Kennedy, author of *Insurance: How Much Do You Need? How Much Is Enough?* (HP Books, $9.95). Kennedy also recommends narrowing your list to companies rated A or better by A.M. Best, a national firm that judges the financial soundness of insurers.

Chances are the list of options you will be offered will make the tax code look like child's play. Examine all the charges and premiums carefully. Remember, you don't need to purchase a policy at the moment you meet with an agent. Ask to take the reading material with you and decide later. As long as you are dealing with a financially strong insurer that generally charges reasonable prices, you should concentrate on studying the exact terms of the coverage. While it is a waste of money to buy insurance that you don't need, the worst bargain is to skimp on the coverage you do need and leave yourself vulnerable to financial disaster.

What Insurance Do You Need?

When you decide to buy insurance, don't rely solely on the advice of insurance agents, who have a natural desire to sell as much coverage as they can. To help you choose policies wisely, *Money* has compiled the following guidelines from financial planners, academics specializing in insurance, and consumer interest groups:

Life. The amount you need hinges on the number of people who depend on you financially. With two young children, you might need insurance worth five times your annual income.

Health. At the minimum, you need a major medical policy that covers 80% of most doctor and hospital bills that exceed your deductible. Make sure the policy has no exclusions for costly diseases such as cancer and that it will pay no less than $250,000 over your lifetime.

Disability. Look for a policy that replaces 60% to 70% of your income if you become disabled. The policy should pay you when you are unable to work at your own occupation, not when you cannot do any type of work. If you have an emergency fund, you can reduce your premium by opting for a long waiting period—90 days, for example—before the insurer begins paying.

Auto. Choose a policy that pays at least $100,000 for a single injury, $300,000 for all injuries, $50,000 for property damage (which includes the costs of liability suits) and costs resulting from fire, theft, and vandalism (so-called comprehensive coverage). If your car has lost more than a third of its initial value—which can happen within three years—collision insurance may not be worthwhile. Before you buy any medical coverage, be sure that you would not be duplicating health insurance you already have. Also check with the Department of Motor Vehicles in your state to find out whether you are required by law to buy protection against uninsured motorists.

Homeowners. You should insure at least 80% of the replacement cost of your home (excluding the land value). In addition, you need coverage of at least $100,000 against liability suits.

Personal liability. The standard liability coverage of auto and homeowners policies may be inadequate if your assets total more than $100,000—especially if you are frequently exposed to potential lawsuits. For example, if you own a pool or throw parties for your children, a $1 million umbrella liability policy may be worth the $100 to $150 annual premium.

Insurance Dos and Don'ts

DO:

• Take the maximum deductible you can afford. Increasing the deductible on your car's collision insurance from $100 to $500 could reduce your premium cost by one-third.

• Ask your agent or company whether you qualify for discounts.

• Consider term life insurance. Such policies are usually 10% to 20% cheaper than whole life contracts.

• Try to get health insurance through a group policy or from your employer, professional association, or union. If you are over 50, check with the American Association of Retired Persons (202-872-4700). Group coverage is almost always cheaper than individual policies.

DON'T:

• Buy policies with narrowly defined coverage, such as travel or cancer insurance. Policies such as these frequently duplicate other coverage.

• Confuse the guaranteed rate with the projected rate used to forecast the future cash value of your policy. Most insurers guarantee a return of only 4% to 5%.

• Switch among cash-value life insurance policies on impulse. Fees and agents' commissions will often outweigh a slightly higher return.

• Buy life insurance principally as an investment. Your primary goal should be the best insurance coverage. One exception: single-premium life insurance may be attractive as a tax-deferred investment.

Colleen Duffley

Personal Finance

These days a quick trip to the bank to get cash for the weekend can entail some fancy footwork. You often have to veer past the discount brokerage kiosk, be careful not to knock over the three-foot sign proclaiming current interest rates on the bank's numerous savings accounts, and sidestep those blinking home-banking demonstration terminals just to reach the wall of card-eating automatic teller machines. Banking has become a bewildering amalgam of services and show biz in the past decade. But the added choices and conveniences that have resulted from deregulation and the advent of new technology are big improvements over the days when your banking options were largely limited to selecting the color of your checkbook cover.

The variety of services and fees differs widely among commercial banks, savings and loans, and credit unions—the three types of institutions loosely called banks. Choosing the one for your checking, borrowing, and saving requires you to assess your particular banking needs and preferences. Start by reading "Ways to Get the Most from Your Bank" and the accompanying box, "Ten Money-Saving Questions for Your Banker."

Indeed, for many people the question isn't which bank to use but rather which combination of banks offers them the most appealing interest rates and least onerous service fees. That's because the place paying the highest rates on savings accounts frequently also charges the most for checking, credit cards, or car loans. The key is to shop selectively for the best deals in your area without unduly complicating the chore of keeping track of your finances. (For help on this task, see "Records Worth Keeping.")

To pull your personal finances together and make the most of what you have, look into so-called asset management accounts, which are offered by many brokers and bankers and are described in "Consider Consolidating Your Assets." A combination of money-market and brokerage accounts, these usually let you earn high interest on your spare cash, buy and sell securities, borrow inexpensively against the market value of your holdings, and write an unlimited number of checks at no extra charge. You also get a convenient monthly statement of all your financial transactions. But it pays to shop around. At pricier institutions, you may be required to deposit cash or securities worth $20,000 or more and to pay annual fees up to $100 to open such a multipurpose account.

Need to borrow money quickly for almost any purpose? One of the best ways to meet such a need is to bypass your banker, who invariably wants to know why, and instead to tap your company-sponsored savings or profit-sharing plan. You often can borrow most of what you personally have put away in the account and at favorable rates. But heed the warnings detailed in "Getting Cash from Your Company Plan" before you hit up your benefits officer at work.

Ways to Get the Most from Your Bank

An array of enticing services is being offered to rebuild customer loyalty—and bank profits.

After years of frosty service and niggling service charges, banks now realize they desperately need to attract new depositors. The reason for this rather sudden change of heart is deep and structural. It has to do largely with changing global cash flows, the souring of Third World debt obligations, and the intrusion of large competitive investment firms and other multinationals into the worldwide lending business. Suffice it to say that American banks have begrudgingly realized that Joe Paycheck is their first, best, and most dependable source of cash.

How can you take advantage of this new attitude? If you are not already enjoying substantially better service at your old bank, then perhaps it's time to look down the street. A survey conducted in 1987 by *American Banker*, the industry trade paper, reveals that service and convenience are overwhelmingly (67%) the chief concerns of most of the bank customers polled and that wrath over rising fees is the third most commonly cited reason for dissatisfied customers to switch banks. As the table on page 139 makes painfully evident, lots of banks have victimized their customers through hidden or partially concealed fees: $15 here for stopping a check, $12 there if you deposit a check that bounces, even $8 a year to maintain your Individual Retirement Account (that is, for sending you quarterly statements).

Recently, however, as customer disgust at

this constant chipping away has grown acute, bankers have gone to work on a variety of new approaches to rebuild loyalty. The major trend has been toward package deals called bundled accounts. Sensing that the customer resented fees and, worse, would flee from them, bankers calculated that if they could just depend upon a depositor to keep a certain amount of money in one or more accounts, the bank could see a tidy and dependable profit from the spread—or cost difference—between what it pays depositors for their money and what it charges borrowers. Thus, bankers would not have to subject the customer to nuisance fees.

Amid all this feverish marketing, you need new moxie to select a bank smartly. First, it is wise to separate banking from investing. True, the wall between investment banking and conventional commercial banking—the durable 1932 Glass-Steagall Act, which forbids banks to underwrite or sell stock—is crumbling. Many banks are already acquiring discount brokerage operations and offering access to mutual funds, while nonbank companies such as American Express, Merrill Lynch, and Sears are offering services that are nearly identical to bank accounts.

Your first consideration should be to pick an institution with which you can establish a sustained banking relationship. You want a bank that's close by, open when you can get to it, accessible by automatic teller machines (ATMs) when it is closed, and a member in good standing of the Federal Deposit Insurance Corporation (FDIC) or the Federal Savings and Loan Insurance Corporation (FSLIC) so that your money will be safe from the next act of the financial follies.

Ten Money-Saving Questions for Your Banker

Whether you want to buy a bundle of banking services or just a single account, here are checklists of questions you should ask about each product.

For checking accounts:

● What are the fees? If no minimum balance is required, you shouldn't pay more than 20 cents a check and $5 a month.

● Is there a minimum amount you must maintain to avoid those fees or qualify for free services? For free checking, $1,000 to $2,000 is the range for a fair minimum.

● What does the monthly statement look like? Does it list cleared checks in numerical order?

● What does the bank charge for money orders or certified checks? (Reasonable charges range from $1 to $3 for money orders and $3 to $6 for certified checks.)

For interest-paying accounts:

● How is interest calculated? The best method for the saver is day of deposit to day of withdrawal. And the more often your interest is compounded, the higher your yield. Daily compounding is best.

● Are there any restrictions on withdrawals, such as only a certain number allowed each month?

● Can you write checks on the account? How many per month?

For credit cards:

● What is the annual percentage rate and the annual fee? If you tend to let your unpaid balance build up, then go for a card with a low rate of interest.

● What is the grace period on the card? Most banks don't charge interest on your balance for at least 25 days, but there has been a trend toward charging from the day of purchase. If you pay off your balance each month, then you want a bank that offers a grace period.

● Does the card also function as a debit card? Once heralded as a new generation of plastic, the debit card is acceptable at retail counters that would reject your personal check, because payments are taken immediately from your checking account. Debit cards have fizzled. Consumers, like bankers, adore the float, the grace period between the moment of purchase and the moment the bank demands payment or starts charging interest.

Once you have narrowed your search to a few handy, well-equipped, fully insured banks, you are ready to drop in and conduct your own on-site inspection. What should you look for? The new face of banking has three beguiling but not always totally satisfying expressions: "personal banker," "one-stop banking," and "automatic teller machine." Here's what is really going on:

Personal Banker

This new trend toward encouraging customers to strike up a one-on-one relationship with a bank staffer is known in the industry as relationship banking. Small banks have the edge in customer rapport, if only because their employees don't get transferred from branch to branch like chess pieces. But even big banks can operate in the intimacy mode. Irving Trust in New York City has offered a personal banker to everyone who has opened an account there since 1978. And Wachovia Bank & Trust in Winston-Salem, North Carolina has made the concept its credo, assigning a customer to one particular staff member who opens accounts, makes all loans, and generally handles all banking business beyond routine transactions.

Any bank's promotion of this fiduciary buddy system is, of course, a calculated strategy. When an institution has a relationship with a customer already, it's easier to sell that second service, then that third. Whatever the motive, such courtesy could result in real savings of time and even money if the banker can help you think more clearly about your accounts. When you come to assess a bank's promise of a personal banker, here are some polite questions to ask:
● How many other clients does my personal banker have? Any number under 100 should be acceptable. Anything higher suggests you might not get the personal attention you seek.
● Does my personal banker have his own office? Discussing the details of your financial life at the busy customer service counter is hardly personal.
● Can I deal with my personal banker over the

telephone? Often this is the fastest and most convenient way to handle many banking matters, even though the salesman in your personal banker would rather do business with you face to face.
● Can my personal banker pass a flash test? See if, for example, you can get a clear explanation of how interest compounds in your savings account. If your banker doesn't know, he or she may not be much help.
● How long will I have the same personal banker? Rapid promotions can create high turnover in the position, leaving you all too frequently with a personal banker you don't know.

One-Stop Banking

Banks are breaking out with a riot of new products. Theirs is a middleman's game. As financial intermediaries, they take money from Peter and pay him for its use, say, 5.25% interest on a NOW account, then lend the money to Paul at 10.75% for a mortgage or, better yet, 18% for revolving credit on a Visa card.

The gaping spread between the savings rate and the lending rate is the field on which bankers reap their profit. The demise of federal ceilings on bank account interest rates in 1980 has widened bankers' profit margins. Rates at both ends of the spread are now basically governed by whatever banks can get. And what a banker can get is bounded only by what he can dream up. For example, Trustcorp Bank of Toledo offers funeral-planning trust accounts through local undertakers. Valley National Bank in Phoenix offers a lifetime safe-deposit box for a one-time fee of $110 if a customer signs up for its checking/savings package. Los Angeles, not to be outdone when it comes to new wrinkles, boasts First Professional Bank, which caters mainly to doctors. Its wrinkle is no teller lines; most transactions are handled by courier service.

The greatest flight of bankerly imagination is bundling. Perhaps you have noticed the proliferation of free checking accounts that require a minimum balance of $1,000 to $5,000. To make that minimum balance seem worth

Reverse Interest: How Banks Nick You on Your Own Money

Total fees paid by depositors at some banks are running as high as $60 a year and rising, according to a Federal Reserve Board study. More and more banks, for example, charge as much as $1 for each use of an automatic teller machine (ATM), and a few are imposing yearly maintenance fees on IRAs. This sampling of 10 major U.S. banks and savings institutions shows the tariff, if any, at branches in the cities named. Outlets in other cities may charge differently or may require that varying balances be maintained to get free services.

	Bank of America, San Francisco	Bay Banks, Boston	Citizens & Southern, Atlanta	First City, Houston	First National of Chicago	Manufacturers Hanover, New York	Mellon Bank, Pittsburgh	North Shore Savings, Milwaukee	Security Pacific, Los Angeles	Southwest Bank, St. Louis
SAVINGS ACCOUNTS										
Minimum to open	$100	$10	$100	$300	$250	None	None	$500	$100	$25
Monthly (M) or quarterly (Q) charge or transaction fee (T) for low balance	$3 (Q)	50¢ (T)	$6 (Q)	$5 (M)	$5 (Q)	$3 (M)	$1 (M)	$5 (M)	$1.50 (M)	$0
Balance that triggers this charge	$500	$250	$100	$300	$250	$400	$100	$500	$200	—
How this balance is defined	Average quarterly	Lowest monthly	Average quarterly	Lowest monthly	Lowest quarterly	Average monthly	Average monthly	Average monthly	Lowest monthly	—
REGULAR CHECKING										
Minimum to open	$100	$10	None	$250	$100	None	None	N.A.	$100	$100
Monthly charge	$5	$0	$0-$3	$0-10	$0-$7	$0-$8	$0-$4	—	$4.50	$0-$5
Per-check charge	$0	$0-30¢	30¢	$0	$0	$0-50¢†	$0	—	$0-30¢	$0
NOW CHECKING ACCOUNT										
Minimum to open	$500	$10	None	$500	$100	None	None	None	$100	$1,000
Monthly charge	$0-$7	$0	$0-$6	$0-$10	$0-$9	$0-$10	$0-$7	$0-$7.50	$0-$5†	$0-$10
Per-check charge	$0	$0-30¢	30¢	$0	$0	$0-50¢†	$0	$0	$0-30¢†	$0
BASIC CHECKING ACCOUNT										
Minimum to open	$100	$10	None	$250	$100	None	None	N.A.	$100	$100
Monthly charge	$0-$2.50	$7	75¢	$5	$0-$2	$4	$0	—	$0-$4.50	$2
Per-check charge (free per month)	50¢ (8)	$0	75¢ (7)	20¢ (0)	30¢ (10)	50¢ (8)	50¢ (4)	—	$0-30¢ (10)††	25¢ (0)
MISCELLANEOUS FEES										
Bounced check On a check that you wrote	$10	$12.50	$15	$17.50	$10	$7	$20	$18‡	$10	$15
On a check written to you	$3	$1	$0	$17.50	$10	$1.25	$0	$5	$4	$1.50
Order to stop payment	$10	$12.50	$12	$15	$12	$10	$10	$10	$10	$11
Money order	$2-$4	$1.50	$3	$2.75**	$0-$2	$2	$1.75	$1	$3	$2
Certified check	N.A.	$5	46	$15	$10	$6	$6	$0	N.A.	N.A.
ATM fee per use on bank's own ATM	$0	$0-30¢	$0-30¢	$0	$0	$0-25¢ a day	$0	$0	$0	$0
On others on its network	$1	50¢-$1	75¢	50¢-$1	$0	$0-25¢	75	$1§	$0-$1	N.A.
IRA maintenance	$8	$5	$0	$0	$0	$0	$0	$0	$0	$0
Microfilm copy of canceled checks Regular and NOW accounts	$0	$5	$5	$2	$2	$4	$5	$3	$2‡‡	$5
Basic checking	$0	$5	$5*	$2	$2	$1.50	$5	N.A.	$2‡‡	$5

N.A. (account not available) *12 free copies a year **Higher for nondepositors †Depending on your balance ‡No miscellaneous fees if total balances exceed $25,000 per household §Out of state only ††Charge for all checks if you write more than 10 ‡‡No charge if you choose not to have your canceled checks returned your while, banks usually pay interest on it or tie the checking account to an interest-bearing savings account. Many banks also throw in a no-fee, low-fee, or low-interest Visa or Master-Card, or offer reduced rates on loans to customers who bundle. Some revert to toaster bribes or confer preferential rights to use special express lines to the tellers' wickets.

One example of bundling is the ChemPlus package at New York City's Chemical Bank. For a minimum balance of $1,000, spread between any two or more accounts (including checking, savings, money market, certificates of deposit, and Individual Retirement Accounts), you get free checking, a 16.8% combined MasterCard and Visa account (free for the first year), reduced rates on loans and mortgage fees, and free 24-hour banking in a network of 18,000 ATM machines around the country.

On the high-end side of relationship banking, Fleet National Bank of Providence offers its Westminster Account, a combination of banking, discount brokerage, and investment advisory services. The price of admission is high, $300,000 of liquid assets plus a fee of 1% of whatever assets Fleet has under management, but the extra benefits are lush. You get free checking on interest-bearing money-market accounts; a free Visa gold debit card; a line of credit secured by the assets in your account or the equity in your home; a personal account executive; a detailed monthly statement showing cash flows in, out, and among all of your accounts, and tabulating the relevant tax consequences of each transaction; and automatic payment of your regular bills.

You could probably beat almost any individual feature of a bundled account as a single product at some other bank. But that's not the point. The real benefits of a good bundle are convenience and service. All your banking paperwork comes to you on a single integrated statement, and you establish a bank relationship that, over time, could pay off in privileged treatment. At the same time, you should get a competitive return on your balance, substantial breaks on a variety of fees, a good rate on a credit card and, in almost every case, free checking.

Automatic Teller Machines

In place at banks since 1971, automatic teller machines (ATMs) can give you 24-hour access to your checking and savings accounts, and let you deposit checks and transfer funds between accounts without ever talking to a teller. Customer satisfaction is high, and not just among computer nuts and night people. Networks of interlinked systems such as MAC, CIRRUS, or TYME are on the march, giving you access to your hometown bank account from ATMs across the country.

Still, problems crop up. One of the most common complaints—"Your machine just took my card"—is not always the bank's fault. Power surges sometimes cause a sort of ATM amnesia in the machine. The plastic cards that activate them get sat on and warped in hip pockets. (If a card gets bowed to a certain degree, it will go into the machine but can't get back out.) Or, face it, you might be a chronic over-withdrawer. Regardless of the culprit, rescue is at hand. Already, Citibank in New York has made it impossible for its machines to eat cards. Customers simply dip them an inch or two into a slot and then pull them out without ever letting go.

Hold the ATM system at a prospective bank to the following minimum standard:

● At least two machines at each ATM location. This is the best insurance against a late-night case of the broken ATM blues.

● Are the machines looking good? Scuzzy facades often indicate secondhand or poorly maintained machines.

● A service phone near the machines you are likely to use when the bank is closed. This can be important not just if you need help completing a transaction, but also if you find yourself late at night holding a wad of cash and looking out the glass door at someone you suspect wants to take it from you. Video cameras in plain sight are also good deterrents.

● No fees. Many banks, including Citibank, lately have begun the loathsome practice of charging their customers for ATM transactions. A quarter, 50 cents, a dollar—any price seems too high for a service that just a few years ago bankers were begging you to try.

Records Worth Keeping

Most of us squirrel away more paper than is necessary.

Warren and Rosemary Wells of Deerfield, Illinois once belonged to the accumulate-and-procrastinate school of record keeping. They saved everything. In their basement and study they had five file cabinets stuffed with important papers such as stock certificates, IRA statements, and the deed to their house—as well as more than 20 years' worth of canceled bankbooks, credit-card and utility bills, and other useless documents. Finally, with the help of certified financial planner Victoria Ross, the couple cleared out the useless documents and organized the records they really did need into one two-drawer file cabinet. "We found things we had totally forgotten about," says Rosemary Wells. "We thought stock we had inherited years earlier might be worth $5,000 or $6,000, but we turned up certificates actually worth more than $20,000."

You can't expect that kind of reward from cleaning the clutter out of your life, but it's still worth doing—for its own sake, as well as for the possibility of saving some money. "We have people coming in with boot boxes full of papers and receipts," says Brad Greer, a certified financial planner at First National Bank in Albuquerque. "If your accountant or financial planner charges by the hour, organizing and weeding your records before you turn them over could reduce your bill by about 10% to 20%."

You can start by throwing out worthless documents. Follow this rule of thumb: If you don't need the record for tax purposes or if you are sure it can easily be replaced, don't save it. For example, keep your monthly credit-card statement only until your bank returns the canceled check verifying that you paid the bill. Then get rid of both the statement and the check. In fact, you can throw out all canceled checks except the ones you need as tax records.

Monthly mutual fund and brokerage statements can be discarded once you receive your comprehensive year-end accounting, which lists all of your transactions for the 12 months. But save every stock trade confirmation and fund dividend-reinvestment statement to figure the cost basis of an investment. That way you will avoid overpaying taxes when you sell the security. Receipts for minor daily purchases such as groceries can routinely be tossed but not receipts for expensive purchases such as jewelry and furniture. You will need them to settle insurance claims in case of loss, theft, or damage.

Most of your records can be kept at home. A shoebox may be sufficient for some people, but you are probably better off paying about $50 for a sturdy, fireproof file box, which can typically hold at least six years' worth of documents. Hard-to-replace records such as stock certificates, a divorce decree, or a power of attorney should be stored in a safe-deposit box. Banks charge about $25 to $50 a year for a three-inch-by-five-inch-by-24-inch box, sufficient for most families.

The records you must safeguard at home or at your bank can be divided into the following two groups, depending on how long you must keep them:

Hold for six or more years. If the IRS hasn't begun an audit of your tax return six years after you file it, you can reward yourself by tossing out copies of the return and of the records that prove your income, deductions, and other entries for the year. (Only if you are suspected of filing a fraudulent return is there no statute of limitations on an IRS audit.)

Similarly, investment records such as annual mutual fund accountings and partnership K-1 statements must be kept until six years after you have sold the asset. That same holding period applies to receipts and canceled checks for improvements to your home and to documents identifying nondeductible contributions to an Individual Retirement Account. Without verification of the amount and date of the nondeductible contribution, you could be hit with a stiff tax bill when you make withdrawals from your IRA.

Hold for life. A copy of your will can be stored in a safe-deposit box, but keep the original at home or with your lawyer. In many states your safe-deposit box will be sealed when you die, making it hard for relatives to take from it your will and funeral instructions. Moreover, financial planners generally suggest you keep up-to-date photos and fingerprints of your children, in case of emergency.

Finally, make a list of all your records, as well as the names, addresses, and phone numbers of advisers such as your accountant, broker, financial planner, insurance agents, and lawyer. Copies should be kept in the safe-deposit box and with your lawyer or planner.

Getting Cash from Your Company Plan

If you need money fast, you can tap your savings at the office. But read this before you try to do it.

More and more Americans are discovering that the best place to raise cash for nearly any purpose may be their company's employee-benefits office. You can often tap your savings account at work and collect most of what you have put away—sometimes much more. In fact, a growing number of businesses have made it easier for employees to borrow against their plan balances.

For example, one benefits consulting firm estimated that 59% of companies with 401(k) salary-reduction plans allowed loans in 1987, compared with 44% in 1986. What's more, the interest charges and repayment terms on company-plan loans are often more generous than those of other lenders. At the same time, the alternative to borrowing—withdrawing money from company plans—has become tougher and costlier because of new restrictions and penalties added by Congress and the Internal Revenue Service.

These changes have turned answering what was once a fairly simple question—whether you are better off withdrawing or borrowing money from your company plan—into a complicated exercise that often requires the assistance of your benefits department. The answer depends on your tax bracket, when you contributed the money and, most important, what kind of company savings plan you want to take the money from.

There are three types of plans, all offering tax-free compounding of investment earnings until you withdraw the money. Your contributions are vested automatically; they belong to you irrevocably. Employers have their own vesting rules for money they contribute to your account, but usually the money is yours to keep after three years or so. Briefly, the three plans are:

401(k) plans. These are the most popular tax shelters sponsored by employers. Every dollar you invest through payroll deductions reduces your taxable income by a dollar. Last year you could contribute $7,313 tax-free to a 401(k)—the maximum rises annually with inflation. Many employers match some or all of the money you invest, most commonly 50 cents on the dollar. You can typically put your money in one or more of several investments, including a growth-stock fund and a fixed-income fund. Usually you can borrow against your account and, in the event of financial hardship, withdraw money from it. Expect to wait one to three months for the check. (So-called 403(b) plans for employees of schools, hospitals, and other nonprofit groups have similar policies on withdrawals and loans.)

After-tax savings plans. You must pay taxes on the money that you invest in these profit-sharing or savings plans. They offer employer-matching and investment choices similar to those of 401(k) plans. Many after-tax plans permit withdrawals and loans.

Employee stock ownership plans (ESOPs). Usually funded exclusively by the employer, these plans invest in the firm's own shares. Few ESOPs permit employees to borrow against their accounts or take out cash until they quit or retire.

Now for the main question: If you have a choice between withdrawing cash from your plan or borrowing, which is preferable?

Unless you have exhausted other sources of quick cash, withdrawing money from a company plan makes sense only if it is an after-tax account and you are taking out money you contributed before 1987. Although most companies that have after-tax plans permit withdrawals, some limit the number to one or two a year. In addition, your employer might force you to wait six months or longer before you can start contributing again to the plan.

As a result of the 1986 tax reform law, with-drawals of money you invested after 1986 in an after-tax plan generally must include a prorated portion of your account's earnings and, if the money was matched, employer contributions. Suppose you withdraw $1,000 from an after-tax plan in which you have a $10,000 balance—$7,000 from your own 1987 and 1988 contributions and $3,000 from earnings and your employer's contributions. Of the money you take out, $700 will be considered a nontaxable withdrawal of after-tax contributions and $300 will be taxed at your bracket. If you are under age 59½, you will also owe a 10% penalty ($30 in this example).

Your company may permit you to withdraw money from a 401(k) plan. But it is an option you should generally decline because the price is too high. By law, if you are under age 59½, you can take out contributions and earnings from a 401(k) only if you can prove to your employer that you have a financial hardship. Then all withdrawals are taxable and subject to the 10% penalty. The fine is waived, however, if you use the money for unreimbursed medical expenses exceeding 7.5% of your adjusted gross income. Employees older than 59½ are permitted by law to make withdrawals without proving financial hardship. Their money is taxed, but the 10% penalty is waived. With-drawals from 401(k)s will be even harder to swing beginning this year, when you will be able to take out just the amount you contributed but not earnings or your employer's contributions.

What qualifies as a financial hardship? A survey by the Wyatt Co., a benefits consulting firm in Washington, D.C., showed that 93% of employers offering 401(k)s allow hardship withdrawals for medical expenses, 89% for the purchase of a primary residence, and 86% for education costs. The IRS, however, has issued regulations that define hardship as a "heavy and immediate" expense for which no other resources are reasonably available.

Taking out a loan against your plan assets may be a better alternative to withdrawing money because no tax or penalty is involved. Generally, plans permitting loans allow employees to borrow for any purpose. By law, any loans must be repaid within five years, although your employer can extend the period, usually to 10 or 15 years, if you borrow to buy a principal residence. And you will owe interest, lately as high as 11% a year. Actually, you will in effect be paying yourself—the interest is deposited into your plan account. But you probably won't come out ahead because you will have less money earning interest or dividends in the plan than you would if you hadn't taken out the loan.

The maximum amount that you can borrow at any time is the lesser of (1) $50,000 minus your highest outstanding loan balance over the previous 12 months or (2) half of your vested plan balance or $10,000, whichever is greater. To illustrate, suppose you have $40,000 vested in your 401(k) plan account and you owed as much as $25,000 during the past year on an existing loan. The maximum you could borrow now would be $20,000. That amount is the lesser of (1) $50,000 minus $25,000 or (2) one-half of $40,000.

Company plan loans have one especially fetching advantage over other borrowing sources—you will not be turned down, no matter how deeply in hock you may be to other lenders. The reason: Since repayments will be deducted directly from your paycheck, your company has no need to review your credit record.

Most plan loans carry fixed interest rates of 8% to 11%, or four to 11 percentage points below that of bank or credit-card loans. Many plans link what they charge to the prime rate (recently about 10%), adding one or two percentage points. In contrast, most home-equity loans have fluctuating rates—they lately averaged 11%—that could cause your payments to escalate or shrink depending on the vagaries of the credit markets.

On the other hand, you can deduct all of the interest on a home-equity loan of up to $100,000. None of the interest on a 401(k) loan made after December 31, 1986 is deductible, while employees generally can write off only 40% of the interest they pay on loans from after-tax plans in 1988, 20% in 1989, 10% in 1990, and nothing after that. A fully deductible 10% home-equity loan costs the equivalent of 7.2% after taxes for someone in the 28% tax bracket—just below the nondeductible 8% on the least expensive 401(k) loan.

Some companies that permit loans against savings plans impose their own barriers on employees. For example, you may need a minimum balance in your account—usually $1,000—to get a loan. You also might not be allowed to have more than one loan at a time.

Consider Consolidating Your Assets

Cash management accounts can simplify your life.

Pssst! Want a sure thing in the stock market? Brokers are practically giving it away. And it can make your financial life a breeze. No, it isn't a stock tip; it is a street-name brokerage account.

These accounts have brand names such as Merrill Lynch CMA, Prudential-Bache Command, Schwab One, and Fidelity USA. They are versions of an investment and cash management tool invented by Merrill Lynch in 1977. Merrill's CMA and its several hundred imitators combine a brokerage margin account, which gives you instant borrowing power against your securities, with a money-market account, a checking account, and a credit card. All of these services in one bundle can consolidate and greatly simplify your household finances even if you seldom trade securities.

Americans now maintain about 2.5 million such multipurpose accounts at brokerages as well as mutual fund management companies and banks with discount brokerage affiliates. The yearly fee ranges no higher than $100 for Shearson Lehman Hutton's Financial Management Account with an American Express Gold Card. And the fee is zero for a Schwab One account, from the Charles Schwab & Co. discount brokerage, or a Unisave account, from Unified Management, an Indianapolis financial services subsidiary of Mutual of New York. To open a multipurpose account you may need as much as $20,000 in cash or securities at Merrill Lynch or as little as $1,000 at Unified Management.

High-fee, high-balance accounts generally welcome clients who may want them mainly for household money management. No-fee, low-balance plans are aimed at active investors. If you use a Schwab One account only to write checks, for example, you may be asked to leave.

Most asset management accounts include free checking, with no limit on the size or number of checks you write. The plastic that comes with the account is usually not a true credit card but rather a debit card—your purchases are deducted from your account. A debit card can also be used to extract cash from automatic teller machines at thousands of banks and other locations in the U.S. and abroad. For a few dollars extra a month, some accounts, including Pru-Bache's and many banks', will pay your fixed monthly bills automatically and your other bills when you phone them in. Every transaction shows up in your monthly statement.

If you overdraw your cash supply, you automatically borrow against the value of securities or certificates of deposit in your account. The interest rate, from one-half to 2.5 points above the broker loan rate, which is what banks charge brokers, was recently 10% to 13%, compared with 18% or more on credit-card balances at most banks.

Open a multipurpose account and you will never mislay a stock or bond certificate or puzzle over where to keep it simply because you need never again get one. After you sign up for an account, you send the securities you own to your broker, who re-registers them as property of Cede & Company. This is, quite literally, the street name. Securities so registered come under the administration of a Wall Street institution called the Depository Trust Company, which serves as custodian for more than $2.8 trillion of stocks and bonds.

All that wealth exists at Depository Trust only on computer tape. Billions of dollars of interest and dividends flow electronically through the company to financial institutions for allotment to the accounts of the true owners of the stocks and bonds held in street name. The invisible hand of the computer sweeps your dividends and interest, $100 at a time, either daily or weekly into a money-market account. In many cases you can choose a taxable or tax-free fund. Some brokers and all banks offer a third choice—a federally insured money-market account.

When you sell a security, possession changes electronically. Your monthly statements tell you how much income your account earned, what you bought or sold, and how much your investments were lately worth. Toward tax filing time, you will receive a year-end statement that totals all your investment income, which you can enter on one line of Form 1040.

Investors whose confidence in brokers plunged with the stock market's crash may still prefer to clutch parchment to their bosoms rather than entrust it to Wall Street. William J. Fitzpatrick, general counsel of the Securities Industry Association, a trade group, argues persuasively, however, that securities are safer with a broker than they would be at home or in a bank. If your broker goes under, holdings in the firm's name are covered by the Congressionally chartered Securities Investor Protection Corporation for $500,000 and at many brokerages by additional commercial insurance as high as $9.5 million. In contrast, the contents of safe-deposit boxes are not even insured for fire and theft unless you buy your own policy.

Nevertheless, there are some drawbacks to

holding stocks in street name: Corporate financial reports are late in arriving because they must be relayed to you by Depository Trust and your broker. You cannot participate in the automatic dividend-reinvestment plans that many companies offer their shareholders. And you lose financial privacy. A curious broker can call up your account statement on a computer screen and find out how you have been spending your money.

Above all, don't open a street-name account if you are overly susceptible to brokers' recommendations. The inconveniences of keeping your stocks in your own name and most of your cash in the bank will help squelch any impulse to follow hot tips.

How to Move Your Belongings—and Preserve Your Sanity

Your employer can help, but a little foresight does even more.

Of the 40 million Americans who change addresses each year, many make the move with only normal wear and tear on their persons and personal effects. But a host of others file claims for damaged or lost possessions, verifying the old armed forces axiom, "three moves equals a fire."

Also, about 8% of pickups are late, as are 15% of deliveries. Last year, a West Coast family that transferred to the Midwest had to bed down on the floor of their new home in sleeping bags for two weeks because the driver had stopped off in Las Vegas for a dalliance with a girlfriend. But delays are more typically caused by detours for another shipment (vans can generally hold three or four).

Your chances of a mishap are much reduced if you are being moved by an employer that has a large volume of business with van lines and therefore has muscle with agents, dispatchers, and drivers.

But even if you are among the 30% or so who pay their own way, you can limit the damage to nerves and furniture with planning and foresight. Get names of reputable movers from new arrivals in your community and ask for estimates from at least three van lines. Interstate shipping rates, which vary from company to company but are based on weight and distance, are listed with the Interstate Commerce Commission, as are prices for such extras as packing and unpacking. Discounts for the whole job run as high as 45%, however.

To stay profitable, movers that knock the biggest chunks off their prices may also chip away at the corners of their service. For example, the driver may wrap mirrors in pads instead of crating them. So don't automatically hire the lowest bidder. Bargain hard but base your decision on the care and courtesy shown by the agents, as well as on their estimates.

What you finally pay may be rather different from the estimate. To determine the actual price, the driver will weigh your shipment. At your destination, if you are footing the bill, you must pay in cash or traveler's checks before a stick of furniture is unloaded. Some lines accept credit cards, but no personal checks, please. Worse yet, there is a 28% chance that the bill will exceed the estimate. In that case, the ICC lets the driver demand as much as 110% of the estimated charges on the spot. If you can't raise that much in two hours, the driver can put your load in storage at your expense.

So take plenty of traveler's checks with you. Or request what's known as a binding estimate—often at no extra cost. Then, unless you add to your shipment after the price has been set, the mover cannot make you pay more than the estimate.

In preparation for moving day, make sure the agent gives you the free ICC pamphlet, *When You Move: Your Rights and Responsibilities.* If you have further questions or a complaint, phone the nearest ICC office. For total hand-holding, buy *Jan Dickinson's Complete Guide to Family Relocation* (Dickinson Consulting Group, 6175 S.W. 112th Ave., Beaverton, OR 97005; $19.95).

To head off delays, give the mover as much advance notice as you can. If possible, move in the off-season, which runs from November through May. This improves your chances of getting an experienced crew. At any time of year, avoid the last week of the month, when demand is heaviest.

Also, consider buying the mover's optional full-replacement-value insurance coverage. Ordinarily, your limit on claims equals $1.25 per pound of goods shipped—$6,250 for a typical 5,000-pound load—when, in fact, household possessions generally average about $3.25 a pound in worth. You pay $5 per $1,000 for this standard protection—$31.25 for that 5,000-pound load—and settlements are based on the depreciated value of damaged goods.

In contrast, the full-replacement-cost coverage pays for new furniture equivalent to the old stuff if it can't be completely restored. The extra cost varies with the mover. Wheaton Van Lines, for example, charges $8 per $1,000 of estimated value—$130 for a typical 5,000-pound shipment.

But even the best coverage for damage may be no more generous than the person sent out by the mover to view the ruins. Some adjusters take the attitude that the homeowner is guilty until proven innocent, despite the fact that a 1985 Consumers Union study showed people who did their own packing reported damage only about half as often as when the mover packed. To head off an impasse, ask your mover for an arbitration agreement in your contract (called the bill of lading).

Measuring A Move's Costs

When the boss is paying the freight, people pile just about everything they own onto the van. Families paying their own way tend to be far more frugal. These average prices for interstate moves in 1986, the latest compiled, include packing, insurance, and all other extras.

MILES TRAVELED	Employer-paid (average weight: 8,098 pounds)	Self-paid (average weight: 4,766 pounds)
Up to 800	$2,691	$1,703
800 to 1,000	3,299	1,866
1,001 to 1,500	3,633	2,037
1,501 to 2,000	4,821	2,358
2,001 to 2,500	5,052	2,741
2,501 or more	5,479	2,984

Source: Household Goods Carriers' Bureau

Your Future

Consider the following statistic: A baby born in America this year will turn 65 in a geriatric society with one in every five persons that age or older. This is the inexorable result of major demographic changes occurring all around us. The age seesaw of our population, once weighted by the young, will gradually tilt heavily toward the old because fewer children are being born, the baby boomers are maturing, and the average life span is increasing. Since 1965, life expectancy at birth has jumped from 70 to more than 75 today and could reach 80 by the year 2000.

What does this trend mean to you, regardless of your age? It means that extended families no longer will be primarily horizontal, comprising brothers and sisters and cousins. Instead, they gradually will turn vertical: three and four generations of a single family will be alive at once. Already the average married couple in the U.S. has more living parents than children. It means that spouses will spend more years together after their children have left home than they did raising them. It means that the average woman today will spend more years caring for her aging mother than she will have spent caring for a child.

Even more significant, it means that whole new stages are being added to our life cycles. Once we were only young, middle-aged, or old. Now there are bright new stops along the way. Take, for example, the young-old, an ebullient group stretching roughly from age 55 to 75. These are vigorous people who are moving from one career to another, stepping aside for a semester or two of education, experimenting with phased-in retirement, or raising venture capital for a company of their own. To them, the idea of a quarter-century of R&R sounds ridiculous—and it is.

There are many steps you have to take to prepare for successful retirement. First, you have to decide when to retire; you could spend many bitter nights regretting the wrong decision. You also have to worry about whether there will be enough money to live on until the end of your life and your spouse's. If you are to get a pension lump sum, you must agonize over whether you'll invest it poorly and live out your fourth quarter as a burden to your children. Even if you invest your nest egg wisely, you must submit to the nightmare of all retirees: no matter how smart and provident you are, inflation hurts you in the end.

Fortunately, the survival strategies for the future are at hand. Those families that learn to talk to one another candidly about some sensitive topics—Does Dad have a will? Shall we ask the children about moving?—will thrive. So will people who see retirement as a glorious mixture of work, play, and learning. After the agonies of growing up and the terrible pressures of succeeding at both career and family life, they are about to come into their own.

Figuring What You Will Need

The essentials are Social Security, a pension, and a disciplined plan.

Of all the major milestones in life—graduating from college, say, or getting married—retiring from work may be the only one in which the decisive consideration is whether you can afford to do it. Indeed, financial independence does not come cheap. It means being able to support your pre-retirement standard of living for as long as three decades in the face of an unpredictable economy and implacable inflation. Financial security in retirement is not a birthright; to get it you have to plan for it.

As with any financial plan, you need to set a specific monetary target, and the worksheet on page 152 will help you do that. By measuring your income needs against the resources you will have in retirement, such as Social Security and your company pension, you can calculate how much capital you must accumulate.

Equally important, you can also estimate how much to start saving now.

The first step in setting your goals is to decide how much income you will require in retirement. If you are more than 10 years away from calling it quits, you obviously won't be able to predict your retirement expenses accurately. But you can be reasonably sure that certain current outlays will dwindle or vanish. For example, you can budget less for workaday expenses such as transportation, lunches, and a dress-for-success wardrobe.

You can also count on a lower tax bill in retirement. Leaving the payroll means you no longer have to pay the Social Security tax, which last year siphoned as much as $3,380 from a worker's salary and $5,860 from self-employment income. Your Social Security benefit may be partly taxable if you take in more than $32,000 ($25,000 if you are single), but at least half your benefit still escapes the tax man. The pleasantly surprising conclusion is that you generally can expect to live as well in retirement as you do now on 70% of your current income.

As you get closer to retirement and can estimate your budget more accurately, you are likely to find that you can get by on even less. By the time you are ready to retire, for example, you may well have paid off your home mortgage and the bills for your children's education. With your kids finally grown and presumably self-sufficient, you may feel free to reduce your life insurance. And if you move to a warmer climate, you can expect to save on heating bills. On the other hand, be sure to allow for larger discretionary expenditures such as travel and education. Be prepared also to spend about 30% more on medicine and health insurance.

Fortunately, you won't have to produce your retirement income entirely from your own investments. For all the justifiable concern about the long-term fiscal health of Social Security, you can still count on Uncle Sam to pay benefits through at least the first few decades of the next century. The size of your benefits will depend on how long you have worked and how much you earned on the job. If over the past 29 years you made at least the maximum Social Security base salary—which rises each year with average wages and is currently $45,000—you would be entitled to the maximum $10,056 benefit in 1988.

Your spouse usually can receive a check equal to 50% of your benefits at age 65 if he or she does not collect his or her own Social Security benefits. Thus, if you retired last year and qualified for the maximum benefit but your spouse did not work, your household's annual Social Security checks would be about $15,000 instead of $10,056. When you reach age 60, your local Social Security office can tell you with some accuracy what your benefit will be. Last summer, the Social Security Administration began testing a personalized benefits statement that lists all your annual earnings and estimates your retirement benefit for those 45 and older. Or you can calculate the figure

yourself using a pamphlet called *Estimating Your Social Security Retirement Check*, which is available at your local Social Security office.

The other source of monthly retirement income is your company's pension. Like your Social Security benefit, the size of your pension will depend on your salary and length of service. Pension formulas vary widely, but a typical arrangement awards you an annual benefit equal to 1.25% to 1.5% of your average salary over your last five years of employment times the number of years you worked for the company, minus half of your Social Security benefit. Your company benefits department can usually project your benefits for you at any age.

Chances are slim that the combination of Social Security and pension benefits will give you the income you need. Even if you spend a couple of decades with a fairly generous employer, you can generally expect the combination to replace no more than 40% to 60% of your salary in the first year you are retired. The rest will have to come from the capital you build up in your Individual Retirement

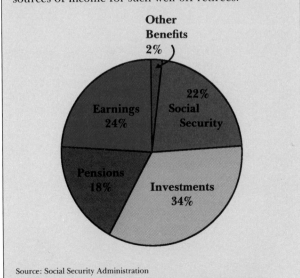

Who Will Pay for Your Retirement?

Americans hoping to retire with an income of $20,000 or more a year should not count on Social Security to provide very much. Here are the current sources of income for such well-off retirees.

Other Benefits 2%

Earnings 24%

Social Security 22%

Pensions 18%

Investments 34%

Source: Social Security Administration

Accounts, your Keogh plan, your personal investments, and any capital-accumulation plan offered by your employer, such as a profit-sharing or 401(k) account.

The unpleasant surprise of retirement planning is how much capital it takes to make up that income gap. A married couple retiring at age 65 should figure on about $179,000 of capital for each $10,000 that their pension and Social Security benefits fall short of their yearly income needs. Thus, if you need to replace $25,000 of annual income in retirement, the price of a worry-free retirement would be nearly $450,000.

Part of the reason you require so much capital is that the money has to last as long as you do. The median life expectancy is 20 years for a man at age 60 years and 25 for a woman. Thus, you have a 50% chance of outliving the median life expectancy assigned to you when you retire. As a result, you may want to base your planning on the assumption that you will live longer than 85% of the people your age. (That assumption has been incorporated into the worksheet below.) So, a 60-year-old man could feel secure with savings sufficient to meet his income needs to age 90; a woman of the same age should lay in enough to reach 94.

The other contingency that boosts the cost of financial independence is inflation. Because

Making the Numbers Add Up

The worksheet at right will tell you roughly how much you need to start saving now to hold on to your standard of living in retirement. The multipliers used in lines 7, 9, and 11 allow for inflation by assuming your investments will grow at three percentage points over the inflation rate, before and after retirement.

Line 3: If you and your spouse are over 60, you can ask your local Social Security office to estimate the annual benefits you each have earned, or you can calculate them yourself with the help of a Social Security pamphlet called *Estimating Your Social Security Retirement Check.* (For a very rough estimate of your benefit, fill in $10,000 if you make $45,000 or more; if you make between $18,000 and $45,000, enter between $7,500 and $10,000.)

Line 4: Your company benefits department may be able to estimate your pension. Make sure the estimate assumes that you continue working until your retirement age

AGE AT WHICH YOU EXPECT TO RETIRE	MULTIPLIER A	
	men	women
55	22.1	23.5
56	21.8	23.2
57	21.4	22.8
58	21.0	22.5
59	20.6	22.1
60	20.2	21.8
61	19.8	21.4
62	19.3	21.0
63	18.9	20.6
64	18.4	20.2
65	17.9	19.8
66	17.4	19.3
67	16.9	18.9

TIME UNTIL YOU EXPECT TO RETIRE	MULTIPLIER B	MULTIPLIER C
1 year	1.03	1.00
3 years	1.09	.324
5 years	1.16	.188
7 years	1.23	.131
9 years	1.30	.098
11 years	1.38	.078
13 years	1.47	.064
15 years	1.56	.054
20 years	1.81	.037

your Social Security benefits increase in step with the consumer price index, your benefits will continue to provide the same proportion of your retirement income in later years as in the year you left work. Almost no private employers' pensions are indexed to inflation, however. Consequently, your capital must be large enough so that it earns more than you need to live on, leaving you a surplus to reinvest. Later, as inflation pushes your expenses ahead of your investment earnings, you will have enough stashed away to meet the added need by dipping into principal without having to worry about running out of money ahead of schedule.

While the sums you may have to save for retirement may seem imposing, the job of accumulating them need not be—if you start early. Assuming your investments grow at the conservative pace of three percentage points over the inflation rate—which recently was about 4.6% annually—you could build a retirement chest of $179,000 (in 1988 dollars) by saving only $6,600 a year. (The calculation includes the amounts your employer contributes to your capital-accumulation plan at work, if you began 20 years before you retire.) If you postpone saving until you are only 10 years from the finish line, you would have to set aside more than $15,600 a year.

1. Current gross income _____

2. Annual income needed in retirement, in 1988 dollars (70% of line 1) _____

3. Annual Social Security retirement benefits _____

4. Annual pension benefits _____

5. Guaranteed annual retirement income (line 3 plus line 4) _____

6. Additional retirement income needed (line 2 minus line 5) _____

7. Capital required to provide additional retirement income (line 6 times multiplier from column A at left) _____

8. Amount you have saved already

_____ + _____ + _____ = _____

| personal retirement portfolio | IRA/Keogh | employer-sponsored savings plans | total savings |

9. What your current investments will have grown to by the time you retire (total from line 8 times multiplier from column B at left) _____

10. Additional retirement capital required (line 7 minus line 9) _____

11. Total annual savings still needed (line 10 times factor from column C at left) _____

12. Annual employer contributions to your company saving plans _____

13. Amount you need to set aside each year (line 11 minus line 12) _____

at your current salary. That will somewhat understate your likely eventual payout but will help by keeping the figure in 1988 dollars.

Line 7: The multipliers in column A incorporate the cautious assumption that men will live to 90 and women to 94—longer than 85% of them do now. Single men should use the multiplier under "men." Women and couples should use the one under "women," since wives usually outlive their husbands.

Line 8: Your personal retirement portfolio includes any investments you have specifically earmarked for retirement, aside from your IRA or Keogh. For your employer-sponsored savings plans, check the most recent statement from your 401(k), profit-sharing, thrift, or stock ownership plan and total your vested balance in each.

Line 12: Consult the most recent annual statement from these plans to find the amount your company contributed on your behalf to each of the plans last year. Enter the total.

Great Places to Retire

From golf-intensive Prescott to intellectual Amherst, one may be just the town for you.

Your freedom in retirement can be awesome. Not only can you do anything you want, but you can also live anyplace you please. Only one in four retirees is as yet daring enough to follow the sun or some other long-harbored fantasy. But migration analysts say the likelihood of your making such a major move increases each year.

One reason is financial: retirees are receiving fatter pensions and higher prices for their houses than ever before, even adjusted for inflation. Another is the trend among affluent retired people to sojourn—that is, to live in one home half the year and in another the rest. Furthermore, as families grow farther apart geographically, retirees have less reason to stick close to the old homestead.

Choosing where to live in retirement could be the most critical housing decision of your life. You may be less flexible financially than when you were younger, and the new place could be your home for the next 25 years. If grandchildren are nearby, a big move may only show you just how indispensable that proximity has been. Start your search by determining why you might want to move. The most popular reason, according to one survey, is to reduce expenses, followed by the desire for a smaller home or to eliminate maintenance chores.

Your reasons could be quite different. You might seek a warmer climate, a smaller city, an area suited to your hobbies or a place where your friends live. To help you better assess your options, *Money* recently identified six top retirement locations, selected on the basis of geographical diversity, climate, cultural and recreational activities, and the cost of living. They were culled from interviews with retirees and authors of books about retirement locations, as well as U.S. Census migration statistics and reporters' visits to the areas. (A table on page 156 estimates living costs in the six locations as well as 14 other popular retirement spots.)

Prescott, Arizona. No one researches retirement places as exhaustively as does Peter Dickinson, author of *Sunbelt Retirement* (American Association of Retired Persons), *Retirement Edens Outside the Sunbelt* (AARP), and a monthly newsletter on retirement places (*The Retirement Letter*, 44 Wildwood Dr., Prescott, AZ 86301; $57 a year). Dickinson has appraised more than 800 such spots from Aberdeen, South Dakota ("great pheasant hunting") to Zurich, Switzerland ("excellent quality of life—if you can afford it"). So when Dickinson bought *his* future retirement house in Prescott in 1987, that was about the most towering testament a town could get.

Dickinson had been falling in love with Prescott's mountainous beauty and moseying pace since he first passed through in 1949. But once he figured out how inexpensive retirement there is today, he was sold. "I paid $117,000 for a three-bedroom house on a third of an acre with a spectacular view of the Thumb Butte ridge of the Bradshaw Mountains," he says. "The house and land are comparable to what I owned in Larchmont, New York worth

$500,000. My property taxes will be $900 a year versus $6,000 in New York. I can live on 50% to 70% of my New York income and have the same lifestyle. I just had to give up the New York ballet. But Phoenix is only 102 miles away, and it is home to Ballet Arizona, an up-and-coming troupe."

He is hardly the only retiree to fall for little Prescott (pop. 25,000). The past decade has seen a steady stream of retired people settling into this tidied-up throwback to the Old West whose nostalgic downtown strip, known as Whiskey Row, draws its character from a sprinkling of 19th-century saloons that are now bars and boutiques and equally antique hotels that have been lovingly restored. The crisp, clean air is another strong lure. Credit belongs partly to Prescott's position one mile high. The altitude makes Prescott far cooler in the summer than Phoenix (average daytime temperature of 70° versus 88°) and permits year-round golfing at the two local public courses. On winter mornings, you may need to scrape frost off your car's windshield, then drive with the top down by 2 p.m.

Prescott is a mostly white, middle-class town. But the lack of diversity is balanced somewhat by the happy contrast between its two major demographic blocs: A third of the population are retired and a third are students at three colleges—Yavapai, Prescott, and Embry-Riddle. Yavapai welcomes retirees the most. They pay $12 to $35 a course while full-time students pay roughly $400 a semester.

Chapel Hill, North Carolina. Of all U.S. college towns, Chapel Hill (pop.35,000) is home to the most retired people—about 11,000. The University of North Carolina is here, Duke is a 10-minute drive away in Durham, and North Carolina State in Raleigh is a half-hour drive.

The 20 square miles of rolling countryside that surrounds the three cities is called the Research Triangle or sometimes simply the Triangle. Durham, a former tobacco town, is transforming itself into a regional medical center, and Raleigh, like many other state capitals, is pushing for more commercial growth. Chapel Hill is the most courtly city in the Triangle, partly because of the predominance of campus life, partly because it is the smallest of the three.

Many of its retirees are well-to-do Northerners who settled in Chapel Hill to enjoy the cultural comforts of home without the hectic pace and harsh winters (February's temperature averages 42°). The campus setting has proved fertile ground for educational innovation. For example, more than 300 retirees both teach and attend classes held at local churches in programs known as Shared Learning and Peer Learning.

Bibliophilia notwithstanding, the fun begins at the drop of a divot. North Carolina has 400 golf courses, including 60 in the renowned Pinehurst area, a 1½ hour drive south of Chapel Hill. Both the Atlantic Ocean and the Blue Ridge Mountains are three hours away and provide blessed relief from the hot, sticky summers (average temperature: 77°; average humidity: 71%). The hottest tickets during the fall and winter seasons are college football and basketball; Tar Heels and Blue Devils games are typically sold out.

The medical care is exceptional. The doctor-patient ratio in the area far surpasses the national average. For example, in Durham there are seven doctors per 1,000 residents—nearly quadruple the national average. Nearby Duke University Medical Center has one of the largest cardiac rehabilitation programs in the United States. Its doctors perform about 1,500 open-heart operations a year.

Sarasota, Florida. Welcome to the retirement capital of America. Almost a third of Sarasotans (pop. 244,364) are 65 and older, and most have migrated from outside Florida. What attracted them and kept them loyal is a report card of attributes that gives this city straight A's in climate, cultural and recreational activities, and services.

Start with soft Gulf Coast winters in which the temperature averages 62°. In the summer the thermometer can jump to a sticky 86°, but even that is mitigated by cooling bay breezes in the evening and omnipresent air conditioning. Golf, tennis, and boating abound, and local beaches—particularly Lido Beach—are said to have the whitest, finest sand in the state.

Sarasota's streets sparkle, a matter of civic pride. The city maintains some Spanish flavor

Living Costs in 20 Attractive Towns

As this table shows, the cost of living varies enormously in 20 popular retirement locations. In Honolulu, a condominium sells on average for more than four times a house price in Provo, Utah. Even Seattle and Tacoma, while only 25 miles apart, are distinct in many ways, not least of all the 22% difference in the price of a house. A pattern is hard to find. For example, Honolulu has the highest rents and steak and egg prices, but its greens fees and energy bills are among the lowest. The house-price figures represent what a retired person would pay for a house or condominium —typically two bedrooms—whichever is most common in the area. Greens fees cited here are for 18 holes of golf on a public course (private in Palm Springs, where the cart is also included).

	House price	Property taxes	Rent	Monthly energy bill
ALBUQUERQUE	$85,000	$400	$395	$99
AMHERST, MASSACHUSETTS	190,000	2,300	520	125
BLOOMINGTON, INDIANA	80,000	850	360	124
CHAPEL HILL, NORTH CAROLINA	135,000	1,500	440	105
FORT LAUDERDALE	62,500	400	540	130
HONOLULU	190,000	980	1,550	53
KERRVILLE, TEXAS	80,000	850	410	97
MYRTLE BEACH, SOUTH CAROLINA	80,000	640	390	72
PALM SPRINGS, CALIFORNIA	85,000	950	590	117
POINT PLEASANT, NEW JERSEY	150,000	1,600	850	65
PORTLAND, OREGON	85,000	2,500	355	75
PRESCOTT, ARIZONA	68,500	655	340	65
PROVO, UTAH	45,000	405	310	85
ST. PAUL	90,000	1,600	500	125
SAN ANTONIO	88,000	1,350	325	117
SAN DIEGO	150,000	1,500	850	86
SARASOTA	77,500	850	390	35
SEATTLE	98,000	1,000	430	59
TACOMA, WASHINGTON	80,000	700	415	70
TUCSON	100,000	825	455	83

Top state income tax rate	Sales taxes	Hospital room	Doctor's visit	One pound of steak	One dozen eggs	Greens fees
8.50%	5.25%	$238	$25	$3.79	$0.69	$8.00
5.00	5.00	337	30	4.99	1.10	5.50
3.40	5.00	215	20	4.42	0.77	10.00
7.00	5.00	197	30	5.22	0.68	7.00
—	6.00	249	30	4.44	0.78	10.00
10.00	4.00	241	40	5.69	1.55	6.00
—	7.50	118	25	3.92	0.81	6.50
7.00	5.00	200	25	5.23	0.72	30.00
9.30	6.00	296	40	4.05	1.32	70.00
3.50	6.00	200	40	4.99	1.09	10.00
9.00	—	307	25	4.24	0.76	10.00
15.00	7.00	205	40	3.98	0.89	7.50
7.70	6.25	236	20	3.05	0.69	9.00
8.00	6.00	312	25	3.86	0.58	5.25
—	7.50	175	30	4.43	0.78	6.50
9.30	6.00	300	30	3.33	1.31	9.00
—	6.00	227	30	3.78	0.71	11.00
—	8.10	266	40	4.86	0.70	8.50
—	7.80	295	25	4.49	0.85	12.75
15.00	7.00	248	30	4.13	0.77	12.50

in older buildings, but that is being gradually upstaged by modern residential communities in lush green settings, often with their own golf courses and tennis courts.

What sets Sarasota apart from so many other Florida cities is its cultural life. Art and theater lovers, in fact, have nearly as much to choose from here as they do in Baltimore, more than three times the size. The Ringling Museum of Art has one of the largest Rubens collections in the world. The St. Louis Symphony, Bobby Short, and Itzhak Perlman all performed in Sarasota during one month last winter. The Van Wezel Performing Arts Hall, Asolo State Theater, and Florida West Coast Music Inc. are just some of the distinguished arts presences in the area.

Spring in Sarasota has a special sweetness. So many people watch the Chicago White Sox at spring training that a new stadium with seating for 7,800 and expanded parking will replace smaller Payne Park. The Pittsburgh Pirates play at McKechnie Field in Bradenton, just a 15-minute drive north.

Classes in subjects from fitness to religion to architecture are offered at the Longboat Key Adult Education Center for about $50 a course. The Sarasota Institute of Lifetime Learning holds 35 lecture series just for retirees on literature, politics, religion, and history. For $20, you can attend an unlimited number of lectures.

Amherst, Massachusetts. Calling Amherst (pop. 36,000) a college town is an understatement. Perhaps that's poetic justice for a place whose personality is as elegantly understated as if it never forgot that Emily Dickinson lived her entire life here. Amherst and the surrounding Pioneer Valley in western Massachusetts are home to Amherst College, Hampshire College, Mount Holyoke College, Smith College, and the University of Massachusetts. Yet this place also manages to deliver cosmopolitan living, the amenities of a first-class suburb, a ravishing rural setting, many services designed specifically for retirees, and a friendliness for which New England towns are definitely not renowned.

As you might have guessed, the price of such a package of superlatives comes high.

Housing costs are a shock, as in much of economically vibrant Massachusetts. An Amherst voter referendum to slow growth through a two-year moratorium on new-home construction, which ended last May, has sent the median house price up 34% annually since 1986 to $190,000. Bob Mitchell, director of Amherst's planning department, expects house price increases to moderate this year with appreciation of perhaps 5% annually. Apartments are hard to come by (typical monthly rent for a two-bedroom apartment: $520), but they come with a special tax break. Tenants may deduct half their annual rent, up to $2,500, from their state income taxes.

Downtown, serious browsers will find a bookstore practically every 50 yards. Dozens of retirees take classes at UMass, where day and evening courses providing college credits are tuition-free for anyone 60 or older. Roughly a third of the area's 3,000 retirees have ties to one of the valley's colleges, according to John Clobridge, executive director of the local council on aging. In the summer, groups of retired residents often take a scenic 1½-hour drive west through the Berkshires to concerts at Tanglewood or dance performances at Jacob's Pillow.

Although only about 8% of Amherst's population are retirees, the town makes special efforts to reach out to them. Amherst's cable-television channel lists activities at the local senior center. Free vans take retirees to any personal appointments upon request. The 90,000-volume public library is known throughout the region for its collection of 1,850 large-print books. With both town and campus police, Amherst is notably safe, too. Its crime rate is half that of a typical U.S. metropolitan area.

Bloomington, Indiana. If you are one of those Renaissance folks who relish Bob Knight, grand opera, Kurt Vonnegut, and ice fishing, this lively university town (pop. 53,045) is made for you. Bloomington caught its worst case of Hoosier fever in decades in 1987, when the Indiana University basketball team, flogged to a frenzy by Coach Knight, won the national collegiate championship. Even if you are not much of a fan, you could turn to the university for a feast of cultural opportunities. The school of music, one of the best in the country, mounts professional and student opera, jazz, ballet, theater, and musical productions almost every evening. Many are free. A season's subscription to the opera costs as little as $36—less than the price of a single ticket in some cities. IU also offers a noncredit adult education program with 37 courses from Greek to computer programming for $16 to $80.

Recreational activities tend to be vigorous. The city operates 35-acre Riddle Point Park at Lake Lemon, which is 15 miles northeast of Bloomington and has camping and beach facilities. And at Lake Monroe, the state's largest park with nearly 26,000 acres of land and water, activities span the seasons from ice fishing for large mouth bass and bluegill to some of the finest sailing in the Midwest.

Seattle/Sequim, Washington. Seattle's setting is extravagant, with gleaming Puget Sound to the west and two mountain ranges—the Olympics and the Cascades—towering to the west and north. Downtown is dotted with parks. The waterfront bustles with stylish shops and restaurants. Pioneer Square has lovingly restored buildings dating from before the Gold Rush.

Seattle (pop. 493,000) is also the cultural center of the entire Northwest. The Seattle Symphony is 85 years old; there's a Gilbert & Sullivan Society, and a professional ballet company, Pacific Northwest Ballet. There are about a dozen professional and semiprofessional theaters.

Yet what if you are picky enough to object to two drawbacks: the weather (156 rainy days a year) and Seattle's fairly fast pace? Then head 70 miles northwest, via a scenic half-hour ferry ride over Puget Sound and an hour's drive. There you will find what some airplane pilots call "the blue sky of the Northwest." Sequim (pronounced *squim*) has a population of 3,300, and nestles in a valley protected by the Olympic Mountains. So it gets only 16 inches of rain annually, compared with Seattle's 50. Summer temperatures in Sequim rarely exceed 80°, and the winter average is 32°.

Sequim transplants claim to have seen 100-pound halibut and 40-pound salmon landed in the vicinity. Clamming and crabbing are cherished pastimes. When residents tire of Sequim's lone moviehouse, two 18-hole golf-courses, and four seafood restaurants, they can always retreat to Seattle. They may not even have to do that much longer for specialized medical care: the Olympic Memorial Hospital in Port Angeles, 15 miles away, will soon open a cardiac and radiation center in Sequim.

Medical Musts for Serious Trekkers

Six months exploring the Indian subcontinent? A jaunt up the 1,600-mile Orinoco? Hiking the Himalayas? Exotic, exciting, and extended describe the kind of trips that appeal to retirees today. But with more adventurous travel comes greater risk of illness and injury.

Fortunately, you can avoid disaster by taking precautions. You might start with a pretrip travel clinic. Many big-city hospitals have such a service. At the travel and immunization center of Long Island Jewish Medical Center in New Hyde Park, New York, for example, you pay $25 for a consultation that includes advice tailored to your health and your destination. For additional fees ranging from $15 to $35 each, you can get all the recommended shots. "Travel clinics are probably better equipped than general physicians are to offer specialized advice on such matters as tropical diseases and food precautions," says Beth Weinhouse, author of *The Healthy Traveler* (Pocket Books, $6.95).

Or you can research the perils particular to your destination on your own. For the most current health warnings, consult your state or local health departments. A strain of malaria that recently appeared in West Africa, for example, may require that you take one type of medicine before you leave and bring another along with you for treatment should you need it. Health departments can also tell you whether the water is safe to drink, what precautions to take if it isn't, and what kinds of special immunizations and preventive medicines you will need.

How to Retire on the House

Trading down is the best way to raise cash from your home.

More and more people are turning to the family residence, its value fattened by inflation, to buttress their retirement income. About 75% of Americans over 65 own their own homes, with an average of more than $50,000 in equity waiting to be tapped. Most retirees living on fixed incomes, however, don't earn enough to qualify for conventional home-equity loans, the simplest way to exploit this burgeoning asset. But selling out and buying or renting a smaller place—trading down—is usually the smartest move anyway. On balance, it also outperforms such alternatives as taking a reverse mortgage, which is a loan against home equity that allows the borrower to defer repayment, or just staying put (See the table on page 161).

What's best for you depends greatly on whether you need to raise money from your home—and how much. Your retirement costs probably will come to about 70% of your pre-retirement expenses. If your expected income from investments, Social Security, pensions, and other sources falls well short of your requirements, you may have little choice but to tap your prime asset. But executing a trade-down calls for careful planning. Financial planners and housing specialists advise you to:

Estimate your profit in advance. Before you sell your old house, try to find out what you will need to spend for a suitable replacement. If your potential profit is small, trading down might not be worth the trouble and expense. Be sure to take into account any savings you will realize from reduced maintenance and property taxes on a smaller home. Lower costs and taxes might make it worthwhile to move even if your profit from the trade-down is slim.

Time your sale to take advantage of tax benefits. If you or your spouse are 55 or older, you may be able to exclude from taxes up to $125,000 of the capital gain on the sale of your home. Should your gain exceed $125,000, you can defer tax on the excess by reinvesting the money in a new residence. If you have lived in your home for less than three of the five years preceding the sale, however, you do not qualify for the exclusion. In that case, it's probably worth delaying the sale until you can take the tax break.

Consider lending the buyer part of the purchase price. Interest payments on the loan will provide more income than you would receive if you sold for cash and invested the proceeds conservatively, such as in five-year Treasury notes, recently paying 8.7%. The reason is that fixed-rate mortgages lately have been about two percentage points higher. Insist on a down payment of at least 20%. That will protect your principal if the buyer defaults on the loan and, in fact, is an incentive for him *not* to default.

Pay cash for your new home. You could take out a mortgage and invest your house profits elsewhere, but the returns on conservative investments would not cover the loan payments. Just be sure that you leave yourself enough cash to meet emergencies and that you have other investments to offset the risk that your house might lose value. When you tie up all of your cash in a house, you lose the protection of a diversified portfolio. If you must borrow to pay for your new home, get a mortgage with a fixed rate so that you never have to worry about payments rising sharply.

One alternative to trading down is selling and renting permanently. In the long run, selling your house and becoming a tenant might be less financially rewarding than trading down. But it might well provide enough cash to defray your housing costs and free considerable cash for travel and other expenses. And if you decide to move again, you won't be pinned down by the task of selling a home, which could prove difficult if the real estate market in your area goes soft.

Of course, you may be among the homeowners who, like impoverished nobility in an English novel, wouldn't think of abandoning their castle, even if they have to sell all the silver to pay the upkeep. In that case, you may want to consider one of the following techniques to hold on to the old place. Some of them are limited to certain regions, and others require the cooperation of relatives or outside investors.

Reverse mortgages. They pay the borrower a fixed monthly amount and defer repayment. Reverse mortgages come in several forms, with closing costs of typically 2.5% of the total loan. The most attractive type offered is the Individual Reverse Mortgage Account (IRMA), whereby the lender receives part or all of the value of your home, including its appreciation during the term of the loan, in return for deferring repayment until you move or die. (In the latter case, your estate pays off the loan.) American Homestead, a Mount Laurel, New Jersey mortgage bank, offers IRMAs in California, Connecticut, Delaware, Maryland, Massachusetts, New Jersey, Ohio, Pennsylvania, and Virginia.

Your income from an IRMA depends on the size of the mortgage and the life expectancies of you and your spouse. If you live beyond your life expectancy at the time you signed the mortgage agreement, your lifetime payments from an IRMA may exceed the value of your home. But if you die soon after you enter the program, your estate must repay the lender all of the monthly checks you received, with interest, plus all of the appreciation in the house since the mortgage was signed.

Why Trade-downs Work Best

The tables below show three options available to a 65-year-old couple with a mortgage-free house worth $250,000.

TRADE-DOWN

Year	Additional income	Annual housing costs	Home equity and principal
1	$13,500	$3,200	$254,000
5	13,500	3,744	271,665
10	13,500	4,555	298,024
15	13,500	5,541	330,094
20	13,500	6,742	369,112
25	13,500	8,203	416,584

The couple get the biggest payoff if they sell the house and buy a smaller one for $100,000. Then they can invest their $150,000 gain in a diversified portfolio of investments, in this case yielding 9%. The income will more than cover their housing costs.

REVERSE MORTGAGE

Year	Additional income	Annual housing costs	Home equity
1	$5,676	$8,000	$223,312
5	5,676	9,359	185,293
10	5,676	11,386	106,979
15	5,676	13,853	0
20	5,676	16,855	0
25	5,676	20,506	0

The couple can take out an Individual Reverse Mortgage Account, which provides payments of $5,676 a year for life. If they live for at least 15 years, their estate will owe the lender an amount equal to the home's value.

DO NOTHING

Year	Additional income	Annual housing costs	Home equity
1	0	$8,000	$260,000
5	0	9,359	304,164
10	0	11,386	370,061
15	0	13,853	450,236
20	0	16,855	547,781
25	0	20,506	666,459

If they stay put and leave their equity intact, the couple will retain the full value of their property, which increases by 4% a year in our example. But they will need income from other sources to meet rising costs, including maintenance, insurance, and property taxes.

SOURCES: HOUSTON ASSET MANAGEMENT; AMERICAN HOMESTEAD

One variant on this type of loan, called a term reverse mortgage, is downright dangerous for most homeowners. With a term reverse mortgage, the lender makes monthly payments to a homeowner for a given period of time, typically seven years. At the end of that term, the homeowner must repay the loan, which often means selling the house. But occasionally, the loans do make sense. For example, an elderly person who is on a waiting list for a nursing home might take out a term reverse mortgage to meet his expenses in the interim.

Sale-leasebacks. Here is how this type of arrangement worked for a California widow, age 79, who sold her home in 1984 to an investor for $92,400. She received a down payment of $25,000 and granted the investor a 13-year mortgage that pays her $825 a month. Just over $400 goes for the rent she pays to the investor, who qualifies for tax benefits because of the house's status as a rental property. The rest supplements her income from Social Security and the violin lessons she gives to local children. The mortgage payments will stop in 1997, when she turns 89. To ensure that her income continues indefinitely, she took the precaution of investing $6,800 from the down payment in a single-premium deferred annuity, which will begin paying her $825 a month when the mortgage payments stop. Meanwhile, the lease limits her annual rent increases to 2%, and she has managed to set aside some money for her heirs.

With a sale-leaseback, the buyer generally agrees to a 10% to 20% down payment and 15-year mortgage. The buyer also covers the cost of property taxes, insurance, and maintenance. For example, a typical sale-leaseback with a 10% down payment and a 15-year mortgage on a $250,000 house might generate $32,000 in income to the seller, who would pay about $21,000 in rent during the first year. The income would remain constant, but the rent might climb to about $36,000 by the end of the mortgage term. As an added precaution, you probably should invest part of the down payment in a deferred annuity so that you will continue to receive income should you outlive the mortgage.

Finding an investor to take part in a sale-leaseback may be difficult, unless your children or other family members can afford to make the investment. Either way, enlist the help of an experienced attorney. Local bar associations and real estate boards will probably recommend professionals who can help you structure a typical deal for approximately $1,500 to $2,000 and for $45, the National Center for Home Equity Conversion (110 E. Main St., Room 605, Madison, WI 53703) will send you its booklet, *Sale Leaseback Guide and Model Documents*.

Charitable donations. If you can't find an investor to do a sale-leaseback and you have no children, you might try an institution such as a school, hospital, or charity. They will sometimes grant you a lifetime annuity in exchange for a remainder interest in your property. You continue to own it, but when you die it's all theirs.

Accessory apartments. If you have rooms to spare in your home, you might consider turning them into an apartment that you can rent out. Before you do anything, find out if zoning regulations in your community permit such an arrangement. If so, ask a contractor to estimate the cost and real estate agents how much rent you will be able to charge.

Ask your local agency on aging if your area has a household matching service, which helps bring people with extra rooms together with prospective tenants. The service might help you find a suitable tenant; otherwise, try real estate agents. The book, *Creating an Accessory Apartment* (McGraw-Hill, $16.95) by Patrick H. Hare and Jolene N. Ostler, includes a sample lease and other useful information.

While you're weighing these options, give careful consideration to the emotional impact each will have on you as well. Anything that makes you uncomfortable is not worth doing, no matter how smart it may be in dollars and cents.

Tending to Your Pension and Savings Plans

Who's supposed to protect that nest egg from harm? Your employer? Less and less. You? More and more.

For millions of employees, October 1987's Wall Street meltdown rudely reaffirmed some tired truths about the stock market—and some fresh ones about their companies' retirement packages. Chief among the lessons is that old-fashioned corporate paternalism is waning, and with it the cozy promise that if you put in your time, your company would look after your retirement. Today the amount of money you take with you when you retire depends on how well *you* manage your interest in your company plans.

This shift toward employee self-reliance was under way well before Black Monday. Over the past decade, capital-accumulation plans, including profit-sharing, thrift, and 401(k) accounts—in which the employee, not the employer, bears the investment risk—have grown three times as fast as traditional pensions. The 401(k) has spread most rapidly: more than 82% of large and medium-size employers now offer one, up from less than 2% in 1983.

As long as the stock market kept going up, the growing significance of these plans was easy to overlook. But not anymore. The crash was a powerful lesson in how crucial your management of the plans can be in achieving a successful retirement. Fortunately, Black Monday sent a far more forgiving message about the other half of many employees' retirement package, their pension. No matter how hard you were hit in your capital-accumulation plans, the crash did not cost you a penny in pension benefits. That's because your employer guarantees your pension benefit, boom or bust.

The two types of retirement plans thus demand very different strategies. With regard to your pension, your task is simply to understand how your benefits build and to use that knowledge to capitalize on a valuable asset. In your capital-accumulation plans, the challenge is more active: to balance investment risks with your desire for high return on your contributions and your employer's. The following should help make the decisions a little easier.

Your Pension

Your employer typically calculates the size of your pension by multiplying a percentage of your final salary—say, 1%—by the number of years you were on the payroll.

There is little you can do to manage your interest under this arrangement. Almost all employers fund their pensions entirely out of their own pockets, and all of them bear the responsibility both for investing the pension fund and for ensuring that the money to pay your retirement benefits is there when you need it, regardless of the fund's investment performance. In the rare event that your company were to go bankrupt with an underfunded pension, a quasi-governmental insurance agency, the Pension Benefit

Guaranty Corporation, would guarantee your benefits up to $1,900 a month.

A far more serious threat to many employees' future retirement income is their own readiness to change jobs. In most pensions, you are entitled to a certain retirement payout—that is, you become vested—after 10 years. Starting in 1989, companies must begin to vest employees fully after their fifth year or gradually between their third and seventh year of service. The shorter vesting schedule will help job hoppers become vested in more pensions, but it may not boost their retirement income appreciably. That's because when you leave a pension in mid-career, your benefits are frozen as of your departure. When you eventually start collecting checks from that pension, generally no earlier than age 55, inflation may have drastically eroded their value. So, if you are within a decade of retirement, you should not change jobs or accept an early-retirement package without taking into account the value of the pension benefits you would forfeit.

How can you tell the value of what is essentially just a series of monthly checks beginning at some time in the future? The answer: Your pension's current worth is the amount of money your employer would theoretically have to set aside today to pay you your promised

A Primer for Nine Common Retirement Plans

The nine varieties of retirement plans listed below are all that most wage earners need to concern themselves with. But they are enough.

With the exception of the defined-benefit pension, all of the plans require some caretaking—from occasional to intense.

	Major source of funding	Usual form of benefits	Where invested
Defined-benefit pension	Employer	Annuity	Diversified among stocks, bonds, cash and sometimes real estate
Money-purchase pension	Employer, employee contributions sometimes allowed	Lump sum or installments	Same as defined-benefit pension
Profit-sharing plan	Employer, employee contributions usually optional*	Lump sum	Usually employee's choice of diversified stock fund, fixed-income account or company stock
Savings plan	Employee*: company usually matches a portion of employee contributions	Lump sum	Same as profit-sharing plan
Employee stock-ownership plan (ESOP)	Employer	Single payment of stock shares	Company stock
Tax-sheltered annuity (TSA or 403[b] plan)	Employee**: employer may contribute in some plans	Employee's choice of lump sum or annuity	Usually employee's choice of mutual funds or insurance company annuities
IRA	Any salary or wage earner	Lump sum or periodic withdrawals	Account with bank, brokerage, insurance company, mutual fund, credit union, savings and loan or independent trustee
Keogh plan	Self-employed people	Same as IRA	
Simplified employee pension (SEP)	Company: employee contributions may be optional††	Same as IRA	

*Employee contributions are tax deductible if the plan is set up as a 401(k).   **Employee contributions are tax deductible.
†Those not covered by a company retirement or Keogh plan or who have adjusted gross income less than $25,000 ($45,000 for married couples)
††Employee contributions are tax deductible in some SEPs.

monthly checks over your expected life span in retirement. This is roughly the same sum an insurance company would charge for an annuity equal to your pension benefit. Thus, your accountant or financial planner can easily estimate the value of your pension from insurance company annuity tables.

To use this technique to evaluate an early-retirement offer, ask your employee-benefits department to tell you what your benefit would be if you retired now and what it would be if you retired at the time you had planned to leave. For example, a 56-year-old executive currently earning $70,000 who had been with a typical company for 15 years might normally

be entitled to $1,300 a month. That benefit would require a pension reserve of $156,000. If the executive were to stay on the job until age 62 and received raises of 7% a year, he would retire on $3,310 a month. The fund would then need $343,000 when he reached age 62. That's the equivalent of $222,000 today, assuming the money was invested at 7.5%. An early-retirement package would have to offer him an additional $66,000 ($222,000 minus $156,000) just to compensate him for foregone pension benefits.

The moral is that each year you continue working you earn far more in pension benefits than you might think. In a typical plan, the value of your pension would quadruple between ages 55 and 65. The reason is that every year you work, your payout grows because it is based on an ever-larger percentage of an (presumably) ever-larger salary.

Your Savings Plan

Unlike pensions, capital-accumulation plans do not guarantee any particular retirement income. Instead, your employer establishes an investment account on your behalf and promises only to chip in a specified sum periodically. Otherwise, the responsibility for managing your account falls largely on you. You decide how to invest your account in the plan, and you take the consequences. If your investments go sour, no kindly corporate patriarch stands by to make up the loss.

A consolation for shouldering the investment risk is that you can change jobs without gutting your payout. Your benefit—the sum that has built up in your account—simply leaves with you. You can either roll it over into an Individual Retirement Account or into the capital-accumulation plan offered by your new employer, if that plan permits. Whichever you choose, your money continues to grow.

The first decision you need to make in piloting a capital-accumulation plan is whether to get on board at all. There is a reason to hesitate aside from the investment risk. Once you have money in the plan, it is quite difficult to get it out. In 401(k)s, for example, you can

Remarks

Benefits depend on salary and length of service

Benefits depend on size of contributions and investment performance of pension fund

Company contributions depend on size of company profits

Employees may be permitted to borrow a portion of vested benefits

Starting at age 55, employees must be given a choice of other investments for a portion of their account balance

Offered only by schools and nonprofit institutions

Contributions are tax deductible for some IRA holders†

Contributions are tax deductible

Designed for small businesses

withdraw tax-deductible assets only in the case of financial hardship, and even then, if you are younger than 59½, you will owe the tax man a 10% penalty tax on top of his usual cut.

Financial planners brush this demurral aside, however. One way or another, you have to save for your own retirement, they point out, and capital-accumulation plans give you impressively more benefit for the buck than other methods of saving. At the very least, they allow your money to grow tax-free, which builds capital faster than similar investments outside the shelter of a company plan. In a 401(k) plan, moreover, the first $7,313 you stash away in 1988 is not subject to income tax (The maximum tax-free contribution rises annually with inflation). That means that if you are in the 28% tax bracket, it effectively costs you only $72 of spendable income to save $100. The 401(k) advantage turns even more

enticing if your contributions are matched by your employer. In the most common formula, the employer kicks in 50 cents for each dollar you contribute—an instant, guaranteed 50% return.

Assuming that you do decide to participate in the plan, which investments should you choose? Generally, you must select among two to four funds. These might include some relatively risky growth investments—such as a diversified stock fund or a fund invested entirely in the employer's stock—and one or two safer choices, such as a government securities fund or one consisting of guaranteed investment contracts (GICs), which are virtually risk-free investments similar to bank certificates of deposit but backed by an insurance company. Rather than trying to manage your retirement savings to take advantage of—or reduce your exposure to—changing market conditions, you

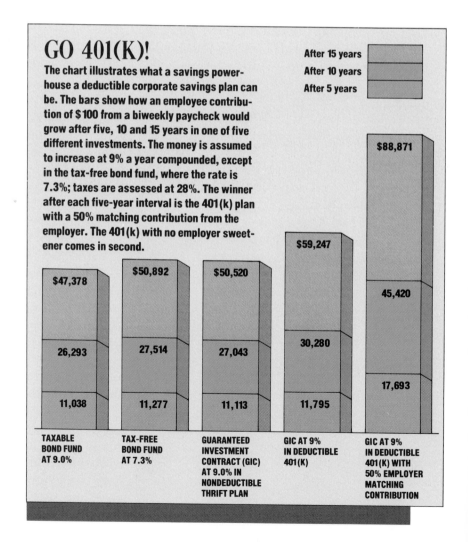

GO 401(K)!

The chart illustrates what a savings power-house a deductible corporate savings plan can be. The bars show how an employee contribution of $100 from a biweekly paycheck would grow after five, 10 and 15 years in one of five different investments. The money is assumed to increase at 9% a year compounded, except in the tax-free bond fund, where the rate is 7.3%; taxes are assessed at 28%. The winner after each five-year interval is the 401(k) plan with a 50% matching contribution from the employer. The 401(k) with no employer sweetener comes in second.

After 15 years
After 10 years
After 5 years

TAXABLE BOND FUND AT 9.0%	TAX-FREE BOND FUND AT 7.3%	GUARANTEED INVESTMENT CONTRACT (GIC) AT 9.0% IN NONDEDUCTIBLE THRIFT PLAN	GIC AT 9% IN DEDUCTIBLE 401(K)	GIC AT 9% IN DEDUCTIBLE 401(K) WITH 50% EMPLOYER MATCHING CONTRIBUTION
$47,378	$50,892	$50,520	$59,247	$88,871
26,293	27,514	27,043	30,280	45,420
11,038	11,277	11,113	11,795	17,693

are better off adopting a conservative, diversified portfolio and sticking to it. Don't think of your company plan in isolation; ideally, the investments in the plan should blend in with your outside holdings to create an overall retirement portfolio that reflects your risk tolerance and your goals.

If your personal holdings are large enough, it makes sense to keep most of your stocks there and to put safer, income-producing investments in your company plan. That way, you can soften the impact of setbacks in the stock market by writing off capital losses on your income tax return. You don't have that option if you suffer losses inside tax-sheltered retirement plans.

Because of the limited investment choices that asset-accumulation plans offer, they may not blend smoothly with the rest of your portfolio. This is particularly true if—as is the case for many corporate employees—your capital-accumulation accounts make up the bulk of your retirement portfolio and absorb most of your annual retirement savings. In that event, you must construct a diversified portfolio that matches your goals as best you can with the choices available to you. If you are more than a decade from retiring, your focus should be on building your assets; your best course then is to keep half to two-thirds of your account in a growth-oriented fund and the rest in fixed income. If your plan offers two or more investments in a category—you may have a choice of both a general stock fund and a growth stock fund, for example—split your allocation among them.

As you move to within five years of retirement, shift two-thirds or more of your account into the income fund. Note that you probably will not be able to make the move all at once. Most capital-accumulation plans forbid you to rearrange your account more often than quarterly. Many also limit the fraction of your account that you can move between investments at one time. In this case, however, such restrictions can have a benign effect. By forcing you to make portfolio switches gradually, they may prevent you from cashing out at what later turns out to have been a temporary market bottom.

Are You on Your Way to a Comfortable Retirement?

By age 50, most people are planning seriously for retirement. But younger people often lack a specific strategy. If you are under 50, this quiz will tell you whether you are doing enough for your retirement. Give yourself a point for each yes answer.

1) If you are under 40, are you saving 10% of your annual salary? If you are 40 or older, are you setting aside 10% of your salary specifically for retirement?

2) Is part of your savings in a tax-deferred account, such as an Individual Retirement Account or 401(k) plan?

3) Do you have three to six months' worth of living expenses in a cash account available for use in emergencies?

4) If you are under 35, do you own growth investments that you plan to leave untouched for at least a decade? If you are 35 or older, do you have a well-diversified portfolio that includes cash, bonds, and real estate?

5) If you have children, have you established a college tuition fund? (If you have no children, count this as a "yes.")

6) Do you own your own home? If not, and you are under 35, are you saving to buy a home?

7) If you are under 35, do you work for a company with a pension plan? If you are 35 or older, do you have a vested pension?

HOW YOU RATE

1 point or less: You are in the pits when it comes to retirement planning. Start putting money away using techniques such as payroll deductions.

2 to 4 points: You're off to a good start. Once you have an emergency fund, invest for long-term growth.

5 to 7 points: Pat yourself on the back. After filling in any cracks, all you will need is the discipline to stay the course.

How to Handle a Plump Payout

The real homework begins after you decide which way to take your retirement money.

So you served your time, built up your pension credits, religiously stashed a part of your paycheck in the company savings plan and tended it wisely all these years. Now comes the gut-wrenching part: deciding how to take the money. At stake is probably the bulk of your retirement wealth. And since most choices open to you are irrevocable, if you choose wrong you are stuck with the consequences for the rest of your life. For these reasons you probably will want to have a financial planner or accountant help you wrestle with the numbers and keep you from tripping over the tax laws. Together you might consider the following questions:

Should you take your payout as a lump sum or an annuity? If your only company retirement plan is a pension, this decision has probably already been made for you. That's because most pensions pay benefits only in the form of a monthly annuity, which means equal monthly payments for the rest of your life. Only about one in five pension plans allows employees to take a lump sum instead. You are most likely to face the choice if your retirement package includes a capital-accumulation plan such as profit sharing or a 401(k). Though such plans normally pay benefits as lump sums, your company may let you convert your account balance into an annuity. And even if your savings plan requires you to take a lump sum, you can always use the money to buy an annuity from an insurance company.

With an annuity you don't have to worry about squandering your retirement money on a bad investment or spending it all before you die. The annuity is guaranteed to last as long as you do. On the other hand, even with moderate inflation of 5% or so, fixed monthly payments will decline in purchasing power over the years. A 5% annual price rise will halve the real value of your checks after only 14 years.

If you take a lump sum, however, you could put a portion in growth investments to preserve the purchasing power of your assets. Also, you may lean toward a lump sum if you want to leave money to your heirs.

In converting your benefits to a lump sum, a pension plan's administrator calculates the amount it would take to pay you a check every month for the rest of your expected life, as determined by actuarial tables, assuming the money earns a particular rate of interest, say around 8%. But pension payments stop at the end of your life (or your surviving spouse's), not at the end of the actuarial life expectancy assigned to you at retirement.

Thus, an annuity turns out to be a bargain if you manage to live longer than average, while a lump sum wins out if you die shortly after you retire. So if you are chronically ill you should consider taking a lump sum; conversely, if you or your spouse are descended from a long line of nonagenarians, you might lean toward the annuity. If you're somewhere in between, read on. Note, too, that in calculating lump-sum conversions, employers use unisex life expectancy tables that understate life expectancies of women, who as a group live longer than men. All else being equal, that makes an annuity a better deal for a woman than for a man.

Interest rates can also determine whether a lump sum or an annuity is more advantageous. The higher the rate the plan's actuaries assume it can earn, the smaller the lump sum needed to pay a benefit. For example, in July 1984, when interest rates were around 10.5%, a pension of $1,000 a month for a 60-year-old man translated to a lump sum of $93,000. In March 1988, when interest rates were 8%, the same benefit produced $109,000.

Many pension managers assume a conservative interest rate at the beginning of the year and stick with it. Thus, in a year of rising interest rates, a lump sum offered by your plan late in the year could be disproportionately large. One simple way to tell would be to ask your life insurance agent how large an annuity benefit you could buy with the lump sum your pension is offering. To be competitive, an insurance company has to change its interest-rate assumptions frequently to match prevailing rates in the economy. So if interest

Lump Sum Versus Annuity

To decide how to take your retirement money, you should project the financial consequences of each option. This table, put together with the help of Paul Westbrook, a retirement planner in Watchung, New Jersey, reviews the choices open to a couple, both 65, who are faced with a $250,000 benefit.

The first option would be to leave the money in the pension plan, which would pay them an annuity of $24,000 ($17,280 after taxes). The payments would continue as long as they lived; however, with 5% inflation, by the time the couple reached age 75, the check would be worth only $10,346 in 1988 dollars.

The remaining four options all require the couple to take the $250,000 as a lump sum and invest it either in a tax-free municipal bond fund, paying 7.3% a year, for example, or a taxable bond fund yielding 9%. In each case, they could then withdraw $17,280 after taxes in

the first year and increase the payout by 5% a year to counteract inflation. Thus, at age 75, they would still receive the same amount of money in 1988 dollars that they did at age 65.

If the couple needed income right away, they could pay the tax up front, taking advantage of the favorable 10-year forward-averaging rate. Invested in the tax-free fund, the remaining money would last them to age 78. Two less desirable options are paying the initial tax at the less favorable five-year averaging rate and postponing the tax by rolling over the entire sum into an IRA. The disadvantage is that both options would exhaust the couple's capital when they reached age 77.

The best course, if the couple can let the money grow untouched for five years, would be an IRA rollover. In that case, the sum—invested in the taxable bond fund—would last to age 86.

Option	Initial tax	Net sum invested	Income* at age 65	Income* at age 75	Balance at age 75	Age when income ends
Pension	$0	$0	$17,280	$10,346	$0	death
Lump sum with 10-year averaging	50,770	199,230	17,280	17,280	85,330	78
Lump sum with five-year averaging	60,110	189,890	17,280	17,280	66,436	77
IRA rollover with immediate withdrawals	0	250,000	17,280	17,280	108,882	77
IRA rollover with no withdrawals for five years	0	250,000	0	17,280	372,865	86

*In after-tax 1988 dollars, assuming inflation of 5% a year

rates are rising, you might be able to obtain a higher monthly payment from an insurer's annuity than from your pension, in spite of the insurer's sales charges and profit margin.

If you want an annuity, what kind should it be? The most common annuities are life only, which pays you a certain monthly amount until your death; joint and survivor, which assures that if you die first your spouse will continue to receive a certain amount until he or she dies; and life and period certain, which pays benefits for your lifetime or for a specified period—15 years, say—whichever is longer.

The option you choose will affect the size of your monthly checks. Life-only annuities pay the largest pensions but stop once you die; the other options continue to provide checks for your beneficiaries at the cost of reducing your income by 10% to 15% during your lifetime. One possible compromise: Select the life-only option and buy a life insurance policy. Then when you die and the pension payments cease, the insurance benefits will provide for your spouse. (Under federal law, a married person cannot choose the life-only option without the written consent of his or her spouse. To make the insurance tactic work, get a notarized waiver of the joint-and-survivor option from your spouse.)

Take the example of a 63-year-old manager who must choose between a life-only pension of $30,000 or a $25,700 joint-and-survivor pension with his 63-year-old wife as beneficiary. Were he to select the life-only option and then buy a whole life policy that has an initial face value of about $130,000 (Level-premium whole life is required because term insurance becomes prohibitively expensive at older ages) the couple could pocket an extra $50 a month in retirement income after subtracting the cost of the insurance. Upon his death, his wife would get the same income as under the joint-and-survivor pension option. To reduce the cost of this strategy, insist on a policy with minimum cash value buildup and a face value that decreases over time. That way, as your beneficiary ages, he or she needs less life insurance proceeds to provide the same income because his or her life expectancy is growing shorter.

Which tax option should you take for a lump sum? A lump-sum distribution need not be very large to push you into the top tax bracket of 33%, which in 1988 was triggered by a taxable income of $43,150 if you were single, $71,900 if you were married. Luckily, the tax code lets you use one of two tax-saving tactics. First, if the lump sum makes up at least 50% of the value of your interest in a specific plan, such as a 401(k), you can roll over the distribution into an Individual Retirement Account within 60 days after receiving it. Your money will compound tax-free until you make withdrawals, which will be taxed as ordinary income. Thus, if you don't need to begin withdrawing money from the IRA for three to five years, the rollover is probably the better choice.

Second, you can use a tax-saving device called forward averaging if you meet these conditions: (1) your payout represents your entire interest in a plan; (2) you have participated in the plan for at least five years; and (3) you are 59½. If you are 52 or older in 1989, you get a special break: you don't have to wait until you reach 59½ to use forward averaging. But if you aren't at least 55, you will be socked by a 10% early-withdrawal penalty.

If your lump sum makes it past all these checkpoints, it is taxed as if you had received it over five years instead of all at once. This is known as five-year forward averaging. If you were born before January 1, 1936, you can choose an even more capacious break, 10-year forward averaging. In both cases, you pay the total tax in the year you get the money but at a much lower rate than if the sum were taxed the way the rest of your income is.

For example, with five-year forward averaging, a married couple with $30,000 of other income who received a lump sum of $150,000 would pay $30,398 in taxes—an effective tax rate of 20%—instead of the $45,867 (31% rate) they would pay under ordinary tax tables. With 10-year forward averaging, you figure your taxes at 1986 rates, when brackets were as high as 50%. The couple in this example would pay a tax of $24,570 on their lump sum—an effective rate of about 16.4%.

People over age 52 who participated in their

How Does Your Company Plan Stack Up?

Unless you are independently wealthy, your company retirement plan will be an important source of income one day. Although wise management of your employer's retirement plans will improve your eventual payoff, nothing beats having a generous package to begin with. To help you judge yours, *Money* asked employee-benefits experts what features distinguish a solid gold handshake from a brass imitation. Their answers:

A generous pension formula. Pension plans usually compute your retirement benefits by multiplying a percentage of your salary by the number of years you worked for the company. As a rule, the most generous formulas, known as final-pay pensions, use your salary during your highest-paid three to five years. According to a survey of 812 large and medium-size employers by the benefits consulting firm Hewitt Associates of Lincolnshire, Illinois, about one in six companies bases its pension payout on your average salary over your entire career, a formula that tends to penalize employees who rise through the ranks. In practice, however, many of these companies voluntarily update their plans to make them competitive with final-pay pensions.

A typical final-pay formula would award you retirement income equal to 1% of your average salary during your three to five highest-paid years times the number of years you spent with the employer. Be pleased if the pension gives you 1.5% or more for each year of service; if you get 2% or more—as do employees of Morgan Guaranty and PepsiCo—feel free to brag about it. On the other hand, if your plan follows a career-average pay formula, a typical multiplier of 1.5% would produce only about as much retirement income as a three-quarters of 1% to 1% final-pay pension, because the salary used in the formula would be smaller. Few companies using career-average-pay plans, however, go much higher. Two that do: Ford, which employs an accrual rate of 2%, and American Honda, which uses 2.5%.

If you are tempted to leave work before your company's standard retirement age, note that most formulas will reduce your pension. If you have been with your employer for 30 years, for example, three out of four companies surveyed by Hewitt would trim your benefits—by 4% a year on average—if you left before age 62.

Adjustments for inflation. Less than 5% of pension plans guarantee periodic inflation raises to retirees. And though many companies voluntarily increased pension payments during the roaring inflation of the 1970s, the practice has faded in recent years. Companies have either adopted a new tough corporate philosophy or simply no longer fear inflation as much. If your employer, like AT&T, Kodak, and Lockheed, has boosted retirees' income in the past four years of comparatively low inflation, take it as an encouraging sign.

More than one plan. Since even a long-term employee can expect his combined pension and Social Security benefits to replace only about 40% to 60% of his salary, it helps to have a supplementary capital-accumulation plan, such as profit sharing or a 401(k). According to Department of Labor statistics, only about two of five packages offer at least two plans, but multiple plans are far more prevalent among large employers. Hewitt Associates found that 92% of such companies backed employees with at least a pair of plans. About one in six toss in two capital-accumulation plans, such as a 401(k) and an employee stock ownership plan. Having a combination of plans could make a difference in your lifestyle after retirement.

A 401(k) with matching contributions. In more than two-thirds of the 401(k) plans in the Hewitt Associates survey, the employer offers to chip in a certain percentage of your contribution, most commonly 50 cents on the dollar. One in five of them matches you dollar for dollar, however, and one in 100 gives you more. Two magnanimous matchers: National Westminster Bank, which hands over to its employees $1.50 for every dollar they contribute, and Bankers Trust, which matches two dollars for one.

employer's pension plan before 1974 have yet another option. They can elect to have the portion of the sum attributable to their pre-1974 contributions taxed as capital gains at the top 1986 rate of 20%. Your company benefits department can tell you exactly how much qualifies as capital gains. Taxpayers in this category can then use five-year or 10-year forward averaging for the remainder of their payout.

What methods give you the least tax? If none of your distribution qualifies as capital gains, the answer is easy: 10-year averaging if your payout is less than $473,700. Above that amount the lower tax rates used in five-year averaging outweigh the greater bracket-lowering power of 10-year averaging. For other situations, the only way to choose between forward averaging and a rollover is to project the consequences of both into the future and see which alternative rewards you with the most after-tax income.

What Can You *Really* Count on from Social Security?

A new government document spells out your benefits.

One of the biggest aggravations in retirement planning used to be getting an accurate estimate of your Social Security benefits. If you knew the right questions, you could write to the Social Security Administration, which months later would send back, piecemeal, the scraps of information you had specifically requested. No longer. Last year the agency began spelling out your whole basket of benefits in an eight-page document called a "Personal Earnings and Benefit Estimate Statement."

To get one, you simply call a toll-free number (800-937-2000) and request Form SSA-7004. This is a questionnaire asking you for a number of facts about yourself, including your name, Social Security number, date of birth, previous year's earnings, current year's estimated earnings, the age at which you plan to retire, and your projected earnings from now to retirement. About four to six weeks after you send in the form, you can expect to receive this list of estimated benefits:

● Your monthly retirement check from Social Security, in today's dollars, at your stated retirement age. To arrive at this figure, the Social Security Administration computer assumes that your future annual earnings, net of inflation, will rise at the national average of 1% a year. The earliest you can collect your check is at age 62, if you are willing to settle for 80% of what your benefit would be if you worked to 65.

● The full benefit you could get by waiting until you are age 65 to retire. Under Social Security regulations, 65 will remain the standard retirement age until 1999. After that, the age for collecting a full benefit will start to rise at the rate of nearly one month per year. Someone born in 1939, for example, will have to wait four months after his or her 65th birthday to be eligible for a full retirement benefit. From that point on, the full-benefit retirement age keeps increasing until it gets to age 67 in 2027. There it will remain.

● The 33% larger benefit available to people your age who continue working until they are 70 years old.

• Your survivors' monthly benefits if you die during the current calendar year. Children of Social Security taxpayers are likely to be eligible for these benefits until they reach 18 or 19, depending as a rule on when they finish high school. A spouse who stays at home with the children can also collect survivors benefits until the youngest child is 16. By taking an outside job, however, a widow or widower will probably forfeit Social Security income. Last year, for example, the loss was equal to $1 for every $2 earned in excess of $8,400 a year for those recipients between 65 and 70.

• Your disability benefits if you will be unable to work for at least a year or if you are terminally ill. Like survivors benefits, Social Security disability benefits include income for dependent children.

• A year-by-year statement of your earnings that were subject to Social Security taxes and of the Social Security taxes that you paid. Since the Social Security Administration has been known to make an occasional error in figuring benefits, you should check the numbers you get by matching them against your own earnings records.

The Social Security statement also explains briefly but clearly what it takes to become eligible for benefits. Basically, you must work 10 years to earn retirement benefits but generally only five out of the last 10 years to claim disability benefits.

How Social Security Income Builds

These figures represent the approximate yearly income from Social Security benefits for a single person and, on the following line, for a worker and a nonworking spouse of the same age, when they become eligible for full Social Security benefits at age 65 to 67. All of the amounts in the table are Social Security Administration projections in 1988 dollars, based on continuous employment throughout an adult lifetime.

Your earnings in 1987	▶		$20,000	$25,000	$30,000	$35,000	$45,000 or above
Your age in 1988	▼ 25	Individual	11,796	13,548	14,568	15,600	17,652
		Couple	17,688	20,316	21,852	23,400	26,472
	35	Individual	10,896	12,540	13,476	14,436	16,296
		Couple	16,344	18,804	20,208	21,648	24,444
	45	Individual	9,972	11,496	12,360	13,104	14,412
		Couple	14,952	17,244	18,540	19,656	21,612
	55	Individual	9,048	10,344	10,920	11,352	12,036
		Couple	13,572	15,516	16,380	17,028	18,048
	65	Individual	8,100	9,216	9,564	9,792	10,056
		Couple	12,144	13,824	14,340	14,688	15,084

Annual Social Security benefit ▲

The Policy You May Need the Most

The premiums run high, but you can protect your life savings against the cruel cost of long-term care.

Most people's foremost fear in planning their retirement is simply outliving their money. Yet that terror can be tamed by Social Security, a pension, and a well-planned program of personal savings and investments. What *should* rank as the No. 1 financial fear of growing old is the cost of long-term care for people too feeble to look after themselves—a nonstop expense that can quickly deplete resources built up over a lifetime. Now this problem too can be alleviated. Growing numbers of insurance companies are offering long-term-care policies that are more comprehensive and affordable than you might think.

The longer we live, the more likely it is that we will have to pay others to dress and groom us, feed us, and move us around. Americans' life expectancy at age 65 is increasing dramatically. Since 1940, the chances of living another 20 years have doubled, from one in five to two in five, and they are expected to rise to three in five by the year 2030.

With longevity comes a new set of medical problems. Where once disability came largely from strokes, cancer, or other acute diseases, for the over-85 generation, it is more likely to come as a gradual loss of the ability to take care of oneself. Elderly people live for years with chronic ailments such as Alzheimer's disease and osteoporosis, which seldom require long hospital stays but render the victims more and more helpless. In the past, the duty of caring for them fell to their children or other family members. Now, with the generations dispersed geographically, the givers of care tend to be paid strangers. While only 8% of people 65 to 84 years old are in nursing homes, 32% of the 85-plus group are institutionalized. Of the rest, an estimated 23% stay at home with regular assistance from nurses, housekeepers, or meal-delivery services.

The cost can be crushing. At average rates, nursing homes charge $24,000 a year, and the fees are escalating in step with inflation. Expect to pay on average $30 to $50 a day for home-care services, which include physical therapy, administration of drugs, and food preparation. Few people are up to the costs. In 1987 a congressional subcommittee on aging found that 70% to 80% of nursing-home residents used up all of their capital in a year or so and were forced onto welfare. Once impoverished, nursing-home patients usually have to move to less desirable accommodations in the same facility or to a less costly institution.

Most Americans have done little or nothing to prepare for the high risk of needing long-term care—or its rising cost. One reason is that they assume incorrectly Medicare will pick up their nursing-home bills. Medicare pays only for stays in skilled nursing homes—ones staffed with doctors and nurses—and then only if admission follows a hospital stay. Furthermore, this coverage is limited to 100 days per admission. Supplemental Medigap plans, which you can buy from private insurers, pick up part of the medical expenses that Medicare doesn't pay. But Medigap also excludes long-term care. So does the catastrophic coverage that, effective this year, Congress added to

Choosing a Life-Care Community

Just a couple of years ago, you might have been scared off from life-care communities as possible places to live in retirement. They were bright on promise: A stiff entrance fee of, say, $30,000 guaranteed you food, housing and, if necessary, nursing-home care until the day you died. But the industry was marred by financially incompetent and sometimes unscrupulous operators. In the decade to 1985, 40 communities ran into financial difficulties—in a few cases leaving residents bereft of both money and services.

Since then, the life-care industry has undergone a thorough housecleaning. New state laws require communities to have substantial reserves and more fully disclose the condition of their finances to prospective residents. The industry itself has sponsored an accrediting commission to help screen out inept operators. As a result, you stand a better chance than ever of finding financially sound, well-managed life-care communities, also known as continuing-care retirement communities.

Today there are approximately 700 such communities in 45 states, nearly double the number 10 years ago. Specifically geared to the comfort and physical limitations of older people, usually 75 and up, they typically offer studio, one- and two-bedroom units, plus facilities for long-term care. The communities also provide physical therapy and home care and usually feature extra help for housekeeping. One of their most attractive aspects to many older people and their families is that providing needed care and services falls to the communities' social workers, not to inexperienced family members.

Average entrance fees at all-inclusive communities—those that provide shelter plus all medical and support services—range from $37,000 for a studio to more than $100,000 for large apartments. Monthly fees are $700 to $1,100 a person. A majority of these communities fully or partly refund entrance fees to residents if they leave, or to their estates when they die. A continuing-care community with re-

funds, however, may charge entrance fees that are twice those of a nonrefunding facility.

At somewhat lower cost—$27,000 to $85,000 entrance fees and $650 to $750 monthly fees—some communities offer modified continuing-care contracts. They provide all residential and some medical and support services. Typically, 50 or 60 days of nursing-home care might be included in the community's fee or a discount of 15% to 20% on daily, weekly, or monthly rates at the nursing home.

A third type of continuing-care community is the fee-for-service contract. For entrance fees ranging from $21,000 to $56,000 and monthly fees of $570 to $690, you can buy residential apartment space and pay for medical and personal services as you use them. A fee-for-service community can then be combined with a long-term-care insurance policy.

Whatever type of community you find attractive, make sure that you thoroughly understand exactly what expenses are covered and what you will be paying for them over and above the cost of your living unit. Since both your living arrangements and your medical care will be provided by the community, be sure it's capable of doing the job. Check the performance record of the community itself or, if it's brand new, of its sponsors, owners, and managers.

Ask your state attorney general's office whether there are regulations governing reserves and other financial obligations and whether the community meets them. At last count, some 23 states had such regulations, and one industry trade group, the American Association of Homes for the Aging, has been sponsoring accreditation reviews for the past four years. Accreditation assures that the community is financially sound and maintains a high standard of service to residents.

For a list of accredited communities and a useful consumer guide to choosing one, send $2 to American Association of Homes for the Aging, 1129 20th St. N.W., Suite 400, Washington, D.C. 20036 (202-296-5960).

Medicare. This new plan, which will be phased in between 1989 and 1991, is aimed at expenses which result from acute illnesses, such as heart attacks, and injuries, such as bone fractures.

Long-term care necessitated by the gradual enfeeblement of aging rather than acute illness is uncovered except by Medicaid, the medical welfare program for the indigent. Worse yet, many of the most desirable nursing homes discourage—or refuse outright—applicants who are on Medicaid.

What to do? The best protection against long-term care's financial wipeout is a comprehensive, solidly funded life-care community, a retirement residence that provides medical and personal care to the elderly in or out of a nursing home. But you have to pay an entrance fee of at least $20,000—and usually much more. Another alternative, so far open to only a few, is a specialized health maintenance organization (or HMO) that includes long-term care among its prepaid services. The third choice, and the only one for most people, is to buy their own long-term-care insurance policy. The premium is likely to be more than $1,000 a year if you put off the purchase until you are past 70. Fortunately, though, the coverage is becoming more comprehensive and some insurers are abandoning escape clauses that marred earlier policies.

Whether you should sign up for long-term-care insurance depends largely on your age. People under 50 are best advised to do nothing because broader and better solutions, public or private, probably lie ahead. Those past 50, however, or the children who might someday have to support them, can't afford to wait. Since purchase of long-term-care policies is limited to those in good health and few companies sell insurance to anyone over 80, it is prudent to insure yourself by age 60 or so.

About 70 commercial insurers and seven Blue Cross plans now offer coverage for long-term care—generally meaning up to six years—in either a nursing home or the patient's own dwelling. Because the coverage is fairly new, insurers are wary of assuming too much risk, and the few plans offering affordable protection are not available in every state.

(For the names of companies selling long-term-care insurance in your state, write to the Health Insurance Association of America, 1025 Connecticut Ave. N.W., Washington, D.C. 20036.) Take a close look at the following characteristics of any policy you might consider buying:

Costs and benefits. Annual premiums for long-term-care insurance range from $100 or so for those in their thirties to more than $3,000 for the broadest coverage on people nearing 80. Almost all policies have one major drawback: they indemnify you for a fixed dollar amount per day, no matter how much you are paying for services or how much their cost may rise over the years. An antidote provided optionally in a few policies is an inflation provision at extra charge, typically 1% more a year for each 1% of additional benefits. In contrast, hospital and major-medical insurance pays all or a high percentage of each bill.

On average, U.S. nursing homes charge $65 a day, and top rates are more than twice that. The daily amount reimbursed by most nursing-home policies is up to you. The higher the premium you pay, the higher the benefit, with twice the coverage generally doubling your cost. For instance, American Republic Insurance in Des Moines would charge a 70-year-old $800 annually for a $50 daily benefit lasting 1,500 days and $1,600 for $100 a day. Once you become insured, however, your premium should remain constant unless it includes inflation protection.

Deductibles and duration of benefits. How many days of care come out of your pocket before your benefits begin and how long they continue will greatly influence the premium you pay. Most insurers offer at least two choices of waiting periods, typically 20 or 100 days. Selecting a 100-day waiting period can reduce your premium by as much as 30%. So choose as long a waiting period as you can afford. At the other end, though, more coverage is worth paying for. Since the majority of policy-holders will need care for less than a year, benefits that quit after 12 months or so may cost only half as much as those continuing for the six-year maximum many policies currently offer. The extra coverage, however, can mean the difference between solvency and bankruptcy for the minority whose confinement continues for years.

Benefit prerequisites. Many policies require hospitalization for three days or so before benefits begin. Yet the need for paid care is often the result of a deteriorating condition such as arthritis, which may not put you in the hospital at all. The most worthwhile policies require only that a doctor certify the need for care.

Types of services covered. Some people require medical services; others just need personal care. Some people can get along in their own home; others have to be in a nursing home. Ideally, a long-term-care policy should offer the widest possible options, including nursing homes in three categories of medical care: skilled homes; intermediate homes, which provide rehabilitative therapy; and custodial homes, which offer little more than practical nursing. The best policies also pay for care at home, adult day-care centers and brief intermittent care at a nursing home, also known as respite care.

The policy should offer those benefits in nearly equal amounts so as not to bias your choice. A policy that covers nursing-home care for years but home care for only a month or so forces you to opt for institutionalization or to skip benefits. The fewer the types of care covered and the more heavily the choice is skewed toward one type of care, the less useful the policy is. Most companies now cover home care. But some, such as CNA of Chicago, charge extra for it or, like Amex Life of San Rafael, California, reduce the payments over time. Amex's plan pays for home care only after you have been in a nursing home and only for as many days as you were there. Furthermore, Amex cuts the daily benefit after 30 days. While companies insist that this practice keeps premiums down, you should carefully compare premiums and policies to make sure that less coverage actually costs less.

Exclusions. Alzheimer's disease can leave victims helpless for 15 years or longer. That's why some insurers exclude "organic brain disease" from the conditions their policies cover and why you shouldn't buy any such policy. (All of the policies in our table cover organic brain disease.) Most policies have a six-month or so waiting period before they start paying benefits for diseases you had before paying the insurance. This pre-existing illness clause is standard, and you can't avoid it.

Renewability. Be sure your coverage will continue for as long as you want it to and that your premiums can't be hiked unless everybody's are raised in your area. In the language of insurance, such a policy is guaranteed renewable. An examination of premiums indicates that you pay little or no more for this highly desirable feature. If you live in Arizona, Hawaii, Indiana, Iowa, Kansas, Nebraska, North Carolina, North Dakota, Oklahoma, or Virginia, you are protected by law against cancellation of a long-term-care policy because of age or deteriorating health. Any policy that can cut you off just as liability begins to increase is a bad deal.

How to Buy Drugs by Mail

Mail-order sales of prescription drugs have leaped 30% to 50% annually for five years and now account for $900 million of the $25 billion retail drug market. Small wonder. Mail-order suppliers claim that the prices of their predominantly generic drugs run as much as 50% below those of the brand-name equivalents.

Some people hesitate to shop long distance for drugs. While the National Association of Mail Service Pharmacies insists that the odds of a drug mishap are extremely low, you can exercise extra quality control when ordering by mail in several ways:

● Check the reputation of your supplier by phoning the appropriate state board of pharmacy, which regulates mail-order drug sellers located in its state.

● Stick with a supplier that has an 800 number you can call to consult with a staff pharmacist if you have questions.

● Be certain the supplier keeps a computerized medication profile for each customer and consults it before filling new prescriptions. This could head off a bad reaction from combining drugs.

An Anatomy Lesson on Six Policies

Because long-term-care insurance is expensive, you should be able to customize your coverage. Some policies offer a few flexible options. Others allow you to pick nearly every feature. Ideally, you want to pay for only the types of care you think you will require and to keep benefits flowing for as long as you are likely to need them. The policies dissected here pay benefits primarily for nursing home care. They share these four strong points:

■ All are guaranteed renewable; your coverage cannot be canceled if you pay the premiums on time.
■ All will cover you for Alzheimer's disease.
■ All can be written to pay benefits for at least four years.
■ And all are available in most states.

The rates shown here apply if you are in good health; certain ailments may be insurable at a higher rate. Where inflation protection is optional, we include the cost of one year's increased coverage. After that, the premium rises when the benefit is hiked. Highly desirable features are marked with a check.

Company	Policy (number of states where it is sold)	
Aetna Life & Casualty Hartford 203-273-4510	**Long-term care** (35)	**Plan A**
		Plan B
AIG Life Wilmington 302-594-2000	**Nursing-home insurance** (28)	
American Republic Insurance Co. Des Moines 800-247-2190 Ext. 2175	**Americare** (all but Alaska and Minnesota)	**Low Option**
		High Option
CNA Insurance Chicago 800-262-1919 In Illinois, 800-325-1843	**Long-term care** (all but Kansas and Minnesota)	**Low option**
		High option
John Hancock Mutual Life Boston 617-421-3517	**ProtectCare** (35)	**Basic**
		Comprehensive
The Travelers Hartford 203-277-9101	**Group long-term-care plan** (29)	

* 60-day wait
† Three days in the hospital required before benefits are paid to new buyers 80 or older, and benefits last only one year

Covers custodial nursing homes, home care, and day care, except as noted	No prior hospital stay required, unless otherwise noted	Inflation protection available	Annual premiums for $50 per day of benefits, after a 90-day wait, at ages 60 to 79	Comments
	Three days	Optional at extra cost	$299 to $1,918	Inflation protection boosts benefits 5% a year for 15 years and adds 5% a year to the premium.
		Optional at extra cost	$393 to $3,514	
Home-care benefit requires 30 days in a nursing home; no day care	Three days	No	$272 to $1,616	Primarily nursing-home coverage
Covers only skilled and intermediate-care homes		No	$367 to $1,037*; $1,563 at age 85	One of the few plans available to people who sign up at age 85 or older
Home care only		No	$419 to $1,171*; $1,781 at age 85	
Home care costs extra; no day care	Three days	Optional at extra cost	$299 to $1,608; $556 at age 80†	Plan can be tailored to several levels of coverage. High-option premium includes home care.
No day care		Optional at extra cost	$447 to $3,094; $668 at age 80†	
	14 days in a skilled nursing home	Optional at extra cost	$277 to $1,550	Extra coverage is offered every three years to keep pace with inflation.
		Optional at extra cost	$367 to $2,733	
		No	$474 to $2,283	Available only to large, employer-sponsored groups

Leaving a Lasting Legacy

A short but essential course on wills, trusts, and estate taxes.

It's strange but true: about seven of 10 adults have life insurance, but only a third have wills. The most plausible explanation for such faulty forward planning is that insurance is sold and wills are not. Since lawyers don't hawk their services door-to-door, you will just have to motivate yourself to provide a secure financial future for your family. Start by considering the consequences if you decide to do nothing:

Thy will won't be done. Should you die without a will, your heirs' inheritances will be determined under state laws of intestacy, which may not even begin to match your own notion of who should get what. In most states your assets are apportioned among your spouse and children, often with half to two-thirds going to your kids.

The tax man grabbeth. Even if you write a will, your estate may not escape taxation. By using trusts, however, a married couple can pass as much as $1.2 million to their heirs free of federal estate tax, with its grim-reaper rates running as high as 55%.

Suffer ye children. A carefully drawn estate plan will protect and preserve property that you leave to young children or disabled heirs. You can also spare your heirs the inconvenience of probate, the legal process in which your will is proved valid and your assets are inventoried in court.

To accomplish all of this, you will need the help of an attorney who is well versed in estate planning. Unfortunately, finding a lawyer who is experienced in this specialty may be difficult. Ask your friends, relatives, accountant or financial planner for recommendations, or call your city's bar association and ask for the telephone number of the local estate planning council, which is an association of lawyers, accountants, insurance agents, financial planners, and bank trust officers who specialize in estate planning. You will be able to communicate more effectively with your lawyer if you understand the fundamentals of estate planning discussed below.

A Simple Will

Many people never get around to writing a will for fear of confronting their own mortality. Others figure they don't need one if they own all of their assets jointly. But their survivors eventually learn that joint ownership is no substitute for a well-drafted will.

Assume, for example, that an elderly widow puts her son's name on her bank account, making him joint owner of the balance, so he can deposit checks for her. She may tell him to divide the money equally with his siblings after she's gone. But what happens if he decides to keep the cash? His brothers and sisters can sue, but litigation is costly and time consuming and may not be worthwhile unless a large amount of money is at stake.

Married couples shouldn't rely solely on joint ownership either. If a childless couple were involved in an accident in which the husband was killed while the wife survived for another day, the husband's half of the couple's joint property would automatically pass to his wife. But unless she managed somehow to scribble a will as she lay on her deathbed, all of the couple's assets would go to the wife's relatives after her death, leaving his family with nothing.

Couples with minor children also need wills, despite the fact that their jointly held property will go to their children under state laws of intestacy if they die together. It's in a will that you nominate guardians to care for your children and manage their inheritances. If you don't name caretakers for your kids, the probate judge will appoint guardians of his or her own choosing for the children and their assets.

You also nominate the executor of your estate in your will. It is his or her responsibility to pay your debts, file tax returns, and disburse assets to your heirs after you are gone. (For more about the duties of an executor, see box below.) The peace of mind that a will provides comes at a modest price. Simple wills for a husband and wife cost $50 to $200. If

Advice for Executors

Congratulations! Your father wants you to serve as the executor of his estate. No doubt you won't think of this honor again until your father dies. But you will be able to settle your father's estate more quickly and economically if you prepare for the task well in advance. First, you must discuss your father's financial affairs and intentions with him. You should ask him to maintain an up-to-date inventory of his assets and liabilities, which he can leave for you in a specified place. Your father doesn't have to give you a copy of the will, but he should tell you where the original is and who prepared it so you can find it later.

When you file the will in probate court, a judge will officially appoint you executor of the estate. The court may require you to post a bond—the size is typically equal to the value of an estate's cars, furnishings and other personal property—to safeguard the financial interests of your father's other heirs, unless your father waived the bond in his will. The bond premium is paid out of the estate.

Your first duty is to identify and determine the value of the estate's assets. Then, with an attorney's aid, you must shepherd the estate through probate proceedings. You needn't hire the lawyer who prepared your father's will, but you may want to do so if he or she is familiar with your father's financial affairs. The attorney's fee, as well as those of appraisers and accountants, comes out of the estate.

If your father rented a safe-deposit box, you may have to inventory its contents under the watchful eyes of a state tax collector. It's also your responsibility to file claims for any life insurance or veterans' and Social Security benefits that are due. If your father died in an accident or because of medical malpractice, you should see to it that any necessary lawsuits are filed.

In the meantime, you must invest and protect the estate's assets, perhaps seeking advice from a stockbroker, investment adviser, or bank trust officer. Finally, you must pay your father's outstanding debts, file any required income, federal estate and state death tax returns, and distribute what's left over to your father's heirs. It's your prerogative to determine which assets to sell to raise cash to pay debts, taxes, and bequests. Throughout, you must keep careful records because most probate courts require a detailed accounting of all money received, spent, and held by the estate.

Your load may be lightened considerably if your father has named a bank or trust company as co-executor. The institutional executor will make investment decisions and file tax returns, relying on you to interpret your father's wishes. But don't count on such assistance unless your father's estate is both large and complicated. Most banks and trust companies won't handle estates of less than $75,000. An institutional executor's fees generally range from 2% to 5% of the total value of the estate.

What's in it for you? Your commission, which may be set by state law or the probate court, is 1% to 5% of the estate. But you can waive the fee, accepting instead the gratitude of your fellow heirs.

you already have a will, examine it periodically to make sure it still reflects your wishes.

Caring for Heirs

If your heirs are very young, disabled or simply disinclined to manage money, you will shortchange them if you do nothing more than write a rudimentary will. Say that you and your spouse die and leave your assets to your minor children. The guardian of their property named in your will must report expenditures and investments on the children's behalf to a judge. This prevents the guardian from stealing or dissipating the children's inheritances. But it also gives a judge who is unfamiliar with your financial goals and investment philosophy power over how your legacy is managed and spent.

That's one reason why it's advisable to create a trust in your will to hold your children's inheritances. If you do, you needn't name a guardian of your children's assets because a trustee you select will follow instructions that you set down in your trust document. Another advantage of creating a trust is that you can keep the trust principal out of your children's hands until you think they will be mature enough to manage money. If you leave property to your children in your will, on the other hand, they can claim their inheritances when they reach the age of majority, which is 18 in most states.

Many people, however, shy away from trusts because they associate them with the super-rich. In reality, a married couple might pay as little as $250 for wills that establish trusts for their children. Trusts are quite flexible, and a lawyer can draft yours to fit your family's particular needs.

A trust is a legal device that holds property placed in it by a person called the grantor for the benefit of one or more beneficiaries. The grantor sets forth instructions for the management of the trust and the disbursement of its income and principal in a document called the trust agreement, which is drawn up by an attorney. The grantor also chooses a trustee to carry out his wishes.

There are two basic types of trusts, testamentary and living (sometimes called *inter vivos*). A testamentary trust is created in your will and takes effect upon your death. A living trust starts to operate during your lifetime. In addition, living trusts may be either revocable or irrevocable. With a revocable trust, you continue to control the trust property, meaning you can change the trust's provisions, terminate it or, in some cases, even serve as trustee.

Once you establish an irrevocable trust, you cannot control assets in it or tinker with its provisions. As a result, property in an irrevocable trust isn't included in your estate for the purpose of calculating estate taxes. (You may, however, incur gift tax when you put property into an irrevocable trust.) Assets in a revocable trust are part of your taxable estate. A testamentary trust for your minor children that becomes irrevocable upon your death is included in your taxable estate because you controlled the property in it during your lifetime.

A trust is only as effective as the trustee you choose. The ideal trustee is financially savvy and has your children's best interests at heart. Your relatives and friends will probably agree to serve without any compensation. Institutional trustees such as banks and trust companies will generally levy annual fees of about 1% of a trust's assets up to $1 million. After that, the larger the trust, the smaller the trustee's percentage.

Estate Taxes

If you fail to draw up an airtight estate plan, the Internal Revenue Service may claim a more than generous share of your estate. The top estate tax rate was supposed to fall to 50% in 1988. But it was frozen at 55% on taxable estates of more than $3 million until 1993 in a little-publicized provision of the 1987 tax law. Congress also slapped a 5% surtax on estates above $10 million. In addition, state death taxes range from zero to 30%.

Yet with proper planning, most estates can escape federal and state taxation. Your $600,000 exclusion from federal taxes includes the sum of taxable gifts you make while you are alive as well as the estate you leave when you die. You can make tax-free gifts of as much as $10,000 a year each to as many people as you would like; married couples giving jointly may bestow as much as $20,000. You can also make unlimited tax-free gifts to charity and payments to health-care and educational institutions to cover a relative or friend's medical or tuition bills.

Furthermore, you may make gifts of any size and leave an estate of any value to your spouse tax-free. If your spouse is not adept at money management, you might want to leave assets to him or her in a trust that qualifies for the marital deduction, meaning that its contents aren't subject to estate tax. There are two basic types of marital deduction trusts: With a general power of appointment trust, your spouse decides which heirs get the trust's assets after he or she dies. With a QTIP (qualified terminable interest property) trust, you choose your spouse's eventual heirs.

If you leave everything to your spouse, however, you may succeed only in postponing estate taxes until his or her death. As a result, more complicated tax planning may be necessary. You can eliminate or at least reduce estate taxes by removing assets from your estate. One way to accomplish this is to make tax-free gifts during your lifetime; a married couple can pass as much as $1.2 million to their heirs tax-free if both spouses fully utilize their $600,000 exemptions.

You can also trim your tax liability by placing property in an irrevocable living trust. The hitch is that few people can afford to relinquish control of real estate, securities or other assets years before their death. Instead, many people transfer the ownership of their life insurance policies to an irrevocable life insurance trust. Upon your death, your life insurance proceeds go into such a trust untaxed. Your spouse typically receives income from the trust for life and can even tap its principal if necessary. After he or she dies, the assets go to the heirs named in your trust agreement.

There's one catch, however. If you die within three years of establishing an irrevocable life insurance trust, the insurance proceeds

are included in your taxable estate. For that reason, attorneys often include a clause in the trust agreement stating that should you die within three years, the insurance will go directly to your spouse or into a trust for his or her benefit. The trust is included in his or her estate.

You can also remove assets from your taxable estate by making gifts to charity during your lifetime or in your will. You can even give assets to a charity and keep on getting income from them by establishing a trust or buying an annuity from the charity. Of course, because you retain income from your gift, the tax deductions you receive will be smaller than what you might have gotten with an outright gift.

If you establish a charitable remainder unitrust, for example, you receive an amount determined annually by multiplying a fixed percentage that you select when you create the trust—typically 7% to 9%—by the market value of the trust's assets. After your death, payments end or a beneficiary that you name can continue to receive the income from the trust. When he or she dies, the trust's property passes to the charity. In general, charities welcome only sizable remainder unitrusts—worth $25,000 or more.

Charitable remainder annuity trusts work much like unitrusts but pay out a fixed amount each year, usually 7% to 9%. Appreciated property producing little or no income makes the best gift. If you sold it and reinvested the proceeds for higher income, you would incur a taxable capital gain. But if a charitable trust sells the property, no tax is due. For smaller donors, some charities offer pooled income funds that operate much like mutual funds. Many such funds accept initial donations as small as $5,000.

Altruists whose hearts are bigger than their bank accounts should also consider charitable gift annuities. Many tax-exempt organizations issue these contracts for contributions as small as $1,000. In exchange for your donation, the charity pays you a fixed amount each year for life. The younger you are when you buy the annuity, the lower your return. For example, a 50-year-old would receive 6.5% for life while a 90-year-old would collect 14%. You would receive more income if you bought an annuity from an insurance company, but you would not get any income tax deductions or an estate tax break.

One last point: It is important to leave a liquid estate. If yours is loaded with real estate or fine art, your heirs may be forced to sell your assets at fire-sale prices to satisfy the tax man. Your survivors will not face a liquidity crisis if you leave them enough life insurance to pay the estate taxes. Also, insurance proceeds are not subject to probate, so your executor will be able to get his or her hands on cash fast.

If you wait until you are on your deathbed to act, you will not be able to buy life insurance but you can purchase special U.S. Treasury obligations called flower bonds. They generally yield only 4% but bloom at your death, when they can be redeemed at face value to pay federal estate tax.

Probate

In some counties, probate court is a 20th-century version of *Bleak House.* Probate is less horrific in other locales, but it always takes time and costs money.

Depending upon the efficiency of your executor and the local court, your heirs may have to wait six months to two years for their inheritances. If they fight over who gets what, the process can drag on for much longer. Court costs, attorneys' and executors' fees vary by locale, but they will probably add up to about 5% of your estate. Worst of all, if you own property in more than one state, your executor will have to contend with two or more legal proceedings. And probate court records are public, so nosy neighbors and relatives can find out how much you left to your loved ones.

Your share of assets that are jointly owned or have named beneficiaries—such as life insurance policies, pensions, profit-sharing plans, and Individual Retirement Accounts—escapes probate. But you shouldn't put property in joint names just to avoid probate. This could, for example, trigger federal estate tax after the second spouse's death if he or she leaves an estate worth more than $600,000.

A better solution is to create a revocable living trust. Property in such trusts also bypasses probate. A married couple should expect to pay $1,500 to $2,500 for a pair of living trusts that include so-called pour-over wills, which state that any property you forgot to place in your living trust should go there after your death. Those assets will be subject to probate, but most states have simplified, less costly probate procedures for small estates (those totaling $500 to $60,000).

Revocable living trusts are flexible. You can keep any or all income such a trust produces, change its provisions or terminate it. You can even act as your own trustee. Consequently, property in a revocable living trust is included in your taxable estate. After your death, the trust can remain intact for your survivors or it can end with assets distributed to your heirs. Your wishes, which you set down in your trust agreement, are carried out by the trustee or, if you served as trustee during your lifetime, by the successor trustee you appoint. A relative, friend or one of your beneficiaries may agree to serve for free. If the trust terminates at your death, banks and trust companies generally charge a one-time fee equal to 1% of the trust principal.

A living trust can also benefit you while you are alive. If your physician certifies that you are no longer capable of handling your own finances, your successor trustee takes over. This is less expensive and often more satisfactory than the alternative, a court-appointed conservatorship. A conservator must present an annual accounting to the court and may have to get approval to make major expenditures and investment decisions. Your successor trustee simply follows the instructions in your trust agreement.

After you have grasped the basics of estate planning, it's time to act. Much of the humor in the dour field of estate planning has to do with poor planning—like the *New Yorker* cartoon in which an elderly gent thumbs through a copy of *How to Avoid Probate!* on his deathbed. Good estate planning is a continuing process, not something that can be done at the last minute.

Mutual Fund Rankings

Thomas Sweeney had his hands full. The Fidelity Capital Appreciation Fund he runs was continuing to fall—and panicky investors were making it worse. "Black Monday was over," the manager says of 1987's frightening fourth quarter. "But shareholders were still checking out." So Sweeney sold some stocks to meet redemptions. Then he had to sell some more. He sold so many, in fact, that by October 31, 1987, Fidelity Capital had shrunk in assets to $850 million from $1.5 billion pre-crash.

For investors who kept their cool, however, the tale has a warmer ending. True, Fidelity Capital Appreciation shareholders lost 24% in that quarter. But the fund rebounded so fast—up 32% in the first nine months of 1988—that those who hung in are ahead, albeit by a slim 0.2%, for the 12 months to October 1988. Under normal circumstances, that would be nothing to crow about. But during that same period, Standard & Poor's 500-stock index fell 12.4%. Stock funds, on average, did not do as well as Fidelity Capital, but they did finish two full percentage points ahead of the S&P. Concludes Sweeney: "Investors would be a lot better off if they had stayed put."

Yet, unconvinced shareholders continue to pull assets out of stock funds *and* bond funds (even though the average fixed-income portfolio was up 10.6% for the 12 months to October 1988). According to the Investment Company Institute, a fund industry trade group, Americans yanked more money out of stock and bond portfolios ($1.6 billion net) in August

1988 than they had in any month since that darkest of Octobers.

A consensus of experts interviewed by *Money* says enough already. Kurt Brouwer, author of *Mutual Funds: How to Invest with the Pros* (John Wiley & Sons, $19.95), reports that too many former fund buyers are spending too much time mourning their losses. They are sulking in certificates of deposit and money-market funds, he says, and putting off the business of building life savings and protecting themselves against an inflation risk more threatening over the decades than the vagaries of stocks. At recent levels of about 4.6% a year, inflation can halve the purchasing power of your money in about 17 years. If last year taught us anything, it was that emotions can run as wild as markets. In that post-crash year and over the long term, the wisest course has been to stay calm and ride out drops, however violent. "There will always be market cycles," according to veteran international fund manager John Templeton, 75, who has weathered 48 years' worth of them as a portfolio adviser. "I think maybe some of the younger investors didn't stop to think about that."

So the first lesson of the crash is do not panic when everyone else does. While there was much (and justifiable) consternation about the tie-up of funds' telephone switch lines on October 19, shareholders who gave up on getting through and then resisted the urge to bail out of stock funds in the weeks that followed were better off.

Investors deal themselves a double whammy

by joining a sell-off stampede. For one thing, they may get out near the market low. For another, they all but assure themselves of missing the market's eventual upswing. Says senior portfolio strategist Mark Dollard of Amivest Corporation, a New York City management firm: "The markets are so volatile, I don't think anybody can time them." That is Lesson No. 2. If you keep your horizons long enough, you don't have to try to do what even many pros regard as impossible.

Just look at the table below. All of the 17 fund categories listed there have rung up returns in excess of 86% over the past 10 years. Examine the maximum-capital-gains category in particular. It placed 16th, or second to last, during both the crash quarter and the past one-year period. But over the long haul, maximum-capital-gains funds have been standouts, ranking first among the 17 categories in the 10 years to October 1988 (up 362%). And in that longer run, this crash-smashed category was joined at the top by other growth groups that had dismal or, at

Don't Let One Lousy Little Year Cloud Your Long View

Despite the crash, stock funds have furnished the greatest returns to investors over the past decade, as illustrated in the table below, which ranks 17 domestic mutual fund categories over four different time periods. Because their gains (or losses) are often heavily influenced by currency moves, averages for fund categories that make significant overseas investments are not included here. In the 10 years to October 1, 1988, international equity funds were up 335%. Globals, whose portfolios include both foreign and U.S. holdings, soared 384%.

FUND CATEGORY	% gain (or loss) to October 1, 1988							
	10 years	Rank	12 months	Rank	1988	Rank	Crash quarter	Rank
Maximum capital gains	362.0	1	(13.4)	16	11.4	6	(22.1)	16
Growth	318.3	2	(11.7)	13	13.1	3	(21.9)	15
Growth and income	303.8	3	(7.4)	12	14.0	2	(18.7)	12
Gold	286.2	4	(35.1)	17	(17.6)	17	(21.8)	14
Equity income	280.5	5	(0.7)	9	11.8	5	(11.0)	9
Small-company growth	274.3	6	(12.4)	14*	16.4	1	(24.7)	17
Balanced	266.1	7	(3.7)	10	9.6	9	(12.2)	10
Sector	237.9	8	(12.4)	14*	10.2	7*	(20.6)	13
Option income	196.2	9	(6.3)	11	12.6	4	(16.6)	11
High-grade corporates	165.5	11	12.5	1*	7.1	10	5.1	3
High-yield corporates	174.2	10	9.3	4	10.2	7*	(0.7)	8
U.S. Governments	161.2	12	11.4	3	5.9	14	5.2	2
Short-term Treasuries	144.6	13	8.8	5	5.0	15	3.7	5
Mortgage-backed securities	131.7	14	12.5	1*	6.8	11*	5.4	1
High-yield tax-exempts**	105.8	15	6.9	7	6.8	11*	3.2	6
High-grade tax-exempts**	100.1	16	7.0	6	6.6	13	5.0	4
Immediate-term tax-exempts**	86.7	17	5.2	8	4.4	16	2.7	7
S&P 500 index	319.1		(12.4)		13.1		(22.8)	
Salomon Bros. Inv. grade bond index	—		13.4		7.2		5.8	

*Tie   **Returns cover periods to September 1, 1988

best, middling performances in 1987's traumatic fourth quarter.

All this is not to take away anything from investors who had the perspicacity or the blind luck to ride out most of the past year in either the crash quarter's best-performing category, mortgage-backed securities funds (up 5.4%), or in the overall one-year leaders, high-grade corporate bond and mortgage-backed funds (both up 12.5%). But it does illustrate a third lesson: don't play follow the leader, chasing the category winner *du jour*. Over the past decade, high-grade corporate bond funds ranked a modest 11th as a group. Ginnie Mae funds were even deeper in the second division, in 14th place. A rotten 12 months is too short a period to judge any manager by. The same goes for a sterling 12 months. The ultimate lesson of the past year, not to mention of all fund history, is that investing for the long term is the best way to win and the surest way not to lose.

Despite the dangers of placing too much emphasis on any short period, the past 12 months have given investors an excellent opportunity to test their portfolio managers. Marvels Don Phillips, editor of the newsletter, *Mutual Fund Values*, published in Chicago: "Look at what a great chance investment advisers have had to react to both overpriced and undervalued situations."

Although small-company growth funds led the pack in the first nine months of 1988, many other strong performances were posted by value-oriented veterans who look for stocks selling for less than they're worth. True maximum-capital-gains-oriented Columbia Special, which buys small-cap shares, was No. 1 among the 850 funds in *Money*'s data base with a nine-month gain of 35%. But several esteemed fund-runners, who oversee money in other investment categories, have fared exceptionally well. For instance, John Templeton's bargain-minded Global I, Growth, World, and Global II funds—up 27%, 20%, 18%, and 18%, respectively, for the nine months—edged out typical globals by as much as 21 percentage points. Then too, Vanguard's John Neff, who was voted by his peers in a 1987 *Money* survey as the manager they would most trust with

their own cash, has piloted the Windsor Fund's growth and income portfolio to a nine-month return of 27%—a figure 13 percentage points ahead of his category's average. (Good news: Windsor and Vanguard executives are discussing reopening the fund to new investors in the future.) Finally, Stephen Lieber, the value-oriented founder of the venerable Evergreen Fund, guided his growth fund to a 25% gain over the nine months, compared with a category-average return of 13%.

Do these double-digit rebounds suggest that good times are beginning another roll? The pros are divided. John Templeton feels that recession fears have already been built into stock prices today and that the Dow will probably climb from its October 1988 level of around 2150 to as high as 2500 this year. On the other hand, Mark Dollard of Amivest is more cautious, pointing out that bond prices, which are significant stock bellwethers, have lately been too erratic to allow anyone to decipher a trend.

One fund category many advisers urge caution on is high-yield or junk-bond funds, which Dollard warns are as "risky as stock funds." What most troubles fund watchers like editor Gerald Perritt of the *Mutual Fund Letter* in Chicago is the inevitable next recession. "An economic downturn could wreak havoc," he says. Advice: If you insist on putting money in junk-bond funds, a workable strategy now is to do it via a fund family and be ready to make a swift switch into another fund if recession fears rekindle.

Another current concern of some fund authorities is that investors, especially novices, have been permanently spooked by the October 1987 stock market crash. "Probably 80% of all mutual fund investors before October 19 had never seen a bear market," estimates Tyler Jenks, research director for Kanon Bloch Carre in Boston. Even so, over the long haul stocks are the place to be. Sadly, that's a lesson investors forget after a crash. The value theorists see keen opportunities right now. "It is a better time to invest in stock funds than it has been for some time now," says Windsor's John Neff. "Unfortunately, that is not what is happening."

How to Use the Fund Rankings

The *Money* rankings of 850 mutual funds are divided into stock and taxable bond funds and tax-exempt bond funds. Individual fund records can be measured against the category averages boxed on page 186, the market benchmarks provided on the first page of each ranking section and, for simplest comparison, the column labeled *Five-year ranking within category*. A designation of *high* means the fund placed in the top 20% of its peers; *middle* denotes the intermediate 60%; and *low* signals a subpar return in the bottom 20%.

Pay special attention to the column marked *Five-year expense projection*. The dollar amount you will find there reflects all front- and back-end sales loads, management fees and other charges that an investor would incur on a $1,000 investment that compounds annually at 5% and is redeemed after five years. This cost measure, now required in fund prospectuses, is calculated according to new rules established by the Securities and Exchange Commission. But since funds need not report the data until the start of their next fiscal year, figures for some funds were not available.

You'll note the wide divergence, with some funds breaking into the expensive three digits. The lesson: Read prospectuses carefully before you invest, and don't go for a fund with unusually high charges unless you think they are justified by superior management and performance potential.

Stock Funds

ABBREVIATIONS

Bal Balanced; **Eql** Equity income; **G&I** Growth and income; **Glo** Global; **Gold** Gold and precious metals; **Gro** Growth; **HGC** High-grade corporates; **HYC** High-yield corporates; **Intl** International; **Max** Maximum capital gains; **MBS** Mortgage-backed securities; **OpInc** Option income; **SCG** Small-company growth; **Sec** Sector; **STT** Short-term taxables; **USG** U.S. Government bonds

BENCHMARKS FOR INVESTORS

		% gain (or loss) to Oct. 1, 1988			
	1988	One year	Five years	10 years	% yield
S&P 500-stock index	13.1	(12.4)	98.7	319.1	—
Dow Jones industrial average	12.1	(15.5)	110.6	303.1	—
Lipper growth fund index	13.9	(10.4)	66.2	272.7	—
Lipper growth and income fund index	16.7	(6.8)	83.3	302.6	—
Salomon Bros. investment-grade bond index	7.2	13.4	81.7	—	9.6
Shearson Lehman Hutton Treasury index	6.0	12.0	75.7	186.5	8.7

FUND NAME	Type	% gain (or loss) to Oct. 1, 1988				Five-year ranking within category	% yield	Five-year expense projection	Telephone	
		1988	One year	Five years	10 years				Toll-free (800)	In state
ABT Emerging Growth	Max	17.3	(13.9)	39.3	—	Middle	0.0	$130	289-2281	—
ABT Growth & Income Trust	G&I	20.8	(4.1)	84.4	327.4	Middle	3.4	111	289-2281	—
ABT Utility Income	Sec	13.4	8.6	65.9	111.3	Middle	6.4	111	289-2281	—
Acorn Fund	SCG	21.4	(3.9)	103.2	399.5	High	1.3	46	—	312-621-0630
Advest Advantage Gov. Securities	USG	3.8	5.8	—	—	—	8.1	97	243-8115	800-842-3807 (Conn.)
Advest Advantage Growth	Gro	12.6	(11.7)	—	—	—	1.8	123	243-8115	800-842-3807 (Conn.)
Advest Advantage Income	Eql	11.7	(0.6)	—	—	—	6.3	107	243-8115	800-842-3807 (Conn.)
AIM High-Yield Securities	HYC	6.2	4.4	50.3	151.4	Low	13.5	114	231-0803	800-392-9681 (Texas)
AIM Summit Investors	Gro	17.2	(16.0)	44.6	—	Middle	0.9	55	231-0803	800-392-9681 (Texas)
Alliance Balanced Shares	Bal	12.4	(1.1)	108.9	265.9	High	3.5	121	221-5672	—
Alliance Bond–High Yield Portfolio	HYC	8.6	4.8	—	—	—	12.8	116	221-5672	—
Alliance Bond–Monthly Income Portfolio	HGC	7.3	11.8	77.7	151.4	Middle	9.5	129	221-5672	—
Alliance Bond–U.S. Gov. Portfolio	USG	5.7	9.5	—	—	—	10.8	111	221-5672	—
Alliance Canadian	Intl	15.2	(5.0)	48.8	219.9	Low	0.7	147	221-5672	—
Alliance Convertible	Eql	16.6	(3.5)	—	—	—	6.6	132	221-5672	—
Alliance Counterpoint	G&I	19.8	(8.8)	—	—	—	1.7	139	221-5672	—
Alliance Dividend Shares	G&I	13.3	(9.8)	95.7	295.9	Middle	3.7	102	221-5672	—
Alliance Fund	Gro	14.9	(12.2)	61.9	237.5	Middle	1.4	95	221-5672	—
Alliance International	Intl	16.8	(11.4)	168.1	—	Middle	1.2	122	221-5672	—
Alliance Mortgage Securities	MBS	8.7	14.5	—	—	—	10.9	115	221-5672	—

FUND NAME	Type	% gain (or loss) to Oct. 1, 1988			Five-year ranking within category	% yield	Five-year expense projection	Telephone	
		1988	One year	Five years	10 years				Toll-free (800)	In state
Alliance Quasar	SCG	24.7	(8.6)	66.9	537.7	Middle	0.0	$119	221-5672 —
Alliance Surveyor	Gro	25.1	(8.1)	48.9	248.5	Middle	0.0	132	221-5672 —
Alliance Technology	Sec	1.0	(22.7)	31.9	—	Middle	0.0	125	221-5672 —
AMA Classic Growth	Gro	8.2	(17.1)	47.0	120.5	Middle	1.6	87	262-3863 —
AMA Classic Income	HGC	5.7	8.9	54.2	119.7	Low	7.4	85	262-3863 —
AMA Global Growth	Glo	16.2	(8.6)	—	—	—	3.4	79	262-3863 —
AMA Income–Global Short Term	Glo	3.7	6.6	—	—	—	6.3	87	262-3863 —
AMCAP Fund	Gro	7.0	(12.4)	66.6	379.3	Middle	2.1	99	421-9900 714-671-7000 (Calif.)
American Balanced	Bal	11.2	(0.6)	91.5	257.5	Middle	5.9	100	421-9900 714-671-7000 (Calif.)
American Capital Comstock	Max	11.2	(19.5)	51.6	392.9	Middle	3.0	114	847-5636 —
American Capital Corporate Bond	HGC	11.4	14.2	82.0	157.0	High	10.8	85	847-5636 —
American Capital Enterprise	Gro	9.1	(19.2)	44.9	340.3	Middle	2.3	114	847-5636 —
American Capital Federal Mortgage	MBS	6.3	11.6	—	—	—	8.4	125	847-5636 —
American Capital Government Securities	USG	6.0	11.2	—	—	—	10.0	104	847-5636 —
American Capital Harbor	EqI	12.5	(10.5)	52.4	289.4	Low	6.8	116	847-5636 —
American Capital High Yield	HYC	12.8	10.0	71.5	—	Middle	14.0	104	847-5636 —
American Capital OTC Securities	SCG	6.8	(34.9)	—	—	—	0.0	N.A.	847-5636 —
American Capital Pace	Max	9.3	(19.6)	51.7	496.0	Middle	2.7	119	847-5636 —
American Capital Venture	Max	2.7	(18.2)	15.0	314.5	Low	3.2	N.A.	847-5636 —
American Growth	Gro	7.3	(15.4)	32.4	246.8	Low	2.4	150	525-2406 303-623-6137 (Colo.)
American Investors Growth	Gro	16.7	(18.1)	(10.9)	61.9	Low	0.8	84	243-5353 203-531-5000 (Conn.)
American Leaders	G&I	10.3	(5.9)	100.6	335.6	Middle	3.4	98	356-2805 —
American Mutual	G&I	11.4	(3.2)	95.7	384.3	Middle	4.7	90	421-9900 714-671-7000 (Calif.)
American National Growth	Gro	5.1	(17.7)	40.6	267.5	Middle	2.2	N.A.	231-4639 800-392-9753 (Texas)
American National Income	EqI	8.8	(11.6)	55.8	306.4	Low	4.2	N.A.	231-4639 800-392-9753 (Texas)
AMEV Capital	G&I	4.6	(14.4)	60.7	452.6	Middle	1.4	139	872-2638 800-328-1001 (Minn.)
AMEV Growth	Max	6.3	(19.1)	51.2	486.8	Middle	0.5	135	872-2638 800-328-1001 (Minn.)
AMEV U.S. Government Securities	USG	6.8	12.7	65.6	164.5	Middle	9.3	93	872-2638 800-328-1001 (Minn.)
Analytic Optioned Equity	OpInc	12.2	0.3	65.6	205.2	Middle	2.7	64	— 714-833-0294
Axe-Houghton Fund B	Bal	7.2	(12.5)	80.6	216.4	Middle	5.5	70	431-1030 914-333-5200 (N.Y.)
Axe-Houghton Income	HGC	7.2	11.1	85.9	197.3	High	9.7	84	431-1030 914-333-5200 (N.Y.)
Axe-Houghton Stock	Gro	1.8	(35.0)	10.2	186.5	Low	0.7	83	431-1030 914-333-5200 (N.Y.)
Babson Bond Trust	HGC	5.2	10.7	69.8	156.3	Middle	10.4	54	422-2766 816-471-5200 (Mo.)
Babson Enterprise	SCG	33.6	(4.0)	—	—	—	0.3	75	422-2766 816-471-5200 (Mo.)
Babson Growth	Gro	13.2	(12.0)	77.9	223.3	Middle	2.4	71	422-2766 816-471-5200 (Mo.)
Bartlett Basic Value	G&I	22.7	(2.0)	87.2	—	Middle	3.3	68	543-0863 800-327-4363 (Ohio)
Bartlett Fixed Income	HYC	7.5	10.5	—	—	—	8.6	55	543-0863 800-327-4363 (Ohio)
Benham Government–GNMA	MBS	8.2	15.2	—	—	—	9.1	41	472-3389 —
Blanchard Strategic Growth	Max	2.3	(9.6)	—	—	—	2.1	164	922-7771 212-779-7979 (N.Y.)
Bond Fund of America	HGC	9.7	15.3	85.0	199.0	High	9.4	79	421-9900 714-671-7000 (Calif.)
Boston Co. Capital Appreciation	Gro	17.7	(5.7)	111.6	320.4	High	1.1	59	225-5267 —
Boston Co. Managed Income	HYC	8.0	11.1	81.9	—	Middle	8.8	59	225-5267 —
Boston Co. Special Growth	Gro	20.4	(9.3)	40.0	—	Middle	3.6	88	225-5267 —
Bull & Bear Capital Growth	Gro	12.5	(19.2)	30.7	201.6	Low	0.0	118	847-4200 —
Bull & Bear Gold Investors	Gold	(15.8)	(36.5)	11.6	189.3	Middle	0.0	125	847-4200 —
Bull & Bear High Yield	HYC	5.4	(1.7)	36.7	—	Low	12.6	93	847-4200 —
Bull & Bear U.S. Gov. Guar. Securities	MBS	4.6	9.6	—	—	—	10.4	106	847-4200 —
Calamos Convertible Income	EqI	6.6	(10.0)	—	—	—	6.8	66	323-9943 —
Calvert Social Inv. Man. Growth	Bal	9.8	(2.6)	82.0	—	Middle	4.2	113	368-2748 301-951-4820 (Md.)
Capital Pres. Treasury Note	USG	5.1	11.1	63.1	—	Middle	7.6	42	472-3389 —
Cardinal Fund	G&I	15.8	(3.8)	98.1	337.9	Middle	4.6	116	848-7734 800-282-9446 (Ohio)
Cardinal Government Guaranteed	MBS	6.8	12.7	—	—	—	9.7	84	848-7734 800-282-9446 (Ohio)
Carnegie Cappiello–Growth	Gro	30.4	(0.6)	—	—	—	2.7	133	321-2322 —
Carnegie Cappiello–Total Return	G&I	18.8	(1.6)	—	—	—	6.6	132	321-2322 —
Carnegie Gov. Sec.–High Yield	USG	5.9	11.2	69.1	—	Middle	7.6	112	321-2322 —
Century Shares Trust	Sec	19.6	(2.1)	106.1	292.0	High	2.9	45	321-1928 617-482-3060 (Mass.)
Charter Fund	G&I	2.5	(17.0)	52.5	301.8	Low	2.3	111	231-0803 800-392-9681 (Texas)

N.A. Not available. Fund is not required to report these data until the end of its fiscal year.

FUND NAME	Type	\% gain (or loss) to Oct. 1, 1988				Five-year ranking within category	\% yield	Five-year expense projection	Telephone	
		1988	One year	Five years	10 years				Toll-free (800)	In state
Cigna Government Securities	USG	5.9	9.1	—	—	—	8.5	$104	562-4462	—
Cigna Growth	Gro	7.8	(17.4)	54.9	252.8	Middle	1.7	98	562-4462	—
Cigna High Yield	HYC	13.5	14.4	88.8	199.4	High	11.7	102	562-4462	—
Cigna Income	EqI	7.4	13.9	78.3	168.4	Middle	8.5	98	562-4462	—
Cigna Value	G&I	15.1	(6.5)	—	—	—	1.7	104	562-4462	—
Colonial Advanced Strategies Gold	Gold	(11.0)	(29.8)	—	—	—	2.6	156	426-3750	—
Colonial Diversified Income	OpInc	12.9	(5.6)	56.9	191.3	Middle	5.7	121	426-3750	—
Colonial Fund	G&I	18.5	(0.9)	100.6	302.0	Middle	4.2	117	426-3750	—
Colonial Government Securities Plus	USG	6.6	14.6	—	—	—	8.4	126	426-3750	—
Colonial Growth Shares	Gro	21.1	(5.6)	82.2	351.7	Middle	1.9	119	426-3750	—
Colonial High Yield Securities	HYC	11.6	11.6	82.9	198.5	High	11.5	111	426-3750	—
Colonial Income	EqI	10.3	11.5	70.8	151.7	Middle	10.5	109	426-3750	—
Colonial Income Plus	OpInc	10.0	(9.1)	—	—	—	3.2	125	426-3750	—
Colonial Small Stock Index	SCG	30.3	(9.6)	—	—	—	0.5	125	426-3750	—
Colonial U.S. Equity Index	Gro	12.3	(13.0)	—	—	—	2.2	119	426-3750	—
Columbia Fixed Income Securities	HGC	7.2	13.4	69.7	—	Middle	8.4	46	547-1037	800-452-4512 (Ore.)
Columbia Growth	Gro	9.1	(9.4)	64.1	395.7	Middle	1.6	57	547-1037	800-452-4512 (Ore.)
Columbia Special	Max	35.5	(2.8)	—	—	—	0.0	79	547-1037	800-452-4512 (Ore.)
Common Sense Government	USG	5.5	9.4	—	—	—	8.4	115	888-3863	—
Common Sense Growth	Max	10.9	(18.0)	—	—	—	0.0	144	888-3863	—
Common Sense Growth & Income	G&I	6.6	(15.6)	—	—	—	2.7	133	888-3863	—
Composite Bond & Stock	Bal	13.1	2.9	67.4	236.7	Low	5.5	128	541-0830	800-572-5828 (Wash.)
Composite Growth	G&I	16.0	(1.7)	78.2	311.6	Middle	4.5	88	541-0830	800-572-5828 (Wash.)
Composite Income	HYC	6.6	9.0	71.0	138.5	Middle	10.7	93	541-0830	800-572-5828 (Wash.)
Composite U.S. Government Securities	USG	7.3	13.1	64.4	—	Middle	9.3	87	541-0830	800-572-5828 (Wash.)
Constellation Growth	Max	16.4	(15.0)	49.7	417.3	Middle	0.0	119	231-0803	800-392-9681 (Texas)
Continental Option Income Plus	OpInc	9.5	(12.0)	—	—	—	6.9	144	626-3863	212-440-3863 (N.Y.)
Continental U.S. Government Plus	USG	5.4	10.5	—	—	—	9.1	135	626-3863	212-440-3863 (N.Y.)
Cowen Income & Growth	EqI	14.2	(3.5)	—	—	—	4.5	122	—	212-495-6000
Criterion Commerce Income Shares	EqI	4.9	(6.3)	63.2	248.9	Low	5.5	N.A.	999-3863	—
Criterion Investment Quality Interest	HGC	5.6	11.5	73.4	—	Middle	9.5	107	999-3863	—
Criterion Lowry Market Timing	Max	(0.7)	(9.8)	—	—	—	5.0	N.A.	999-3863	—
Criterion Pilot	Max	(0.9)	(23.4)	22.5	199.2	Middle	0.4	135	999-3863	—
Criterion Sunbelt Growth	Gro	6.3	(16.0)	33.3	—	Low	1.1	N.A.	999-3863	—
Criterion U.S. Government High Yield Trust	USG	5.4	10.0	—	—	—	9.7	104	999-3863	—
Dean Witter American Value	Gro	8.2	(10.9)	50.6	—	Middle	2.2	108	221-2685	212-938-4554 (N.Y.)
Dean Witter Convertible Securities	EqI	5.1	(19.4)	—	—	—	3.4	N.A.	221-2685	212-938-4554 (N.Y.)
Dean Witter Developing Growth	SCG	11.7	(11.8)	3.5	—	Low	0.0	N.A.	221-2685	212-938-4554 (N.Y.)
Dean Witter Dividend Growth	G&I	14.2	(5.9)	95.7	—	Middle	3.8	103	221-2685	212-938-4554 (N.Y.)
Dean Witter Government Plus	USG	5.0	10.9	—	—	—	8.2	N.A.	221-2685	212-938-4554 (N.Y.)
Dean Witter High Yield Securities	HYC	9.1	4.7	64.4	—	Middle	15.0	N.A.	221-2685	212-938-4554 (N.Y.)
Dean Witter Natural Resource Dev.	Sec	10.2	(12.2)	34.2	—	Middle	2.1	118	221-2685	212-938-4554 (N.Y.)
Dean Witter Option Income	OpInc	10.9	(8.4)	—	—	—	1.9	N.A.	221-2685	212-938-4554 (N.Y.)
Dean Witter U.S. Government Securities	MBS	6.1	11.0	—	—	—	10.1	N.A.	221-2685	212-938-4554 (N.Y.)
Dean Witter World Wide	Glo	5.8	(11.8)	—	—	—	0.5	134	221-2685	212-938-4554 (N.Y.)
Delaware Fund	G&I	17.9	(14.3)	60.7	318.3	Middle	2.2	N.A.	523-4640	215-988-1333 (Pa.)
Delaware Group—Decatur I	EqI	16.2	(5.8)	105.0	386.6	High	5.6	N.A.	523-4640	215-988-1333 (Pa.)
Delaware Group—Decatur II	G&I	21.3	(6.0)	—	—	—	4.1	N.A.	523-4640	215-988-1333 (Pa.)
Delaware Group—Delcap I	Max	17.8	(2.3)	—	—	—	3.1	N.A.	523-4640	215-988-1333 (Pa.)
Delaware Group—Delchester Bond I	HYC	11.7	13.9	89.8	193.0	High	12.3	N.A.	523-4640	215-988-1333 (Pa.)
Delaware Group—Gov. Income Securities	MBS	6.1	11.8	—	—	—	9.3	N.A.	523-4640	215-988-1333 (Pa.)
Delaware Group—Trend	Max	22.2	(16.0)	6.1	257.6	Low	0.0	145	523-4640	215-988-1333 (Pa.)
Delaware Treasury Rsvs.—Investors Ser.	USG	5.0	7.4	—	—	—	7.4	N.A.	523-4640	215-988-1333 (Pa.)
Drexel Burnham Fund	G&I	9.3	(3.4)	101.1	330.8	High	4.4	88	272-2700	212-232-2888 (N.Y.)
Drexel Series—Convertible	EqI	5.1	(14.9)	—	—	—	4.9	127	272-2700	212-232-2888 (N.Y.)
Drexel Series—Government Securities	USG	4.0	11.6	—	—	—	7.4	118	272-2700	212-232-2888 (N.Y.)
Drexel Series—Growth	Gro	13.8	(8.8)	—	—	—	2.5	132	272-2700	212-232-2888 (N.Y.)

N.A. Not available. Fund is not required to report these data until the end of its fiscal year.

FUND NAME	Type	1988	One year	Five years	10 years	Five-year ranking within category	% yield	Five-year expense projection	Toll-free (800)	In state
Drexel Series–Option Income	OpInc	12.1	(6.4)	—	—	—	1.5	$128	272-2700	212-232-2888 (N.Y.)
Dreyfus A Bond Plus	HGC	7.4	14.3	71.2	177.1	Middle	8.8	49	645-6561	718-895-1206 (N.Y.)
Dreyfus Capital Value	Max	5.8	3.3	—	—	—	1.2	N.A.	645-6561	718-895-1206 (N.Y.)
Dreyfus Convertible Securites	EqI	18.8	(5.0)	92.3	257.4	Middle	5.3	47	645-6561	718-895-1206 (N.Y.)
Dreyfus Fund	G&I	6.3	(9.0)	74.0	275.9	Middle	5.3	56	645-6561	718-895-1206 (N.Y.)
Dreyfus General Aggressive Growth	Max	16.2	(12.7)	—	—	—	1.0	89	645-6561	718-895-1206 (N.Y.)
Dreyfus GNMA	MBS	6.4	11.6	—	—	—	8.9	56	645-6561	718-895-1206 (N.Y.)
Dreyfus Growth Opportunity	Gro	13.6	(12.7)	61.6	265.6	Middle	4.0	50	645-6561	718-895-1206 (N.Y.)
Dreyfus Leverage	Max	1.4	(17.6)	96.3	338.8	High	2.9	N.A.	645-6561	718-895-1206 (N.Y.)
Dreyfus New Leaders	SCG	24.3	(10.9)	—	—	—	0.4	77	645-6561	718-895-1206 (N.Y.)
Dreyfus Strategic Aggressive Investing	Max	7.1	4.9	—	—	—	0.0	137	648-9048	718-895-1347 (N.Y.)
Dreyfus Strategic Income	HYC	8.6	17.0	—	—	—	9.6	N.A.	648-9048	718-895-1347 (N.Y.)
Dreyfus Strategic Investing	Max	(5.5)	(11.1)	—	—	—	1.3	N.A.	648-9048	718-895-1347 (N.Y.)
Dreyfus Third Century	Gro	18.7	(4.1)	68.2	267.4	Middle	2.0	N.A.	645-6561	718-895-1206 (N.Y.)
Dreyfus U.S. Gov. Intermediate	USG	5.7	11.2	—	—	—	9.5	N.A.	645-6561	718-895-1206 (N.Y.)
Eaton & Howard Stock	G&I	12.4	(7.1)	93.8	267.2	Middle	3.4	124	225-6265	617-482-8260 (Mass.)
Eaton Vance Gov. Obligations	USG	6.5	10.8	—	—	—	10.1	121	225-6265	617-482-8260 (Mass.)
Eaton Vance Growth	Gro	7.1	(15.2)	68.8	304.7	Middle	1.0	100	225-6265	617-482-8260 (Mass.)
Eaton Vance High Income Trust	HYC	12.4	11.4	—	—	—	12.1	136	225-6265	617-482-8260 (Mass.)
Eaton Vance High Yield	HYC	13.2	11.6	90.5	180.4	High	11.9	102	225-6265	617-482-8260 (Mass.)
Eaton Vance Income of Boston	EqI	12.1	9.4	90.7	216.2	Middle	13.3	114	225-6265	617-482-8260 (Mass.)
Eaton Vance Investors	Bal	8.5	(4.8)	70.0	255.3	Middle	5.1	95	225-6265	617-482-8260 (Mass.)
Eaton Vance Special Equities	Gro	10.3	(10.4)	23.1	264.3	Low	0.0	134	225-6265	617-482-8260 (Mass.)
Eaton Vance Total Return Trust	G&I	9.7	(13.2)	99.4	—	Middle	8.9	81	225-6265	617-482-8260 (Mass.)
Eclipse Equity	SCG	10.4	4.0	—	—	—	4.8	65	872-2710	404-631-0414 (Ga.)
Enterprise Growth Portfolio	Gro	11.0	(9.9)	62.0	349.5	Middle	1.2	133	443-3521	404-521-6545 (Ga.)
Equitec Siebel Aggressive Growth	Max	7.7	(14.2)	—	—	—	5.1	123	826-7194	—
Equitec Siebel Total Return	G&I	6.8	(9.7)	—	—	—	2.0	110	826-7194	—
Equitec Siebel U.S. Government	USG	6.8	8.0	—	—	—	9.8	113	826-7194	—
EuroPacific Growth	Intl	11.1	(10.3)	—	—	—	1.9	126	421-9900	714-671-7000 (Calif.)
Evergreen Fund	Gro	25.0	(1.9)	81.8	458.2	Middle	2.0	57	235-0064	—
Evergreen Total Return	EqI	15.6	(1.4)	97.4	429.1	Middle	4.6	56	235-0064	—
Fairfield Fund	SCG	10.6	(16.4)	23.1	222.2	Middle	2.4	N.A.	223-7757	212-661-3000 (N.Y.)
Fairmont Fund	Max	7.9	(20.1)	68.0	—	Middle	1.1	65	262-9936	—
FBL Series–Growth Common Stock	G&I	10.6	(15.5)	32.7	144.9	Low	1.0	N.A.	247-4170	800-422-3175 (Iowa)
Fenimore International–Equity Series	Intl	2.8	(28.0)	—	—	—	0.0	159	272-2700	212-232-2888 (N.Y.)
Fidelity Balanced	Bal	13.8	5.7	—	—	—	5.7	90	544-6666	617-523-1919 (Mass.)
Fidelity Capital Appreciation	Max	32.0	(0.2)	—	—	—	0.1	N.A.	544-6666	617-523-1919 (Mass.)
Fidelity Contrafund	Gro	20.5	(14.2)	61.1	243.0	Middle	0.0	55	544-6666	617-523-1919 (Mass.)
Fidelity Convertible	EqI	14.4	(4.8)	—	—	—	6.0	N.A.	544-6666	617-523-1919 (Mass.)
Fidelity Destiny I	Gro	17.5	(10.9)	102.2	463.4	High	2.0	N.A.	225-5270	617-328-5000 (Mass.)
Fidelity Destiny II	Gro	22.5	(7.9)	—	—	—	0.5	N.A.	225-5270	617-328-5000 (Mass.)
Fidelity Equity-Income	EqI	20.4	(1.3)	92.7	477.2	Middle	5.7	N.A.	544-6666	617-523-1919 (Mass.)
Fidelity Europe	Intl	(2.3)	(27.0)	—	—	—	0.0	N.A.	544-6666	617-523-1919 (Mass.)
Fidelity Flexible Bond	HGC	6.9	12.5	66.2	141.1	Low	8.8	N.A.	544-6666	617-523-1919 (Mass.)
Fidelity Freedom**	Max	16.4	(13.0)	95.8	—	High	1.8	N.A.	544-6666	617-523-1919 (Mass.)
Fidelity Fund	G&I	15.1	(11.0)	79.1	325.2	Middle	3.1	38	544-6666	617-523-1919 (Mass.)
Fidelity Global Bond	Glo	(0.7)	13.8	—	—	—	1.8	N.A.	544-6666	617-523-1919 (Mass.)
Fidelity GNMA Portfolio	MBS	7.0	12.8	—	—	—	8.5	N.A.	544-6666	617-523-1919 (Mass.)
Fidelity Government Securities	STT	5.6	10.2	63.0	—	Middle	9.2	48	544-6666	617-523-1919 (Mass.)
Fidelity Growth & Income	G&I	20.7	(4.9)	—	—	—	4.3	N.A.	544-6666	617-523-1919 (Mass.)
Fidelity Growth Company	Gro	14.1	(13.3)	62.2	—	Middle	0.1	88	544-6666	617-523-1919 (Mass.)
Fidelity High Income Bond	HYC	10.7	10.0	88.0	227.2	High	11.6	N.A.	544-6666	617-523-1919 (Mass.)
Fidelity Intermediate Bond	HGC	6.1	10.8	71.6	204.1	Middle	9.0	N.A.	544-6666	617-523-1919 (Mass.)
Fidelity International Growth & Income	Intl	3.8	(15.1)	—	—	—	0.3	N.A.	544-6666	617-523-1919 (Mass.)
Fidelity Magellan	Gro	19.6	(10.0)	114.6	1,105.7	High	0.7	N.A.	544-6666	617-523-1919 (Mass.)
Fidelity Mortgage Securities	MBS	6.8	12.4	—	—	—	8.5	N.A.	544-6666	617-523-1919 (Mass.)

N.A. Not available. Fund is not required to report these data until the end of its fiscal year.   **Open to retirement plans only

FUND NAME	Type	% gain (or loss) to Oct. 1, 1988				Five-year ranking within category	% yield	Five-year expense projection	Telephone	
		1988	One year	Five years	10 years				Toll-free (800)	In state
Fidelity OTC	SCG	24.3	(8.3)	—	—	—	0.1	N.A.	544-6666	617-523-1919 (Mass.)
Fidelity Overseas	Intl	2.1	(15.7)	—	—	—	0.0	N.A.	544-6666	617-523-1919 (Mass.)
Fidelity Pacific Basin	Intl	2.7	(9.2)	—	—	—	1.0	N.A.	544-6666	617-523-1919 (Mass.)
Fidelity Puritan	EqI	17.0	(0.2)	103.5	359.8	High	7.2	$59	544-6666	617-523-1919 (Mass.)
Fidelity Real Estate	Sec	11.2	1.5	—	—	—	7.6	N.A.	544-6666	617-523-1919 (Mass.)
Fidelity Select—American Gold	Gold	(12.1)	(30.0)	—	—	—	0.4	N.A.	544-6666	617-523-1919 (Mass.)
Fidelity Select—Biotechnology	Sec	6.8	(24.3)	—	—	—	0.0	N.A.	544-6666	617-523-1919 (Mass.)
Fidelity Select—Chemicals	Sec	17.9	(11.4)	—	—	—	0.0	N.A.	544-6666	617-523-1919 (Mass.)
Fidelity Select—Computers	Sec	(2.4)	(37.2)	—	—	—	0.1	N.A.	544-6666	617-523-1919 (Mass.)
Fidelity Select—Energy	Sec	11.4	(15.9)	33.8	—	Middle	0.2	N.A.	544-6666	617-523-1919 (Mass.)
Fidelity Select—Financial Services	Sec	18.6	(9.6)	94.9	—	High	0.4	N.A.	544-6666	617-523-1919 (Mass.)
Fidelity Select—Health Care	Sec	9.2	(21.9)	85.9	—	Middle	0.0	N.A.	544-6666	617-523-1919 (Mass.)
Fidelity Select—Industrial Materials	Sec	7.4	(23.5)	—	—	—	0.2	N.A.	544-6666	617-523-1919 (Mass.)
Fidelity Select—Leisure	Sec	23.9	(7.1)	—	—	—	0.0	N.A.	544-6666	617-523-1919 (Mass.)
Fidelity Select—Precious Metals	Gold	(26.1)	(43.2)	(11.8)	—	Middle	0.4	N.A.	544-6666	617-523-1919 (Mass.)
Fidelity Select—Technology	Sec	(2.1)	(36.9)	(29.3)	—	Low	0.0	N.A.	544-6666	617-523-1919 (Mass.)
Fidelity Select—Telecommunications	Sec	20.0	(2.0)	—	—	—	0.1	N.A.	544-6666	617-523-1919 (Mass.)
Fidelity Select—Utilities	Sec	14.5	4.9	108.9	—	High	1.7	N.A.	544-6666	617-523-1919 (Mass.)
Fidelity Short-Term Bond Portfolio	STT	4.7	7.8	—	—	—	8.9	51	544-6666	617-523-1919 (Mass.)
Fidelity Trend	Gro	21.7	(10.7)	71.7	229.6	Middle	1.2	27	544-6666	617-523-1919 (Mass.)
Fidelity Value	Max	24.5	(8.6)	46.1	—	Middle	0.0	63	544-6666	617-523-1919 (Mass.)
Fiduciary Capital Growth	SCG	19.7	(11.1)	28.6	—	Middle	0.9	60	—	414-271-6666
Financial Bond Shares—High Yield	HYC	11.8	11.8	—	—	—	11.8	48	525-8085	—
Financial Dynamics	Max	13.4	(19.5)	29.1	233.6	Middle	0.3	57	525-8085	—
Financial Industrial	G&I	6.8	(19.4)	43.8	227.9	Low	1.8	43	525-8085	—
Financial Industrial Income	EqI	13.2	(6.0)	98.8	342.8	High	4.5	43	525-8085	—
Financial Strategic—Gold	Gold	(21.6)	(48.2)	—	—	—	1.2	N.A.	525-8085	—
Financial Strategic—Pacific Basin	Intl	10.5	(19.8)	—	—	—	0.6	70	525-8085	—
Fin. Independence—U.S. Gov. Securities	MBS	7.2	14.3	—	—	—	8.2	124	543-8721	800-582-7396 (Ohio)
First Investors Bond Appreciation	HYC	10.3	(5.7)	42.4	160.7	Low	11.4	148	423-4026	—
First Investors Discovery	SCG	19.8	(22.4)	(39.6)	69.1	Low	0.0	148	423-4026	—
First Investors Fund for Growth	Gro	9.5	(23.5)	(31.1)	74.5	Low	0.7	141	423-4026	—
First Investors Fund for Income	HYC	10.9	7.8	49.2	125.6	Low	12.7	140	423-4026	—
First Investors Government	MBS	8.5	16.1	—	—	—	8.6	135	423-4026	—
First Investors High Yield	HYC	11.3	8.4	—	—	—	11.7	137	423-4026	—
First Investors International Securities	Glo	6.8	(13.4)	96.1	—	Middle	0.0	168	423-4026	—
First Investors Option	OpInc	12.3	(12.1)	35.9	148.8	Low	4.2	134	423-4026	—
First Trust U.S. Government	USG	7.3	13.9	—	—	—	8.8	N.A.	621-4770	—
Flex-funds Retirement Growth	Max	(10.8)	(22.4)	24.6	—	Middle	2.7	73	325-3539	—
Fortress High Quality Stock	G&I	10.9	(10.6)	—	—	—	2.8	N.A.	245-2423	—
Founders Blue Chip	G&I	6.2	(16.4)	73.1	235.4	Middle	2.7	54	525-2440	800-874-6301 (Colo.)
Founders Growth	Gro	3.9	(16.8)	52.3	368.4	Middle	1.7	69	525-2440	800-874-6301 (Colo.)
Founders Special	Max	9.0	(16.4)	25.9	303.9	Middle	0.6	63	525-2440	800-874-6301 (Colo.)
FPA Capital	Gro	26.8	(3.5)	91.2	261.5	High	1.9	111	421-4374	—
FPA Paramount*	G&I	21.2	1.7	109.2	415.7	High	2.2	119	421-4374	—
FPA Perennial	G&I	17.4	(1.6)	—	—	—	3.4	124	421-4374	—
Franklin AGE High Income	HYC	11.1	10.8	65.9	167.9	Middle	13.0	71	342-5236	—
Franklin DynaTech Series	Sec	5.2	(16.4)	14.0	202.4	Low	0.6	85	342-5236	—
Franklin Equity	Gro	22.2	(9.5)	117.5	319.6	High	1.9	77	342-5236	—
Franklin Gold	Gold	(14.5)	(33.9)	16.4	461.2	Middle	4.6	78	342-5236	—
Franklin Growth Series	Gro	6.9	(3.1)	91.0	247.0	Middle	2.1	82	342-5236	—
Franklin Income Series	EqI	8.0	6.5	85.4	321.6	Middle	10.4	72	342-5236	—
Franklin Option	OpInc	14.8	(2.6)	62.1	252.1	Middle	2.8	85	342-5236	—
Franklin Rising Dividend	G&I	19.4	2.1	—	—	—	3.1	133	342-5236	—
Franklin U.S. Government Series	MBS	7.3	12.2	72.3	127.3	Middle	10.0	68	342-5236	—
Franklin Utilities Series	Sec	10.1	4.6	91.8	263.8	High	7.6	74	342-5236	—
Freedom Global	Glo	0.9	(29.6)	—	—	—	0.0	141	225-6258	800-392-6037 (Mass.)

*Currently closed to new investors.   N.A. Not available. Fund is not required to report these data until the end of its fiscal year.

FUND NAME	Type	1988	One year	Five years	10 years	Five-year ranking within category	% yield	Five-year expense projection	Toll-free (800)	In state
Freedom Global Income Plus	Glo	10.3	16.2	—	—	—	7.3	$121	225-6258	800-392-6037 (Mass.)
Freedom Gold & Government	Gold	0.8	2.1	—	—	—	5.0	118	225-6258	800-392-6037 (Mass.)
Freedom Government Plus	USG	6.2	14.7	—	—	—	8.0	70	225-6258	800-392-6037 (Mass.)
Freedom Regional Bank	Sec	29.9	6.7	—	—	—	1.2	136	225-6258	800-392-6037 (Mass.)
Fundamental Investors	G&I	13.6	(11.5)	105.7	344.9	High	2.7	97	421-9900	714-671-7000 (Calif.)
Fund for U.S. Government Securities	MBS	7.1	11.4	67.2	142.1	Middle	9.4	96	356-2805	—
Fund of America	G&I	11.5	(17.5)	55.8	387.1	Low	2.1	121	847-5636	—
Fund Source Government Sec. Income	USG	4.2	9.2	33.5	—	Low	8.0	N.A.	845-8406	—
Fund Source International Equity	Intl	5.4	(12.8)	—	—	—	0.0	N.A.	845-8406	—
FundTrust–Aggressive Growth	Max	10.3	(12.8)	—	—	—	1.6	N.A.	845-8406	—
FundTrust–Growth	Gro	12.7	(7.4)	—	—	—	2.8	N.A.	845-8406	—
FundTrust–Growth & Income	G&I	16.3	(3.4)	—	—	—	4.9	N.A.	845-8406	—
FundTrust–Income	HYC	7.5	7.9	—	—	—	9.1	N.A.	845-8406	—
Gateway Option Index	OpInc	16.2	(2.9)	48.7	155.2	Middle	1.4	81	354-6339	—
Government Income Securities	USG	7.0	12.0	—	—	—	8.8	55	245-2423	—
Gradison Established Growth	Gro	11.6	(3.5)	114.7	—	High	4.1	150	543-1818	800-582-7062 (Ohio)
Growth Fund of America	Gro	16.8	(5.0)	75.3	423.5	Middle	0.2	100	421-9900	714-671-7000 (Calif.)
Growth Fund of Washington	Gro	15.6	(4.2)	—	—	—	1.1	140	972-9274	202-842-5300 (D.C.)
Growth Industry Shares	Gro	7.0	(10.0)	37.1	294.8	Middle	1.8	48	635-2886	800-635-2840 (Mass.)
G.T. Pacific Growth	Intl	15.5	(8.7)	149.4	210.9	Middle	0.0	150	824-1580	—
Guardian Park Avenue	Gro	19.0	(5.5)	117.9	439.4	High	2.6	119	221-3253	—
Harbor Growth	Gro	16.1	(11.1)	—	—	—	0.9	75	422-1050	—
Hartwell Emerging Growth	Max	21.7	(16.4)	13.6	306.6	Low	0.0	135	645-6405	212-308-3355 (N.Y.)
Heartland Value	Max	25.5	(9.7)	—	—	—	0.4	123	558-1015	800-242-1001 (Wis.)
Heritage Capital Appreciation	Max	16.4	(0.2)	—	—	—	0.6	140	—	813-573-8143
Hidden Strength Government	MBS	6.7	11.6	—	—	—	9.6	150	822-8252	212-956-7030 (N.Y.)
Hidden Strength Growth	Gro	20.4	(11.0)	—	—	—	0.3	156	822-8252	212-956-7030 (N.Y.)
Hutton Inv. Series–Basic Value	Gro	9.9	(12.9)	—	—	—	3.0	86	—	212-528-2744
Hutton Inv. Series–Bond & Income	HGC	6.8	16.5	80.2	—	High	9.1	68	—	212-528-2744
Hutton Inv. Series–Gov. Securities	USG	8.2	10.4	—	—	—	9.2	77	—	212-528-2744
Hutton Inv. Series–Growth	Gro	3.4	(18.2)	50.2	—	Middle	3.1	85	—	212-528-2744
Hutton Inv. Series–Option Income	OpInc	11.8	(9.3)	—	—	—	9.9	172	—	212-528-2744
Hutton Inv. Series–Precious Metals	Gold	(14.1)	(30.3)	—	—	—	2.3	98	—	212-528-2744
Hutton Special Equities	SCG	9.9	(21.5)	23.0	—	Middle	0.0	136	—	212-528-2744
IAI–Bond	HGC	6.0	11.3	70.9	170.5	Middle	7.6	42	—	612-371-2884
IAI–Regional	Gro	15.4	(3.1)	105.5	—	High	1.3	46	—	612-371-2884
IAI–Reserve	USG	5.0	6.7	—	—	—	6.3	45	—	612-371-2884
IAI–Stock	Max	5.1	(13.0)	78.8	299.0	High	1.8	46	—	612-371-2884
IDEX Fund*	Gro	15.9	(9.5)	—	—	—	1.8	146	237-3055	800-282-8842 (Fla.)
IDEX II*	Gro	18.0	(8.0)	—	—	—	1.4	151	237-3055	800-282-8842 (Fla.)
IDEX III	Gro	14.4	(10.0)	—	—	—	1.4	159	237-3055	800-282-8842 (Fla.)
IDS Bond	HYC	8.5	12.5	76.8	185.9	Middle	9.4	88	328-8300	—
IDS Discovery	SCG	16.8	(9.1)	10.5	—	Middle	1.6	84	328-8300	—
IDS Equity Plus	G&I	7.9	(14.1)	67.2	264.1	Middle	2.8	87	328-8300	—
IDS Extra Income	HYC	11.2	10.3	—	—	—	11.3	92	328-8300	—
IDS Federal Income	USG	7.8	13.5	—	—	—	8.0	92	328-8300	—
IDS Growth	Gro	7.1	(19.0)	27.7	418.4	Low	1.3	84	328-8300	—
IDS International	Intl	3.8	(21.9)	—	—	—	0.0	119	328-8300	—
IDS Managed Retirement	G&I	3.8	(16.5)	—	—	—	1.8	97	328-8300	—
IDS Mutual	Bal	11.0	0.8	105.1	283.8	High	6.4	83	328-8300	—
IDS New Dimensions	Gro	5.9	(9.5)	76.0	488.9	Middle	1.5	97	328-8300	—
IDS Pan Pacific Growth	Glo	4.1	(20.6)	—	—	—	0.0	N.A.	328-8300	—
IDS Precious Metals	Gold	(16.2)	(34.8)	—	—	—	1.7	108	328-8300	—
IDS Progressive	Max	18.7	(9.5)	70.3	311.5	Middle	3.4	87	328-8300	—
IDS Selective	HGC	8.0	14.4	76.3	185.0	Middle	8.8	88	328-8300	—
IDS Stock	G&I	7.7	(11.1)	74.1	249.0	Middle	3.3	81	328-8300	—
IDS Strategy–Aggressive Equity	Max	9.1	(17.3)	—	—	—	0.0	119	328-8300	—

*Currently closed to new investors   N.A. Not available. Fund is not required to report these data until the end of its fiscal year.

| FUND NAME | Type | % gain (or loss) to Oct. 1, 1988 | | | | Five-year ranking within category | % yield | Five-year expense projection | Telephone | |
		1988	One year	Five years	10 years				Toll-free (800)	In state
IDS Strategy—Equity Portfolio	G&I	22.0	5.8	—	—	—	3.4	$113	328-8300	—
IDS Strategy—Income Portfolio	HGC	7.9	13.6	—	—	—	8.9	113	328-8300	—
Income Fund of America	EqI	12.7	4.0	96.7	287.0	Middle	6.9	94	421-9900	714-671-7000 (Calif.)
Integrated Capital Appreciation	Gro	28.8	(7.4)	—	—	—	0.8	112	821-5100	—
Integrated Equity—Growth	Gro	20.1	(9.7)	—	—	—	0.6	146	821-5100	—
Integrated Home Investors Gov. Guar.	MBS	7.2	13.4	62.7	—	Middle	8.3	112	821-5100	—
Integrated Income—Convertible Securities	EqI	14.2	(7.7)	—	—	—	4.8	136	821-5100	—
Integrated Income—Government Plus	USG	7.1	12.7	—	—	—	10.7	173	821-5100	—
Integrated Income Plus	HYC	12.6	12.0	—	—	—	10.9	122	821-5100	—
International Investors	Gold	(25.8)	(42.0)	5.2	443.3	Middle	3.7	121	221-2220	212-687-5200 (N.Y.)
Investment Co. of America	G&I	11.2	(9.7)	105.2	346.9	High	3.8	88	421-9900	714-671-7000 (Calif.)
Investment Portfolio—Equity	Gro	6.5	(17.1)	—	—	—	0.7	128	621-1048	—
Investment Portfolio—Government Plus	USG	4.2	9.5	—	—	—	10.8	117	621-1048	—
Investment Portfolio—High Yield	HYC	10.6	11.8	—	—	—	12.9	123	621-1048	—
Investment Portfolio—Option Income	OpInc	12.4	(11.0)	—	—	—	15.7	123	621-1048	—
Investment Portfolio—Total Return	Bal	8.9	(9.7)	—	—	—	3.2	127	621-1048	—
Investment Trust of Boston	G&I	7.2	(14.1)	53.7	197.0	Low	3.2	132	888-4823	617-578-1093 (Mass.)
Investors Research	Max	(3.4)	(20.5)	52.6	315.6	Middle	1.3	N.A.	—	213-595-7711
ISI Trust	G&I	12.7	0.8	57.6	157.5	Low	2.6	111	441-9490	302-652-3091 (Del.)
Ivy Growth	Gro	9.9	(12.7)	82.1	436.4	Middle	2.8	70	235-3322	—
Janus Fund	Max	14.8	(3.9)	62.9	440.7	Middle	2.7	56	525-3713	303-333-3863 (Colo.)
Janus Venture	SCG	19.9	(0.4)	—	—	—	0.5	77	525-3713	303-333-3863 (Colo.)
Japan Fund	Intl	6.6	6.1	260.9	366.5	High	0.8	50	535-2726	—
John Hancock Bond	HGC	8.0	13.7	78.1	143.0	Middle	9.4	127	225-5291	617-572-4120 (Mass.)
John Hancock Global Trust	Glo	4.1	(17.2)	—	—	—	0.3	N.A.	225-5291	617-572-4120 (Mass.)
John Hancock Growth	Gro	9.6	(13.1)	64.2	298.7	Middle	1.8	136	225-5291	617-572-4120 (Mass.)
John Hancock High Income—Federal Sec.	USG	4.7	7.8	—	—	—	9.5	111	225-5291	617-572-4120 (Mass.)
John Hancock High Income—Fixed Income	HYC	10.7	11.6	—	—	—	12.1	112	225-5291	617-572-4120 (Mass.)
John Hancock—U.S. Gov. Guar. Mortgages	MBS	6.7	12.8	—	—	—	8.6	N.A.	225-5291	617-572-4120 (Mass.)
John Hancock—U.S. Gov. Securities	STT	5.1	9.7	66.2	144.6	Middle	8.9	134	225-5291	617-572-4120 (Mass.)
Kemper Growth	Gro	10.4	(15.2)	55.7	329.0	Middle	2.8	N.A.	621-1048	—
Kemper High Yield	HYC	11.9	14.2	100.5	239.7	High	12.4	N.A.	621-1048	—
Kemper Income & Capital Preservation	HGC	9.3	13.7	80.8	171.7	High	10.9	N.A.	621-1048	—
Kemper International	Intl	6.6	(10.4)	140.9	—	Middle	1.3	N.A.	621-1048	—
Kemper Option Income	OpInc	14.5	(11.2)	34.7	158.7	Low	15.1	N.A.	621-1048	—
Kemper Summit	SCG	8.0	(17.3)	42.4	325.1	Middle	3.7	N.A.	621-1048	—
Kemper Technology	Sec	4.7	(21.8)	50.3	264.3	Middle	2.8	N.A.	621-1048	—
Kemper Total Return	Bal	5.3	(19.2)	51.7	296.9	Low	4.1	N.A.	621-1048	—
Kemper U.S. Government Securities	MBS	5.8	11.0	78.5	142.4	High	10.7	N.A.	621-1048	—
Keystone America Government	USG	3.6	8.8	—	—	—	8.2	122	225-2618	617-338-3400 (Mass.)
Keystone America High Yield	HYC	8.4	5.5	—	—	—	11.7	117	225-2618	617-338-3400 (Mass.)
Keystone America Investment Grade	HGC	3.6	9.7	—	—	—	8.8	122	225-2618	617-338-3400 (Mass.)
Keystone B-1	HGC	5.6	10.8	58.9	158.2	Low	8.5	85	225-2618	617-338-3400 (Mass.)
Keystone B-2	HYC	9.3	10.8	62.4	188.0	Middle	10.3	91	225-2618	617-338-3400 (Mass.)
Keystone B-4	HYC	10.3	3.9	47.3	163.7	Low	12.5	90	225-2618	617-338-3400 (Mass.)
Keystone International	Intl	3.3	(15.3)	117.2	278.5	Low	1.2	116	225-2618	617-338-3400 (Mass.)
Keystone K-1	EqI	9.7	(3.1)	76.5	239.2	Middle	7.3	104	225-2618	617-338-3400 (Mass.)
Keystone K-2	Gro	5.8	(20.8)	54.6	234.3	Middle	2.2	114	225-2618	617-338-3400 (Mass.)
Keystone Precious Metals	Gold	(16.4)	(37.2)	9.1	294.1	Middle	1.4	100	225-2618	617-338-3400 (Mass.)
Keystone S-1	G&I	5.7	(20.7)	55.2	179.7	Low	2.7	118	225-2618	617-338-3400 (Mass.)
Keystone S-3	Gro	12.2	(16.0)	43.0	244.9	Middle	1.9	110	225-2618	617-338-3400 (Mass.)
Keystone S-4	Gro	10.6	(21.2)	0.1	159.4	Low	0.0	64	225-2618	617-338-3400 (Mass.)
Kidder Peabody Equity Income	EqI	(0.1)	(16.0)	—	—	—	3.0	106	—	212-510-5552
Kidder Peabody Government Income	USG	7.2	12.3	—	—	—	8.0	94	—	212-510-5552
Kidder Peabody MarketGuard*	Sec	4.1	(1.9)	—	—	—	6.2	97	—	212-510-5552
Legg Mason Special Investment	SCG	22.4	(11.9)	—	—	—	0.8	133	822-5544	800-638-1107 (Md.)
Legg Mason Total Return Trust	Gro	19.2	(9.4)	—	—	—	2.3	123	822-5544	800-638-1107 (Md.)

*Currently closed to new investors   N.A. Not available. Fund is not required to report these data until the end of its fiscal year.

FUND NAME	Type	% gain (or loss) to Oct. 1, 1988				Five-year ranking within category	% yield	Five-year expense projection	Telephone	
		1988	One year	Five years	10 years				Toll-free (800)	In state
Legg Mason Value Trust	Gro	24.2	(6.6)	96.7	—	High	1.8	$106	822-5544	800-638-1107 (Md.)
Lehman Capital	Max	(3.5)	(30.2)	33.8	397.6	Middle	0.0	111	221-5350	212-668-8578 (N.Y.)
Lehman Investors	G&I	13.6	(12.9)	63.9	325.1	Middle	2.8	81	221-5350	212-668-8578 (N.Y.)
Lehman Opportunity	Max	21.8	(1.9)	108.0	—	High	3.1	64	221-5350	212-668-8578 (N.Y.)
Lexington Global	Glo	8.4	(3.0)	—	—	—	0.1	113	526-0057	—
Lexington GNMA Income	MBS	6.9	13.5	63.6	114.9	Middle	7.7	54	526-0057	—
Lexington Goldfund	Gold	(17.2)	(31.3)	41.5	—	High	0.6	70	526-0057	—
Lexington Growth	Gro	11.6	(15.3)	41.4	148.1	Middle	0.0	73	526-0057	—
Lexington Research	G&I	9.6	(13.2)	58.8	263.4	Low	1.7	53	526-0057	—
Liberty High Income Securities	HYC	13.0	12.8	73.7	180.1	Middle	12.6	100	356-2805	—
Lindner Fund	Gro	15.7	(3.2)	94.8	541.0	High	3.7	59	—	314-727-5305
LMH Fund	G&I	13.6	(0.7)	67.6	—	Middle	12.3	N.A.	422-2564	800-522-2564 (Conn.)
Loomis-Sayles Capital Development*	Gro	(2.2)	(24.6)	91.9	619.7	High	0.3	46	345-4048	617-578-4200 (Mass.)
Loomis-Sayles Mutual	Bal	0.3	(14.1)	104.9	295.4	High	4.1	52	345-4048	617-578-4200 (Mass.)
Lord Abbett Affiliated	G&I	10.1	(12.3)	95.9	348.8	Middle	5.1	N.A.	223-4224	212-848-1800 (N.Y.)
Lord Abbett Bond Debenture	HYC	11.9	6.5	61.2	176.2	Middle	10.8	106	223-4224	212-848-1800 (N.Y.)
Lord Abbett Developing Growth	SCG	6.9	(15.7)	(9.5)	166.5	Low	0.0	120	223-4224	212-848-1800 (N.Y.)
Lord Abbett U.S. Government Securities	USG	7.7	15.0	75.5	181.5	High	11.0	N.A.	223-4224	212-848-1800 (N.Y.)
Lord Abbett Value Appreciation	Gro	15.7	(11.1)	76.0	—	Middle	2.7	121	223-4224	212-848-1800 (N.Y.)
Mackay-Shields Capital Appreciation	Max	3.5	(23.8)	—	—	—	0.0	175	522-4202	—
Mackay-Shields Convertible	EqI	8.9	(4.5)	—	—	—	4.6	165	522-4202	—
Mackay-Shields Government Plus	USG	5.3	8.7	—	—	—	10.5	124	522-4202	—
Mackay-Shields High Yield Bond	HYC	13.6	13.8	—	—	—	11.6	139	522-4202	—
MacKenzie Option Income	OpInc	3.6	(14.8)	—	—	—	15.8	138	222-2274	800-824-6067 (Fla.)
Mass. Capital Development	Gro	6.7	(19.2)	28.5	398.9	Low	1.1	110	225-2606	617-423-3500 (Mass.)
Mass. Financial Bond	HGC	7.3	13.3	75.3	171.3	Middle	8.8	112	225-2606	617-423-3500 (Mass.)
Mass. Financial Development	G&I	10.5	(15.6)	57.1	322.0	Low	2.1	N.A.	225-2606	617-423-3500 (Mass.)
Mass. Financial Emerging Growth	SCG	12.8	(20.7)	25.7	—	Middle	0.0	139	225-2606	617-423-3500 (Mass.)
Mass. Fin. Government Guaranteed	MBS	5.8	10.2	—	—	—	9.3	109	225-2606	617-423-3500 (Mass.)
Mass. Fin. Gov. Securities High Yield	USG	4.6	11.0	—	—	—	10.0	N.A.	225-2606	617-423-3500 (Mass.)
Mass. Financial High Income Trust I*	HYC	10.8	7.3	63.1	228.8	Middle	12.8	111	225-2606	617-423-3500 (Mass.)
Mass. Fin. International Trust–Bond	Glo	(1.2)	16.4	114.0	—	High	15.2	130	225-2606	617-423-3500 (Mass.)
Mass. Fin. Lifetime–Capital Growth	Max	14.6	(13.2)	—	—	—	0.9	N.A.	225-2606	617-423-3500 (Mass.)
Mass. Fin. Lifetime–Dividends Plus	G&I	12.0	(2.3)	—	—	—	6.3	N.A.	225-2606	617-423-3500 (Mass.)
Mass. Fin. Lifetime–Emerging Growth	SCG	7.0	(22.8)	—	—	—	0.0	N.A.	225-2606	617-423-3500 (Mass.)
Mass. Fin. Lifetime–Global Equity	Glo	(2.0)	(12.0)	—	—	—	0.0	N.A.	225-2606	617-423-3500 (Mass.)
Mass. Fin. Lifetime–Gov. Income Plus	USG	4.1	10.4	—	—	—	9.1	N.A.	225-2606	617-423-3500 (Mass.)
Mass. Fin. Lifetime–High Income	HYC	11.0	9.5	—	—	—	10.0	N.A.	225-2606	617-423-3500 (Mass.)
Mass. Fin. Lifetime–Managed Sectors	Sec	4.0	(23.8)	—	—	—	0.7	N.A.	225-2606	617-423-3500 (Mass.)
Mass. Financial Managed Sectors Trust	Sec	3.0	(25.3)	—	—	—	1.0	123	225-2606	617-423-3500 (Mass.)
Mass. Financial Special	Max	25.1	(8.3)	58.4	—	Middle	1.2	140	225-2606	617-423-3500 (Mass.)
Mass. Financial Total Return Trust	Bal	12.2	(1.7)	102.4	300.6	High	6.0	105	225-2606	617-423-3500 (Mass.)
Mass. Investors Growth Stock	Gro	3.8	(20.3)	45.6	254.0	Middle	1.7	N.A.	225-2606	617-423-3500 (Mass.)
Mass. Investors Trust	G&I	8.6	(16.5)	76.1	266.0	Middle	3.3	96	225-2606	617-423-3500 (Mass.)
Mathers Fund	Gro	11.8	8.6	97.6	377.2	High	2.8	54	962-3863	312-295-7400 (Ill.)
Medical Technology Fund	Sec	5.9	(19.2)	25.3	—	Middle	0.0	99	262-3863	—
Merrill Lynch Basic Value	G&I	19.9	(1.9)	117.4	423.9	High	4.1	96	637-7455	—
Merrill Lynch Capital	G&I	12.5	(5.4)	101.0	386.8	Middle	2.6	96	637-7455	—
Merrill Lynch Corporate–High Income	HYC	10.8	10.8	75.9	—	Middle	12.1	75	637-7455	—
Merrill Lynch Corporate–High Quality	HGC	7.2	13.8	76.0	—	Middle	9.0	72	637-7455	—
Merrill Lynch Corporate–Intermed. Bond	HGC	6.8	12.2	71.8	—	Middle	8.8	53	637-7455	—
Merrill Lynch Eurofund	Intl	(1.7)	(23.4)	—	—	—	9.9	110	637-7455	—
Merrill Lynch Federal Securities	MBS	7.5	13.4	—	—	—	9.2	94	637-7455	—
Merrill Lynch Fund for Tomorrow	Gro	19.0	(8.4)	—	—	—	1.2	101	637-7455	—
Merrill Lynch International	Glo	3.4	(12.1)	—	—	—	4.2	137	637-7455	—
Merrill Lynch Natural Resources	Sec	(7.6)	(30.6)	—	—	—	4.7	99	637-7455	—
Merrill Lynch Pacific	Intl	12.3	(18.7)	255.3	507.7	High	4.4	114	637-7455	—

*Currently closed to new investors   N.A. Not available. Fund is not required to report these data until the end of its fiscal year.

FUND NAME	Type	% gain (or loss) to Oct. 1, 1988				Five-year ranking within category	% yield	Five-year expense projection	Telephone	
		1988	One year	Five years	10 years				Toll-free (800)	In state
Merrill Lynch Phoenix	G&I	30.3	6.0	127.3	—	High	5.5	$125	637-7455	—
Merrill Lynch Retirement Benefit	Bal	6.3	(6.4)	—	—	—	5.0	94	637-7455	—
Merrill Lynch Retirement Equity	G&I	16.0	(2.5)	—	—	—	2.6	107	637-7455	—
Merrill Lynch Retirement Global Bond	Glo	(3.0)	13.5	—	—	—	12.8	96	637-7455	—
Merrill Lynch Retirement Income	MBS	6.8	12.1	—	—	—	8.4	75	637-7455	—
Merrill Lynch Science-Tech. Holdings	Sec	2.7	(15.7)	51.0	—	Middle	0.4	137	637-7455	—
Merrill Lynch Special Value	Gro	17.5	(14.2)	11.2	130.5	Low	2.0	96	637-7455	—
Metlife–State Street Capital Appreciation	Max	20.4	(12.3)	—	—	—	0.7	N.A.	882-0052	
MetLife–State Street Equity Income	EqI	13.5	(3.3)	—	—	—	6.1	N.A.	882-0052	
MetLife–State Street Gov. Income	USG	6.1	11.0	—	—	—	9.7	57	882-0052	
MetLife–State Street Gov. Securities	USG	5.7	10.9	—	—	—	8.5	111	882-0052	
MetLife–State Street High Income	HYC	13.6	13.9	—	—	—	11.8	111	882-0052	—
MidAmerica Mutual	Gro	8.0	(9.9)	70.6	258.1	Middle	3.7	131	553-4936	800-342-4490 (Iowa)
Midwest Income–Intermediate-Term Gov.	STT	4.7	8.8	54.5	—	Low	7.5	74	543-8721	800-582-7396 (Ohio)
Mutual of Omaha America	USG	6.7	13.2	60.1	137.4	Middle	8.5	54	228-9596	800-642-8112 (Neb.)
Mutual of Omaha Growth	Gro	21.2	(9.3)	61.9	213.0	Middle	0.9	136	228-9596	800-642-8112 (Neb.)
Mutual of Omaha Income	EqI	9.8	6.0	79.7	175.4	Middle	8.5	120	228-9596	800-642-8112 (Neb.)
Mutual Qualified	G&I	27.0	6.3	141.6	—	High	5.1	38	553-3014	—
Mutual Shares	G&I	27.9	7.0	137.9	528.2	High	4.7	39	553-3014	—
National Aviation & Technology	Sec	21.0	(12.7)	45.1	158.4	Middle	1.1	100	654-0001	—
National Bond	HYC	6.6	3.7	44.7	113.8	Low	16.2	108	223-7757	212-661-3000 (N.Y.)
National Federal Securities Trust	USG	3.7	10.5	—	—	—	10.5	112	223-7757	212-661-3000 (N.Y.)
National Growth	Gro	9.3	(16.3)	7.0	110.7	Low	2.7	119	223-7757	212-661-3000 (N.Y.)
National Industries	G&I	10.7	(11.1)	34.3	128.8	Low	0.8	N.A.	367-7814	303-220-8500 (Colo.)
National Stock	G&I	18.4	(8.4)	82.2	263.1	Middle	4.1	111	223-7757	212-661-3000 (N.Y.)
National Telecom. & Technology	Sec	7.3	(19.4)	15.0	—	Low	1.1	125	654-0001	—
National Total Income	EqI	13.4	4.0	100.0	318.8	High	5.6	119	223-7757	212-661-3000 (N.Y.)
National Total Return	EqI	9.1	(7.9)	73.2	301.3	Middle	4.8	116	223-7757	212-661-3000 (N.Y.)
Nationwide Bond	HGC	6.2	12.5	65.7	—	Low	10.8	N.A.	848-0920	800-282-1440 (Ohio)
Nationwide Fund	G&I	14.9	(10.3)	102.1	251.8	High	3.5	N.A.	848-0920	800-282-1440 (Ohio)
Nationwide Growth	Gro	18.6	(5.0)	110.5	372.1	High	4.9	N.A.	848-0920	800-282-1440 (Ohio)
Neuberger & Berman Energy	Sec	12.6	(12.4)	59.1	250.4	Middle	2.8	48	237-1413	—
Neuberger & Berman Guardian Mutual	G&I	27.2	(2.4)	94.9	390.4	Middle	3.1	41	237-1413	—
Neuberger & Berman Limited Mat. Bond	STT	5.6	8.2	—	—	—	7.3	36	237-1413	—
Neuberger & Berman Manhattan	Max	15.8	(14.3)	103.1	418.4	High	1.9	55	237-1413	—
Neuberger & Berman Partners	Gro	12.8	(7.2)	97.6	456.2	High	3.4	53	237-1413	—
Neuwirth Fund	Gro	28.0	(7.6)	48.4	246.1	Middle	0.0	90	225-8011	—
New Beginning Growth	SCG	12.1	(12.6)	68.8	—	Middle	0.0	66	—	612-332-3223
New Economy	Gro	13.0	(9.2)	—	—	—	1.8	96	421-9900	714-671-7000 (Calif.)
New England Bond Income	EqI	7.0	11.7	67.7	129.9	Low	7.9	127	343-7104	—
New England Equity Income	G&I	6.8	(14.6)	71.7	281.8	Middle	2.4	145	343-7104	—
New England Government Securities	USG	5.9	13.0	—	—	—	7.4	130	343-7104	—
New England Growth	Gro	(0.1)	(21.4)	71.2	564.1	Middle	0.0	130	343-7104	—
New England Retirement Equity	G&I	(3.9)	(23.4)	82.5	313.4	Middle	0.6	129	343-7104	—
New Perspective	Glo	4.6	(14.3)	107.8	374.8	Middle	2.4	99	421-9900	714-671-7000 (Calif.)
Newton Growth	Gro	12.4	(21.0)	30.0	279.5	Low	1.3	66	247-7039	800-242-7229 (Wis.)
New York Venture	Gro	19.1	(2.8)	99.6	493.2	High	4.2	101	545-2098	505-983-4335 (N.M.)
Nicholas Fund	Gro	18.5	(1.3)	80.5	466.4	Middle	3.2	48	—	414-272-6133
Nicholas Income	EqI	10.1	11.4	73.4	146.6	Middle	9.7	48	—	414-272-6133
Nicholas Limited Edition	Gro	22.6	6.7	—	—	—	0.8	N.A.	—	414-272-6133
Nicholas II	SCG	18.4	(1.5)	—	—	—	1.8	41	—	414-272-6133
Nomura Pacific Basin	Intl	4.2	(4.6)	—	—	—	0.4	70	833-0018	—
Northeast Investors Trust	EqI	12.5	10.5	93.0	197.3	Middle	16.0	43	225-6704	—
Omega Growth Portfolio	Max	11.1	(10.5)	70.1	239.6	Middle	0.0	N.A.	237-5047	—
Oppenheimer Asset Allocation	Bal	13.8	(2.9)	—	—	—	4.3	132	525-7048	800-356-3556 (Colo.)
Oppenheimer Directors	Max	18.3	(13.2)	13.8	—	Low	2.8	N.A.	525-7048	800-356-3556 (Colo.)
Oppenheimer Equity Income	EqI	11.0	(3.0)	94.5	379.5	Middle	7.2	N.A.	525-7048	800-356-3556 (Colo.)

N.A. Not available. Fund is not required to report these data until the end of its fiscal year

FUND NAME	Type	% gain (or loss) to Oct. 1, 1988				Five-year ranking within category	% yield	Five-year expense projection	Telephone	
		1988	One year	Five years	10 years				Toll-free (800)	In state
Oppenheimer Fund	Gro	7.6	(20.0)	18.9	158.9	Low	2.6	N.A.	525-7048	800-356-3556 (Colo.)
Oppenheimer GNMA	MBS	6.6	12.1	—	—	—	9.5	N.A.	525-7048	800-356-3556 (Colo.)
Oppenheimer Global	Glo	10.0	(25.2)	74.5	427.9	Low	0.3	N.A.	525-7048	800-356-3556 (Colo.)
Oppenheimer Gold & Special Minerals	Gold	3.3	16.4	67.3	—	High	1.7	N.A.	525-7048	800-356-3556 (Colo.)
Oppenheimer High Yield	HYC	10.2	7.6	61.3	155.9	Middle	13.0	N.A.	525-7048	800-356-3556 (Colo.)
Oppenheimer OTC	SCG	16.6	(7.1)	—	—	—	0.3	N.A.	525-7048	800-356-3556 (Colo.)
Oppenheimer Premium Income	OpInc	2.4	15.1	90.9	253.7	High	1.7	N.A.	525-7048	800-356-3556 (Colo.)
Oppenheimer Regency**	Max	8.9	(13.8)	19.3	—	Low	1.1	$141	525-7048	800-356-3556 (Colo.)
Oppenheimer Special	Gro	16.7	(0.9)	31.9	259.6	Low	2.3	N.A.	525-7048	800-356-3556 (Colo.)
Oppenheimer Target	Max	31.1	(10.4)	15.8	—	Low	1.2	108	525-7048	800-356-3556 (Colo.)
Oppenheimer Time	Max	11.4	(10.4)	66.7	413.7	Middle	0.8	N.A.	525-7048	800-356-3556 (Colo.)
Oppenheimer Total Return	G&I	10.1	(6.3)	81.5	216.9	Middle	4.5	95	525-7048	800-356-3556 (Colo.)
Oppenheimer U.S. Government Trust	USG	6.5	11.6	51.7	—	Low	10.1	N.A.	525-7048	800-356-3556 (Colo.)
Over-the-Counter Securities	SCG	26.7	(8.6)	49.9	357.8	Middle	0.6	117	523-2578	—
Pacific Horizon Aggressive Growth	Max	(0.2)	(20.3)	—	—	—	0.8	64	332-3863	—
Paine Webber America	G&I	17.3	(5.0)	—	—	—	3.6	N.A.	544-9300	—
Paine Webber Asset Allocation	G&I	9.5	12.8	—	—	—	5.4	127	647-1568	—
Paine Webber Atlas	Glo	8.6	(18.3)	—	—	—	4.4	N.A.	544-9300	—
Paine Webber Fixed Income—GNMA	MBS	7.1	13.7	—	—	—	9.0	N.A.	544-9300	—
Paine Webber High Yield	HYC	8.3	2.2	—	—	—	13.9	N.A.	544-9300	—
Paine Webber Investment Grade Bond	HGC	7.0	14.2	—	—	—	8.8	N.A.	544-9300	—
Paine Webber Master Global	Glo	5.4	17.8	—	—	—	7.9	N.A.	647-1568	—
Paine Webber Master Growth	Gro	14.9	(11.8)	—	—	—	0.0	130	647-1568	—
Paine Webber Master Income	EqI	6.9	13.2	—	—	—	7.7	123	647-1568	—
Paine Webber Olympus	Gro	18.2	(13.1)	—	—	—	0.7	N.A.	544-9300	—
Pax World	Bal	10.3	(4.5)	71.8	214.3	Middle	4.3	61	343-0529	—
PBHG Growth	Max	6.6	(15.9)	—	—	—	0.0	111	262-6631	—
Penn Square Mutual	G&I	10.8	(10.8)	70.1	270.7	Middle	3.6	45	523-8440	800-222-7506 (Pa.)
Pennsylvania Mutual	SCG	23.6	3.1	87.3	383.7	High	2.8	55	221-4268	212-355-7311 (N.Y.)
Permanent Portfolio	Sec	(0.7)	(4.0)	20.9	—	Low	0.0	184	531-5142	512-453-7558 (Texas)
Philadelphia Fund	G&I	11.5	(8.7)	47.5	211.5	Low	1.9	N.A.	221-5588	212-668-8111 (N.Y.)
Phoenix Balanced Series	Bal	2.1	(6.9)	99.9	354.2	Middle	5.1	122	243-4361	—
Phoenix Convertible	EqI	3.1	(5.4)	73.9	342.7	Middle	7.0	122	243-4361	—
Phoenix Growth Series	Gro	5.7	(8.1)	103.8	610.8	High	4.0	121	243-4361	—
Phoenix High Yield Series	HYC	10.5	10.1	71.9	—	Middle	11.5	86	243-4361	—
Phoenix Stock Series	Max	4.0	(11.8)	83.3	600.5	High	3.0	124	243-4361	—
Pilgrim GNMA	MBS	7.6	12.8	—	—	—	9.6	99	334-3444	—
Pilgrim High Yield	HYC	10.8	6.7	61.8	154.7	Middle	12.1	119	334-3444	—
Pilgrim MagnaCap	Gro	14.2	(10.7)	112.3	342.4	High	1.7	127	334-3444	—
Pine Street	G&I	14.1	(11.9)	66.0	248.8	Middle	4.7	65	225-8011	816-283-1700 (Mo.)
Pioneer Bond	HGC	6.7	11.9	65.1	—	Low	9.0	93	225-6292	617-742-7825 (Mass.)
Pioneer Fund	G&I	15.6	(10.3)	70.6	264.8	Middle	3.0	121	225-6292	617-742-7825 (Mass.)
Pioneer II	G&I	18.5	(12.0)	71.7	356.5	Middle	2.6	126	225-6292	617-742-7825 (Mass.)
Pioneer Three	G&I	25.9	(5.9)	72.3	—	Middle	2.7	124	225-6292	617-742-7825 (Mass.)
Piper Jaffray Government Income	USG	6.5	14.3	—	—	—	8.7	108	333-6000	—
Piper Jaffray Sector	Sec	6.4	(20.0)	—	—	—	1.3	106	333-6000	—
T. Rowe Price Capital Appreciation	Max	17.5	5.9	—	—	—	3.3	82	638-5660	301-547-2308 (Md.)
T. Rowe Price Equity Income	EqI	24.9	7.5	—	—	—	4.5	71	638-5660	301-547-2308 (Md.)
T. Rowe Price GNMA	MBS	6.2	9.8	—	—	—	10.2	54	638-5660	301-547-2308 (Md.)
T. Rowe Price Growth & Income	G&I	23.0	(2.5)	57.5	—	Low	3.8	58	638-5660	301-547-2308 (Md.)
T. Rowe Price Growth Stock	Gro	3.3	(18.8)	71.2	173.3	Middle	2.3	41	638-5660	301-547-2308 (Md.)
T. Rowe Price High Yield Bond	HYC	14.8	13.0	—	—	—	12.2	57	638-5660	301-547-2308 (Md.)
T. Rowe Price International Bond	Glo	(8.1)	7.3	—	—	—	9.8	58	638-5660	301-547-2308 (Md.)
T. Rowe Price International Stock	Intl	6.9	(11.5)	175.9	—	Middle	1.5	64	638-5660	301-547-2308 (Md.)
T. Rowe Price New America Growth	Gro	20.2	(9.0)	—	—	—	0.0	82	638-5660	301-547-2308 (Md.)
T. Rowe Price New Era	Sec	7.1	(14.0)	90.0	368.9	Middle	3.1	49	638-5660	301-547-2308 (Md.)
T. Rowe Price New Horizons	SCG	14.5	(15.4)	10.5	213.3	Middle	0.4	44	638-5660	301-547-2308 (Md.)

**Open to retirement plans only   N.A. Not available. Fund is not required to report these data until the end of its fiscal year.

FUND NAME	Type	% gain (or loss) to Oct. 1, 1988				Five-year ranking within category	% yield	Five-year expense projection	Telephone	
		1988	One year	Five years	10 years				Toll-free (800)	In state
T. Rowe Price New Income	HGC	6.3	12.3	66.1	166.7	Low	9.6	$48	638-5660	301-547-2308 (Md.)
T. Rowe Price Short-Term Bond	STT	4.2	8.1	—	—	—	8.4	53	638-5660	302-547-2308 (Md.)
Primary Trend	G&I	14.7	0.4	—	—	—	6.0	66	443-6544	414-271-7870 (Wis.)
Principal Preservation Government Plus	USG	5.5	13.3	—	—	—	8.3	108	826-4600	—
Princor Capital Accumulation	Max	12.4	(13.3)	103.9	330.0	High	2.4	113	247-4123	—
Princor Government Securities Income	USG	8.4	15.9	—	—	—	8.5	106	247-4123	—
Princor Growth	Gro	7.7	(18.8)	58.8	232.4	Middle	1.7	115	247-4123	—
Provident Fund for Income	EqI	9.6	(11.0)	59.4	247.7	Low	7.4	112	847-5636	—
Pru-Bache Equity	Gro	11.9	(14.7)	82.7	—	Middle	1.5	101	225-1852	—
Pru-Bache Equity Income	EqI	18.4	(7.2)	—	—	—	2.9	102	225-1852	—
Pru-Bache Global	Glo	0.6	(21.1)	—	—	—	0.7	128	225-1852	—
Pru-Bache GNMA	MBS	5.6	11.1	60.9	—	Low	7.7	100	225-1852	—
Pru-Bache Government–Intermed. Term	STT	5.0	9.9	67.6	—	High	9.4	40	225-1852	—
Pru-Bache Government Plus	MBS	5.2	12.2	—	—	—	7.2	97	225-1852	—
Pru-Bache Government Plus II	USG	4.8	12.7	—	—	—	7.4	102	225-1852	—
Pru-Bache Growth Opportunity	Gro	23.9	(10.8)	32.2	—	Low	0.4	98	225-1852	—
Pru-Bache High Yield	HYC	10.5	10.0	74.1	—	Middle	11.1	83	225-1852	—
Pru-Bache IncomeVertible Plus	Sec	10.8	(0.7)	—	—	—	6.3	118	225-1852	—
Pru-Bache Option Growth	OpInc	10.9	(7.5)	67.9	—	High	1.8	102	225-1852	—
Pru-Bache Research	Gro	8.6	(15.0)	69.0	—	Middle	1.2	108	225-1852	—
Pru-Bache Utility	Sec	18.9	6.1	168.6	—	High	4.2	93	225-1852	—
Putnam Convertible Income & Growth	EqI	10.2	(11.1)	60.0	310.8	Low	6.7	133	225-1581	—
Putnam Energy Resources	Sec	14.7	(9.7)	28.7	—	Middle	3.1	164	225-1581	—
Putnam (George) Fund of Boston	Bal	10.7	(4.4)	72.6	270.6	Middle	5.4	122	225-1581	—
Putnam Global Government Income	Glo	8.1	20.9	—	—	—	10.0	126	225-1581	—
Putnam GNMA Plus	MBS	5.8	11.9	—	—	—	9.5	101	225-1581	—
Putnam Fund for Growth & Income	G&I	15.3	(7.5)	100.8	361.3	Middle	6.1	121	225-1581	—
Putnam Health Sciences Trust	Sec	12.1	(13.5)	65.7	—	Middle	0.6	140	225-1581	—
Putnam High Income Government	USG	4.3	12.0	—	—	—	8.8	103	225-1581	—
Putnam High Yield	HYC	10.7	11.1	70.5	203.9	Middle	12.8	99	225-1581	—
Putnam High Yield Trust II	HYC	12.1	13.7	—	—	—	11.7	124	225-1581	—
Putnam Income	HGC	8.6	14.6	75.2	171.7	Middle	10.5	109	225-1581	—
Putnam Information Sciences	Sec	3.7	(22.8)	24.6	—	Middle	0.0	196	225-1581	—
Putnam International Equities	Glo	1.3	(16.9)	161.6	407.0	High	1.4	97	225-1581	—
Putnam Investors	Gro	6.8	(16.5)	61.1	281.3	Middle	3.5	118	225-1581	—
Putnam Option Income	OpInc	19.8	(10.6)	60.6	204.3	Middle	4.7	129	225-1581	—
Putnam Option Income II	OpInc	16.3	(6.7)	—	—	—	2.8	128	225-1581	—
Putnam OTC Emerging Growth	SCG	13.8	(12.4)	82.2	—	High	0.0	150	225-1581	—
Putnam U.S. Gov. Guaranteed Securities	MBS	7.1	12.3	—	—	—	9.9	78	225-1581	—
Putnam Vista Basic Value	Max	12.0	(12.9)	59.5	414.3	Middle	2.5	141	225-1581	—
Putnam Voyager	Max	8.3	(13.6)	74.8	387.2	Middle	0.2	139	225-1581	—
Quest for Value	Max	18.2	(6.7)	82.7	—	High	0.6	120	862-7778	212-667-7587 (N.Y.)
Rea-Graham Fund	Bal	9.6	3.9	66.0	—	Low	3.8	139	433-1998	213-471-1917 (Calif.)
Reich & Tang Equity	Gro	20.1	(1.3)	—	—	—	2.6	61	221-3079	212-370-1240 (N.Y.)
Rightime Fund	G&I	2.3	4.0	—	—	—	2.1	N.A.	242-1421	—
RNC Convertible Securities	EqI	9.4	(9.4)	—	—	—	4.7	165	225-9655	800-233-6483 (Calif.)
Rodney Square Growth	G&I	18.8	(8.2)	—	—	—	0.8	95	225-5084	—
Royce Value	SCG	22.9	0.6	73.7	—	High	1.4	113	221-4268	212-355-7311 (N.Y.)
Safeco Equity	G&I	23.1	(9.9)	84.7	242.2	Middle	2.7	54	426-6730	800-562-6810 (Wash.)
Safeco Growth	Gro	20.0	(1.5)	48.5	259.2	Middle	3.1	51	426-6730	800-562-6810 (Wash.)
Safeco Income	EqI	18.1	(4.6)	97.6	347.8	High	6.8	52	426-6730	800-562-6810 (Wash.)
Safeco U.S. Government	USG	5.7	9.1	—	—	—	9.6	58	426-6730	800-562-6810 (Wash.)
SBSF Growth	Gro	17.2	(5.6)	—	—	—	3.4	N.A.	422-7273	—
Scudder Capital Growth	Gro	24.5	(5.6)	93.9	359.1	High	1.2	49	225-2470	—
Scudder Development	SCG	11.5	(13.7)	21.3	215.9	Middle	0.0	70	225-2470	—
Scudder Global	Glo	13.5	(13.2)	—	—	—	1.7	100	225-2470	—
Scudder GNMA	MBS	7.0	12.0	—	—	—	9.1	57	225-2470	—

N.A. Not available. Fund is not required to report these data until the end of its fiscal year

FUND NAME	Type	% gain (or loss) to Oct. 1, 1988				Five-year ranking within category	% yield	Five-year expense projection	Telephone Toll-free (800)	In state
		1988	One year	Five years	10 years					
Scudder Growth & Income	G&I	7.7	(10.9)	68.6	249.2	Middle	3.5	$49	225-2470	—
Scudder Income	EqI	7.4	13.0	71.8	157.7	Middle	6.3	52	225-2470	—
Scudder International	Intl	6.7	(18.1)	151.3	346.7	Middle	2.2	66	225-2470	—
Security Action	Gro	12.6	(15.7)	38.0	—	Middle	1.8	N.A.	888-2461	—
Security Equity	Gro	14.8	(10.8)	58.0	294.0	Middle	4.9	125	888-2461	—
Security Income—Corporate Bond	HGC	5.1	9.5	68.2	150.5	Middle	10.5	100	888-2461	—
Security Investment	G&I	7.7	(11.0)	29.2	184.0	Low	6.5	123	888-2461	—
Security Ultra	Max	18.6	(21.0)	26.3	243.8	Middle	2.5	130	888-2461	—
Selected American Shares	G&I	20.6	(2.5)	124.6	316.7	High	2.8	61	553-5533	—
Selected Special Shares	Gro	19.9	(10.4)	54.6	209.2	Middle	4.8	61	553-5533	—
Seligman Capital	Max	2.5	(23.4)	22.5	329.2	Low	0.0	98	221-2450	800-522-6869 (N.Y.)
Seligman Comm. & Information	Sec	3.2	(16.7)	61.2	—	Middle	0.0	135	221-2450	800-522-6869 (N.Y.)
Seligman Common Stock	G&I	9.4	(11.7)	82.1	338.5	Middle	3.6	79	221-2450	800-522-6869 (N.Y.)
Seligman Growth	Gro	6.1	(15.7)	51.3	223.2	Middle	1.8	80	221-2450	800-522-6869 (N.Y.)
Seligman Hi. Inc.–High Yield Bond	HYC	8.6	13.3	—	—	—	11.5	110	221-2450	800-522-6869 (N.Y.)
Seligman Hi. Inc.–Securities Mort. Income	MBS	7.1	14.3	—	—	—	9.9	111	221-2450	800-522-6869 (N.Y.)
Seligman Hi. Inc.–U.S. Gov. Guaranteed	USG	6.9	15.5	—	—	—	8.6	108	221-2450	800-522-6869 (N.Y.)
Seligman Income	EqI	9.9	6.9	78.5	224.9	Middle	8.0	89	221-2450	800-522-6869 (N.Y.)
Sentinel Balanced	Bal	9.1	(3.4)	97.1	268.7	Middle	5.9	135	282-3863	802-229-3900 (Vt.)
Sentinel Common Stock	G&I	10.6	(11.9)	105.5	361.6	High	3.6	124	282-3863	802-229-3900 (Vt.)
Sentinel Government Securities	USG	6.9	13.1	—	—	—	8.5	133	282-3863	802-229-3900 (Vt.)
Sentinel Growth	Gro	3.5	(19.9)	50.8	346.2	Middle	2.1	139	282-3863	802-229-3900 (Vt.)
Sentry Fund	Gro	16.7	(10.7)	61.2	248.5	Middle	2.0	115	533-7827	—
Sequoia Fund*	Gro	9.2	(1.8)	110.1	396.5	High	3.6	56	—	212-245-4500
Shearson Aggressive Growth	Max	7.5	(17.9)	—	—	—	0.0	108	—	212-528-2744
Shearson Appreciation	Gro	10.6	(10.8)	96.4	470.0	High	2.2	97	—	212-528-2744
Shearson Fundamental Value	Gro	20.3	(7.3)	72.1	—	Middle	4.1	113	—	212-528-2744
Shearson Global Opportunities	Glo	2.5	(25.9)	—	—	—	0.2	118	—	212-528-2744
Shearson High Yield	HYC	10.2	9.7	71.8	—	Middle	12.5	89	—	212-528-2744
Shearson Lehman–Intermed. Term	STT	4.0	7.4	—	—	—	6.1	96	—	212-528-2744
Shearson Lehman–International Equity	Intl	1.7	(24.7)	—	—	—	0.0	151	—	212-528-2744
Shearson Lehman–L.G. Gov. Securities	USG	4.7	10.3	—	—	—	7.5	90	—	212-528-2744
Shearson Lehman Precious Metals & Min.	Gold	(18.7)	(38.6)	—	—	—	0.0	155	—	212-528-2744
Shearson Lehman–Special Growth	Gro	18.2	(3.2)	—	—	—	2.1	124	—	212-528-2744
Shearson Lehman Spl. Inc.–Conv. Securities	EqI	13.4	1.4	—	—	—	6.6	105	—	212-528-2744
Shearson Lehman Spl. Inc.–Global Bond	Glo	(0.5)	13.4	—	—	—	2.1	126	—	212-528-2744
Shearson Lehman Spl. Inc.–Hi. Inc. Bond	HYC	11.4	12.1	—	—	—	11.0	102	—	212-528-2744
Shearson Lehman Spl. Inc.–Mort. Securities	MBS	5.7	8.4	—	—	—	8.4	113	—	212-528-2744
Shearson Lehman Spl. Inc.–Opt. Income	OpInc	23.7	1.3	—	—	—	2.9	106	—	212-528-2744
Shearson Lehman Strategic Investors	G&I	15.3	1.9	—	—	—	3.4	125	—	212-528-2744
Shearson Managed Governments	MBS	6.0	9.9	—	—	—	8.9	91	—	212-528-2744
Sigma Capital Shares	Max	10.6	(13.1)	71.3	366.3	Middle	1.1	115	441-9490	302-652-3091 (Del.)
Sigma Income Shares	HGC	8.3	8.3	77.7	154.9	Middle	7.3	124	441-9490	302-652-3091 (Del.)
Sigma Investment Shares	G&I	9.4	(10.1)	96.3	312.3	Middle	2.7	108	441-9490	302-652-3091 (Del.)
Sigma Trust Shares	Bal	11.0	(0.5)	81.3	222.0	Middle	4.9	116	441-9490	302-652-3091 (Del.)
Sigma Venture Shares	SCG	4.3	(24.4)	6.2	199.6	Middle	0.0	122	441-9490	302-652-3091 (Del.)
Smith Barney Equity	Gro	(1.3)	(16.6)	64.1	287.2	Middle	3.7	85	544-7835	—
Smith Barney Income & Growth	G&I	14.5	(5.2)	91.2	375.8	Middle	5.9	83	544-7835	—
Smith Barney U.S. Gov. Securities	MBS	8.6	16.2	—	—	—	9.3	63	544-7835	—
SoGen International	Gro	10.0	(6.0)	116.8	479.5	High	4.8	109	334-2143	212-832-3073 (N.Y.)
Southeastern Growth	Gro	15.6	(13.6)	—	—	—	0.0	127	321-0038	—
Sovereign Investors	G&I	9.6	(6.1)	98.4	315.4	Middle	5.2	95	—	215-254-0703
State Bond Common Stock	Gro	9.2	(15.7)	56.3	177.4	Middle	1.9	140	328-4735	—
SteinRoe Discovery	SCG	10.1	(19.2)	22.4	—	Middle	0.0	82	338-2550	—
SteinRoe Equity Trust–Cap. Opportunities	Gro	1.5	(23.3)	21.5	310.9	Low	0.2	53	338-2550	—
SteinRoe Equity Trust–Stock	Gro	0.5	(25.7)	28.0	247.4	Low	1.7	37	338-2550	—
SteinRoe Equity Trust–Total Return	Bal	6.5	(5.9)	65.5	190.4	Low	5.9	45	338-2550	—

*Currently closed to new investors   N.A. Not available. Fund is not required to report these data until the end of its fiscal year.

FUND NAME	Type	% gain (or loss) to Oct. 1, 1988				Five-year ranking within category	% yield	Five-year expense projection	Telephone Toll-free (800)	In state
		1988	One year	Five years	10 years					
SteinRoe Equity Trust–Universe	Max	5.6	(22.3)	12.3	—	Low	0.1	$75	338-2550	—
SteinRoe Government Plus	USG	7.0	12.8	—	—	—	7.8	55	338-2550	—
SteinRoe High-Yield Bond	HYC	10.1	15.1	—	—	—	9.9	53	338-2550	—
SteinRoe Managed Bond	HGC	6.8	13.4	73.0	—	Middle	8.2	36	338-2550	—
SteinRoe Special	Max	18.0	(5.0)	82.4	492.9	High	1.5	53	338-2550	—
Strategic Investments	Gold	(45.2)	(56.7)	(57.8)	121.0	Low	8.6	161	527-5027	214-484-1326 (Texas)
Strategic Silver	Gold	(10.2)	(33.4)	—	—	—	0.0	161	527-5027	214-484-1326 (Texas)
Stratton Monthly Dividend Shares	Sec	10.6	(0.5)	77.4	182.0	Middle	7.4	67	634-5726	—
Strong Income	EqI	10.4	10.3	—	—	—	9.7	61	368-3863	—
Strong Investment	Bal	6.6	(0.1)	68.3	—	Middle	5.7	72	368-3863	—
Strong Opportunity	Max	14.8	(7.7)	—	—	—	3.5	100	368-3863	—
Strong Total Return	G&I	13.1	(1.6)	103.0	—	High	6.2	71	368-3863	—
Templeton Foreign	Intl	14.8	(4.5)	139.3	—	Middle	5.7	123	237-0738	800-282-0106 (Fla.)
Templeton Global I*	Glo	27.4	(6.3)	78.6	—	Middle	4.5	111	237-0738	800-282-0106 (Fla.)
Templeton Global II	Glo	17.9	(11.5)	55.9	—	Low	4.8	114	237-0738	800-282-0106 (Fla.)
Templeton Growth	Glo	20.4	(6.4)	99.4	326.6	Middle	5.2	117	237-0738	800-282-0106 (Fla.)
Templeton Income	Glo	4.0	5.5	—	—	—	8.3	134	237-0738	800-282-0106 (Fla.)
Templeton World	Glo	18.3	(4.6)	103.4	385.7	Middle	5.9	118	237-0738	800-282-0106 (Fla.)
Thomson McKinnon–Global	Glo	5.2	(14.1)	—	—	—	0.0	N.A.	628-1237	212-482-5894 (N.Y.)
Thomson McKinnon–Growth	Gro	8.3	(14.8)	—	—	—	0.8	N.A.	628-1237	212-482-5894 (N.Y.)
Thomson McKinnon–Income	HGC	7.9	10.0	—	—	—	10.1	N.A.	628-1237	212-482-5894 (N.Y.)
Thomson McKinnon–Opportunity	Max	15.3	(9.0)	—	—	—	0.2	N.A.	628-1237	212-482-5894 (N.Y.)
Thomson McKinnon U.S. Government	USG	5.6	10.8	—	—	—	9.3	N.A.	628-1237	212-482-5894 (N.Y.)
Transatlantic Growth	Intl	8.7	(11.3)	154.2	285.4	Middle	0.0	108	233-9164	212-687-2515 (N.Y.)
Tudor Fund	Max	12.5	(17.6)	45.8	418.6	Middle	0.1	57	223-3332	212-908-9582 (N.Y.)
Twentieth Century Growth	Max	(0.6)	(27.7)	54.0	435.2	Middle	0.4	54	345-2021	—
Twentieth Century Select	Gro	5.0	(19.3)	57.9	493.9	Middle	1.7	54	345-2021	—
Twentieth Century Ultra	Max	12.4	(17.6)	18.8	—	Low	0.0	54	345-2021	—
Twentieth Century U.S. Governments	USG	5.0	9.1	54.8	—	Middle	8.7	54	345-2021	—
Twentieth Century Vista	Max	6.3	(21.5)	—	—	—	0.0	54	345-2021	—
United Accumulative	Gro	14.1	(3.9)	85.7	367.4	Middle	5.0	116	—	816-842-1075
United Bond	HGC	6.2	11.6	81.1	164.7	High	9.1	119	—	816-842-1075
United Continental Income	Bal	9.9	(8.6)	83.5	278.2	Middle	5.8	128	—	816-842-1075
United Gold & Government	Gold	(7.5)	(32.1)	—	—	—	2.8	145	—	816-842-1075
United Government Securities	USG	6.0	12.2	—	—	—	7.9	83	—	816-842-1075
United High Income*	HYC	9.5	6.6	73.2	—	Middle	13.0	124	—	816-842-1075
United High Income II	HYC	12.2	11.0	—	—	—	11.4	131	—	816-842-1075
United Income	EqI	16.3	3.3	125.8	366.2	High	4.0	118	—	816-842-1075
United International Growth	Intl	4.2	(10.8)	127.4	468.7	Low	2.0	141	—	816-842-1075
United New Concepts	SCG	5.1	(21.0)	34.0	—	Middle	1.2	145	—	816-842-1075
United Retirement Shares	G&I	15.2	(2.5)	60.2	243.4	Middle	4.8	131	—	816-842-1075
United Science & Energy	Sec	7.7	(11.5)	72.3	275.6	Middle	2.6	128	—	816-842-1075
United Services Gold Shares	Gold	(41.2)	(51.4)	(43.0)	208.1	Low	8.1	72	873-8637	—
United Services New Prospector	Gold	(19.5)	(43.1)	—	—	—	0.8	79	873-8637	—
United Services Prospector*	Gold	(18.3)	(44.1)	(20.1)	—	Middle	0.0	N.A.	873-8637	—
United Vanguard	Gro	11.8	(8.5)	61.6	536.2	Middle	3.1	132	—	816-842-1075
U.S. Trend	Gro	9.2	(14.0)	51.1	285.9	Middle	2.6	110	262-6631	—
USAA Cornerstone	Sec	5.3	(13.4)	—	—	—	2.2	67	531-8000	—
USAA Gold	Gold	(18.4)	(48.9)	—	—	—	0.6	76	531-8000	—
USAA Growth	Gro	3.2	(18.3)	24.7	179.1	Low	3.2	N.A.	531-8000	—
USAA Income	EqI	8.9	15.9	77.7	181.0	Middle	9.5	N.A.	531-8000	—
USAA Income Stock	EqI	16.7	(0.1)	—	—	—	4.1	N.A.	531-8000	—
USAA Sunbelt Era	SCG	16.0	(9.7)	13.6	—	Middle	0.7	N.A.	531-8000	—
U.S. Gov. Guaranteed Securities	USG	6.5	13.2	—	—	—	9.7	100	421-9900	714-671-7000 (Calif.)
Value Line Aggressive Income	HYC	5.0	(1.2)	—	—	—	12.3	67	223-0818	—
Value Line Convertible	EqI	14.7	(6.1)	—	—	—	6.3	59	223-0818	—
Value Line Fund	G&I	7.6	(12.8)	44.2	263.5	Low	2.0	39	223-0818	—

*Currently closed to new investors   N.A. Not available. Fund is not required to report these data until the end of its fiscal year.

Fund Name	Type	% gain (or loss) to Oct. 1, 1988				Five-year ranking within category	% yield	Five-year expense projection	Telephone Toll-free (800)	In state
		1988	One year	Five years	10 years					
Value Line Income	EqI	10.9	(6.7)	54.7	279.5	Low	8.8	$42	223-0818	—
Value Line Leveraged Growth	Max	4.3	(20.4)	42.6	257.5	Middle	1.6	60	223-0818	—
Value Line Special Situations	Gro	3.8	(24.3)	(14.7)	141.1	Low	0.5	56	223-0818	—
Value Line U.S. Government Securities	USG	7.6	13.8	74.2	—	High	11.4	40	223-0818	—
Vance Sanders Special	Gro	6.6	(18.5)	(9.1)	125.9	Low	1.5	104	225-6265	617-482-8260 (Mass.)
Van Eck Gold Resources	Gold	(21.0)	(42.9)	—	—	—	0.2	139	221-2220	212-687-5200 (N.Y.)
Van Eck World Income	Glo	7.7	14.4	—	—	—	8.6	155	221-2220	212-687-5200 (N.Y.)
Van Eck World Trends	Glo	(0.5)	(12.9)	—	—	—	1.7	153	221-2220	212-687-5200 (N.Y.)
Vanguard Bond Market	HYC	6.3	12.5	—	—	—	8.8	20	662-7447	—
Vanguard Convertible	EqI	13.6	(5.6)	—	—	—	6.4	47	662-7447	—
Vanguard Explorer*	Sec	25.2	(7.5)	(1.2)	247.5	Low	0.4	35	662-7447	—
Vanguard Explorer II	SCG	18.7	(12.1)	—	—	—	0.3	35	662-7447	—
Vanguard Fixed Income—GNMA	MBS	8.5	15.8	75.1	—	Middle	9.4	20	662-7447	—
Vanguard Fixed Income—High Yield	HYC	11.2	13.1	78.5	—	Middle	11.9	23	662-7447	—
Vanguard Fixed Income—Invest. Grade	HGC	8.1	16.3	73.3	164.6	Middle	9.5	20	662-7447	—
Vanguard Fixed Income—Short-Term Bond	STT	5.8	9.2	65.5	—	Middle	7.9	19	662-7447	—
Vanguard Fixed Income—U.S. Treasury	USG	7.2	15.8	—	—	—	8.4	18	662-7447	—
Vanguard High Yield Stock*	EqI	24.8	4.8	138.5	542.3	High	10.4	28	662-7447	—
Vanguard Index Trust—500 Portfolio	G&I	12.9	(12.8)	94.8	300.2	Middle	3.3	17	662-7447	—
Vanguard Naess & Thomas Special	SCG	23.9	(14.3)	(0.4)	201.9	Low	0.0	51	662-7447	—
Vanguard Preferred Stock	EqI	6.9	6.8	70.6	152.3	Middle	11.5	36	662-7447	—
Vanguard Quantitative Portfolio	G&I	14.2	(11.6)	—	—	—	3.0	35	662-7447	—
Vanguard Specialized Portfolio—Energy	Sec	14.6	(12.4)	—	—	—	5.3	34	662-7447	—
Vanguard Special. Portfolio—Gold & PM	Gold	(18.0)	(36.5)	—	—	—	3.6	41	662-7447	—
Vanguard Special. Portfolio—Health Care	Sec	25.8	(6.4)	—	—	—	1.8	41	662-7447	—
Vanguard STAR	Bal	17.2	4.4	—	—	—	6.0	N.A.	662-7447	—
Vanguard Trustees' Commingled—Intl.	Intl	9.0	(4.0)	200.2	—	High	3.3	$27	662-7447	—
Vanguard Trustees' Commingled—U.S.	G&I	22.9	(9.9)	71.1	—	Middle	3.5	28	662-7447	—
Vanguard Wellesley Income	EqI	12.2	10.3	96.3	254.7	Middle	8.1	27	662-7447	—
Vanguard Wellington	Bal	13.8	(0.4)	98.5	316.1	Middle	5.9	24	662-7447	—
Vanguard Windsor	G&I	27.1	3.4	137.7	494.0	High	6.3	24	662-7447	—
Vanguard Windsor II	G&I	22.0	(3.6)	—	—	—	4.7	27	662-7447	—
Vanguard W. L. Morgan Growth	Gro	22.3	(7.3)	68.1	305.1	Middle	1.8	26	662-7447	—
Vanguard World—International Growth	Intl	2.9	(10.4)	198.8	—	Middle	1.2	36	662-7447	—
Vanguard World—U.S. Growth	Gro	9.2	(15.1)	48.7	247.2	Middle	4.1	36	662-7447	—
Van Kampen Merritt Growth & Income	G&I	13.9	(10.5)	—	—	—	2.7	116	225-2222	—
Van Kampen Merritt High Yield	HYC	9.7	7.9	—	—	—	12.3	113	225-2222	—
Van Kampen Merritt U.S. Government	MBS	7.1	15.3	—	—	—	9.5	83	225-2222	—
Venture Income Plus	HYC	8.3	0.3	56.6	—	Middle	13.3	107	545-2098	505-983-4335 (N.M.)
Venture Ret. Plan of America—Bond	HYC	5.7	13.1	55.6	100.2	Middle	10.8	124	545-2098	505-983-4335 (N.M.)
Washington Mutual Investors	G&I	14.9	(7.0)	109.9	397.3	High	5.3	96	421-9900	713-671-7000 (Calif.)
Weingarten Equity	Gro	9.3	(14.5)	78.7	530.8	Middle	0.1	110	231-0803	800-392-9681 (Texas)
Winthrop Focus Growth	Gro	10.6	(15.0)	—	—	—	0.5	77	225-8011	816-283-1700 (Mo.)
WPG Fund	Max	9.1	(14.4)	62.8	—	Middle	1.2	65	223-3332	212-908-9582 (N.Y.)
WPG Government Securities	USG	6.7	12.5	—	—	—	7.9	49	223-3332	212-908-9582 (N.Y.)
WPG Growth	SCG	9.9	(20.9)	—	—	—	0.1	55	223-3332	212-908-9582 (N.Y.)

*Currently closed to new investors N.A. Not available. Fund is not required to report these data until the end of its fiscal year.

Notes and Cautions: To be included in the listings on pages 188 through 203, a fund must accept a minimum initial investment of $10,000 or less, have assets of at least $25 million as of June 30, 1988, be available to the general public in at least 25 states and have a performance record of at least one year. A fund's gain (or loss) is calculated by the growth of an investment from the start of each period shown and includes reinvestment of dividends. The prospectuses of bond funds in the high-grade categories require them to invest primarily in issues rated BBB or better by Standard & Poor's or Moody's. Short-term taxables have average weighted maturities of up to five years. Intermediate-term tax exempts have average weighted maturities of less than 10 years. Yields are the latest 12 months' dividends divided by the latest share prices. Performance figures were compiled by Lipper Analytical Services.

Tax-Exempt Bond Funds

| | % gain (or loss) to Sept. 1, 1988 | | | | |
	1988	One year	Five years	10 years	% yield

BENCHMARKS FOR INVESTORS

	1988	One year	Five years	10 years	% yield
Shearson Lehman Hutton municipal bond index	6.2	6.9	74.4	—	7.5
S&P 500-stock index	13.1	(12.4)	98.7	319.1	—

FUND NAME	Type	% gain (or loss) to Sept. 1, 1988 — 1988	One year	Five years	10 years	Five-year ranking within category	% yield	Five-year expense projection	Telephone Toll-free (800)	In state
Alliance Tax-Free Income—High Bracket	HGT	7.7	7.4	—	—	—	6.9	$98	221-5672	—
Alliance Tax-Free Income—High Income	HGT	9.0	10.4	—	—	—	7.7	67	221-5672	—
American Capital Muni Bond	HGT	7.4	5.8	64.0	80.8	Low	8.0	81	847-5636	—
American Capital Tax-Exempt—High Yield	HYT	5.1	6.7	—	—	—	9.0	92	847-5636	—
American Capital Tax-Exempt—Insured	HGT	4.6	2.0	—	—	—	6.8	92	847-5636	—
Benham National Tax-Free—Long-Term	HGT	6.7	4.2	—	—	—	7.3	28	472-3389	—
Calvert Tax-Free Reserves—Limited-Term	ITT	4.6	5.6	39.8	—	Middle	5.6	61	368-2748	301-951-4820 (Md.)
Calvert Tax-Free Reserves—Long-Term	HGT	6.1	4.8	—	—	—	7.3	89	368-2748	301-951-4820 (Md.)
Cigna Municipal Bond	HGT	6.6	8.3	72.3	92.6	Middle	7.1	96	562-4462	—
Colonial Tax-Exempt High Yield	HYT	6.7	6.4	50.2	—	Middle	8.1	104	426-3750	—
Colonial Tax-Exempt Insured	HGT	6.4	6.0	—	—	—	6.9	107	426-3750	—
Composite Tax-Exempt Bond	HGT	6.7	7.2	67.5	75.7	Middle	7.5	85	541-0830	800-572-5828 (Wash.)
DBL Tax-Free—Limited	ITT	4.8	5.9	—	—	—	6.7	52	272-2700	212-232-2888 (N.Y.)
DBL Tax-Free—Long-Term	HGT	7.1	3.9	—	—	—	7.2	105	272-2700	212-232-2888 (N.Y.)
Dean Witter Tax-Exempt Securities	HGT	7.6	7.4	74.8	—	Middle	7.6	N.A.	221-2685	212-938-4554 (N.Y.)
Delaware Group Tax-Free—USA	HGT	8.3	8.9	—	—	—	7.6	N.A.	523-4640	215-988-1333 (Pa.)
Delaware Group Tax-Free—USA Insured	HGT	5.8	7.3	—	—	—	7.0	N.A.	523-4640	215-988-1333 (Pa.)
Dreyfus Insured Tax Exempt Bond	HGT	5.5	5.4	—	—	—	7.0	50	645-6561	718-895-1206 (N.Y.)
Dreyfus Intermed. Tax Exempt Bond	ITT	4.9	4.9	59.0	—	Middle	7.5	N.A.	645-6561	718-895-1206 (N.Y.)
Dreyfus Tax Exempt Bond	HGT	6.7	6.3	65.9	85.3	Low	7.6	N.A.	645-6561	718-895-1206 (N.Y.)
Eaton Vance High Yield Muni Trust	HYT	7.0	6.3	—	—	—	7.9	123	225-6265	—
Eaton Vance Muni Bond	HGT	7.1	8.2	76.3	104.2	Middle	7.5	91	225-6265	—
Fidelity Aggressive Tax-Free	HYT	8.6	7.3	—	—	—	8.1	N.A.	544-6666	617-523-1919 (Mass.)
Fidelity High Yield Muni	HYT	6.6	5.1	70.2	105.8	Middle	7.6	40	544-6666	617-523-1919 (Mass.)
Fidelity Insured Tax-Free	HGT	6.2	6.8	—	—	—	6.8	N.A.	544-6666	617-523-1919 (Mass.)
Fidelity Limited Term Muni	ITT	5.1	5.4	61.9	97.1	High	6.5	41	544-6666	617-523-1919 (Mass.)
Fidelity Municipal Bond	HGT	7.2	6.9	69.9	80.4	Middle	7.1	N.A.	544-6666	617-523-1919 (Mass.)
Fidelity Short-Term Tax-Free	ITT	3.0	3.1	—	—	—	5.1	N.A.	544-6666	617-523-1919 (Mass.)
Financial Tax-Free Income Shares	HGT	7.7	7.6	73.7	—	Middle	7.3	43	525-8085	—
First Investors Tax Exempt	HGT	5.6	7.2	68.0	107.0	Middle	7.4	130	423-4026	—
Franklin Federal Tax-Free Income	HGT	8.2	8.6	—	—	—	8.4	68	342-5236	—
Franklin High Yield Tax-Free Income	HYT	8.9	11.3	—	—	—	9.3	75	342-5236	—
Franklin Insured Tax-Free Income—Nat.	HGT	7.2	8.2	—	—	—	7.9	73	342-5236	—
GIT Tax-Free—High Yield	HYT	5.8	6.5	67.4	—	Middle	7.2	63	336-3063	703-528-6500 (Va.)
Hutton National Muni Bond	HGT	7.7	7.6	83.9	—	High	7.9	34		212-528-2744
IDS High Yield Tax-Exempt	HYT	6.2	7.7	76.7	—	High	7.8	81	328-8300	—
IDS Insured Tax-Exempt	HGT	5.2	8.1	—	—	—	6.7	93	328-8300	—
IDS Tax-Exempt Bond	HGT	4.9	7.0	71.7	91.7	Middle	7.3	82	328-8300	—
Integrated Insured Tax-Free—STRIPES	HGT	7.1	7.2	—	—	—	6.8	114	821-5100	—
John Hancock Tax-Exempt Income	HGT	6.3	7.1	75.4	73.5	Middle	6.7	91	225-5291	617-572-4120 (Mass.)

N.A. Not available. Fund is not required to report these data until the end of its fiscal year.

FUND NAME	Type	% gain (or loss) to Sept. 1, 1988				Five-year ranking within category	% yield	Five-year expense projection	Telephone	
		1988	One year	Five years	10 years				Toll-free (800)	In state
Kemper Municipal Bond	HGT	4.5	6.3	78.2	111.5	High	7.7	N.A.	621-1048	—
Keystone America Tax-Free Income	HGT	4.8	3.3	—	—	—	7.3	$114	225-2618	617-338-3400 (Mass.)
Keystone Tax-Exempt Trust	HGT	6.7	6.3	—	—	—	7.1	90	225-2618	617-338-3400 (Mass.)
Keystone Tax-Free*	HGT	6.3	6.2	68.9	108.0	Middle	7.8	114	225-2618	617-338-3400 (Mass.)
Liberty Tax-Free Income	HGT	5.9	7.1	66.2	81.1	Low	7.2	95	356-2805	—
Limited Term Muni–National Portfolio	ITT	5.2	6.7	—	—	—	6.5	89	847-0200	505-984-0200 (N.M.)
Lord Abbett Tax-Free Income–National	HGT	7.1	8.3	—	—	—	7.2	N.A.	223-4224	212-848-1800 (N.Y.)
Mackay-Shields Tax-Free Bond	HGT	5.5	5.6	—	—	—	6.7	118	522-4202	—
Mass. Fin. Lifetime–Man. Muni Bond	HGT	8.0	7.2	—	—	—	6.2	N.A.	225-2606	617-423-3500 (Mass.)
Mass. Fin. Man. High Yield Muni Bond*	HYT	4.3	4.3	—	—	—	8.8	102	225-2606	617-423-3500 (Mass.)
Mass. Fin. Managed Muni Bond	HGT	6.8	7.7	76.3	167.3	Middle	7.1	N.A.	225-2606	617-423-3500 (Mass.)
Merrill Lynch Muni–High Yield	HYT	7.1	6.9	75.1	—	Middle	7.6	70	637-7455	—
Merrill Lynch Muni–Insured	HGT	6.3	7.2	69.4	—	Middle	7.4	71	637-7455	—
Merrill Lynch Muni–Limited Maturity	ITT	3.9	5.0	34.1	—	Low	5.6	30	637-7455	—
Mutual of Omaha Tax-Free Income	HGT	6.7	7.2	79.5	90.8	High	7.3	112	228-9596	800-642-8112 (Neb.)
National Securities Tax-Exempt	HGT	6.4	7.0	77.3	86.0	Middle	7.5	87	223-7757	212-661-3000 (N.Y.)
Nationwide Tax Free	HGT	5.7	5.8	—	—	—	6.8	N.A.	848-0920	800-282-1440 (Ohio)
New England Tax-Exempt Income	HGT	6.3	7.0	71.3	101.9	Middle	6.4	97	343-7104	—
Nuveen Municipal Bond	HGT	5.7	8.3	74.2	102.0	Middle	7.1	76	621-7210	312-917-7844 (Ill.)
Oppenheimer Tax-Free Bond	HGT	5.8	7.0	79.5	109.3	High	7.5	90	525-7048	800-356-3556 (Colo.)
Paine Webber Tax-Ex. Inc.–National	HGT	6.5	7.1	—	—	—	7.2	N.A.	544-9300	—
T. Rowe Price Tax-Free–High Yield	HYT	7.4	6.7	—	—	—	7.5	55	638-5660	301-547-2308 (Md.)
T. Rowe Price Tax-Free Income	HGT	5.7	4.7	54.3	102.5	Low	6.8	38	638-5660	301-547-2308 (Md.)
T. Rowe Price Tax-Free Short-Intermed.	ITT	3.2	4.3	—	—	—	5.4	43	638-5660	301-547-2308 (Md.)
Principal Preservation–Tax-Exempt Plus	ITT	3.9	(1.2)	—	—	—	7.1	108	826-4600	—
Pru-Bache National Muni	HGT	6.4	5.0	71.2	—	Middle	7.1	66	225-1852	—
Putnam Tax-Exempt Income	HGT	6.8	8.5	76.0	153.2	Middle	7.4	73	225-1581	—
Putnam Tax-Free High Yield	HYT	7.3	7.0	—	—	—	7.0	132	225-1581	—
Putnam Tax-Free Insured	HGT	5.9	6.9	—	—	—	6.2	142	225-1581	—
Safeco Municipal Bond	HGT	7.6	8.0	75.1	—	Middle	7.4	34	426-6730	800-562-6810 (Wash.)
Scudder High Yield Tax Free	HYT	8.1	7.3	—	—	—	8.5	22	225-2470	—
Scudder Managed Muni Bond	HGT	7.4	7.7	66.6	101.1	Low	7.8	35	225-2470	—
Scudder Tax-Free Target–1990	ITT	3.4	4.4	44.8	—	Middle	5.8	45	225-2470	—
Scudder Tax-Free Target–1993	ITT	3.8	4.6	58.5	—	Middle	6.2	45	225-2470	—
Scudder Tax-Free Target–1996	ITT	5.1	6.2	—	—	—	6.7	64	225-2470	—
Seligman Tax-Exempt–National	HGT	8.0	8.0	—	—	—	7.3	87	221-2450	800-522-6869 (N.Y.)
Shearson Lehman Spl. Inc.–Tax-Ex. Inc.	HGT	6.8	7.4	—	—	—	6.9	94	—	212-528-2744
Shearson Managed Muni	HGT	6.9	7.6	74.9	—	Middle	7.6	80	—	212-528-2744
Smith Barney Muni Bond–National Port.	HGT	7.2	7.3	—	—	—	8.1	56	544-7835	—
State Bond Tax-Exempt	HGT	5.3	7.7	—	—	—	7.3	90	328-4735	—
SteinRoe High-Yield Muni	HYT	8.8	8.5	—	—	—	7.7	42	338-2550	—
SteinRoe Intermediate Municipal	ITT	3.9	4.9	—	—	—	5.7	44	338-2550	—
SteinRoe Managed Muni	HGT	6.0	8.7	87.7	129.3	High	7.0	36	338-2550	—
Tax-Exempt Bond of America	HGT	4.8	6.7	67.4	—	Low	6.9	85	421-9900	714-671-7000 (Calif.)
Thomson McKinnon Tax Exempt	HGT	5.2	5.5	—	—	—	6.1	N.A.	628-1237	212-482-5894 (N.Y.)
United Municipal Bond	HGT	8.0	8.8	83.1	86.7	High	7.1	74	—	816-842-1075
United Municipal High Income	HYT	4.5	2.9	—	—	—	8.9	88	—	816-842-1075
USAA Tax Exempt–High Yield	HGT	6.7	8.3	70.5	—	Middle	9.0	29	531-8000	—
USAA Tax Exempt–Intermed.-Term	ITT	5.8	7.8	59.2	—	Middle	8.4	31	531-8000	—
USAA Tax Exempt–Short-Term	ITT	3.9	6.3	40.8	—	Middle	6.9	31	531-8000	—
UST Master Intermed.-Term Tax-Exempt	ITT	4.4	7.9	—	—	—	6.4	39	233-1136	—
Value Line Tax Exempt–High Yield	HGT	7.1	6.4	—	—	—	7.9	36	223-0818	—
Vanguard Muni Bond–High Yield	HYT	7.5	8.0	74.9	—	Middle	7.7	15	662-7447	—
Vanguard Muni Bond–Insured Long	HGT	7.1	7.8	—	—	—	7.4	15	662-7447	—
Vanguard Muni Bond–Intermed.	ITT	6.0	7.2	64.7	79.2	High	6.8	15	662-7447	—
Vanguard Muni Bond–Long Term	HGT	6.7	7.6	71.0	79.6	Middle	7.4	15	662-7447	—
Vanguard Muni Bond–Short Term	ITT	3.7	4.9	34.7	83.8	Low	5.2	15	662-7447	—
Van Kampen Merritt Ins. Tax Free Inc.	HGT	7.0	8.4	—	—	—	7.2	90	225-2222	—
Van Kampen Merritt Tax Free High Inc.	HYT	6.4	7.4	—	—	—	8.6	90	225-2222	—
Venture Muni Plus	HYT	7.9	8.4	43.3	—	Low	8.5	N.A.	545-2098	505-983-4335 (N.M.)

*Currently closed to new investors   N.A. Not available. Fund is not required to report these data until the end of its fiscal year.

Index